# FUNDAMENTALISM IN THE MODERN WORLD

## VOLUME 2

# FUNDAMENTALISM IN THE MODERN WORLD

## VOLUME 2

Fundamentalism and Communication:
Culture, Media and the Public Sphere

Ulrika Mårtensson, Jennifer Bailey,
Priscilla Ringrose and
Asbjørn Dyrendal

I.B. TAURIS
LONDON · NEW YORK

Published in 2011 by I.B.Tauris & Co Ltd
6 Salem Road, London W2 4BU
175 Fifth Avenue, New York NY 10010
www.ibtauris.com

Distributed in the United States and Canada
Exclusively by Palgrave Macmillan
175 Fifth Avenue, New York NY 10010

International Library of Political Studies 45

ISBN 978 1 84885 331 7

A full CIP record for this book is available from the British Library
A full CIP record for this book is available from the Library of Congress

Library of Congress catalog card: available

Printed and bound in Great Britain by CPI Antony Rowe
Camera-ready copy edited and supplied by the author

# CONTENTS

# ILLUSTRATIONS

## Figures

# CONTRIBUTORS

## Editors

**Ulrika Mårtensson**, Theol. Dr., is Associate Professor of Religious Studies at the Norwegian University of Science and Technology (NTNU), Trondheim. She works on the translatability of Islamic concepts, concerning theories of knowledge, of interpretation and of the state in medieval and modern contexts, and on the establishment of Islam as a public religion in Scandinavia.

**Jennifer L. Bailey**, PhD, is Professor of Political Science, NTNU. Her research interests concern comparative and international politics (international norms, new social movements, issue-framing and advocacy groups) and US politics, especially the role of religion in US politics and foreign affairs.

**Priscilla Ringrose**, PhD, is an Associate Professor in the Departments of Modern Foreign Languages and of Interdisciplinary Studies of Culture, NTNU. Her research interests are within francophone literature, feminist theory and Internet studies.

**Asbjørn Dyrendal**, PhD, is Associate Professor of the History of Religions at NTNU. His main research interests revolve around contemporary 'occulture', with a focus on conspiracy culture and Satanism.

## Contributors

**Jennifer L. Bailey** is Professor of Political Science at the Norwegian University of Science and Technology (NTNU), Trondheim. Her research interests concern comparative and international politics (international norms, new social movements, issue-framing and advocacy groups) and US politics, especially the role of religion in US politics and foreign affairs.

**Stefano M. Bisighin,** PhD, works in the University of Bologna and in the Italian Ministry of Cultural Heritage at the National Archives of Bologna (Ministero per i Beni e le Attività Culturali, Archivio di Stato di Bologna). His research interests concern the history and sociology of religions; semiotics and communication; archival sciences and record management; and information technology applied to archivists.

**Petra Hedberg,** MPhil, is a Lecturer in the Department of Philosophy, University of Bergen, Norway. Her research concerns German philosophy from Kant and Hegel to Gadamer, Habermas and Apel.

**Soraj Hongladarom,** PhD, is an Associate Professor in the Department of Philosophy and Director of the Center for Ethics of Science and Technology, Chulalongkorn University, Bangkok, Thailand. His main research interests concern the roles of science and technology in society, the impact of the Internet on cultures and religions, and relationships between Buddhism and science.

**Krisadawan Hongladarom,** PhD, was an Associate Professor in the Department of Linguistics, Chulalongkorn University, until retirement in 2007. Her fields of research include discourse analysis and pragmatics. She is currently President of the Thousand Stars Foundation, a non-profit organisation that promotes mutual understanding between Thai and Tibetan Buddhist traditions.

**Ahmed Abidur Razzaque Khan,** MPhil, is a PhD candidate in the Human Rights and Peace Studies Program, Mahidol University, Thailand, and Coordinator of Knowledge Management Systems (KMS) of the SEARCH (South East Asia Regional Cooperation in

Human Development)-CIDA project based in Bangkok, Thailand. His research fields are media and performing arts in the service of human rights development.

**Oddbjørn Leirvik** is Professor of Interreligious Studies in the Faculty of Theology, University of Oslo, Norway. His main fields of research are Islam and Christian-Muslim Relations, and Interreligious Dialogue.

**Gavin N. Picken**, PhD, is a Lecturer in Islamic Studies and Arabic in the University of Edinburgh, UK. His teaching and research concern the Islamic tradition in the formative period, with special reference to jurisprudence, theology, spirituality and mysticism in the context of the evolution of Islamic intellectual history.

**Priscilla Ringrose,** PhD, is Associate Professor in the Departments of Modern Foreign Languages and of Interdisciplinary Studies of Culture, NTNU. Her research interests are within francophone literature, feminist theory and Internet studies.

**Lionel Sacks** holds a PhD in physics from the University of London and a Diploma in Economics from the Open University, UK. He is an independent researcher with an interest in religious communication, especially where it concerns economics and science.

**Jakob Skovgaard-Petersen**, PhD, is Professor of Modern Islam in the Institute for Cross-Cultural and Regional Studies, University of Copenhagen. He works on the modern history of Muslim scholars (*al-ulama*), in particular in relation to the state and modern media in the Arab world.

**Moshe Terdman**, PhD, is a research analyst in the Orient Research Group Ltd. He was the Director of the Islam in Africa Project as well as a senior research fellow in PRISM (the Project for Research on Islamist Movements), the GLORIA Center, Herzliya, Israel. He is an expert on the subject of Islam in Africa and the Caribbean Basin as well as on the social issues addressed by Islamic movements.

**May Thorseth**, PhD, is Professor in the Department of Philosophy and Director of the Programme for Applied Ethics, NTNU. Her research concerns ethical and political dimensions of communication and development, online deliberation and multi-cultural conflicts.

**Michael Trainor**, PhD, is a Senior Lecturer in the School of Theology at Flinders University, South Australia. His main research interest concerns biblical literacy, and the interface between archaeology and early Christian literature.

# INTRODUCTION

# FUNDAMENTALISM AND COMMUNICATION: CULTURE, MEDIA AND THE PUBLIC SPHERE

## Ulrika Mårtensson, Jennifer Bailey, Priscilla Ringrose, Asbjørn Dyrendal

### Introduction

This book is about 'fundamentalism talk'. It is the second of two volumes which have emerged from a conference arranged in 2006 by the Globalisation programme at the Norwegian University of Science and Technology, on the theme 'Global Communication of Fundamentalist Knowledge'. The conference sought to explore how fundamentalist concepts of the nation, the state and the people are related to methodologies of science and interpretation, and how these concepts and methodologies are communicated in global society. In the Introduction to the first of these two volumes, 'Fundamentalism, Politics and History: The State, Globalisation and Political Ideologies', the origins and definitions of the term fundamentalism were explored in relation to the paradigmatic American Fundamentalist movement, to the University of Chicago's *Fundamentalism Project* (Marty and Appleby (eds.) 1991–95), and to other leading research in the field. Against this background, the objective of these two volumes is to explore fundamentalism in terms of ideologically-inspired methodologies related to the 'formation' and 're-formation' of nations, states and communities, and in terms of a specific mode of communicating in national and global public spheres. Hence, if 'fundamentalism' signifies 'return to the sources' and its objective is to form society and individual life according to what the sources are believed to dictate, then the corresponding methodology is to interpret the sources according to a specific doctrinal authority, so that they produce the desired outcome. While the first volume concentrates on the implications of fundamentalism for community, nation and state formation, this second volume focuses on the communication of fundamentalism in the public sphere, which means that the general theme of community, nation and state formation is approached with regard to how national and cultural identities are publicly communicated and debated.

As our point of departure, we take the 'fundamentalist family resemblance traits' produced by the University of Chicago's *Fundamentalism Project*. Accordingly, 'fundamentalism' refers to religious movements sharing most of the following nine characteristics (Almond et al 1995: 399–424):

> a response to religion's social marginalisation;
> the selective use of tradition and modernity;
> moral dualism;
> absolutism and inerrancy of essential texts;
> millennialism;
> elect membership;
> sharp boundaries;
> authoritarian organisation; and
> strict behavioural requirements.

These traits are here taken to support the position that fundamentalism is about the formation and re-formation of community, nation and state. In such formative processes, drawing and defending boundaries and asserting authoritarianism are strategies which uphold doctrinal purity – those with wrong views are kept outside, even if they belong to the same religious faith, so that the insiders can form an exclusive

and easily identifiable community with a distinct message and a programme for social action (Ammerman 1990). If fundamentalism is
viewed in this way, fundamentalist communication can be said to
serve a double purpose: to define 'the other' and *thereby* to attract supporters. Privately, fundamentalists are of course as much involved in
deliberation and compromise as anyone else, but their public communication does not permit the idea that the defined 'other' could add
anything of value to one's own point of view. The sharp boundaries
which fundamentalists draw between their own community or nation
and 'others' are thus matched by equally sharp boundaries between
private and public communication; anyone who publicly approaches
the 'other' side is therefore 'cast out' of the fundamentalist community. Consider, for example, the history of the American Fundamental
Baptist Fellowship International (FBF), as presented on its official
website:

> The FBF traces its roots to the formation of the Fundamentalist
> Fellowship of Northern Baptists in 1920. A more militant seg-
> ment of these early Fundamentalists formed the Baptist Bible
> Union in 1923, which in 1932 separated from the Northern
> Baptist Convention (NBC) and formed the General Association
> of Regular Baptist Churches. The Fundamentalist Fellowship
> men, however, stayed in the NBC and tried to reform it until
> the 1940s, when they were practically forced out. The issue that
> caused much of the conflict was the foreign mission society's
> adherence to the 'inclusive policy', which meant that it approved
> liberal as well as evangelical missionaries.
>
> In 1943 the Fundamentalist Fellowship (FF) was instrumen-
> tal in starting the Conservative Baptist Foreign Mission Society.
> In 1946 the FF changed its name to the Conservative Baptist
> Fellowship (CBF), and in 1951 by public resolution it disavowed
> any further relations with the American Baptist Convention (for-
> merly the Northern Baptist Convention).
>
> In 1948 the CBF organized an association of churches, the
> Conservative Baptist Association of America, and two years later
> it helped bring into existence the Conservative Baptist Home

Mission Society. In the Conservative Baptist movement, the CBF stood against the ecumenical evangelism, exemplified by Billy Graham, and New Evangelicalism and its compromise with liberalism. The beginning of the end of the CBF's involvement with Conservative Baptists occurred in 1961, when it helped to form a mission board that would appoint only premillennial missionaries, the World Conservative Baptist Mission (now Baptist World Mission).

In 1967 the CBF felt compelled to break all ties with the Conservative Baptist movement it had founded. The Conservative Baptist Fellowship was finally completely independent. To distance itself from the Conservative Baptist movement, the CBF changed its name to the Fundamental Baptist Fellowship. Since that time it has continued and prospered as a loose fellowship of individual like-minded Baptists. (2009)

For the FBF, then, doctrinal purity, which is absolutely central to its identity, hinges on the right approach to liberalism and millennialism. Those who accommodate liberal values and ecumenism (intercommunal dialogue), and those who have the wrong beliefs concerning the return of Christ, have been successively 'cast out', so that in the end only a small but hard core of anti-liberal pre-millennial believers remain. And this is not a random posting on the FBF website: it is a marketing strategy, communicating the message that, for those in search of 'the one', this is the Fundamentalist Community, prepared to 'cast out the softies'.

The rejection of liberalism is something which fundamentalists have in common across religious divides. Rejecting liberal principles also means assuming that there is only one valid view, namely one's own, and this is the point where fundamentalism differs from established religious orthodoxies prepared to enter into dialogue and to subject their beliefs to criticism from others; as Jürgen Habermas and his colleagues succinctly put it:

Every religious doctrine is based on a dogmatic kernel of belief. Sometimes there is a religious authority such as the

Pope or the Roman congregation, which determines what interpretations deviate from this dogma and, therefore, from orthodoxy. Such orthodoxy first veers toward fundamentalism when the guardians and representatives of the true faith ignore the epistemic situation of a pluralistic society and insist – even to the point of violence – on the universally binding character and political acceptance of their doctrine. (Habermas et al 2003: 31)

The general public's impressions of fundamentalist communication, as one of assertiveness and strength, often overestimate the extent of its influence. When various national fundamentalist communications are conflated, say in the interest of media reports or academic studies, this impression is even further amplified, with the result that fundamentalists appear to constitute an increasingly powerful and world-wide political force (Marty and Appleby 1997; Juergensmeyer 1993; 2008; cf. Berger 1999). Of course, no one would deny that fundamentalism represents a formidable force in some countries, for example: Hindu nationalists in India; Buddhist nationalists in Sri Lanka and Myanmar; the state ideologies of the Islamic republics of Iran and Sudan; the Taleban and Lashkar-i Toiba in Afghanistan and Pakistan; the Muslim Brotherhood in Egypt and Hamas in Palestine; the Jewish religious settler movement in Israel and Palestine; and Serbian and Islamic fundamentalism during the Balkan wars in the 1990s. Still, there is as yet no evidence that fundamentalists pose a threat to global world order and global institutions, in spite of their communication on the subject.

Fundamentalists' communication on liberalism often includes a critique of globalisation as a conveyor of liberal values, politics and economics world-wide, and as a force that interferes in national or community affairs through international and national law. Peter Beyer (2006) is one researcher into globalisation who holds that it has not reduced the importance of the nation-state. On the contrary, the nation-state is the basic building block in what Beyer terms 'global society'. In Europe, the nation-state emerged gradually from the Treaty of Westphalia in 1648 with its 'new order' of territorial states and national churches, and the idea that citizens' rights were premised on belonging to a territorially-defined community, the nation (Sassen 2006). Through the processes of colonisation and national liberation, the nation-state model has also become the dominant political structure in the Americas, Africa and Asia (Kedourie 1971; 1987). The global institutions which produce international law, together with economic and other policies, invariably execute the will of the nation-states of which they are composed – although the power distribution between those states is not equal. Hence, global society is a society whose most basic institution is the nation-state, from which is developed various other institutions. Globalisation has thus not reduced the significance of nations but rather enhanced it, by providing institutions through which various constellations of nations can collaborate. However, just as fundamentalist organisations do not engage in religious dialogue if this involves submitting their beliefs to critical examination by others, the fundamentalist nation-state is often averse to international institutions and laws which would force it to collaborate and to negotiate its interests with others; and if it boycotts the institutions and rejects their laws, it risks failing to win the contest and so facing international humiliation and sanctions. While some fundamentalist-governed nations, such as Sudan, oppose the international order for pragmatic reasons – e.g. because they are involved in conflicts that they want to handle without international 'interference' – extremists such as Ayman al-Zawahiri, architect of the jihad-for-caliphate doctrine, reject the nation-state structure entirely as far as Islamic countries are concerned. Al-Zawahiri also rejects the major bodies of the global order, represented by:

(1) The United Nations. (2) The friendly rulers of the Muslim peoples. (3) The multinational corporations. (4) The international communications and data exchange systems. (5) The international news agencies and satellite media channels. (6) The international relief agencies, which are used as a cover for espionage, proselytization, coup planning and the transfer of weapons. (al-Zawahiri 2001, Pt. 11, cited in Sageman 2004: 20)

A vital part of a modern and democratic nation is its 'public sphere'. In Habermas's definition, this refers to:

> ... a realm of our social life in which something approaching public opinion can be formed. Access is guaranteed to all citizens. A portion of the public sphere comes into being in every conversation in which private individuals assemble to form a public body. They then behave neither like business or professional people transacting private affairs, nor like members of a constitutional order subject to the legal constraints of a state bureaucracy. Citizens behave as a public body when they confer in an unrestricted fashion – that is, with the guarantee of freedom of assembly and association and the freedom to express and publish their opinions – about matters of general interest. (Habermas 1974: 49)

Over time, the main channels of public-opinion formation have moved from coffee houses and bourgeois salons to the public media. Since the institutions and the media which are necessary for a public sphere to emerge have now become virtually global, national public spheres have become institutional parts of what could be called a 'global public sphere'. Moreover, the topics of national public debates have also taken on global relevance, since national politics and public affairs are connected with global institutions and the latter's policies, laws and values, as well as with the international actions of nation-states.

Marshall McLuhan has classically described mass media – like all social artefacts – as products of human *physical* labour and therefore as extensions of the human body and senses. The mass-media messages are physical sensations which stimulate the recipients and move them in new directions of social action and labour (McLuhan 1997). In other words, the media are not forces outside of individuals and society but extensions of the people who make up society. As such, they express society's self-perception and its deliberations over where to move next. Given, as McLuhan would have it, that 'the medium is the message' and that the media are now to a large extent global, the national dialogue is automatically in the global public sphere.

With respect to the fields of media and religion, Stewart Hoover (2006) has developed McLuhan's approach further, exploring the dynamic relationship between mass media, society and individual identity. In the USA and Europe (and increasingly in other parts of the world as well), the emergence of the modern mass media has taken place within a broader social and cultural context of increased social mobility and individualism: the individual self has changed from being seen as a given into an ongoing project with no determined outcome, and depending simply on choices of education, career and lifestyle. The latest forms of interactive 'new media' (websites, blogs, discussion boards and social-networking sites) are perfectly suited for this project, as they allow individuals to use such media to describe themselves as they wish. For religion, this broader social change has meant that the authority of traditional religious institutions has receded in the wake of a personal, experiential kind of religiosity, even among those who remain members of established churches and communities. This personal religiosity is intrinsically related to the concept of the self as an on-going project, and thus religion is increasingly being perceived as one of several, interchangeable parts of the progressive self. The new interactive media also communicate religion in this way – as an on-going project of self. In this latest phase, the media has become increasingly 'public', in Habermas's sense. Whereas the phrase 'the mass media' refers to broadcasting media which communicate *to* the masses, the new interactive media allow individual media-consumers to become co-producers and to take part in public debates *through* media, albeit on a bi-directional, interpersonal scale (Hoover 2006: 45–8). Hence, the global public sphere is where individuals from all over the world share the same mediatised information, and are able to debate it through interactive web technologies.

All this has a bearing on fundamentalism. Protestantism was the first 'fundamentalism' in the basic sense of the term as 'return to the sources'. Its spread was intrinsically connected to the introduction of the printing press, to growing literacy and to the translation of the Bible into vernacular languages. In the same manner, modern fundamentalist movements have made extensive use of the mass media, and have actively taken part in modern mass politics and public debates. Thus American fundamentalism manifested itself first in the form of printed pamphlets (*The Fundamentals*, 1910–15), and from the 1980s in televised mass sermons and popular cultural products such as *The Left Behind* series. Earlier still, the pan-Islamic movement first took shape in print form as al-Afghani's and Muhammad 'Abduh's Arabic-language monthly journal, *al-'Urwa al-Wuthqa* ('the most trustworthy bond'), distributed from Paris in 1884. In Egypt, 'Abduh's disciple, the journalist Rashid Rida, developed pan-Islam into what he termed a Salafi programme for national reform and a transnational caliphate, through his journal *al-Manar* ('the Lighthouse', 1898–1935). In these cases relating to Islam, as well as in the case of Hindu nationalism, which also emerged in the early 1900s, a generic turn away from theological treatises and towards the mass media took place, involving the reshaping of religious discourse from religious philosophy, law and ethics to a political ideology in which religion is enlarged from 'merely religion' to a programme for social and national reformation and rebirth (Hamzah, forthcoming 2011; Nussbaum 2007). This is also correlated with processes of religious individualisation, as both the leaders and the rank and file of Islamic and Hindu fundamentalist movements are drawn mainly from the modern professions, and their conceptions of religion are defined independently of, and as a direct challenge to, traditional religious authorities. However, although these conceptions are a product of the *social process* of individualisation, this does not mean that fundamentalists *ideologically* adopt the view of the self as an autonomous project with unpredictable outcomes; on the contrary, they perceive the self as bound by religious ethics.

One of countless examples of how the new media are currently being used by 'moderate' Islamic fundamentalists is in evidence on the Muslim Brotherhood's official English website (*www.ikhwanweb.com*), which contains news, columns and blogs of readers' comments. The debate is lively and conflicting views are aired, often on whether Islam is compatible with political liberalism, human rights, democracy and pluralism. Judging from the website, the Muslim Brotherhood does not conform to Habermas's definition of fundamentalists as those who reject religious dialogue and public debate. For example, *Ikhwanweb* posted a column on 'The fraternity of civilizations: prospects for dialogue' by Maryam Sakeenah, a Pakistani student of International Relations, which was originally posted on the left-wing website *Dissident Voice: A Radical Newsletter in the Struggle for Peace and Social Justice*. Sakeenah criticises Samuel Huntington's notorious theory about an imminent clash between religiously-identified civilisations (Huntington 1993; 1996) because he, according to Sakeenah, assumes that civilisations clash because they are different. However, Sakeenah argues, difference is not in itself the source of conflict, it is the refusal of 'the West' to respect the difference between itself and Islam and its attempts to impose its non-Islamic politics, economics and values on Islamic countries which gives rise to conflict. If the West would engage in dialogue with real Muslims and not just 'believers in a "moderated" Islam which does not enjoy any sizeable following in the Muslim world' and who 'are all the representatives of a "modern" Islam (whatever that means)' (Sakeenah 2009, ref. to Senghaas 2002: 105), this would become clear to them:

> [A] danger the West needs to guard against for a genuine dialogue between civilizations is the belief in one's own culture to be essentially unique and exclusive. The West must pull itself out of the Cold War mentality of creating and bloating up enemy images in order to direct an ambitious foreign policy at an adversary – real or imagined. The West should reject attempts at demonization of the enemy and understand that its version of modernity cannot be imposed on the Muslim world. It must allow other communities to develop according to their own orientation and essential values. Besides, the West must engage with authentic, popular representatives of the Muslim world ... Where, then, does a Clash emerge? It emerges as a corollary to interventionist, adventurist, exploitative policies vis-a-vis the Muslim world by the ascendant West steeped in the compulsions of its espoused Materialism and Capitalism. The Clash is not inevitable, but it can become possible if such policies are mindlessly and relentlessly pursued by the West and if the Muslim world does not engage in self criticism and undertake

a rediscovery of the pristine message of Islam. As long as the
West keeps pursuing its ill advised course, insecurity and militant responses will proliferate among the Muslims. In such a
case, Muslim opinion leaders will be compelled to rally together
their people for strengthening, fortifying and gearing up for
the West's assault on what is most precious to them. Given the
insensitivity and superficial grasp of the West over the prevalent
mood in the Muslim world, the vicious cycle of hostility will go
on. This is exactly the self-destructive path towards the Clash
of Civilizations which in the long run will be in the interest of
none. (Sakeenah 2009)

In fact, this is identical with Huntington's argument claiming that
Islamic civilisation, unlike Western civilisation, is not democratic
and that consequently US policy to democratise Islamic countries will
result in a violent 'clash of civilisations' as Muslims defend their essential values (Huntington 1996). Our columnist has already determined
that dialogue should focus on the essential differences between 'the
West' and 'Islam', and about how to cultivate these differences peacefully. This is not quite what Habermas means by public debate in a
pluralistic context, for in such a context the terms and outcomes cannot be determined beforehand. Habermas's approach also implies that
Muslim individuals should be free to define 'Islam' as they wish, with
religion being understood as part of a developing self, and that those
who see Islam as compatible with 'Western' liberal democracy and
capitalism should not be deemed less authentic than other Muslims.
But fundamentalists who believe in the need to reform the nation and
the community will typically define what constitutes the right understanding of religion and count those who disagree with them as less
than true believers, if not outright non-believers.

However, as far as pluralism is concerned, there are significant differences between fundamentalists of different religions. Because of its
feudal origins, the traditional sharia does not have a concept of citizenship and civil rights independent of religion, although more liberal
members of the Muslim Brotherhood are currently trying to accommodate such rights within the framework of the sharia (Rutherford

2008). However, because pre-modern Islamic states governed empires with multi-religious populations, the sharia has always had religious pluralism as a premise. Non-Muslim communities entered into legal contractual relations with the Islamic state, according to which their lives, property and religion were protected by Islamic law, while in all other matters they were governed by their own religious hierarchies. Therefore *religious* pluralism in the sense of different communities living together is not inimical to Muslim fundamentalism; our columnist again:

> Despite the essential differences between Islamic and Non Islamic tradition, historically Islam has never had 'adjustment problems' or difficulties in creating pluralistic societies where peoples of diverse religious traditions have lived together and prospered. In fact, Islam has a rich pluralistic tradition unsurpassed by any other civilization. It has a vast experience of interaction and alliance with non Muslim communities. (Sakeenah 2009)

Compare this with an American fundamentalist's comment on a *Washington Post* news report about President Obama's appointment of an evangelical scientist, Francis Collins, as the new head of the National Institute of Health. Collins has reconciled evolution theory with belief in divine creation, and the *Washington Post* reporter consequently had titled his report 'Francis Collins signals maturity for evangelicalism'. This response was posted on the web forum *Christianity Today: A Magazine of Evangelical Conviction*, where the blogger Alan M commented, picking up on the mention of 'maturity':

> Let us be sure that this so called maturity is worldly wisdom that is antithetical to true spiritual maturity and godly wisdom. We need to be careful not become worldly in order to gain the world to Christ. This only results in the world gaining us to itself.
>
> The issue is not whether or not an idea is popular or unpopular with the modern (and worldly) mind, the question is to know if the idea is biblical, if so we uphold it no matter the cost and

ridicule while making sure that we do not go beyond what is written. I am a young earth creationist (on exegetical and theological grounds), I do not crusade for what I see as a secondary doctrine (this is not part of the gospel per se), but I do not shy away when somebody asks me where I stand and how the doctrine fits in the overall history of salvation.

What is next? A redefinition of sin (i.e. the homosexuality debate), a naturalistic or mythical explanation of miracles (which are equally offensive to the modern mind), abortion as viable method of birth control, *religious plurality?* How far should we go for the world to consider us 'mature' and equally worldly? 'Guard against self-deception, each of you. If someone among you thinks he is wise in this age, let him become foolish so that he can become wise. For the wisdom of this age is foolishness with God. As it is written, "He catches the wise in their craftiness".' And again, 'The Lord knows that the thoughts of the wise are futile.' (Alan M 2009: 1Co 3:18–20 NET; emphasis added)

For this evangelical blogger, religious plurality is a vice, on a par with homosexuality and abortion, while for the Muslim Maryam Sakeenah religious plurality is taken for granted.

In the long run, the problem which fundamentalists have with pluralism and public debate in Habermas's liberal sense may prove to have consequences for their political influence. The numbers of American fundamentalists are declining relative to the population at large as well as to the Protestant community. This is due to the immigration of people belonging to other faith communities (primarily Catholics and Muslims), and to a slow but steady increase in the number of citizens without religious affiliation (Smith and Kim 2005; Pew Forum 2008). In short: American fundamentalists are neither reproducing themselves nor achieving enough conversions to keep up with changes in national demographics and in religious development. It is also possible that their exclusive view of the nation and religion is becoming less attractive, as it alienates believers from mainstream society. According to Ammerman, surveys show that conservative American fundamentalists are predominantly farmers and blue-collar workers, whereas those with more liberal views are predominantly professionals and entrepreneurs. The latter group of professionals and entrepreneurs makes up the expanding part of the national economy which requires of individuals a spirit of creativity, independence and cooperation – and these values are understood in ways which put them on a collision course with fundamentalist core values (Ammerman 1990: 129). In the context of the Arab world, popular support for the Muslim Brotherhood in Egypt and for other opposition Islamist political parties in Jordan and Morocco also seems to be dwindling. In Egypt this could be explained in terms of several factors: the government's increasingly repressive measures which deter both voters and supporters, and the Muslim Brotherhood's failure to form viable alliances with secular opposition parties (*The Economist*, 25 July 2009: 11; Rutherford 2008: 196). Hence, both American and 'moderate' Islamic fundamentalists might now be entering a phase of decline, due to their programmes no longer being able to meet the changing aspirations of their respective communities. It will be most interesting to see whether such organisations are able to address and adapt to changing preferences in the populations.

Within the last decade or so, issues related to fundamentalist activities have informed public debates on multiculturalism in the USA, Canada, Australia and Europe. Both fundamentalism and multiculturalism engage with and have implications for concepts of liberal rights and freedoms. In part, public debates about multiculturalism have been triggered by '9/11', by the attacks in Spain 2004 and in Britain in 2005, and by the ensuing national concerns about security and the social integration of Muslim immigrants and citizens. But the debates also concern broader issues of national identity and culture. Muslims now constitute the largest religiously-identifiable group of immigrants in Europe, and therefore often become the focus of public debates about national identity and national values, which in their turn often revolve around the perceived disadvantages of multiculturalism and the threat of Islamic fundamentalism.

In a report published in Britain by the Runnymede Trust's Commission on the Future of Multi-Ethnic Britain (2000), report director Bhikhu Parekh defines multiculturalism as a social policy according to which citizens of and immigrants to a country have the right to develop cultural lifestyles without encountering any kind of discrimination in education, housing and job markets, or pressure from one's own cultural group (Parekh 2000). Formulated in this manner, multiculturalism is grounded in the individual's right to choose, and is therefore more than anything else a liberal project. As Tariq Modood puts it:

[M]ulticulturalism presupposes the matrix of principles, institutions and political norms that are central to contemporary liberal democracies; but multiculturalism is … also a challenge to some of these norms, institutions and principles. In my view, multiculturalism could not get off the ground if one totally repudiated liberalism; but neither could it do so if liberalism marked the limits of one's politics. Multiculturalism is a child of liberal egalitarianism but, like any child, it is not simply a faithful reproduction of its parents. (Modood 2007: 7ff)

Multiculturalism challenges liberal institutions by implying that individuals may choose to live according to cultural norms that restrict people's movements, educational and professional choices, sexual orientation, and reproduction in ways which clash with liberal norms of freedom of choice, gender equality and equal opportunities. But at the same time, it challenges 'restrictive' communities because, if conflicts arise, they must allow their members to choose other norms and ways of life than those of their community.

As far as concepts of citizenship and nationhood are concerned, multiculturalism is in line with the liberal principle of *jus soli* ('the right of territory'), which means that 'the people' consists of all those who live on the nation's territory and are consequently entitled to full civil rights and liberties The opposite principle is *jus sanguinis* ('the right of blood'), according to which 'the people' are defined in ethnic and linguistic terms so that anyone who is not part of the ethno-linguistic groups is excluded from nationhood (Hastings 1997: 13). This position is associated with ethno-nationalist concepts of the nation as exclusively 'monocultural', as opposed to 'multicultural'. However, there are cross-over cases: France, which formally adheres to the principle of *jus soli*, is monocultural in its demand that citizens conform to *laïcité*, the separation of religion from public institutions in all matters, including dress codes – hence the 2003 law which forbids the wearing of religious symbols in public schools. In these contemporary contexts concepts of nationhood function as the frame of reference for public debates about multiculturalism.

Advocates of multiculturalism see cultural diversity as a national asset – if people can cultivate their cultures of choice, they will prosper and contribute to the nation: if they are subject to enforced conformity, they are less likely to identify with the nation, with all the negative consequences this entails. This is the thinking behind Canada's public promotion of her multicultural policy, aimed at attracting work immigrants (Canada 2009). Generally, the public advocates of multiculturalism are liberals and academics, whether of leftist or more conservative orientation. Public critics of multiculturalism include alliances of various ethno-nationalists who see multiculturalism and immigrants as undermining the nation by destroying the unity of the national cultural fabric, and not-so-liberal leftists and secularists who see it as impairing progress by allowing reactionary cultures to flourish. Both kinds of critics are prone to complain that 'political correctness' restricts free debate on the negative aspects of multiculturalism. But their suggested remedies, of course, differ: ethno-nationalists usually want immigrants or 'foreigners' to leave the country (or to live in 'cultural enclaves'), while anti-multicultural leftists prefer to 're-educate' the perceived reactionaries through legal and educational means.

Fundamentalism enters into these debates in several ways. For instance, the 9/11 attacks were carried out by Islamic fundamentalists, and consequently debates related to post-9/11 concerns have been very much centred on ways to combat, contain and generally domesticate Islamic fundamentalism. Both ethno-nationalists and leftist secularists commonly claim that by giving Muslims multicultural rights, Western societies are actually encouraging Islamic fundamentalism, which will eventually become so powerful that it will abolish the freedoms that are essential to 'Western culture'. (For right-wing examples, see e.g.

Stunich 2007; TheOPINIONATOR 2009; for a secularist-humanist example, see e.g. Malik 2002). However, for a number of reasons it is unlikely that multiculturalism spawns fundamentalism. As we have seen above, fundamentalism is at odds with the principles of public debate – in Habermas's sense, that arguments and opinions should always be submitted to others' critique – and as such it also conflicts with multiculturalism as described by Bhikhu Parekh:

> Multiculturalism is sometimes taken to mean that different cultural communities should live their own ways of life in a self-contained manner. This is not its only meaning and in fact it has long been obsolete. Multiculturalism basically means that no culture is perfect or represents the best life and that it can therefore benefit from a critical dialogue with other cultures. In this sense multiculturalism requires that all cultures should be open, self-critical, and interactive in their relations with other each other. (Parekh 2004)

One of many cases of fundamentalist activists is Hindu nationalists, who campaign vigorously against any representation of Hinduism and Hindu culture that contradicts their own ideological definition of it as the ideal human civilisation. This kind of ideology has resulted in revisions of Indian national-history curricula and textbooks under the Bharatiya Janata Party rule (1998–2004), and in organised campaigns to revise chapters on Hinduism in American books on world history, as well as in public attacks by Hindu nationalists on university academics in the USA (Kurien 2007: 184 *passim*; Nussbaum 2007). If successful, such campaigns could result in the propagation of seriously flawed views of Hinduism and the history of the Indian sub-continent (with very hostile and inaccurate representations of Islam and of Indian Islamic civilisation), and of course in the curtailing of freedom of expression. However, in America – arguably a multicultural country – the revisions were thwarted by academic experts on scientific grounds (Kurien 2007: ibid). By means of policy and the law, and by the circumstance that communities and organisations are forced to negotiate their interests with those of other groups, multiculturalism appears to neutralise rather than nurture demands to limit civil rights and freedoms on ethno-cultural grounds. Moreover, attempts to restrict freedom of expression are not specific to fundamentalism but have been a constant in modern societies since the advent of civil liberties: the liberties and their critics are two sides of the same coin – modern democratic society. It is a paradox that those who wish to restrict cultural liberties often claim that restriction is a necessary measure in order to safeguard freedom of expression in the longer term. However, multiculturalism does not imply giving in to those who want restrictions. On the contrary – as some contributors to this volume argue – restriction of free debate is always a fundamentalist practice, by whichever proponent and for whatever reason it is suggested.

## Contributions

The first two chapters treat the philosophical preconditions for public debate, namely communicative procedures and problems of justification and application, illustrated by the global issues of democracy and human rights. **May Thorseth** divests the concept of 'fundamentalism' of its substantive and religious contents, looking instead at formal and procedural characteristics. Fundamentalists are defined as actors who do not accept a plurality of opinions on issues of central concern to them. Democracy presupposes plurality, but many proponents of democracy refuse to recognise others' positions. Both global and national societies need to reflect critically reflect on this if they wish to communicate in a democratic way, Thorseth argues. **Petra Hedberg** brings the debate between Jürgen Habermas and Karl-Otto Apel to bear on two questions: whether human rights are justifiable on a universal level or only within specific cultural and political systems; and the extent to which a universally-justified system of human rights can resolve conflicts between different rights, e.g. freedom of speech versus religious freedom. Against this background, Hedberg explores the tension between a universally-justified system of human rights, premised on the concept of the autonomous individual, and fundamentalist collectivist concepts of the individual and of rights.

In the third chapter, **Stefano M. Bisighin** and **Lionel Sacks** combine Roy Rappaport's anthropological concept of ritual with the semiotic models of Roman Jakobson and Algirdas Greimas into an analytical model of 'public ritual communication', which they apply to four empirical cases. The purpose of the model is to enable definitions of what distinguishes 'fundamentalist' from 'ordinary' ritual communication, by examining the meaning of the ritual's religious symbols in reference to its social context. The conclusions are that while 'ordinary' rituals sanctify society's core institutions through a message of inclusion, 'fundamentalist' public rituals potentially or even actually withhold sanctification through a message of excommunication or self-exclusion from the core institutions.

What do American 'constitutionalists', such as Senator Ron Paul, and the Islamic movement Hizb al-Tahrir, have in common? According to **Lionel Sacks,** both believe in a return to the gold standard and the Constitution. In each case, their arguments are derived from a founding text, augmented with inferred beliefs of the texts' author(s), and bolstered by selective appeal to modern theory or evidence. Further, considering the ideal form for an existing state (the USA) or a prospective state (a caliphate), this ideal takes on the contours of a haven, isolated from global institutions. Money, itself a medium of communication, is employed as a communication sign (the gold standard) in the context of economic turmoil, to signify a return to the ideal and safe age of the texts and Founding Fathers.

**Oddbjørn Leirvik** analyses the different policies employed by the Danish and Norwegian governments in handling the crisis over the published cartoons of the Prophet Muhammad in the period 2005–06. While the Danes refused to enter into dialogue with offended Muslims, the Norwegians held talks with them on both national and international levels. Without compromising the principle of freedom of expression, the Norwegian approach of offering dialogue secured better relations with concerned Muslims than the Danish non-dialogue. Mapping Norwegian critics of their government's approach, Leirvik argues that their approaches coupled non-communication with an exclusively 'monocultural' view of the nation.

**Jennifer L. Bailey** explores the tension between literacy and reading as essentially emancipating practices and fundamentalist 'embedded literacy'. The Protestant stress on every man and woman reading the Bible in their vernacular language is an essentially emancipating practice, correlated to the invention of the printing press and the slow but steady growth of literacy. American Protestant fundamentalists, however, are anxious about emancipation in general and especially with respect to the Bible. In order to manage the tension between the Protestant principle of 'every man's Bible' and their own authoritarian principles, fundamentalists closely direct their members' reading of the Bible, and as far as possible channel their community members to fundamentalist educational institutions.

In his study of fundamentalism in the Roman Catholic Church, **Michael Trainor** finds that on the elite level, the term applies to those who reject the liberal reforms of the Second Vatican Council (1962–65) in favour of the 'counter-reformation' Council of Trent (1545–63). On the popular level, Trainor argues, the deeply conservative assertiveness associated with this latter council is embraced by those who feel estranged from the Church's open-ended intellectual self-reflection and apparent obliviousness to their need for certainty. The way to reduce popular support for elite fundamentalism is thus increased literacy and education and familiarity with intellectual, open-ended enquiry.

In his study of the Bangladesh branch of the trans-national Hizb al-Tahrir (HTB) and the Bangladeshi public sphere, **Ahmed Abidur Razzaque Khan** argues that government authoritarianism, and its sponsorship of state-oriented Islamist parties with little public support, has favoured the HTB and its programme for a global caliphate. Within Bangladesh's illiberal public sphere, and through global new media, HTB has successfully carved out its own 'pseudo-public sphere' where it communicates its messages without having to confront critics. A genuinely liberal public sphere, Khan argues, would make it harder for HTB to sell their programme to the Bangladeshi people.

**Soraj** and **Krisadawan Hongladarom** explore the emergence of 'Cyber Buddhism' on Thai Internet sites, including a 'fundamentalist' lobby group which argues that Thailand's constitution should specify that Theravada Buddhism is the national religion, that it should be protected from foreign cultural influences and that the special relationship between the state and Buddhism should also be expressed in law. This group communicates its message about a Buddhist national identity through a website which (like those of other Cyber Buddhists) is considerably more dynamic than the ones set up by the traditional Buddhist institutions, but which (unlike those of still other Cyber Buddhists) is highly authoritarian in the way it moderates debate.

In order to arrive at a more nuanced understanding of contemporary Islamic fundamentalist ('Wahhabi') polemics against Sufism, **Gavin N. Picken** conducts a historical survey of thinkers within the Hanbalite School, showing that Hanbalites often displayed multifaceted approaches to Sufism rather than the commonly-held rejectionist response. He continues with a study of how this historical discourse is carried on by both Wahhabis and Sufis in Europe and the USA, and via new media. Consequently, such medieval debates are now part of the global public sphere where these historical discussions regarding 'tradition' and 'orthodoxy' continue to be relived.

Surveying the landscape of Arabic Islamic TV channels which express Islamist and Salafi 'fundamentalist' visions of Islam as an all-encompassing system, **Jakob Skovgaard-Petersen** brings to our attention certain significant facts. Firstly, the Islamist channels in particular are approaching religion and morality in increasingly individualistic ways, exploring – like Oprah Winfrey – personal experiences and offering advice on personality development. Secondly, while the vision of an all-encompassing Islam is central to these programmes, the facts that the Islamic channels are only one option among many others, and that there are differences among the Islamic channels, communicate the message that Islam is but one sector of social life, and that Islamic programmes may address only some of the viewers' desires for entertainment and personal growth. Thus, 'fundamentalist' channels promote a 'compartmentalised' view of religion even as they repeat the message that Islam is a comprehensive system.

Using Zadie Smith's novel *White Teeth* (2000) as a source, **Priscilla Ringrose** explores the formation of the fictitious KEVIN ('Keepers of the Eternal Victory of the Islamic Nation') in the borderland between (at least) three equally globalised phenomena: American-style 'gangsta' culture', Islamic Salafi fundamentalism, and British multicultural (but in places also racist) society. The novel is a powerful and complex commentary on subjects debated in European public spheres: notably, 'integration', generational change and conflicts, and, not least, that the wannabe gangsta-fundamentalist, Millat, is perhaps the character with the fewest resources to participate in public debates.

**Moshe Terdman** provides an insight into the radical Islamist and jihadi Salafi movements and their fraught relationship with the perhaps most popular of all global sports: football. Jihadi Salafis want football banned on principle, as a corrupting Western influence and a form of 'idolatry'. But because of the sport's immense popularity, and because it has been declared lawful by slightly more moderate Islamists, the jihadis have been forced to accept it in practice, so as not to alienate 'the masses' completely. Consequently, they also allow themselves to watch football, pouring scorn over their enemies' teams (especially those of Iran and Saudi Arabia). Thus it seems that global sports and media move even jihadis in new directions.

## Bibliography

Alan M. (2009) at *http://blog.christianitytoday.com/ctpolitics/2009/07/gerson_francis. html*, 15 July 2009. Accessed 29 July 2009.

Almond, Gabriel A., Emmanuel Sivan and R. Scott Appleby (1995) 'Fundamentalism: genus and species'. In Marty, Martin E. and R. Scott Appleby (eds.) *Fundamentalisms Comprehended*. Vol. 5 of *The Fundamentalism Project*. Chicago: The University of Chicago Press, pp. 399–424.

Ammerman, Nancy (1990) *Baptist Battles: Social Change and Religious Conflict in the Southern Baptist Convention*. New Brunswick, NJ: Rutgers University Press.

Berger, Peter (ed.) (1999) *The Desecularization of the World: Resurgent Religion and World Politics*. Washington, DC: Ethics and Public Policy Center.

Beyer, Peter (2006) *Religions in Global Society*. London: Routledge.

Canada (2009) 'About Canada: multiculturalism in Canada'. At *http://www.mta. ca/about_canada/multi/*. Accessed 6 August 2009.

*The Economist* (25 July 2009) *A Special Report on the Arab World*, pp. 3–16.

FBF (Fundamental Baptist Fellowship International) (2009) *http://www.fbfi.org/ content/view/2/2/*, accessed 29 July 2009.

Habermas, Jürgen, Giovanna Borradori and Jacques Derrida (2003) *Philosophy in a Time of Terror: Dialogues with Jürgen Habermas and Jacques Derrida*. Chicago: The University of Chicago Press.

Habermas, Jürgen (1974) 'The public sphere: an encyclopedia article (1964)'. *New German Critique*, Vol. 3 (1974), pp. 49–55.

Hamzah, Dyala (forthcoming, 2011) 'From *'Ilm* to *Sihafa* or the politics of the public interest (maslaha): Muhammad Rashid Rida and his journal al-Manar (1898–1910)'. In Dyala Hamzah, Dyala (ed.) *The Making of the Arab Intellectual: Empire, Public Sphere and the Colonial Coordinates of Selfhood.* London: Routledge.

Hastings, Adrian (1997) *The Construction of Nationhood: Ethnicity, Religion and Nationalism.* Cambridge: Cambridge University Press.

Hoover, Stewart (2006) *Religion in the Media Age.* London: Routledge.

Huntington, Samuel (1996) *The Clash of Civilizations and the Remaking of World Order.* New York: Simon & Schuster.

Juergensmeyer, Mark (1993) *The New Cold War? Religious Nationalism Confronts the Secular State.* Berkeley, CA: University of California Press.

—— (2008) *Global Rebellion: Religious Challenges to the Secular State.* Berkeley, CA: University of California Press.

Kedourie, Elie (ed.) (1970/1971) *Nationalism in Asia and Africa.* London: Weidenfeld and Nicolson.

—— (1956/1987) *England and the Middle East: The Destruction of the Ottoman Empire 1914–1921.* London: Mansell.

Kurien, Prema A. (2007) *A Place at the Multicultural Table: The Development of an American Hinduism.* New Brunswick, NJ: Rutgers University Press.

Malik, Kenan (2002) 'Against multiculturalism'. *New Humanist* (summer). *http://www.kenanmalik.com/essays/against_mc.html*, accessed 4 August 2009.

Marty, Martin E. and R. Scott Appleby (eds.) (1991–95) *The Fundamentalism Project.* 5 vols. Chicago: The University of Chicago Press.

Marty, Martin E. and R. Scott Appleby (eds.) (1997) *Religion, Ethnicity, and Self-Identity: Nations in Turmoil.* Hanover, NH: University Press of New England.

McLuhan, Marshall (1964/1997) *Understanding Media: The Extensions of Man.* London: Routledge.

Modood, Tariq (2007) *Multiculturalism: A Civic Idea.* Cambridge: Polity.

Nussbaum, Martha (2007) *The Clash Within: Religious Violence and the Future of Democracy in India.* Cambridge, MA: Belknap.

Parekh, Bhikhu (2000) *The Future of Multi-Ethnic Britain.* The Runnymede Trust: Report of the Commission on the Future of Multi-Ethnic Britain.

—— BBC News online (2004) 'So what exactly is multiculturalism?', 5 April 2004. At *http://news.bbc.co.uk/2/hi/uk_news/3600791.stm*, accessed 3 August 2009.

Pew Forum on Religion and Public Life (2008) *The US Religious Landscape Survey.* At *http://religions.pewforum.org/reports*, accessed 12 August 2009.

Rutherford, Bruce K. (2008) *Egypt after Mubarak: Liberalism, Islam, and Democracy in the Arab World.* Princeton, NJ: Princeton University Press.

Sageman, Marc (2004) *Understanding Terrorist Networks.* Philadelphia, PA: University of Pennsylvania Press.

Sakeenah, Maryam (2009) 'The fraternity of civilizations: prospects for dialogue'. *Dissident Voice: A Radical Newsletter in the Struggle for Peace and Social Justice.* At *http://dissidentvoice.org/2009/07/the-fraternity-of-civilizations-prospects-for-dialogue* and *http://www.ikhwanweb.com/Article.asp?ID=20914&SectionID=0*, 29 July 2009, accessed 31 July 2009.

Sassen, Saskia (2006) *Territory, Authority, Rights: From Medieval to Global Assemblages.* Princeton, NJ: Princeton University Press.

Senghaas, Dieter (2002) *The Clash Within Civilizations.* London: Routledge.

Smith, Tom W. and Kim Seokho (2005) 'The vanishing Protestant majority'. *Journal of the Scientific Study of Religion*, Vol. 44, No. 2, pp. 211–23.

Stunich, Andrew (2007) 'Internal culture war and self-hatred in the West allow Islamic inroads'. *Islam Watch: Telling the Truth about Islam. http://islam-watch. org/Stunich/Culture-War-and-Self-hatred-West-Allow-Islamic-Inroads.htm*, 6 November 2007, accessed 4 August 2009.

TheOPINIONATOR (2009) 'Islamization on STEROIDS – non-Muslim female British police issued hijabs – veils', 29 July. At *http://theopinionator.typepad. com/my_weblog/multiculturalism/*, accessed 4 August 2009.

al-Zawahiri, Ayman (2001) *Knights Under the Prophet's Banner.* London: Al-Sharq al-Awsat.

# CHAPTER 1

# GLOBAL COMMUNICATION ONLINE AGAINST FUNDAMENTALIST KNOWLEDGE OFFLINE?

## May Thorseth

### Introduction

The term fundamentalism as applied by the media is often used to label certain kinds of behaviours that are implicitly linked to religion. Standard cases include: Muslim reactions to the ironic cartoons of the prophet Muhammad, published in Scandinavian media; religious minorities who refuse to be subordinated to the majority culture (e.g. who demand the right freely to exercise religious practices without interference from the majority society); and terrorist actions undertaken with the stated aim of avenging offences to Muslim religious culture (as on 11 September 2001). In the last case the attack on the Twin Towers was considered by the media to be an act of revenge against the US motivated by Arab religious fundamentalism.

Many people associate fundamentalism with religion, in particular with Islam, which they oppose to Western, democratic and liberal values. From this perspective, it is possible to establish a cultural dividing line between fundamentalist and democratic values, based on the degree to which religion is considered as politicised. This association, I suggest, is unfortunate because it makes us lose sight of an important point, namely that 'Western liberal values' can be highly fundamentalist. So how should we delineate fundamentalism? I argue that it ought to be conceived of in procedural terms. The focus is then shifted from specific (substantive) values to the way values are being treated. Whether or not we are presented with a morally problematic form of fundamentalism depends on whether there is an argumentative disclosure for counter-arguments. We might thus ask: is it possible to argue against a particular cultural norm? Is it open to revision? Can it be refuted? A negative answer to these questions points in the direction of what is here defined as procedural fundamentalism. Such fundamentalism does not allow for counter-arguments, revision or refusal of contested norms. This is precisely why I believe it is relevant to criticise a fundamentalist position.

In several other contexts I have distinguished between legitimate and illegitimate paternalism, using definitions based on procedural criteria (Thorseth 1999: 75–80). Paternalism means potential infringement of an individual's freedom for his/her benefit, an action which may in some cases be morally legitimate;[1] parents' role in their children's upbringing and education is an obvious case in point. Not every kind of parental upbringing is, however, an example of *paternalistic* enforcement – such is the case when there is doubt over whether a certain practice is actually in the child's interest. Forced and arranged marriage – publicly associated with Muslim culture – is another case in point. Some instances of *forced* marriage are obviously both paternalistic and fundamentalist. However, the institution of *arranged* marriages is another matter, since in many cases arranged marriages are freely embraced by women who believe it is for their own good. In these cases the institution of arranged marriage cannot be regarded as paternalist, since it is not connected to enforcement. The institution of arranged marriage, as such, is thus neither fundamentalist nor paternalist, but is still often publicly associated with fundamentalist religious values. This, I would argue, is both unfortunate and unwarranted.

In the light of the above, this chapter explores 'procedural fundamentalism' with reference to public debates about forced and arranged marriages, and through the concepts of global communication and deliberative democracy. The principal case study examined relates to the public debate generated in Scandinavia by the forced marriage and murder in early 2002 of Fadime Shahindal, a young Swedish-Kurdish woman.

## Part I

### Fundamentalism – a procedural approach

Muslim fundamentalists who seek to be acknowledged for their own non-argumentative behaviour towards contested norms render themselves guilty of inconsistency. This is because the claim on non-interference already presupposes argumentative participation. The struggle for recognition of fundamentalist behaviour (for instance, rejection of Western values) is equivalent to demanding respect for criticising these values. Refusal to state one's reasons for withdrawal from discourse, while still claiming the right to be respected for oppressive behaviour towards group members, is an example of non-argumentative fundamentalism. Such fundamentalism is characterised by *argumentative closure*, as opposed to practical discourse associated with argumentative disclosure (Habermas 1990). The morally relevant distinction between argumentative closure and disclosure is *procedural*. Fundamentalism, as described above, can be present anywhere, being characterised by a refusal to enter into critical reflection on any particular way of life that has become contested. This is also an argument against the belief that enforced argumentation is just another kind of fundamentalism.

## 'Traditional' and 'modern' fundamentalism:
## introductory examples

### Fundamentalism as rational behaviour

Increasing fundamentalism within Islam can be understood as a response to fear of negative influences from the West (Thorseth 1994: 6); this is normal given a prevalence of negative rhetoric about the West. One result of this is that religion itself is turned into an argument against Western, secular influence. This might be reflected either in a refusal to argue, or in preventing others within one's own group from arguing, about contested norms. Fundamentalism in this case consists in a refusal to argue about (contested) religious norms.

## Fundamentalism and essentialism

Essentialism is here mainly linked to identity, and is an example of fundamentalism in that it acts as if certain norms and values were beyond revision, for whatever reason (for instance, the aim of preserving a particular way of life). Thus, essentialism becomes one of several kinds of fundamentalism, since there are other kinds which do not particularly relate to identity. The main characteristic of the essentialist fundamentalist is the belief in some non-dialogical or static identity, often attached to ethnicity. The 'modern' Swedish nationalist who wants to preserve a white Swedish majority fits into this category. Another example is one that is discussed by Appiah (1994: 154–5); this concerns Afro-American nationalists who claim recognition for a particular black identity that they wish to preserve, while not recognising that this very identity is developed only in relation to a white majority. Scandinavians who react negatively towards Samis who enter McDonalds dressed in traditional Sami clothes might also fit into this category of essentialism. The common denominator in these examples is the non-argumentative conceptualisation of a particular identity that is regarded as being beyond revision or critical reflection.

## 'Fundamentalism in disguise'

The fundamentalists in the above two examples could be considered 'overt', i.e. they do not pretend to behave in a non-fundamentalist manner, but act more or less strategically in order to realise some particular goal. A different kind of fundamentalist are those who object to such behaviour, while withdrawing some of their own beliefs from critical reflection. The dogmatic Western feminist who criticises the Muslim fundamentalist might be a case in point, if she does not allow any criticism of feminism on the other's part. There are two points I wish to make in connection with this example: first, the feminist and the Muslim are both fundamentalists in respect of particular values; and second they both behave non-argumentatively about those values which they take to be beyond criticism. A common denominator in these examples is the subordination of all arguments under one perspective, along with the raising of some particular norm that is taken to be beyond critical reflection. 'Modern' fundamentalism does not differ from 'traditional' religious fundamentalism as far as such procedural characteristics are concerned, though the 'modern' fundamentalist pretends to be non-fundamentalist and thus rational, as opposed to the 'traditional' fundamentalist. This is why I describe the 'modern' fundamentalist as a 'fundamentalist in disguise'. In order to identify the morally relevant features of fundamentalism, I think it is important to realise that fundamentalism and rationality are not essentially opposites in characterising the difference between the Muslim and feminist fundamentalists in this preceding example.

In sum, across the different instances of fundamentalism there are some common denominators. First, there is the subordination of all criticism under one perspective, and second the withdrawal of some particular norm (religion, belief system, ideology etc) from critical reflection.

## Fundamentalism in the media: the Fadime case

Fundamentalism might be conceived of as the suppression of challenges to particularity, as when a particular cultural practice or narrative is put forward with an unquestionable claim to approval. I will refer to a particular story reported in the Nordic media: in January 2002, a young Swedish-Kurdish woman, Fadime Shahindal, was killed by her father in Sweden. The murder was referred to by the media as an 'honour killing', and explained in terms of Fadime's contesting of the cultural norm of forced marriage. The murder and the ensuing debate have precipitated public reflection on the right to participate in public debate, and also on the practice of referring to immigrants in terms of collective religious or ethnic identities. Moreover, these 'groups' are considered to be represented by certain named representatives. This obscures the fact that practices of forced marriage and honour killings are also contested amongst members of minority societies, just as they are amongst members of society at large.

The murder of Fadime and the subsequent debate in Sweden and Norway clearly demonstrate that Muslims in these two countries cannot and should not be defined on the conceptual basis of a uniform group. Fadime was killed by her father because she loved a Swedish-Iranian man, had refused a marriage arranged by the family, and spoke of her conflict with the family and her opinions of love and marriage openly in the media, arguing publicly against arranged marriages. We might formulate this case as a problem concerning the relation between the particular and the general, in cases where particular arguments are considered to be justified with respect to 'others', but not looked upon as acceptable to 'us'. We may ask: what appeal can be made to general circumstances, and how do such appeals relate to something beyond the particular, something of universal scope?

We may furthermore ask how we should describe the case above. What description would be an accurate one? No matter how we describe it – as an act of honour killing or otherwise – our description will in any case be a normative act, because it represents a solution to what we presuppose are the underlying problems. This act is either an honour killing – Fadime's male family members were saving the family's honour – or it was about a sick man's misdeed, as Fadime's sister Fidan claimed (Eriksson and Wadendal 2002).

In describing this act as an 'honour killing' in the media, a particular appeal is made to particular circumstances about a particular culture. Because of this appeal to the particular, the description can be used either to justify or condemn the act in question. This was exemplified by Shabana Rehman (a Norwegian media personality of Pakistani descent), who was strongly critical, and Norwegian imams, who tended towards justification. Whether this particular description is used for criticism or justification, it encourages segregation. To describe the act as the misdeed of a sick man, as the female members of Fadime's family did, does not, however, appeal to culturally specific circumstances to the same extent as the concept 'honour killing' does. The notion that some people commit sick acts is applicable in any context, and is not necessarily related at all to ethnic or cultural status. The appeal to culturally-specific circumstances is part of the fundamentalism being exercised in this case. The culturally-specific appeal does not, however, necessarily imply a case of fundamentalism, provided that it also includes a more general appeal that transcends the particular circumstances (Dryzek 2000: 57–80).[2]

If the act in question is considered the misdeed of a mentally-ill person, it is turned into something that calls for a more general appeal. By contrast, if the act is described in terms of a particular cultural or religious norm, then not many people can defend it – at least not people in Western, democratic societies. Appealing to the particular also risks giving rise to feelings of disgust within Western society at large. Particular appeals, as an example of procedural fundamentalism, might also enforce a kind of culture relativism that weakens minorities as well as society at large. Ethical argumentation in a global world should strengthen minorities as well as the majority. One means of working towards this is to avoid particular appeals devoid of a universal component.

What we need to establish, in order to avoid particular appeals being turned into fundamentalism, is to establish a link to a universal appeal that transcends what is embedded in the culturally-specific norm or practice. What we should aim at establishing through appeal to the universal is a mutual respect for each other's circumstances. It is thus argued here that disconnecting the conceptual linkage between religion and fundamentalism will enable a better understanding of the procedural features of fundamentalism. The Fadime case illustrates how argumentation might be characterised as fundamentalist by making a particular appeal to a value which cannot be shared by everyone.

## Value pluralism and judgment

The position defended here is a criticism of both procedural fundamentalism and relativism. Part of the problem about moral relativism is that it implies a normative position that is exempted from moral judgment. This is the case if we believe that we can coherently understand practices, without judging them, that many people strongly disapprove of (such as female genital mutilation, or women being banned from education or employment outside the home, or ethnic cleansing). Rather than taking a relativist stance we argue in favour of value pluralism. According to the latter, recognition requires substantive rather than only formal or epistemic judgment.

According to value pluralism, we do not have to commit ourselves to moral relativism. When undertaking a substantive judgment, we show respect for those with whom we disagree by being willing to enter into argumentation with them. It can hardly be argued that we show respect for the plurality of opinions if we leave contested cultural norms unquestioned. The relativist solution would be to leave it exactly there, making an appeal to the claim that moral judgments are only relative to some framework of standards. This raises the important and difficult question of whether or not it is legitimate to interfere in condemnable practices. If we strongly oppose human-rights abuses but choose not to interfere in such cases, this is tantamount to stating that these acts are justified because they are permissible within the moral framework of the people who perform them. This position is hard to defend in a world where we are continuously reminded that norms are not only conflicting in relation to particular cultures – conflicting norms and moral conflicts prevail just as much *within* as *between* cultures. This is essential in dealing with the question of whether or not non-interference demonstrates recognition and respect.

As indicated above, interference is associated with substantive as opposed to merely formal judgment, and hence also demonstrates involvement with the individuals or culture in question. Non-interference is more closely linked to a policy of neutrality, which should not necessarily be identified with recognition and respect: abstaining from substantive judgment is a step in the direction of fundamentalism.

Fundamentalism as described above is here contrasted with communication addressing a global audience, as also with democratic behaviour; thus any form of fundamentalism runs contrary to global democracy. This follows from the procedural criterion that has been discussed above. It is equally important to note that global democracy implies judging as opposed to merely understanding; this follows from the concept of value pluralism discussed above. A third criterion for excluding fundamentalism is that judgments of different moral systems are not purely formal. This last criterion is inherent in the claim that purely formal judgments are insufficient with respect to value pluralism. A preliminary conclusion, then, is that global democracy would require a value pluralism that rules out some moral systems because they are fundamentalist. Non-fundamentalist communication calls for intervention whenever basic human rights are jeopardised. The universal status of human rights is rooted in both the legal and moral aspects of value pluralism.

## Reflective judgment of the particular

From the arguments above we will highlight the following points:

- Treating all values in the same way shows disrespect for differences and undermines value pluralism;
- attributing significance to particular values is a dialogical enterprise that cannot be purely formal; and
- hence value pluralism requires substantive judgment of differences.

The standard by which we make moral judgments is not only substantive as opposed to purely formal. We need a standard for criticising norms and practices that we find intolerable and dehumanising. Different solutions have been suggested, among them some common standard of rationality that applies in particular to the public domain. John Rawls is an exponent of this solution, elaborated in terms of the concept of 'the veil of ignorance' behind which people rationally choose institutions that neither favour nor disadvantage anyone (Rawls 1970). An obvious problem with such a solution is that it is deeply rooted in Western standards of rationality, due to the strong weight that is accorded to individual autonomy. In many Eastern countries collectivism is embraced, and is conceived of as partly incompatible with Western individualism (Madsen and Strong 2003). Charles Taylor's position can be seen as a solution to the problem of reconciling differences between ethical systems:

> The crucial idea is that people can bond not in spite of but because of difference. They can sense, that is, that their lives are narrower and less full alone than in association with each other. In this sense, the difference defines a complementarity. (Taylor 2002, cited in Madsen and Strong 2003: 11)

This does not preclude criticism of moral systems, but instead requires, for the criticism to be valid, that it is predicated on a broad under-standing of what the practices mean in their context (ibid, Madsen and Strong). In order to have knowledge of the practices of alien cul-tures it is necessary to have access to the particular contexts in ques-tion. Online communication appears to be a valuable means of finding such access, mainly because it provides unique possibilities for com-munication across the globe (Coleman and Gøtze 2004; Fishkin 1997; Wheeler 2005; Thorseth 2006).

If we view pluralism in the light of Taylor's politics of recognition, where identity is seen as dialogically established and developed, any recognition will be dependent on the dialogues that constitute the different identities. We may now see that judgments of others also require participation by those making the judgments, due to the rela-tionship which is thereby established with those we are judging. This way of reasoning is also reflected in Stanley Cavell's understanding of how we could criticise, for instance, the institution of slavery without dehumanising those involved in it:

> [W]hat a man who sees certain others as slaves is missing is not something about slaves exactly and not exactly about human beings. He is missing something about himself, or rather something about his connection with these people, his internal relation with them, so to speak. (Cavell 1997: 377, cited in Madsen and Strong 2003: 13)

The important point here is that value pluralism requires admission of a relationship with the others in relation to whom we define our identity. What is at stake is not so much how we judge different others, but rather how we allow others to see us. Value pluralism is then envisaged as a system where the most important enterprise would be to gain recognition of one as viewed by others.

This recognition of oneself links with Kant's concept of the moral law. In Kant's second critique we find several formulations of the categorical imperative: to treat everyone else not merely as a means but also always as an end in herself, and to consider the humanity in every single person as equally worthy of the same kind of respect.[3] In Kant's third critique he speaks of reflective judgment or enlarged thought (Kant 1790/1952: § 40). The Kantian notions of enlarged thought are basic to our understanding of what legitimises a universal appeal of particular judgments. The concept contains a visualisation of how particular judgments gain legitimacy through a kind of universal appeal.

In Kant's conceptual scheme, judgments are of two different kinds: either they are determinant, as when something particular is subsumed under universal laws, or, by contrast, '[i]f only the particular is given and the universal has to be found for it, then the judgment is simply *reflective*' (ibid, Introduction IV: 18). The purpose of reflective judgment is not to determine anything: rather, it is to give itself a law. Hence, validity is gained through reflection of something particular as opposed to something subsumed under universal laws. This is partly because judgment, which is the topic of investigation in Kant's third critique, is about empirical contingencies and not about universal laws of nature or final ends of freedom.[4] Kant's own focal point in his treatment of judgment is taste and the sublime, and applies first and foremost to the aesthetic domain, as distinguished from nature (pure reason) and freedom (practical reason). Hannah Arendt and Seyla Benhabib have, however, extended the notion of reflective judgment to the public and political faculties (Arendt 1968; Benhabib 1992).

The validity of judgments depends on the judging, and it is not valid for those who do not judge. This point is propounded by Hanna Arendt, who claims that validity presupposes communication between self and others; hence a judgment's claim to validity can never extend further than the public realm of those who are members of it (Arendt 1968: 221). There are, in particular, two issues relating to validity that should be noted here. One concerns the relation between the particular and the universal, whereas the other has to do with the public aspect of judgment. Any particular judgment is based on contingent and finite appeals that nevertheless may transcend the subjective conditions of the particular judgment, the potential for which derives from the communicative aspect of all judgments.

The basic point is that communication rather than expression is required in public reason. Part of this claim to make public use of reason builds on the maxims of common understanding: to think for oneself; to think from the standpoint of everyone else, i.e. enlarged thought; and always to think consistently (Kant 1790/1952 § 40: 294). All these maxims about public reason are more profound than any other use of reason, and they are standards for reasoning for addressing 'the world at large' (O'Neill 1989: 48).

In addressing the world at large, reason accepts no external authority. It is this use of reason that is at work in the judgment of particular situations, derived from the human capacity for reflective judgment. Thus, we see how reflective judgment and enlarged thinking is for Kant basic to any other form of communication. This is the important point to be drawn from his model for validation in the public faculty, and it is particularly interesting because it gives an account of how reflection of particular situations and conditions can make a claim to validity. This holds true to the extent that the appeals address a universal audience: Kant speaks of this as the public use of reason. By contrast, appeals addressed to a restricted audience cannot lay claim to being universally communicable. Still, private uses of reason may be legitimate for certain purposes. The important point is that '[t]here are no good reasons for tolerating any private uses of reason that damage public uses of reason' (O'Neill 1989: 49).

Non-fundamentalist value pluralism has to steer a course between relativism, on the one hand, and dogmatic fundamentalism conceived as private use of reason on the other. This implies recognition of (substantive) differences, while also making an appeal to moral claims that are true from a non-relativist point of view.

The distinction between formal and substantive judgment is of critical importance to the argument of this chapter. On the one hand it allows us to establish that fundamentalism can be defined on the basis of procedural rather than substantive criteria, and on the other hand it takes us beyond relativism towards universalism. Thus relativism might turn out to be an instance of fundamentalism if it evades judgment or substantive criticism. In a world of (multi)cultural contestation we need to be capable of distinguishing between morally acceptable and morally unacceptable behaviours and moral systems. For this purpose, Kant's concepts of enlarged thought and public use of reason are helpful. Recalling the Fadime case discussed above, there was a lack of public use of reason in the claim to judge the action of Fadime's father as an honour killing typical of a particular Muslim culture.

## Part II

### Online contexts of global communication

What has been established so far is a prelude to the following discussion of two concepts, global communication and deliberative democracy. Here these concepts are seen as interrelated. The global aspect is present in the vision of communication that transcends borders, whereas the deliberative aspect might best be conceived of as direct communication which aims at qualifying and possibly changing arguments and opinions in the public domain. The outcome of deliberation might be a change of preferences and opinions, due to insights into opposing views of the matters discussed. For example, deliberation has on some occasions been carried out as a controlled test ahead of elections. The theory underlying that project was developed by James Fishkin, and is known as 'deliberative' polling.[5] In the following, we will have a brief look at some other projects aiming at deliberation in the sense described.

### Online deliberation and Democracy Unbound

My contribution to the project Democracy Unbound[6] deals in part with online communication and with the question of the feasibility of

global communication – or worldwide deliberation – across boundaries and across stereotypes, of which fundamentalism is an example.
My philosophical interest relates to public use of reason online. As yet,
there are no conclusive reports supporting the assumption that communication online moves in a more democratic and unbound rather
than a fundamentalist direction. As we shall see, while some research
underlines the democratic and borderless potential of this new technology (Wheeler: 2005; Coleman and Gøtze: 2004), other investigations claim the opposite to be the case (Sunstein 2001). Rather than
discussing these opposing views in any detail, I will focus on the kind
of communication that is contrasted with fundamentalism. One main
objective here is to demonstrate why online communication might
work as an impediment to procedural fundamentalism.

## Deliberative democracy

There are different notions of democracy, some of which are more
demanding than others, depending on the level of participation and
influence of the citizens. Democracy might be representative or direct,
and its scope may vary (local, national or federal, supranational, global). The most fundamental characteristic of *liberal* democracy, however, is the plurality of voices upon which opinions and decisions are
based. How should we make sure that policies pay attention to the
plurality of parties concerned, and how should we safeguard the procedures at work?

The notion of *deliberative* democracy relates to discursive democracy as discussed by John Dryzek (2001), and is partly based upon
Habermas's notion of practical discourse. The ethical norm of a non-
coerced mode of communication, free from both external and internal
obstructions, is a fundamental one. A necessary prerequisite for deliberative democracy is a plurality of parties and opinions, and their accessibility. Furthermore, the final arbiter is public reason itself, which is
the only legitimate authority in policy-making. From this it follows
that any policy decision should be exposed to open and critical public
debate, which should not be limited to political decision-makers. This
is the normative basis for the argument of this chapter.

## Deliberative polling online

The core idea of deliberative polling is to contribute towards a better-informed democracy. The method, as developed by Fishkin (1997), is to use television and public opinion in a new and constructive way. A random, representative sample is polled on the targeted issues. One of many examples of this is the national deliberative poll on health care and education in the US. Results are also available from deliberative polling in different other countries around the world, including China, Greece, Italy and Northern Ireland.[7]

After the first baseline poll, members of the sample are invited to gather in some specific location in order to discuss the issues, together with competing experts and politicians. After the deliberations, the sample is again asked the original questions. The resulting changes in opinion represent the conclusions the public would reach if individuals had opportunities to become more informed and engaged in the issues in question.

## Deliberative polling online

The Public Informed Citizen Online Assembly (PICOLA) project was developed by Robert Cavalier.[8] It takes its point of departure in Fishkin's theory of deliberative polling. PICOLA is primarily a tool for carrying out deliberative polling in online contexts. The user interface allows for a dynamic, multimedia participant environment. The interface relations made possible by this technology is of vital importance to the deliberative process, as it allows for synchronous conversation in real time. Thus it appears to come very close to offline interface communication.

Several other reports on online deliberation are discussed by Coleman and Gøtze (2001). Some of their examples are drawn from tests of deliberation between local politicians and their electors. By and large, they conclude that a dialogical and responding structure of communication is obtained between the parties involved. However, it seems that there is also a clear tendency towards a decline in deliberation as soon as the test period has ended. Besides, the scope of the experiments discussed is limited and local, and they are thus not comparable to communications at a global level.

## Blogs, storytelling and enlarged thought

According to Coleman and Gøtze, the communication which takes place in blogs can be characterised as follows:

> A blog is a powerful way of telling stories that refer to, and make sense of, the documents and messages that we create and exchange in our professional and private lives. It is a simply designed and usable storytelling technology that could represent the next wave of grassroots knowledge and management implementations. Storytelling and blogs share one common ground: grassroots interaction. (Coleman and Gøtze 2001: 34)

The relation between storytelling and blogs is pertinent to our discussion, not only because of bloggers' grassroots interaction, but more importantly because storytelling links to the reflective judgment and enlarged thought as expressed in Kant's third critique. The idea is that something particular – a story – is made explicit, whereas the universal by which it is to be judged is not, and has to be found. This is how Kant characterises reflective as different from determinant judgment. The openness in the structure of reflective judgment is available through the particular. To the extent blogs promote such thought, they support the claim of this chapter that the internet may contribute positively to facilitating modes of communication associated with the particularity at work in reflective thinking.

Some critical voices have argued against this positive characterisation of blogs, mainly with reference to the notion of democracy. This is because blogs run the risk of descending into a chaotic cacophony of voices, a claim put forth by the Swedish media ombudsman Yrsa Stenius.[9] Her main argument against blogs is that they lack the critical and structured kinds of dialogues that are required if media is to work in a democratic way, not least by preventing those in power from exercising a monopoly on choosing the issues to be debated. Against

Stenius, however, it might be argued that the unstructured cacophony could be considered more democratic than structured debates in the media, because dialogues in blogs are, to some extent, not subject to the power relations that determine choices of subject matter in the public media.

Another argument against the democratic potential of blogs is that the storytelling going on there is not democratically relevant, nor necessarily contributing to more enlarged thought. The important question this raises relates to the kinds of topics which should be regarded as relevant for deliberative democracy. If we look at the questions raised in deliberative polls, they concern political and public questions relating to areas such as health policies, traffic or tax regulations. The topics of some blogs relate to similar issues, whereas others deal with more private issues. Despite this, I believe that the potential for blogs to promote enlarged thought derives from the fact that their authors can tell particular stories to people who do not know exactly what they are looking for when they visit any particular blog.

## Virtual and possible judgment online

When Kant talks about reflective judgment, he means possible rather than actual judgment. He introduces the concept *sensus communis*, a public sense and critical faculty that takes into account others' modes of representation, thereby avoiding the illusion that private and personal conditions are taken as objective. By weighing our judgments against the possible judgments of others, and by putting ourselves in their position, we are abstracting from the limitations which contingently affect our own estimate. The power of judgment rests on a potential agreement with others, and judgments derive their validity from this potential agreement. As Arendt has pointed out, judgment must liberate itself from the 'subjective private conditions' which naturally determine the outlook of each individual in privacy. Judgments based on subjective private opinions are legitimate as long as they are only privately-held opinions, but they are not fit to enter the market place, and lack all validity in the public realm (Arendt 1968: 220).

A key to understanding how this argument applies to virtual realities online is contained in the idea of *possible* judgment. The main reference being made is not to some actual context, but rather to something virtual, something it is *possible* for humans to imagine. Second Life is a virtual world online that is interesting in this respect. Visitors set out to create characters, meet, work and discuss within a virtual reality. The capability for imagining virtual scenarios may well be as important as polling and blogs for the purpose of broadening peoples' minds.

## The problem of the public

At the beginning of the 20th century, and therefore long before the technology for blogs and virtual worlds online was developed, Dewey (1927) expressed concern about the conditions for public debate. He pointed to the need, given increased socio-political complexity, for improving methods and conditions of debate, discussion and persuasion. He recognised, in particular, the need for a better-informed public and also for legislators and policy-makers to become better informed about the experiences of the public. Reflective judgment and enlarged thought based on Kant's third critique offer a theoretical framework for dealing with this problem. The liberation of our judgments from subjective private conditions is a necessary condition for weighing our judgments against the possible judgments of others, by putting ourselves in their place.

Kant does not offer a model for dealing with the complexity which concerned Dewey, but he does offer a model for transcending the private conditions of others' judgments. From this perspective, we may reformulate the problem of the public in terms of a problem of how to make people overcome the limitations that contingently affect our own judgments.

We argue that the cacophony of voices need not be a problem; rather, we believe it is in the interests of the public domain as likely to contribute to more enlarged thought, of which the main point is to address a universal audience. New information technologies now offer possibilities for far more extended access to the cacophony of voices than at any previous time. The main question, though, is what structures are required in order for the public to become better informed. Obviously, the fact that there is a plurality of voices is not sufficient. An important hypothesis of this chapter is that the mode of reflection is more important than the plurality of voices *per se*. The solution of the problem of the public is first to reformulate the problem: it is not a problem that there is a plurality of voices, nor is it a problem that the communication is not sufficiently structured: rather, the problem is how to make people more aware of the limitations of their immediate judgments, based as they are on their own private subjective conditions.

We believe that internet communication of different kinds – polling, blogs, virtual realities like Second Life – contribute to improved conditions for reflective judgment due to the following: first, the public cannot avoid awareness of different tastes and judgments, from which it follows, secondly, that it becomes harder to ignore the differences of tastes and opinions. From this, it follows, thirdly, that internet activities, as mentioned above, do have an impact on public reason. Still, there is a concern that lack of regulation or structure weakens democracy in the public domain. The main problem, as it relates to blogs in particular, is that even if they are democratic, they often lack structures for discussing community affairs, and there is therefore a risk of them turning into a cacophony of voices. Against this conclusion we have argued that there is no proof that this cacophony is itself a problem.

## Substantive judgment online – concluding remarks

In the first part of this chapter, we emphasised the importance of substantive judgment and knowledge of particular circumstances for combating fundamentalism. For this purpose, it is also required that communication of the particular contains some universal appeal in order to extend beyond the particular context. In this sense, global democracy presupposes communicative constraints that are not purely formal. This has been discussed in view of Kant's concepts of reflective judgment and enlarged thought.

There are partly divergent reports on the question of whether the internet enhances the kind of deliberative and democratic communication that has been contrasted, above, to fundamentalism. On the one hand, there are reports on the problem of filtering and group polarisation, indicating that global communication online jeopardises democracy (Sunstein 2001). On the other hand, there are more optimistic reports emphasising the importance of global internet communication for the purposes of promoting democracy and empowerment (Wheeler 2005). Despite this divergence, it is maintained here that the internet offers a venue for potentially more democratic and less fundamentalist communication between people of differing opinions. Several experiments have been carried out for examining how people would deliberate in online pollings.[10] Others have reported on equally positive results in cases of electronic set-ups for online deliberation between politicians and their electors, but the problem has often been that the good results prevail only during the period of the trial, and thereafter a decline of activity has been reported (Coleman and Gøtze 2001).

To conclude, I would like to put forward a hypothesis as to how the internet might work as an impediment to the circulation of fundamentalist knowledge. This hypothesis builds on the anticipation that the internet offers a unique possibility for knowledge of particular others across fundamentalist stereotypes. Had the Fadime case been made an object of criticism in different virtual scenarios, the case might have helped in realising the limitations of judgments based on purely 'subjective private conditions'. Taking our point of departure in local and particular judgments we might, in a virtual world, be able to establish a link to the global world encompassing judgments based in local cultures. The means of enabling this would be to have people participate in different virtual scenarios, thereby being able to judge the matter from the perspective of potential others. The interconnectedness of 'the local' and 'the global' would then appear evident. The individual encounters between people of very different backgrounds (religious, cultural, ethnic etc) appear to help people see that conflicting norms and moral conflicts are equally prevalent within as well as between cultures. This is of particular importance in a globalised world. An even more adequate way of putting it would be that in online contexts individuals meet individuals and particular stories rather than abstract conceptions of cultures.

Furthermore, if the encounter between different individuals and circumstances matters more than the differences of the aggregated stereotypes, the encounter as such is perhaps more important than the particular content of the communication. This indicates that it is perhaps not the democratic 'content' of the conversations which matters most when it comes to the question of whether global democracy is feasible. Rather, I would suggest that the possibility of playing different roles and putting oneself in the position of others stimulates the capacity to imagine counterfactual circumstances. From this perspective we might even consider the virtual reality that is offered online as more conducive to non-fundamentalist knowledge than knowledge of reasonable arguments about democratic behaviour. As an illustration of the kind of virtuality we have in mind, there are worlds like 'Second Life' where visitors set out to create characters, meet, work and discuss virtual reality.[11] Such play-acting may well stimulate more creativity and exploit imaginative powers resulting in greater openness towards and appreciation of the plurality of ways of living.

Besides the global potential of reflective judgment which virtuality provides, there is also another interesting way in which Second Life may be of vital importance to global democracy. In 2007, it was reported that a virtual political strike for an increase in salary rates had been started by Italian IBM employees in Second Life:[12] nine thousand employees urged the (nearly) nine million inhabitants of this virtual world to join the strike. The incident is interesting because the multinational giant IBM is one of the companies that have invested most in Second Life. It is, however, even more interesting with respect to the relation between the online and offline worlds. The dividing line between the two seems to disappear when people act in the virtual, online world as they do offline. This new communication-technology tool therefore has a clear potential to engender political action.

More empirical research is needed as to how internet visitors judge the importance of visiting virtual realities. Meanwhile, I believe there is sufficient evidence that more people than ever have access to a plurality of virtual and actual 'others' thanks to the new technology internet offers. It is yet too early to know exactly how internet encounters between people affect offline behaviour. Public criticism of fundamentalism – e.g. the public media representations of the murder of Fadime in 2002 as 'Muslim honour killing' – no doubt contributes to more diversity of opinions and perhaps even more democratic debate. New communication technology works on a global scale and keeps us constantly informed about processes of enlarged thinking that are going on in the public sphere, and thus the technology makes us conscious of the limitations of the private use of reason.

## Notes

1. Paternalism is defined as 'the interference of a state or an individual with another person, against their will, and justified by a claim that the person interfered with will be better off or protected from harm' The Stanford Encyclopedia of Philosophy, Published by The Metaphysics Research Lab, Stanford University. ISSN: 1095–5054.
2. Dryzek here discusses deliberation in the light of two different tests: communication that involves coercion should be excluded; and communication that cannot connect the particular to the general should be excluded.
3. 'Act in such a way that you treat humanity, whether in your own person or in the person of another, always at the same time as an end and never simply as a means' (Kant 1785/1981: 36).
4. Judgment is one among three cognitive faculties, the other two being understanding and reason – the subjects of the first and second of his critiques respectively.
5. See at *http://cdd.stanford.edu/polls/*.
6. At *http://people.su.se/~folke/index.html*.
7. More information on the method and different trials are accessible at *http://cdd.stanford.edu/*.
8. Cavaliers homepage at *http://www.hss.cmu.edu/philosophy/faculty-cavalier.php*. More information on the PICOLA project is accessible at *http://caae.phil.cmu.edu/picola/index.html*.
9. This is a claim put forth by the Swedish media ombudsman Yrsa Stenius, referred to by Lina Lindgren, *Morgenbladet*, 8–14 June 2007.
10. Fishkin (1997) is a valuable reference on this point.
11. Second Life is a virtual 3D world that was established in 2003. It is developed by its users, who establish themselves by a so-called 'avatar', a virtual

figure. The avatar is used for different purposes: communication, dancing, shopping and even striking.

12. Article by E. Løkeland-Stai in *Klassekampen*, Oslo, 25 September 2007, p. 10.

## Bibliography

Appiah, K. Anthony (1994) 'Identity, authenticity, survival: multicultural societies and social reproduction'. In Gutman, A. and C. Taylor (eds.) *Multiculturalism: Examining The Politics of Recognition*. Princeton, NJ: Princeton University Press.

Arendt, Hannah (1968) 'Crisis in culture'. In *Between Past and Future: Eight Exercises in Political Thought*. New York: Meridian.

Benhabib, Seyla (1992) *Situating the Self*. Cambridge: Polity.

Cavell, Stanley (1979) *The Claim of Reason*. Oxford: Clarendon and New York: Oxford University Press.

Coleman, Stephen and John Gøtze (2001) *Bowling Together: Online Public Engagement in Policy Deliberation*. Hansard Society. At *bowlingtogether.net*, accessed October 2004. http://www.bowlingtogether.net/bowlingtogether.pdf.

Dewey, John (1927) *The Public and its Problems*. New York: Holt.

Dryzek, John (2001) *Deliberative Democracy and Beyond: Liberals, Critics, Contestations*. Oxford: Oxford University Press.

Eriksson, Charlotta and Ia Wadendal (2002) 'Pappan: "Det var inget heder-smord"'. *Svenska Dagbladet*, 29 January 2002 (electronic version).

Fishkin, James (1997) *Voice of the People*. New Haven, CT: Yale University Press.

Grimen, Harald (1995) 'Starka värderingar och holistisk liberalism: innledning till Charles Taylors filosofi'. In *Charles Taylor: Identitet, frihet och gemenskap. Politisk-filosofiska texter i urval av Harald Grimen*. Göteborg: Daidalos.

Habermas, Jürgen (1990) 'Discourse ethics: notes on a program of philosophical justification'. In *Moral consciousness and Communicative Action*. Cambridge: Polity.

Kant, Immanuel (1790/1952) *The Critique of Judgment*. Trans. J.M. Meredith. Oxford: Clarendon.

—— (1785/1981) *Grounding for the Metaphysics of Morals*. Indianapolis, IN: Hackett.

Levy, Neill (2002) *Moral Relativism: A Short Introduction*. Oxford: Oneworld.

Løkeland-Stai, Espen (2007) 'Starter streik i Second Life'. *Klassekampen*, 25 September, p. 10.

Madsen, Richard and Tracy B. Strong (eds.) (2003) *The Many and the One: Religious and Secular Perspectives on Ethical Pluralism in the Modern World*. Princeton, NJ, and Oxford: Princeton University Press.

Rawls, John (1970) *A Theory of Justice*. Boston, MA: Harvard University Press.

Taylor, Charles (2002) 'Democracy, inclusive and exclusive'. In Madsen, R., W.M. Sullivan, A. Swidler and S.M. Tipton (eds.) *Meaning and Modernity: Religion, Polity and Self.* Berkeley, CA: University of California Press.

—— (1992) 'The politics of recognition'. In Gutman, Amy (ed.) *Multiculturalism and 'The Politics of Recognition': An Essay by Charles Taylor.* Princeton, NJ: Princeton University Press, pp. 25–75.

Thorseth, May (2006) 'Worldwide deliberation and public reason online'. *Ethics and Information Technology*, Vol. 8, No. 4, pp. 243–52.

—— (1999) *Legitimate and Illegitimate Paternalism in Polyethnic Conflicts.* Acta Philosophica Gothoburgensia 8 (doctoral thesis). Gothenburg: Acta Universitatis Gothoburgensis.

—— (1994) *Filosofi og retorikk: Overbevise eller overtale? Rapport med intervju av Karl-Otto Apel.* Trondheim: SINTEF IFIM.

Wheeler, Deborah (2005) 'Digital politics meets authoritarianism in the Arab world: results still emerging from internet cafés and beyond'. Paper presented at the Annual Meeting of the Middle Eastern Studies Association, Washington, DC, 19–24 November.

# CHAPTER 2

# THE VALIDITY OF HUMAN RIGHTS AND THE PROBLEM OF RELIGIOUS FUNDAMENTALISM

## Petra Hedberg

Fundamentalism presents Western democratic societies with serious challenges. It challenges the core liberal notion of the universality of human rights, confronts the idea of individual rights with that of group rights and pits one liberal right (such as freedom of speech) against another (such as freedom of religion). This chapter explores how Western democracies can respond to these challenges. It takes up two central issues. First, to what extent can human rights be universally justified? The second issue concerns the problem of applying abstract rights to concrete cases: to what extent can a justified system of human rights resolve conflicts between different rights?

The debate between Jürgen Habermas and Karl-Otto Apel is a useful aid in elucidating these questions. The chapter turns first to Habermas's approach to human and democratic rights, which is a comprehensive one based on different levels of reconstruction or 'rational interpretation' – a term he uses synonymously with 'reconstruction'. He claims that all forms of interpretations are rational, since interpreting means to understand the meaning of what is said in terms of the rational claims that are raised (cf. Habermas 1983/1990: 31–2).

In *Faktizität und Geltung* (1992a/1998), Habermas makes use of both classical and modern theories of modernisation/democratisation in order to reconstruct certain basic rights which are both democratic and human rights. According to Habermas, these basic rights are the 'equal right to take part in political processes and associations' and the 'legal protection of the individual'. In addition, political theories, theories of law and philosophical perspectives play a part. On the one hand, Habermas views human rights as enjoying general acceptance within the European tradition; on the other, he recognises that their validity must be established without reference to their historical genesis or their cultural basis.

Justifying human rights is a two-fold topic. Human rights can be accepted as valid if accepted as such by a consensus, including anyone concerned by these norms, as expressed by the general discursive principle – the so-called 'principle of (D)' (Habermas 1992a/1998: 138). Validity also depends upon the validity conditions of any rational discourse, i.e. the conditions that any argumentation must fulfil in order to yield a valid consensus.[1] Reconstructing such conditions draws attention to the possibility of achieving a valid consensus and, accordingly, to a valid justification of norms and rights.

Habermas's position is somewhat ambiguous, since he sees the realisation of human rights as dependent upon the existing liberal culture. The acceptability (and validity) of human rights, therefore, seems to be dependent on the *de facto* acceptance of these rights (Habermas 1996/1998: 177; 1992a/1998: 165).[2] In addition, he calls for stronger supranational bodies in order to strengthen the legal rights of 'world-citizens' (1996/1998: 181–2). A cosmopolitan order, however, needs a moral basis that can justify interference, whether by peaceful or violent means, in internal, national affairs where human rights are being violated. Such actions will, reasonably, be justified in a weaker sense if they rest only upon a *de facto* justification derived from international law.

The first part of this paper clarifies the general presuppositions of Habermas's approach to democracy and human rights. Here I turn to the 'republicans vs. liberals debate', which is used by Habermas (1992a/1998) to reconstruct basic democratic and human rights. The second part examines the relationship between the consensual conditions of the discourse and the possibility of justifying specific human rights. The third part turns more explicitly to the justification and application/implementation of specific human rights, relating to the contradictions inherent in the freedoms of speech and religion. In the fifth and last part, the right to religious freedom will be linked to the problem of religious fundamentalism, and to the question of whether fundamentalist positions are compatible with religious freedom.

The Habermas-Apel debate is central to the last three parts of the paper. It serves a double purpose: it clarifies both philosophers' positions vis-à-vis the possibility of justifying human rights, and offers solutions to the dilemmas posed by religious fundamentalism.

## The reconstruction of rights

Here I take up Habermas's reconstructive approach to democratic and human rights. His account of these rights in *Faktizität und Geltung* (1992) and *The Inclusion of the Other* (1996) will form the vantage point.

### *The liberal-republican debate vs. discourse theory*

Within Habermas's approach, the republican and liberal viewpoints work as correctives to one another. The liberal model is based on a classic 'market model' of society, whereby public law is mainly conceived of as a means of protecting the individual's rights. Competitive aspects of human interaction are stressed at the expense of the cooperative. Liberals tend to view political decisions as the results of bargaining processes in which aggregated individual interests are at stake, while republicans view the democratic process as a cooperative endeavour oriented towards the 'common weal'. Liberals give priority to economic rights, while republicans concentrate on political rights: voting, free expression and taking part in political decision-making.

The republicans vs. liberals debate is central to Habermas's approach to democracy and human rights. He ties the liberal precondition of individual autonomy to the need to protect individual political civil rights rather than seeing it as an expression of a collective value system. The republican view is reflected in the communicative presuppositions of Habermas's discourse theory. Here politics, whether at the institutionalised level of parliamentary bodies or at the informal level of the public sphere, is a deliberative process, and one which, furthermore, is dependent on the basic communicative presuppositions of discourse theory (Habermas 1996/1998: 248–52). Habermas, however, distinguishes between strategic and communicative forms of communication and interaction. Political deliberations are seldom purely 'understanding-oriented', but also contain conflicting interests. The liberal model is based on strategic forms of communication and interaction, while the republican focuses too one-sidedly on the communicative.[3] The republican model also tends to be too contextualised, seeing the formation of public will as too closely tied to the values and norms of an existing political culture and society (Habermas 1992a/1998: 130, 338–9, 359–66). Habermas hence sees the need to combine the liberal and republican viewpoints by combining individual freedom with a communication-oriented approach.

Habermas's 'list of categories', i.e. basic rights that are part of both human and democratic rights, works well with liberal preconditions by emphasising the legal rights of individuals: the 'political autonomy of the citizen', the 'equal right to take part in political processes and associations' and the 'legal protection of the individual' work here as basic premises.[4] These rights are connected to two extended basic rights that include the legal and socio-economic basis of these rights: they must be part of legitimate law and must also be secured by certain social and ecological life-conditions.

### The liberal presuppositions of discourse theory

In *Faktizität und Geltung* (1992a/1998), Habermas emphasises the difference between law and morality. Here, he turns to the basic presuppositions common to human and democratic rights: the preconditions of 'freedom and equal rights'. Both work as basic conditions of human and democratic rights and as part of the validity conditions of practical discourses. They constitute 'meta-norms' and are at work within the general argumentative conditions of discourses, in terms of *chanceng-leiche und symmetrische Teilnahme* (ibid: 282). This 'equal right to take part' is also a constituent of the specifically-formulated discourse-principle of practical discourses (ibid: 138–42, 280–2).

The difference between law and morality is linked to private vs. public autonomy. According to the liberal view, rights are primarily negative rights, and their main function is to safeguard the private autonomy of individuals 'against the tyranny of the majority' (ibid: 130). The materialisation of law caused by the development of the welfare state is seen as a potential threat to the liberty of individuals, since welfare policies are seen as state paternalism. Habermas adopts a more positive stance towards material rights, but emphasises that they must be used in order to enhance, not restrict, the freedom of individuals. By securing certain material rights, such as a minimum standard of living and a minimum level of education, one may enhance the participatory potential of the population (ibid: 501–3; 1996/1998: 260–4).

Habermas's solution to the classic divide between formal and material rights is ambiguous. On the one hand, he claims that the conditions of a valid consensus are purely formal and procedural, and therefore value-neutral. On the other hand, he emphasises that the interests of the participants (such as economic interests) must be taken into consideration. Not only are these difficult to reconcile with each other, but neither the argumentative conditions, nor the basic rights, nor the content of practical discourses, seem value-neutral.


## Justification

This section turns to the question of justifying rights as well as consensual conditions, and ties this question of justification to that of neutrality.


### Moral versus legal norms

In *Faktizität und Geltung* (1992a/1998) Habermas makes a sharp distinction between morality and law by distinguishing between the moral principle of (U) and the general discursive principle of (D): the latter is intended to apply to norms in general, not simply to moral ones.

Human rights enjoy a dual status: they are not simply moral rules, but depend on legal implementation in regulating both interpersonal relations and governmental actions. However, they are supposed to be justified by moral arguments, and not solely by *de facto*, positive law. Unlike democratic rights, which apply to citizens of a politically-restricted area, human rights are supposed to apply to *anyone* (Habermas 1996/1998: 190). How, then, does this dual legal-moral character relate to the difference between (U) and (D)?

Habermas introduces the principle of (D) in order to establish a morally neutral principle applicable to all types of practical discourses, whether moral, pragmatic or legal (ibid: 41–6; 1992a/1998: 138–42). The moral principle is reserved for moral discourses only, but on the other hand is also conceived as 'co-original' with the discursive principle. Apel, in contrast to Habermas, insists on the primordial status of the moral principle, claiming that even theoretical discourses depend on discourse ethical principles, since all discourses presuppose the equal right to take part (Apel 1996: 23–4; 1998: 738, 790–1; 1999: 47). He also claims that Habermas resorts to a functional explanation/justification of legal institutions by stressing the need to implement rights at an institutional level (Apel 1992: 43–4; 1998: 750–8, 828–31; Habermas 1992a/1998: 143; 1996/1998: 179–82).

In Apel's view, Habermas ignores the different levels of justification involved in his own approach. Democratic and legal institutions cannot, after all, be justified to the same extent as the rights that they are to implement. Democratic rights must enjoy a weaker form of justification as long as they are part of specific democratic constitutions (Apel 1992: 54–7; 1998: 761–3). After all, other constitutional solutions may always be at hand, and as Habermas himself points out, constitutional norms are changeable (1996/1998: 255). Human rights must hence be justified at a 'strict' justificatory level, apart from any constitutional and implementational level (cf. also Apel 1999: 88–90).

## Argumentative conditions vs. (U) and (D)

The alleged neutrality of the discursive principle is a challenge, since Habermas claims that basic rights and the discursive conditions are dependent on the very same preconditions of freedom and equal rights. Even human rights seem to rest upon neutral preconditions. But, in what sense can one claim that 'freedom and equal rights' are neutral conditions rather than values of a given (modern, European) culture (cf. Apel 1999: 89)?

Both philosophers distinguish between general argumentative conditions, and the more specific conditions of practical discourses. Discourses in general rely upon basic conditions of uncoerced argumentation and the equal right to raise claims. Discourses also rely upon the validity claims of 'truth', 'rightness' and 'sincerity'. These basic conditions are capable of being proved *via negativa*, since no valid consensus may be established unless argumentation is uncoerced, and unless disputable claims to truth or rightness are raised (Habermas 1972/1989: 166–73; Apel 1996: esp. 22–3). Both consider the argumentative level to be neutral, because these conditions are procedural rules that do not affect the content of the discourse. In addition, only the arguments of the participants are taken into consideration. The ideal model of scientific argumentation excludes arguments related to personal traits or socio-economic interests (Apel 1998: 811; 1999: 59). Here, 'freedom and equal rights' work as a purely argumentative form of freedom and equal rights. Legal and moral discourses, however, do in addition rely on the principles of (U) and (D):

(U) For a norm to be valid, the consequences and side effects of its general observance for the satisfaction of each person's particular interests must be acceptable to all. (Habermas 1983/1990: 197)

(D) Just those action norms are valid to which all possibly affected persons could agree as participants in rational discourses. (Habermas 1992b/1996: 107; 1992a/1998: 138)

The key notion here is that of "interest", since both formulations include the interests of the participants, either in the generalisable sense of (D) or in the particular sense of (U). A demand for impartiality is also present in both (D) and (U). The problem, however, is that a purely argumentative version of 'freedom and equal rights' may easily be confused with 'freedom and equal rights' in the socio-economic sense, implying certain material conditions. Habermas (1992a/1998: 330) also refers to these argumentative conditions more abstractly, as 'symmetry and reciprocity', which distinguishes them from socio-economic conditions. The purely argumentative form of equal rights works as a procedural, formal type of justice along with liberal conceptions of justice, while the socio-economic form works as a distributive form of justice.

The neutrality (impartiality) of the conditions may also be based on the procedural premises of discourse theory that distinguish between form and content, i.e. between the conditions of reaching a consensus and the specific claims agreed upon. Still, the question of neutrality remains. The argumentative conditions are, after all, based on the triple conditions of symmetry, reciprocity and individual autonomy. These conditions fit into a very modern and liberal conception of how to 'reach an (impartial) agreement'. The eurocentric perspective looms large, and is easily attacked by sceptics and relativists. Apel and Habermas provide us with two alternative ways of escaping this problem; Habermas's formula is the following:

> By considering these conditions as neutral in terms of being procedural and not affecting the content of the arguments.
>
>   By also considering them to be neutral in terms of being unavoidable in any discourse aiming at a valid consensus. This is, however, based on the premise that no better solution is at hand within the current human rights debate. (*Menschenrechtsdiskurs*, cf. Habermas 1998: 180–1)

These conditions, however, cannot claim to be neutral just by being 'unavoidable in any discourse aiming at a valid consensus', since Habermas cannot allow a strong universality and necessity in the transcendental, Kantian sense. Apel, on the other hand, may avoid the eurocentric trap by considering the conditions as simultaneously meta-normative and unavoidable. His 'proof' rests on the following premises (cf. Apel 1999: 39–55, esp. 77–83):

> Any reflexively conducted test of these conditions must prove them to be unavoidable, and as such, irreplaceable by other principles.
>
> Any set of principles that tries to accomplish a valid consensus by dispensing with the conditions of symmetry, reciprocity and individual autonomy will get entangled in self-contradictions. Such approaches will have to accept a 'forced acceptance of norms', which might even make the rules of dictatorships into valid rules.

A criterion of consistency is central to Apel's version. Consistency, however, while necessary, is not sufficient. In the case of norms, values and legal rules, certain (meta-) normative criteria are presupposed, since ideas concerning 'the good life' are at stake. The liberal premises of symmetry, reciprocity and individual autonomy seem to be the only premises that are consistently able to secure the individual's very own choice of a 'good life'. Within this conception, a variety of individual choices is possible, as long as the individual does not 'force his/her choices upon others' (cf. Habermas 1992a/1998: 109). This seems to be the strongest argument in favour of a discourse-theoretical (Habermas) and discourse-ethical (Apel) approach to human rights.[5] Liberal premises, however, are not neutral, although they might be the only premises available capable of establishing a consistent system of human rights.[6]

## Justification vs. application

So far, I have dealt with the question of justifying rights at a general level. In the next part of this chapter, I will turn to the problem of justifying specific rights.

### Justifying specific human rights

Given that human rights can be justified by reflexive means, more unitary implementation of them should be possible. This would resolve the dilemmas resulting from differing interpretations of human rights.

Habermas's approach gives rise to several problems, since he leaves the questions of justification and application/implementation to real discourses. In the case of material versus formal rights, the problem stems from the potential for disagreement. Material rights, after all, are tied to specific economies. One cannot expect to achieve a global consensus about the 'proper standard of living' in measurable per capita terms. Political civil rights, on the contrary, may well be justified without reference to economic and political constraints.

Various political civil rights, however, easily come into conflict with one another. 'Freedom of speech' vs. 'freedom from discrimination' and 'religious freedom' are good examples of this. Freedom of speech works contrary to argumentative symmetry and reciprocity when used in order to deprive other individuals of their rights, as in cases of racial discrimination and religious blasphemy. Real discourses, such as political discourses in parliamentary bodies, may choose to privilege religious freedom and freedom from discrimination at the expense of freedom of speech.

There is an additional problem: specific human rights may be interpreted in multiple ways. Collectivist accounts of religious freedom conflict with the presupposition of individual autonomy (Habermas 1998: 183ff; 2005: 277). Rules of command and obedience within a religious community may be seen as part of a collective religious tradition, a tradition that can be defended by the very right to religious freedom. Collectivist accounts, therefore, are likely to contradict the basic preconditions at work in the liberal conception of human rights, i.e. symmetry, reciprocity and individual autonomy. In fact, collectivists have to dispense with the sum total of political civil rights, since none of these rights are applicable to collective subjects as long the latter may violate the rights of other individuals, including individuals who are part of their own group. The Palestinian group Hamas is an exemplary case in this respect: women are only allowed to take part in political activities to a limited extent, because they are not allowed to attend election meetings (cf. Milton-Edwards 2005: 324).

Collectivist positions, consequently, run into contradictions, and hence are easily discredited by 'reflexive means', since they fail by being inconsistent.

Another problem relates to human rights when applied to specific cases. The right to wear religious-cultural symbols in public, such as the headscarves of Muslim women, may be contested on the basis of an 'anti-religious' interpretation of this right: the public space might interpret the right of 'religious freedom' as the right of 'freedom from religious impact'. Religious symbols may also be seen as symbols of an authoritarian culture that should be prohibited in the name of human rights. Such interpretations of religious freedom, nevertheless, conflict with discourse theory/discourse ethics, because they violate the very conception of individual freedom they try to defend.

## The procedural solution

The precondition of individual autonomy is crucial, since the principle of (D) explicitly points to the need to take the 'persons affected by a rule' into consideration (Habermas 2005: 125; Apel 1999: 91;1998: 836–7).

The solution of representative democracies is to leave specific questions to political processes of decision-making, and to let parliamentary bodies decide these matters on a majority basis. The democratic solution, however, is not optimal, since it dispenses with the participatory presupposition embedded in the principle of (D): the 'affected person's equal right to take part in a rational discourse' – the affected person will, reasonably enough, only be able to take part through representatives. However, such as in the case of headscarves, any affected person may consider it to be a woman's human right to decide for herself whether she should wear a headscarf. Bringing democratic procedures to a supranational level ('world parliament') would not resolve this problem, but rather aggravate it, because the debate and decision would be even further removed from the individual.

Habermas relies heavily on a procedural solution, connected to the constitutional basis of law rather than on democratic representational processes (Habermas 1992a/1998: 364–5). Legal rules are intended to safeguard the public and private autonomy of the individual, and not of groups (Habermas 2005: 310, 314–16). Additionally, legal rules should ensure that the individual herself is able to choose (Apel 1998: 781–3;

Habermas 1992a/1998: 514–15). Interference, then, is only legitimate when the person is subject to force. Legal rules should therefore be formulated in favour of the individual's right to decide for herself, and should not restrict the range of individual choices (cf. Habermas 1992a/1998: 299 vs. 536–7).

## Democracy, law and human rights

Human rights are supposed to be justified by moral arguments, but also need to be institutionalised at both national and international levels in order to work efficiently. Implementing the rights, however, does not solve the problem of conflicting rights, nor that of religious fundamentalism in relation to religious freedom and freedom of speech. What kinds of solutions do Habermas and Apel provide to such problems?

### Morality and legality: Habermas vs. Apel

Habermas's arguments against Apel have been based on the point that human rights cannot solely be regarded as moral rules. The 'will to act morally' is not sufficient, since neither individuals nor states can be expected to act morally solely on the prerogative of good will (Habermas 1996/1998: 169–70). Institutionalising these rights is thus necessary.

The differences between morality and democracy are of special importance. Apel here employs the key concept of 'approximation' (Apel 1996: 40–1; Apel 1999: esp. 94). Democratic systems cannot, for different reasons, fulfil the requirements of the discourse principle to the fullest extent. The representational basis of democratic bodies presents one restriction, since the 'affected persons' will not be able to partake themselves. The power monopoly of the state vis-à-vis its citizens is another restriction, since the condition of 'mutual recognition' cannot be said to apply to citizen-state relationships to the fullest degree (cf. Apel 1999: 87; 2002: 24 vs. Habermas 1998: 255). This power monopoly includes the possibility of regulating the actions of the citizens against their own will.

At a more general level, the difference between morality and democracy points to the basic differences between discourses *proper* and political ones. Moral discourses are based on communicative rationality, which is the basic rationality of any understanding- and consensus-oriented argumentation. Political discourses are of ethical, moral and pragmatic kinds, and combine strategic and teleological forms of rationality with an understanding-oriented one (Habermas 1992a/1998: 197–200; Apel 1998: 775; 2002: 22–4). They depend on material conditions of 'power' and 'economy', and cannot rely on communicative 'solidarity' alone. Political negotiations are good examples of this, since they often aim at distributions of wealth and power (cf. Apel 1999: 110–11; 1996: esp. 33). Moral discourses may, therefore, be of the 'proper kind', fulfilling the conditions of the discourse to the fullest degree, in contrast to political discourses, which will only be able to fulfil them to a lesser degree. However, counter-measures are at hand within Apel's approach, since policies based on 'strategic-counter-strategic' actions of different kinds may be implemented in order to enhance the participatory potentials of the population. Welfare policies work as one example in this respect. International interventions also represent counter-measures, if used in order to promote human rights (Apel 1992: 46, 57ff; 1998: 786–9, Apel 1999: 90ff.).

Caution is important here, since humanitarian interventions of the military kind are likely to violate 'the interests of affected persons', and since such interventions may well be motivated by concerns other than purely moral ones. Such an approach works well with Apel, although at the political level it will never be possible to justify interventionary actions to the ultimate extent (cf. Apel 1999: 88, on the case of Kosovo). Apel's position, however, is not contrary to Habermas's: he is not opposed to the need to implement human rights, but simply points out the impossibility of justifying the level of implementation (of legal rules and political actions) to the fullest extent. Legal rules could be formulated contrary to the premises of the principles of discourse ethics, and political actions are, as such, of the approximative kind (Apel 1998: 831ff.). A fallibilist premise is at work in both Apel and Habermas (cf. Habermas 1992a/1998: 514–15, 535; Apel 1992: 55–7). Yet another similarity is detectable: when turning to the public debates between religious and non-religious citizens of the Western democracies, Habermas (2005: 117–118, 123, 125) introduces the key concept of 'tolerance'. This concept is analogous to the meta-normative 'ought' of Apel, where a concept of 'co-responsibility' is formulated as part of the meta-normative conditions of the discourse. Here, participants are co-responsible for the realisation of the discursive conditions (Apel 1992: 29–33; 1996: 34; 1998: 756–8, 831ff; 1999: 63–64; 2002: 22).

### 'The difference that makes the difference'

Habermas's main arguments against Apel have been about the status of argumentative meta-norms. Habermas insists that these norms work as presuppositions on an argumentation-inherent level, and cannot be seen as meta-norms applicable to interpersonal relations and systems at a discourse-external level (cf. Habermas 1992a/1998: 192; 2005: 90). Apel, on the contrary, maintains that the 'ideal community of communication' is to be used in order to identify constraints given in various 'real communities of communication', whether on the small-scale level of social groups or the large-scale level of international relations. Both persons and governments are seen as responsible for taking actions such as tackling the ecological crisis, or strengthening various human rights (Apel 1998: 764–5, 801–23).

Habermas also emphasises the need for criticism, and speaks of the 'critical function of public opinion' as well as 'public opinion as a warning-system' (Habermas 1992a/1998: 435, 447). Since public opinion is informal and not tied to specific institutional (say, economic or administrative) constraints, it has the greatest potential for critique. However, Habermas needs to specify the criteria for a 'critique proper'. Public opinion could raise critical objections against human (and democratic) rights which would contradict the very normative presuppositions of discourse theory/discourse ethics. Habermas, hence, has to presuppose the symmetry- and reciprocity-conditions of discourse theory if the aim is to strengthen human rights. These conditions must, along with Apel, be in use at both discourse-inherent and discourse-external levels. Habermas cannot in fact avoid using meta-norms at a discourse-external level whenever applying the need for 'tolerance' and 'mutual respect' to the phenomenon of 'public opinion' (cf. also Habermas 1992a/1998: 149).

## Public opinion and freedom of speech

In the current world situation, two specific rights have been brought into focus: freedom of speech and religious freedom. In the aftermath of the 9/11 attacks in 2001 and also in the case of the early-1990s decree against Salman Rushdie by Ayatollah Khomeini, these two rights seem to have become opposed to one another. Freedom of speech may seem to be the most important of the two, since this is the very right at stake whenever different forms of criticism are exercised. Religious freedom, on the other hand, implies freedom from religious discrimination, such as in the case of blasphemy.

Both Habermas and Apel call for a 'mutual recognition' that works in favour of non-blasphemous criticism. When used for a critical purpose, freedom of speech will be used in order to strengthen, not weaken, human rights by pointing out violations within various 'real communities of communication'. Based on the meta-norms of human rights and practical discourses, such a critique cannot be conducted without taking the 'interests of the affected persons' into consideration. The 'affected persons' will, evidently, be both leaders and regular members of religious associations. By accepting religious freedom as an individual right, both religious and non-religious citizens must accept that every person has the right to choose whether she/he is to be part of a religious community or not. The various religious leaders must realise that they cannot deny the members of their community this right without violating a principal human right.

The preconditions of communicative symmetry and reciprocity work in favour of 'religious tolerance', since the members are supposed to respect one another's choices. The requirement of consensual conditions, however, imposes certain restrictions on the freedom of speech by excluding polemical, manipulative and rhetorical arguments. The arguments are, after all, supposed to be used in order to accomplish a mutual understanding and eventually a consensus. Blasphemous arguments may, per se, be seen as polemical and manipulative ones, and thereby be excluded from a practical discourse (cf. Apel 1996: 28). The problem is, however, that any kind of arguments directed against religious beliefs and practices may be considered blasphemous by believers. This dilemma can only be solved if religious criticism is accepted on the basis that all forms of human-rights violations, included religious forms, must be subject to criticism.

I believe one may solve the dilemma of freedom of speech vs. religious freedom by sharpening the difference between speech and action. Freedom of speech is, after all, a precondition of the freedom to express religious views. Actions that work contrary to individual liberties should therefore be regulated by legal sanctions, but purely verbal attacks on individual liberties should be accepted. Verbal incitements to physical violence may, hence, be accepted, as long as these remain purely verbal and do not violate the private sphere of other persons. Cases of violence should on the other hand, be brought to court. The same point applies to different political and religious positions: neo-nationalist groups or religious fundamentalists should be allowed to express themselves in public, but legal sanctions should be applied to violent actions. Public criticism, then, should be exercised by directing objections against any 'system of thought' that contains ideas contrary to the basic presuppositions of 'symmetry, reciprocity and individual autonomy'. Such a usage of the freedom of speech would work as a *critique proper*. Such a solution is only consistent with human rights as long as the individual's private autonomy is not violated.

This solution can be linked to the procedural solution. Here, Habermas (1996/1998: 181–2) draws an analogy between the national and international level. At the national, democratic level, individuals can file complaints against other individuals or public bodies. Similarly, human rights should be institutionalised at the international level, allowing individuals to file complaints against their own government in a supranational court. Cases of blasphemy and of ethnic and religious discrimination should, preferably, be handled on an individual basis, rather than following general rules concerning collective rights. Individuals who believe themselves to be discriminated against by blasphemous expressions may then be able to have their case tried on an individual basis. The same point applies to other rights: an international court could sanction member-states in cases of human-rights violations. Complaints would have to be handled by 'appropriate means'; and those means must themselves be justified.

## Religious freedom vs. religious fundamentalism

Fundamentalist positions represent a challenge to liberal democracies, in relation to both religious freedom and freedom of speech. Such positions are incompatible not only with specific rights, but also with the general conditions of both human rights and practical discourses.

Discourse ethics/discourse theory presupposes freedom of choice in terms of the freedom to choose a value-system of one's own. A person should, accordingly, be allowed to choose fundamentalist values. This choice, however, contradicts the meta-normative conditions of discourse ethics/discourse theory, and this is problematic because fundamentalists do not cherish their values on a purely private basis, but are also willing to pursue actions in order to 'change the world', contrary to the interests of other persons. The fundamentalist position contradicts *sum total* discourse-ethical meta-norms. Although fundamentalists may be perfectly sincere about their own belief-system, they are not willing to discuss their own world-views on an equal basis with those who hold opposing beliefs. Neither are they interested in submitting their own claims of rightness to rational discourse, nor willing to take into consideration the claims of others on equal terms. Fundamentalists, then, contradict the procedural conditions of individual autonomy, symmetry and reciprocity. Accordingly, they also oppose the general conditions of human rights. Fundamentalists take an exclusivist stand towards the religious world-views of other belief-systems, and cannot therefore be promoters of religious freedom. Bruce Lawrence proposes the following definition of fundamentalism:

> *Fundamentalism* is the affirmation of religious authority as holistic and absolute, admitting of neither criticism nor reduction; it is expressed through the collective demand that specific creedal and ethical dictates derived from scripture be publicly recognized and legally enforced. (1989: 27)

This definition was based on Lawrence's comparative and historical approach to different religious fundamentalist movements within the USA and other regions of the world.

More recently, Habermas (2005; see also Borradori 2003), has addressed the present world situation. Habermas sees the importance of distinguishing between religious orthodoxy and fundamentalism, and uses the Catholic Church as an example. He points out that dogmas work as a vital part in religions in general, but that dogma is not the distinguishing mark of a fundamentalist belief-system. Dogmas are, after all, compatible with a respectful and tolerant attitude towards other religions:

> [Such] orthodoxy first veers toward fundamentalism when the guardians and representatives of the true faith ignore the epistemic situation of a pluralistic society and insist – even to the point of violence – on the universally binding character and political acceptance of their doctrine. (Habermas, cited in Borradori 2003: 31)

Lawrence's definition also emphasises the collectivism and holism of fundamentalist thinking, two traits that are clearly contrary to the presuppositions of discourse ethics/discourse theory. Of further importance is the political commitment mentioned by both Lawrence and Habermas, which not only reveals the holism/totalitarianism of world-views that try to unite morality, law and politics into one complete system of thought, but also the need to transform thinking into action – even by violent means. The definition excludes a tolerant attitude towards the world-views of others, and also any willingness to subject one's views to a rational discourse. The possibility of reaching a compromise through negotiation, even on minor issues, seems to be ruled out by such a position. The following remarks by Marty and Appleby are of interest in this context:

> When they play politics to influence the policies of the state, fundamentalisms are thus necessarily involved in some measure

of compromise and accommodation. Political involvement may alter the original, exclusivist, dogmatic, and confrontational mode of the fundamentalist to such a degree that the word 'fundamentalism' may no longer seem to apply. (Marty and Appleby 1993: 4)

In other words, fundamentalists may turn away from fundamentalism when their views become more and more open to discussion and revision. Vice-versa, the orthodox may turn into fundamentalists if their views are made part of a system no longer open to discussion and revision.

The Palestinian case shows the complexity of the communicative conditions when linked to the establishment of a democratic state. The situation of Hamas is illustrative: its religious convictions must be balanced against democratic rights, such as the equal rights of men and women to take part in political processes. In this case, both religious dogmas and claims to power compete with the need to cooperate with the more secular Fatah. The Israeli-Palestinian conflict adds to the complexity of the case: Hamas must refrain from promoting terrorist attacks in order earn acknowledgment as a democratic party by the Western world.[7]

Communicative conditions are, for obvious reasons, more easily implemented in Western democracies, since liberal cultures already embody the prerequisite of tolerance. *De facto* acceptance of liberal values must, nevertheless, not be confused with the *acceptability* of liberal conditions *qua* argumentative conditions and basic rights.

### Fundamentalism vs. the claims of liberal democracies

In *Zwischen Naturalismus und Religion: Philosophische Aufsätze* (2005), Habermas advocated the liberal model of democracy: citizens must accept the cultural, religious and political pluralism of modern societies. The state itself must be neutral vis-à-vis different religious positions. The separation of 'state and church' is vital (ibid: 127–9; Borradori 2003: 31). Further on, Habermas stresses the importance of public opinion, both within the boundaries of national, liberal democracies and in the 'global public sphere'. The latter works as a guardian of liberal democracy, since everyone, at least in principle, has an equal right to express his/her opinions.

The citizens of liberal democracies must adopt a certain epistemic attitude. Religious opinions should be translated into secular arguments, and become part of the public debate. Both religious and secular citizens must accept the differences between secular and religious reasons, and be able to give priority to the former within the public debate, since religious dogma is not open to negotiation and compromise. Reasonable disagreements (*Dissens*, Habermas 2005: 146) must be acceptable; religious as well as non-religious citizens must accept that not all disagreements can be solved (ibid: 136–46).

Based on these presuppositions, the differences between fundamentalist and 'moderate' religious world-views are apparent. Fundamentalists are, after all, interested in neither understanding, nor consensus, nor reasonable disagreement. They rely on strategic communication and action in terms of claims on power (superiority), and are willing to use excessive means. In fundamentalist communication, 'open strategic speech acts' are at work rather than communicative speech acts.[8] This is especially so when fundamentalism is linked to the phenomenon of terrorism, where threats and excessive violence are used to achieve 'success'. Understanding-oriented communication, on the other hand, is a condition for both consensus and reasonable disagreement.

In Habermas (2005: 119–20; also cited in Borradori 2003: esp. 34–5), Habermas turns to a historical reconstruction of the contemporary form of terrorism. He points out that terrorism is linked to the colonialism of the past, and to contexts of distorted communication that have resulted from the colonial era. This kind of historical reconstruction may help as a device for understanding the phenomenon of fundamentalist terrorism, although fundamentalist positions and terrorist acts cannot be validly justified by reconstructive, discursive or reflexive means. This may also indicate the limits of religious tolerance, since fundamentalists who favour terrorist action serve as threats to liberal constitutional democracies (cf. Habermas 2005: 261–2). The question is, reasonably enough, whether fundamentalist positions represent a threat as long as they remain part of 'systems of thought' rather than 'systems of action'. Expressing fundamentalist views may still be a part of the right to express oneself freely, as long as 'words do not turn into deeds'. A fundamentalist who is not willing to pursue violent actions may, however, not fit into the fuller definition of fundamentalism offered by Habermas; in such cases, 'dogmatism' may be a better term of choice than 'fundamentalism'.

Habermas (2005) gives the concept of tolerance a principal position: he considers it a prerequisite for the maintenance of a liberal democratic culture (ibid: 265). Tolerance should, accordingly, be actively promoted in order to accomplish mutual understanding between religious and secular citizens, as well as between citizens of different religious convictions. The danger that orthodox persons could turn into fundamentalists may then be reduced. Potential fundamentalists may, respectively, adopt less fundamentalist/dogmatic convictions by letting their views be part of communicative processes where holders of beliefs try to understand the belief-systems of one another. Understanding is, however, not equal to consensus, and the acceptance of reasonable disagreements between holders of different convictions is a vital part of the stabilisation of democracy. With Habermas, human rights need to be constitutionalised on a supranational level in order to become efficient rules of law enforcement. The combination of an active public sphere with constitutionalised rights both at national and supranational levels would thereby strengthen human rights.

## Final remarks

The presuppositions of symmetry, reciprocity and individual autonomy are part of the consensual conditions as well as human rights. In my view, such conditions are heavily burdened with liberal presuppositions.

These conditions may nevertheless be the only conditions available that are able to produce a unitary and consistent system of human rights. Human rights cannot, after all, escape the liberal presupposition of 'equal individual liberties' without running into contradictions. Apel's approach has a further advantage: by accomplishing a clarification of these presuppositions at a justificatory level, one will also be able to produce a more consistent implementation of these rights. The presupposition of individual autonomy is crucial in this respect, since symmetry and reciprocity cannot work unless individual autonomy is presupposed. Collective accounts of human rights tend to neglect the presuppositions of symmetry, reciprocity and autonomy, and are therefore likely to run into contradictions in trying to interpret a human right as a collective right. Fundamentalist religious positions relying on collectivist convictions will, accordingly, be unable to produce any consistent system of human rights.

## Notes

1. Habermas (1981/1997: 42) defines the term 'discourse' in the following way: 'I shall speak of "discourse" only when the meaning of the problematic validity claim conceptually forces the participants to suppose that a rationally motivated agreement could in principle be achieved, whereby the phrase "in principle" expresses the idealizing proviso: if only the argumentation [can] be conducted openly enough and continued long enough.'
2. In Habermas (1992a/1998), the dual concepts of 'acceptance' vs. 'acceptability' are used in order to distinguish between *de facto* and valid consensuses concerning norms/rules (cf. Habermas 1992a/1998: 30–1, 54–5).
3. On the difference between strategic forms of communication and action vs. understanding and consensus-oriented communication, see Habermas 1981/1997, Vol. 1: 279–88, 333–4; Habermas 1999: ch. 2; Apel 1996: 32–4; 1992: 44–5; 1998: 701–25.
4. For the full formulations of these categories, see Habermas 1992b/1996: 122–3; 1992a/1998: 155–8; 2001/2006: 125.
5. See Apel (2002) for comments on the differences between his own discourse-ethical approach and Habermas's discourse-theoretical approach.
6. See Hedberg (2006) for discussion of reflexive vs. discursive forms of justification.
7. See, for instance P.R. Kumaraswamy's (2005: 53–8) analysis of Hamas's attitudes towards Fatah as well as Israel.
8. Cf. esp. Apel (1998: 701–25) on open strategic speech acts (such as threats) vs. covert ones (such as lies and deceptions).

## Bibliography

Apel, Karl-Otto (1992) 'Diskursethik vor der Problematik von Recht und Politik: Können die Rationalitätsdifferenzen zwischen Moralität, Recht und Politik selbst noch durch die Diskursethik normativ-rational gerech-tfertigt werden?' In Apel, Karl-Otto and M. Kettner (eds.) *Zur Anwendung der Diskursethik in Politik, Recht und Wissenschaft.* Frankfurt am Main: Suhrkamp, pp. 29–62.

—— (1996) 'Die Vernunftfunktion der kommunikativen Rationalität: Zum Verhältnis von konsensual-kommunikativer Rationalität, strategischer Rationalität und Systemrationalität'. In Apel, Karl-Otto and M. Kettner (eds.) *Die eine Vernunft und die vielen Rationalitäten.* Frankfurt am Main: Suhrkamp, pp. 17–42.

—— (1998) 'Das Problem des offen strategischen Sprachgebrauchs in tran-szendentalpragmatischer Sicht. Ein zweiter Versuch, mit Habermas gegen Habermas zu denken'. In Apel, K-O (1998) *Auseinandersetzungen in Erprobung des Transzendentalpragmatischen Ansatzes,* Frankfurt am Main: Suhrkamp, pp. 701–25.

—— (1999/2001) *The Response of Discourse Ethics to the Moral Challenge of the Human Situation as Such and Especially Today.* Mercier Lectures, Louvain-la-Neuve, March 1999. Leuven: Peeters.

—— (2002) 'Regarding the relationship of morality, law and democracy: on Habermas's *Philosophy of Law* (1992) from a transcendental-pragmatic point of view'. In Aboulafia, Mitchell, Myra Bookman and Catherine Kemp (eds.) *Habermas and Pragmatism.* London and New York: Routledge, pp. 17–30.

Borradori, Giovanna (2003) 'Fundamentalism and terror: a dialogue with Jürgen Habermas'. In *Philosophy in a Time of Terror: Dialogues with Jürgen Habermas and Jacques Derrida.* Chicago: The University of Chicago Press, pp. 25–43.

Habermas, Jürgen (1972/1989) 'Wahrheitstheorien'. In Habermas, J. *Vorstudien und Ergänzungen zur Theorie des kommunikativen Handelns.* Frankfurt am Main: Suhrkamp, pp. 127–186.

—— (1981/1997) *The Theory of Communicative Action.* Vol. I, trans. McCarthy, T. Cambridge, MA: Polity.

—— (1983/1990) *Moral Consciousness and Communicative Action.* Trans. Lenhardt, C. and Weber Nicholsen, S. Cambridge, MA: Polity.

—— (1992a/1998) *Faktizität und Geltung: Beiträge zur Diskurstheorie des Rechts und des demokratischen Rechtstaat.* Frankfurt am Main: Suhrkamp.

—— (1992b/1996) *Between Facts and Norms: Contributions to a Discourse Theory of Law and Democracy.* Trans. William Rehg. Cambridge, MA: Polity.

—— (1996/1998) *The Inclusion of the Other: Studies in Political Theory.* Trans. Cronin, C. P. Eds. Cronin, C. and De Greiff, P. Cambridge, MA: MIT Press.

—— (1998) *Die postnationale Konstellation.* Frankfurt am Main: Suhrkamp.

—— (1999) *Wahrheit und Rechtfertigung.* Frankfurt am Main: Suhrkamp.

—— (2001/2006) 'Constitutional democracy: a paradoxical union of contradic-tory principles?' In Cronin, C. And Pensky, M. (eds.) *Time of Transitions.* Trans. Ciaran Cronin, C and Pensky, M. Cambridge, MA: Polity Press, pp. 113–28.

Habermas, Jürgen (2005) *Zwischen Naturalismus und Religion: Philosophische Aufsätse.* Frankfurt am Main: Suhrkamp.

Hedberg, Petra (2003) 'Discursive conditions and contextual presuppositions: Habermas versus Apel'. *Sats – Nordic Journal of Philosophy*, Vol. 4, No. 2, pp. 67–92.

—— (2006) 'Justification: reflexive and/or discursive?' *Sats – Nordic Journal of Philosophy*, Vol. 7, No. 1, pp. 107–35.

Kumaraswamy, P.R. (2005) 'The Cairo dialogue and the Palestinian power struggle'. *International Studies*, Vol. 42, No. 1 , pp. 43–59. At *http://isq.sagepub.com/cgi/content/abstract/42/1/43*.

Lawrence, Bruce (1989) *Defenders of God: The Fundamentalist Revolt Against the Modern Age.* San Francisco, CA: Harper & Row.

Marty, Martin E. and R. Scott Appleby (1993) 'Introduction'. In Marty, Martin E. and R. Scott Appleby (eds.) *Fundamentalisms and Society: Reclaiming the Sciences, the Family and Education.* Chicago: The University of Chicago Press, pp. 1–23.

Milton-Edwards, Beverley (2005) 'Prepared for power: Hamas, governance and conflict'. *Civil Wars*, Vol. 7, No. 4, pp. 311–29. At *http://dx.doi.org/10.1080/13698280600682940*.

# CHAPTER 3

# PUBLIC RITUAL AS COMMUNICATION IN THE MASS MEDIA: INCLUSION OR EX-COMMUNICATION

## Stefano M. Bisighin and Lionel Sacks

### Introduction

This paper explores how fundamentalists can use ritual in the mass media to achieve a presence on a par with established organisations. Four case studies of events, three of which concern fundamentalist individuals and movements, are used. These events have quite different profiles, but common features as well as differences are identified between them, by using a semiotic analysis. The first case is a single, peaceful group protest, consisting of a collective prayer by Italian Muslims on 4 January 2009, in front of the Duomo in Milan, the most important Catholic cathedral in northern Italy; an event which intertwined concerns over the Gaza Strip (O'Brian 2009) with the place of Muslims in Italy. The second case is a personal 'pro-life' campaign, although intertwined with a wider movement and various organisations, over many years by a single individual, Randall A. Terry. The case study focuses on his protest demonstration when President Obama spoke at the commencement ceremony (Clark 2009) at the Catholic University of Notre Dame, Indiana. The third case concerns the 11 September 2001 demolition of the World Trade

Centre in New York, and focuses on one of the ring leaders, Mohammed Atta, his relationship with the traditions of Islamic extremism, and his self-sacrifice. The final case is included here as contrast with the three other cases, and covers an organised Muslim prayer gathering on Capitol Hill, Washington, DC, in September 2009.

Although the cases are diverse, the analyses will bring out some common features associated with fundamentalism. Foremost, the cases will be viewed as media events and actions whose primary aim is to communicate by generating news at a level equal to that generated by established institutions. Within this framework, each case will be viewed as a ritual being performed into the media, and specifically as new and public forms of rituals which are normally performed as private or internal community practices. For example, the Muslim prayer, the second pillar of Islam, is a daily ritual performed alone or collectively in a mosque, but rarely in a public space. When performed outside the Duomo in the context of a protest regarding the Gaza strip, the ritual of daily prayers is performed into the public media. The protest by Terry may be viewed as excommunicating or casting Obama out of the Christian faith due to Terry's pro-life stance. In addition to Terry's direct-action protest ritual – he has been arrested 40 times for similar actions – the form of the protest refers to the ritual of communion and its commemoration of Christ's sacrifice. Finally, the behaviour of Atta in the 9/11 attack may be viewed as an act, through ritual self-sacrifice, of excommunicating Muslims who do not participate in violent jihad against those who offend Islam. By being interpreted as news events of public performances of established community rituals, these cases serve as exemplars of how fundamentalist movements use modern media in their attempts to build community. The fourth case study contrasts with these. Although it is also an example of community ritual being performed into media in a public space, and explicitly concerned with building community, the event signifies inclusion without the element of opposition that is central to the three other cases.

All protests, from web campaigns or organised marches through to terrorist attacks, contain both actions and symbols. A placard saying 'ban abortion' is a direct message, and as such it can be contrasted with a placard showing a swastika; the latter is a symbol requiring exten-sive cultural history and context to understand its significance. Rituals themselves, including actions and artefacts, may also be treated as symbolical communication. There are several recipients of such com-munications: other members of the group; associated communities and protagonists; the general public. Analysing the significance of these symbols, when used for communication through media and when the various recipients are taken into account, can reveal important infor-mation about the motivations of the participants, and about the pecu-liarities of 'fundamentalist communication'.

## Considering Fundamentalism

This paper uses the Chicago Fundamentalism Project's 'family resemblance' definition of fundamentalism, adapted to the mass-mediated communication process (Almond, Sivan and Appleby 1995: 399–424). The authors have found five ideological characteristics of fundamentalism:

1.  Reactivity to the marginalization of religion;
2.  Selectivity;
3.  Moral Manichaeism (a dualistic, polarised worldview and morality);
4.  Absolutism and inerrancy;
5.  Millennialism.

And four organizational characteristics:

1.  Elect, exclusive membership;
2.  Sharp boundaries;
3.  Authoritarian organization;
4.  Behavioural requirements.

From the perspective of this chapter, the definition of the group charac-teristics is considered as internal rules of the groups. The relevant char-acteristics are 'moral Manichaeism', 'elect, exclusive membership', and 'sharp boundaries'. According to our perspective, the interaction with the external environment (local and/or global) is the *image* that the fundamentalist movements give of themselves to the other people. Group characteristics are projected through the mass-media, by actions, words, public declarations or protest movements; and the projection is transmitted by the mass-media to the audience. As such, it is a one-way communication from the group actions to the environment, constructed to a degree by mass media's particular characteristics of transmission.

In addition to the Fundamentalism Project's characteristics ('moral Manichaeism', 'elect, exclusive membership', and 'sharp boundaries'), we have found that the following four traits are also part of a 'fundamentalist make-up':

1. The presence of a sacred source (scripture and/or tradition) considered to be infallible;
2. The constitution of an 'orthodoxy/orthopraxy' (list of beliefs and rules for social life, derived from the sacred source);
3. The ritual-like communication (their simple messages have a repetitive form, and are the real transmitter of the truth);
4. Political issues as the place where the sacred truth is entirely applied.

Our focus on fundamentalism, media and communication is not new, as such. Several studies have explored the intrinsic relationship between modern and globalised fundamentalism, mass media, and the new media, among others (Hoover and Kaneva 2009); and (Hoover 1998). This chapter's contribution consists in developing a model that allows us to analyse fundamentalist communication in terms of a transformation of 'ordinary' private or community rituals into what is here called public rituals, and their messages concerning inclusion and exclusion from the community. As a test of our model we have included case study four which has very little direct involvement of a fundamentalist movement or ideologue. This case study is used to help see that the model has differential power – the model does not show up fundamentalist traits in this example as it does in the first three case studies.

The model describes the effect of the dichotomising approaches that characterise fundamentalist thought and actions and which produce a common field of communication that uses bi-polar images such as black/white, life/death, inclusion/exclusion; our three 'fundamentalist' cases serve as metadata (Preiss 2007) expressing this kind of dichotomies. The effectiveness of the model thus depends on the dualistic orthopraxis of fundamentalist thinking and action.

In what follows we will briefly describe the concept of ritual that we apply in the model, and show how the four cases can be analysed as public ritual performances. After that we develop the model by combining the concept of ritual with a semiotics model, and finally we apply the model in a detailed analysis of 'fundamentalist ritual communication'.

## The role of ritual

In his now classic study *Pigs for the Ancestors: Ritual in the Ecology of a New Guinea People* (1984) the anthropologist Roy Rappaport analysed the role of the *kaiko* ritual among the Tsembaga, a community of horticulturalists in New Guinea, as expressing their way of managing natural resources and the ecological environment, so as to perpetuate their social institutions. Rappaport defined ritual as a homeostatic (systemic self-regulation for the sake of maintaining stability) mechanism which preserves the stability of the society and which is intimately tied up with the concept of the social contract. As Rappaport says:

> In attending to ritual's form we must not lose sight of the fundamental nature of what it is that ritual does as a logically necessary outcome of its form. In enunciating, accepting and making conventions moral, ritual contains within itself not simply a symbolic representation of social contract, but tacit social contract itself. As such, ritual, which also establishes, guards, and bridges boundaries between public systems and private processes, *is the basic social act*. (Rappaport 1999:138)

And:

> I will argue that the performance of more or less invariant sequences of formal acts and utterances not entirely encoded by the performers logically entails the establishment of convention,

the sealing of social contract, the construction of the integrated conventional orders we shall call Logoi (singular: Logos ... ), the investment of whatever it encodes with morality, the construction of time and eternity; the representation of a paradigm of creation, the generation of the concept of the sacred and the sanctification of conventional order, the generation of theories of the occult, the evocation of numinous experience, the awareness of the divine, the grasp of the holy, and the construction of orders of meaning transcending the semantic. (Rappaport 1999:27)

Rituals can thus be considered to direct the life journey of a community, or an individual, by marking significant social events and occasions. Rituals also define the fundamental beliefs of a community, build trust and reliance on those beliefs, distinguish one community from another, and foster a sense of group identity through adherence to a basic social contract and its related social institutions. Through the rituals, the social institutions are continuously 'sanctified', as they are being drawn into the frame of reference of what is believed to be sacred.

In the first three fundamentalist cases selected in this chapter, the rituals seek to forge a 'community of true believers' around a political issue. For this purpose, the activists in each case use ritual practices which draw on fundamentalist features as a means of turning ritual into a mode of communication with both the general public and the religious community. In each case a religious community ritual is transformed into a public performance: the Duomo prayer is a version of the Muslim prayer; Randal Terry's demonstration contains a version of Christ's sacrifice – as symbolised in the communion – and of excommunication; and 9/11 is a version of self-sacrifice and excommunication. But what makes these three rituals 'fundamentalist' is the fact that they do *not* sanctify the *established* institutions; on the contrary, they cast them as in opposition to the sacred. The fourth case, the Muslim prayer on Capitol Hill, will bring out this point.

## Ritual and Communication

To understand how media events can be used for community building it is necessary to distinguish between directed communication – transferring information from one party to another – and 'phatic' communication in which information transfer is incidental to the primary intent of social bonding, social cohesion, and such like. Models of the media focus largely on directed communication. The classic communication model is one-to-one, with a sender exchanging symbols to a receiver to convey information, such as telephony or email. Broadcast media, such as news papers and television, extend that model to one single source sending (in mostly a single direction) information to an unspecified multiple of receivers. However, James Carey's view of social communication as transmission and ritual (Carey 1989: 14–23), tells us that a 'ritual view of communication is directed not toward the extension of messages in space but toward the maintenance of society in time; not the act of imparting information but the representation of shared beliefs' (Carey 1989:18–19). It is this kind of phatic communication that takes place in the public rituals which will be analysed in detail below, except – again – that fundamentalist ritual communication seeks to change rather than maintain society.

## Case 1: Muslim prayer becomes the Duomo public ritual

On Saturday, 3 January 2009 anti-Gaza-war protests where held in Milan and Bologna, Italy. The protesters were mostly Muslims from a variety of backgrounds. The protests included stops outside Milan Cathedral (il Duomo), and outside the Basilica of San Petronio; in both places the protesters stopped to pray – to perform the standard Islamic daily prayer – outside the buildings. In addition to the prayer, the protest included particular symbols, such as burning the Israeli flag, and banners equating the Star of David (a key Jewish symbol) with the Nazi swastika. As a result of the provocative demonstrations and the reactions of various actors, the protests were widely reported in the press and discussed in online fora, both in Italy and globally (Hopper 2009; Foschini 2009; O'Brien 2009; Owen 2009).

The manifestation was organized by The Islamic Center of Viale Jenner in Milan, run by imam Abdel Hamid Shaari, notorious for

anti-Western statements. The authorities had required that the manifestation must remain at a distance of some hundred meters away from
the cathedral (at Piazza San Babila), but the crowd carried on walking
right up to Piazza Duomo, just in front of the cathedral, where they
performed the prayer in the context of the provocative demonstration.
In this way the ritual prayer was used to communicate a political message. Two days later, however, the president of the Islamic Culture
Institute in Milan publicly asked for pardon for the demonstration
(Foschini 2009; see also Sheikyermami 2009).

Catholic religious actors displayed a range of reactions. The Vatican
found the event 'troubling for that prayer', that is, for the *context* of the
prayer, particularly the burning of the Israeli flag in front of the cathedral (Squires 2009) – although it was conciliatory towards the prayer
as such. Ernesto Vecchi, vicar general of the Bologna basilica, however, considered the choice of the prayer ritual to be confrontational
in itself (Vecchi 2009; Owen 2009). The Italian far right organisation The Northern League reacted strongly, interpreting the incident
as a direct insult to Italy (Squires 2009); this should be understood
in relation to their generally negative view of immigration, particularly of Muslims. The political establishment was largely negative and
there where proposals to ban all protests outside religious buildings
(O'Brien 2009).

Public marching, banners, flag burning and the Muslim prayer
are examples of rituals, manifest in this event, which were all identified by political groupings and the media. The particular thing about
the prayer is that, in contrast to the other rituals pertaining to the
demonstration, the Muslim prayer is not a traditional public ritual
in Italy, where it is commonly performed within a closed group of
participants, and strengthens their feelings of community. In contrast,
the Duomo event carries another message. While the prayer ritual,
as such, is clearly a religious requirement, this requirement was used
as an excuse for holding the prayers during the march. Equally as
Muslim prayers are quite distinct visually, they are a communicatively
clear model of stating one's affiliation with a particular community
and, in so doing, also expressing non-affiliation – in this case not only
with the acts being carried out in Gaza; but with the largely Catholic

establishment which, the demonstration implied, does not care about the Palestinians' plight.

## Case 2: Randall A. Terry: The communion becomes a public 'pro-life' demonstration

Randall A. Terry is an anti-abortion campaigner in the USA. He founded 'Operation Rescue' in 1987 and 'The Society for Truth and Justice' in 2003, as part of his 'pro-life' campaign. Terry focuses on public direct action against abortionists and attempts to close abortion clinics, and he has been arrested over 40 times. He has also lead anti-homosexuality campaigns and practised as a preacher (Powell 2004). As manifest on his website *www.ahumbleplea.com*, he takes a strongly biblical stance. His relationship with religion is complex. He converted from Protestantism to Catholicism, and became a member of a Charismatic Episcopal church after having been excommunicated, due to his divorce, from the Landmark Church in which he had originally studied and married (Ling 2009). Even his children have reflected his campaign positions. One of his adopted daughters converted to Islam; he denounced another daughter who had been pregnant twice out of wedlock; and one of his sons who came out as homosexual was 'not welcome in my home right now – not because of his homosexuality, but because he could sell us out again' (Terry 2004).

On 1 May 2009, Terry was arrested on the campus of the Catholic Notre Dame University for 'pushing baby carriages with plastic dolls covered with fake blood in protest of the upcoming commencement visit by President Barack Obama' (Randy 2009). The baby carriages had a bumper sticker stating: 'Obama '09 – One Dead baby at a Time – Notre Dame' (Terry 2009). President Obama has taken position in favour of abortion and stem cell research (McCormick 2009), and equal opportunities for homosexuals. To advertise his protest, Terry set up a website (see below), the banner of which combines the logo of Notre Dame University with splatters of blood to spell NO to abortion, next to another picture-text which equates Obama with Pontius Pilate, who condemned

Christ to death:

**Figure 1**   Banner symbol from Terrys www.stopobamanotredame.com website

For Terry, protest and arrest are the key ritual practices he has adopted for his campaigns and protests. But the Notre Dame protest includes another, less explicit ritual – that of 'casting out' or excommunicating from the community the likes of Obama, who do not believe in Terry's 'pro-life' orthopraxy. 'Casting out' as a practice has played a significant role in Terry's private life: he was excommunicated from one church and has denounced two of his own children.

To summarise the basic ritual characteristics of Terry's antiabortion manifestation:

- Community ritual alluded to (1): The blood on the dolls identifies aborted foetus with the sacrifice of Christ that is celebrated ritually in *the communion*, thus equating those who allow abortions with those who killed Christ;
- Community ritual alluded to (2): *Excommunication* of those who allow abortion.

### Case 3: Mohammed Atta – The 9/11 self-sacrifice and excommunication

The terrorist attacks on the World Trade Center, New York, on 11 September 2001, of which Mohammed Atta was a coordinator and perpetrator, have been extensively documented and analysed. Atta's background and motivations have, similarly, been widely researched. Amongst the many views as to his motivations are the established facts relating to his affiliations with Islamic extremist movements. Atta was part of the militant movement called by external observers *Al-Takfir wa'l-hijra* ('Excommunication and withdrawal') (Makarenko 2007:47). The *Takfir* movement originated in Egypt in 1971 as an extremist off-shoot from the Muslim Brotherhood (Makarenko 2007: 46; Arjomand 1995: 183). The ideology includes a Kharijite ('the Seceders') or 'neo-Kharijite' (Arjomand 1995: 184) perspective which dates as far back as the first Islamic century (the late 600s) and not only distinguishes between Muslim believers and non-Muslim infidels, but also identifies infidels *within* the Muslim community, thereby permitting jihad against fellow Muslims. The importance of this perspective to some Islamic fundamentalist and terrorist thinking is identified in Sageman (2004: 28), where the role of this line of thought on the formation of al-Qaeda is explored.

It cannot be expected that details of the ideological make-up of particular terrorist groups is common knowledge for the public. However, within most Muslim communities, the neo-Kharijite perspective is well understood as it goes back to the founding years of Islam and the famous divide between the followers of Ali and of Aisha which gave rise to the Shiite–Sunnite divide. It is also common knowledge that the original Kharijites killed Ali because he would not perform the – in Kharijite view – single-most important duty which distinguishes the faithful from the infidel, i.e. to perform jihad for the sake of raising a righteous caliph to the throne (Von Grunebaum 1970: 60–61). Within these early conflicts which laid the ground for the modern factions within Islam, the Kharijite doctrine was established that a Muslim could declare another Muslim infidel on account of his or her deeds, in contradiction of the Quran (Von Grunebaum 1970: 62):

> [T]he state of grace of the individual was to be seen in his behaviour; the masses in their indifference where no better than heathens; their rejection of the Kharijite conception of Islam excluded them from the true Community and justified their being killed. But even the Kharijite, if he sinned badly, was excluded from the Community ...

The original Kharijites were associated with a number of themes commonly attributed to modern Islamic fundamentalism, which include 'attracting support from the oppressed and disappointed' and 'providing a rallying point for those who felt it important to destroy political and social injustice' by appeal to divine justice; and being 'ready to sell their lives to gain paradise' (Von Grunenbaum 1970: 62). This last point has been developed further by extremist fundamentalists such as Osama bin Laden into the concept of *istishhad* (martyrdom or self-sacrifice for the sake of God) as an obligation for all Muslim individuals (rather than a collective duty under a head of state, as the established doctrine of jihad has it), and Atta 'spoke to [his comrades] of "offering sacrifice and obedience in these last hours"' (Jones 2008: 52). The development of this self-sacrifice into ritual performance is explored by Radler (2009) who argues that for al-Qaeda, 'In their self imposed culture, an armed fight within apocalyptical dimensions is the only way for salvation in the afterlife, and within this neo-religious community it gets institutionalized. Suicide attacks depict an act of divine service and are thus part of a ritual practice. It is in this context that I speak of suicide attacks as a "ritual of modernity"' (Radler 2009:6). The 'Spiritual Manual' found in Mohammed Atta's baggage describes how the action must be carried out and defines the self-sacrifice as sacred acts which are an end in themselves (Kippenberg and Seidensticker 2006). Furthermore, the handbook 'stresses how formal and structured the time-line of the attack were' (Radler 2009:8). According to Ronald Grimes, theoretician of ritual, 'the [9/11] terrorist attack was ritualized. In the newspaper are translated excerpts from the preparation manual. It was a liturgical text prescribing the man's activities ... "They" ritualized the attack. "We" ritualized the counter-attack by flying flags and lighting candles. A moment of silence here, a moment of silence there – several days running' (Grimes 2006:74). According to Atta's thought and al-Qaeda's doctrine, the 9/11 attack was not suicide (*intihar*) but self-sacrifice, a martyrdom operation (*amal istishhadi*) and therefore religiously legitimate (Iannaccone and Introvigne 2004: 79, 92, 107–142).

To summarise the characteristics of Atta's 9/11 attack:

- Community ritual alluded to: Self-sacrifice to destroy the infidels (Americans and Muslims) through a 'Kharijite' ritual of fatal excommunication (*takfir*).

- Symbols: The self-sacrifice itself; the target, i.e. the World Trade Center, symbol of American economic power (the other hit target was the Pentagon, symbol of American military power).

## Case 4: Islam on Capitol Hill

On Friday 25 September 2009, a Muslim congregational prayer was held on the west lawn of Capitol Hill in Washington, DC (*www.islamoncapitolhill.com*). This location is clearly associated with the core federal institutions (the Capitol buildings, the memorials) and the US national rituals (presidential inaugurations, Martin Luther King, Jr.'s 'I have a dream' speech), and even though the west lawn itself is not such an important location, it is popular. The event was attended by around 3000 Muslims, who performed the prayer and gave speeches. There where also manifestations by Christian organisations; some of these where anti-Muslim, but there was also a large Evangelical presence manifesting more inclusive attitudes (Rosenberg 2009; Salmon 2009a; Salmon 2009b).

In contrast to the Duomo prayer, this event did not include any auxiliary protests but concentrated on the message that Muslim-Americans are loyal citizens. The choice of the site accentuates this claim by associating the event with core American institutions which were sanctified through the prayer ritual. Doubt was cast on the agenda of the event in the press and blogosphere by focusing on one of the organisers, Hassen Abdellah, who is president of a mosque and a lawyer who has defended Mahmud Abouhalima, 'one of the men convicted in the 1993 World Trade Centre bombing' (Salmon 2009a). The opposition to the prayer event picked up on this association to assert that the event promoted a more radical agenda (e.g. Dobbs 2009). Such opposing voices took the opportunity to call on Muslims generally to decide whether they are for peaceful coexistence as part of the American society, or for conflict and outsider status; for example:

Well, the time has come for the American public to call Islam to account. The time has come for transformation and reformation within Islam. The time has come for Islam to change. Change needs to start now and means facing the reality that there is a foundational element within Islam that is determined to undermine peace and enforce the strict penal code of Islamic Law upon a society that celebrates liberty and justice for all people. It will be a long, hard road for Islam to get its house in order so that it can coexist peacefully with the rest of society in the 21st century. (Dobbs 2009)

Key features of the Capitol Hill prayer are:

- Community ritual alluded to: The Friday congregational prayer with the accompanying *khutba* ('sermon', in this event in the form of speeches); the Friday prayer traditionally symbolises the community's internal bonds and loyalty with the state;
- Sanctifying central national institutions;
- A self-appointed opposition which either confronted the Muslims with a dichotomy of choices (either in or out), or offered inclusion along with "soft" evangelism.

Before proceeding to the detailed semiotic analysis of these public rituals, the analytical model itself will be constructed in what follows.

## Ritual semiotic analysis

To analyse social action we are obliged to conceptualise the act from within a specific social context; only through the contextual points of reference can the act become significant. If the contextual references can be determined, the meaning of social action is unambiguous. Concerning the protagonists of our four cases – treating all four symmetrically for the moment – their actions constitute ritual performances with stylized choreographies rooted in religious principles. These ritual performances represent the communication of the protagonists' group, and the message is contained inside the performance itself. Therefore, their performances present us with their interpretation of reality, based on a specific religious fundamentalist belief and practice.

Normally, communication follows a circular movement where both the sender and the receiver are involved in a process of encoding, interpreting, and decoding. In this sense, communication involves feedback that maintains and preserves a dynamic balance among its interdependent parts. However, in our case studies, as in *all* ritual communication, the normal circular communication system is modified because communication takes place through ritual which comes from a religious base (Rappaport 1999: 431), in which the social homeostatic equilibrium, distilled from 'the ultimate sacred principles' (USP), is established and maintained.

Rappaport classifies ritual as a linguistic ideology (Rappaport 1999: 7–11; see also Robbins 2001). Ritual is the absolute reference of a given culture and protects the institutionalised communication against ambiguity and double meaning, thereby perpetuating the social institutions themselves (Rappaport 1999: 88–89); consequently, ritual is '*the* basic social act' (Rappaport 1999: 138; emphasis added). Due to its univocal performance, ritual language has only a narrow limit of misinterpretation: its repetitiveness ranks culture hierarchically according to fixed interpretative categories, building a closed communicative cycle in the social ambient.

In any religious ritual communication, the feedback is the answer that the divinity gives to the worshipper through the sacred scripture or tradition, which supplies believers with messages that are symbolically actualised in the ritual. In this way the concept of a divine reply, external to the communicative system and contained in scripture or tradition, modifies the 'ordinary' communicative circuit by introducing a sacred element that is made to speak publicly only through the ritual performance. In this way the ritual perpetuates the social institutions by 'sanctifying' them. If we assume, with Rappaport, that ritual is the basic social act which guarantees institutional communication through a 'sacred' source, feedback from the receiver is redundant, as the sacred source and the ritual communication effectively sanctify the message twice. In this way ritual communication is a one-way message which does not need feedback.

Like other ritual communication, fundamentalist ritual communication also refers to a sacred source. Each message is expressed through the religious symbolic form, when the fundamentalist group performs a particular action which is deduced from the sacred text or tradition. In this way each new social action is 'sanctified', and in the process they pass on the religious message, but in a selective way that makes the sacred source speak for their particular political objective. It is in the political objective that the distinguishing feature of fundamentalism is located: fundamentalists do *not* sanctify the main social institutions. Fundamentalists instead sanctify courses of action that are geared towards re-forming both the community of believers *and* the main social institutions. For this reason fundamentalists perform their ritual communication outside of the rituals that are performed by the established religious institution, in public social contexts which determine how their simultaneously one-way and doubly sanctified message should be understood.

In this way, each fundamentalist public ritual performance transmits the group's definition of the truth of the sacred source, and becomes the vehicle of their political ideology. By expressing their ideology through public performance, fundamentalists make the ritual performance itself very similar to a political action, because like political action the performance seeks to modify the surrounding social reality (Addario 2003: 40–45).

## One-way communication

The hypothesis here is thus that fundamentalist groups use a one-way simplified ritual communication system, where the sender of the message is the decision-maker, and the receiver destination is passive. This mode of transmission is very similar to the broadcasting (one to many) transmission, as in the mass-mediated communication (TV, radio, newspapers, etc.). Inside this linear model, a number of psychological effects are involved in the process of loading symbols with meaning, which we are now going to define from a semiotic point of view.

A well-known representation of the process of meaning inside the communication channel is Roman Jakobson's model and the six functions of the sign. The sign is the smallest unit in the meaning-creating process. The complete process of transmission (Jakobson 1960: 353) works in a specific social context (referential function: the living ambiance) and uses a specialized language (meta-lingual function: the religious codes):

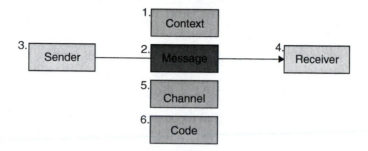

Figure 2    Jakobson's Communication Model

In detail, communication comprises the following levels (Jakobson 1960: 355–356):

| N. | Type: Name of Function | Factor: Oriented Towards | Description of Function |
|---|---|---|---|
| 1 | Referential | Context | Imparting information: the world around the message |
| 2 | Poetic | Message | Foregrounding textual features |
| 3 | Expressive or Emotive | Sender or Addresser or Enunciator | Expressing feelings or attitudes |
| 4 | Conative | Receiver or Addressee or Enunciatee | Influencing behaviour |
| 5 | Phatic | Channel or Contact | Establishing or maintaining social relationships |
| 6 | Meta-lingual | Code | Referring to the nature of the interaction (genre) |

In fundamentalist ritual communication performed into the media, the message comes from a sender (who refers to sacred scripture or tradition), passes through a transmission channel (the media), to the receiver (phatic function). The emotional function is the sign's image generated by the sender, and the conative function is the effect of the message on the receiver. The evocative power of the poetic function delivers religious messages, using knowledge common to community members.

The significance of fundamentalist communication is in the phatic function: the contact between sender and receiver. Fundamentalism modifies Jakobson's transmission model because transmission takes place in a ritual that is performed through religious symbolic actions. The address functions thus acquire extended power, through the religious symbolic actions.

As described by Jakobson, the communication process produces effects on both the transmitter and the receiver. There are the social (public or political) effects of the symbolic communication. At the individual level, the symbolic actions may have psychological consequences, as the performance creates a highly theatrical ambience taking psychological implications to extreme consequences, as in a tragedy.

## The model of fundamentalist ritual communication

Rappaport's concept of ritual provides us with the contextual social frame of reference, which is imagined by fundamentalists in terms of unquestionable principles, for example the obligation to sacrifice oneself in the struggle against infidels. The lack of feedback gives to the fundamentalist public ritual performance a particular unidirectional effectiveness, which is further enhanced because the society they show is the ideal 'sacred' image derived from scripture or tradition. Jakobson's phatic one-way communication model presents us with the elements of the specialized comprehension of the transmitted religious signs: an individual understands the fundamentalist performance as a ritualized message, ruled by a hierarchy of sacred principles, representing a perfect society. By combining Rappaport's concept of ritual with Jakobson's one-way communication model, one may conclude that fundamentalist messages have a strong impact on the public because they are based on the powerful contrast between the ideal and the social reality.

We assume that our four cases exhibit this one-way ritual mode of communication. Rappaport's concept of ritual shows the ritual constitution of fundamentalist communication and allows us to see what the fundamentalist ideal image of society is compared to the established social institutions, while the differences among the four case studies are highlighted by Jakobson's functions of signs.

*Case 1:* The Duomo prayer analysed with Jakobson's categories and Rappaport's concept of ritual:

| Type | Oriented towards | Analysis of the event |
| --- | --- | --- |
| Referential | Context | Gaza strip/Palestinians under attack by Israel. |
| Expressive | Addresser | We are a coherent, angry community who consider Palestinian issues to be Muslim *and* Christian/Italian issues. |
| Conative | Addressee | Confronted: the Catholic church and Italian institutions which treat Israel in terms of *real politik*, not according to sacred principles. |
| Phatic | Contact | Italy should protect Palestinian Muslims' rights, in accordance with its sacred principles, represented by the Church. Israel is Nazism and therefore the anti-thesis of Italy's/the Church's sacred principles, while Islam sanctifies these same principles. |
| Meta-lingual | Code | Muslim prayer sanctifies the same principles as Church rituals. |
| Poetic | Message | Muslim prayer sanctifies Italian institutions, *if* they support Muslims and denounce Israel. |

*Case 2:* Terry's anti-abortion manifestation analysed with Jakobson's categories and Rappaport's terms:

| Type | Oriented towards | Analysis of the event |
| --- | --- | --- |
| Referential | Context | Catholic University (Notre Dame); Obama ceremony for receiving doctorate; debate on abortion. |
| Expressive | Addresser | Randall Terry and the "pro-life" movement. |
| Conative | Addressee | Confronted: Obama as a liberal Christian and "pro-choice" (i.e. allows abortion). |
| Phatic | Contact | Those who killed Christ were against life, but Christ was God's sacrifice for eternal life; those who take life are like those who killed Christ, i.e. are not part of the community. |
| Meta-lingual | Code | Blood on toy doll symbolises Christ's self-sacrifice, executed by Pontius Pilate, and ritually celebrated in the sacred communion. |
| Poetic | Message | Excommunication: We "pro-lifers" sanctify all life, including the life of the unborn, to protect life against "the killers of Christ" who violate the sacred principles. |

*Case 3:* Mohammed Atta's self-sacrifice analysed with Jakobson's categories and Rappaport's terms:

| Type | Oriented towards | Analysis of the event |
|---|---|---|
| Referential | Context | The destruction of a symbol of American economic domination. |
| Expressive | Addresser | The true Muslims who believe that jihad against infidels for the sake of righteous institutions is a sacred principle. |
| Conative | Addressee | Threatened/the infidels: America and its allies, also among Muslims. |
| Phatic | Contact | Demonstrating the commitment of the true Muslim community to the sacred principle through the supreme self-sacrifice. |
| Meta-lingual | Code | This is the supreme sacrifice which sanctifies the *true* Muslim community and institutions. |
| Poetic | Message | Excommunication (*takfir*) of infidels through self-sacrifice. |

*Case 4:* Muslim prayer on Capitol Hill analysed with Jakobson's categories and Rappaport's concept of ritual:

| Type | Oriented towards | Analysis of the event |
|---|---|---|
| Referential | Context | Prayer ritual held at the location of the core state institutions. |
| Expressive | Addresser | Muslim-Americans. |
| Conative | Addressee | The general public, including Muslims and other religions groups. |
| Phatic | Contact | Muslim identity is part of American national identity and institutions. |
| Meta-lingual | Code | Muslim prayer sanctifies American institutions. |
| Poetic | Message | Inclusion: We belong here. |

All three fundamentalist public (cases 1–3) rituals communicate a sharp dichotomy between those who are 'inside' the community and those who are 'outside' it, and the dichotomy implies a profound critique of established institutions. The Duomo prayer aligns itself with the Church and Italian institutions only on the condition that they disavow Israel. Terry's pro-life campaign says that he will only sanctify American institutions and the law, represented by Obama, if they cease to take life. Mohammed Atta's self-sacrifice says that the current Muslim institutions are run by infidels, supported by American money and power, and that everyone who supports this situation has forfeited his or her right to live. In contrast, the prayer on Capitol Hill (case 4) communicates inclusion of Muslims in the nation and their loyalty to the state institutions, without any conditions attached. While the media-reported responses to this prayer communicated both inclusive and exclusive messages, the organizers themselves communicated only inclusion.

By applying Jakobson's model, both the transformation of the ritual and the different levels of meaning in the message become apparent. To begin with, there is simply the ritual: prayer (the Duomo; Capitol Hill); protest demonstration (Terry); and self-sacrifice (Atta), which in itself has only a limited significance. But as the religious signs employed in the ritual are interpreted in reference to the social context and the signs vested in it (at the cathedral; at a catholic university with Obama; targeting the World Trade Center; on Capitol Hill), the political message comes to the fore. This change of significance is located in the choice of context, e.g. when the Muslim prayer is performed in the context of a demonstration in front of the catholic cathedral, instead of inside a mosque or in someone's living room, the ritual's message changes. Yet the same message carries multiple levels of significance. The general public may only understand the obvious political message ('Italian Muslims are outraged over Israel and seek solidarity from the Church'), while someone familiar with the theological and societal implications of the prayer ritual also gets the more subtle message about Muslim affiliation or non-affiliation with Italian institutions. Similarly, Atta's self-sacrifice may be understood by the general public as simply an attack on America, while Muslims also understand the excommunication level of the message. These multiple significances inside the same religio-political message and the complexity of the contextual significance are typical of very narrowly focused messages.

## Greimas' semiotic square

So far, we have explored the religious fundamentalist messages only through 'ordinary' semiotic models, such as Jakobson's. However, the parallel with advertisement invites a more elaborate semiotic analysis. Advertising agencies use logical tools for developing more extended associations of significations, for example, starting from a couple of opposed words (black/white, top/bottom, etc.). To apply this approach to our four cases, we have selected the French semiot-ics theorist Algirdas Greimas' model, or 'Greimas' semiotic square' which, according to Louis Hebert, is particularly suitable to 'exam-ine the dynamics of truth/falseness in any semiotic act' (Hebert 2006: 29).

The use of the communicative power of ritual for transmitting the truth of a given religious message can be seen as an essential part of a strategy to capture mass-mediated visibility. Greimas' semiotic square provides a method for analysing paired semiotic concepts (Greimas 1987: xiv, 49):

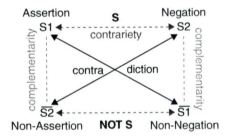

**Figure 3**    Greimas' semiotic square (from Chandler 2003)

In our application of Greimas' semiotic square we consider the S category to represent Jakobson's Addresser/Addressee commutation elements. In each of our cases, we consider the primary instigator of the manifestation to be addressing one or several audiences, and we take the addressee to be the audience made most obvious in reports of the events. We take the 'Not S' category to be the subtext of commu-nication or message(s) conveyed as reflected in Jakobson's Phatic and Conative communication elements, which is where the community meaning of rituals appear. We will apply this model to examine opposite pairs of religious concepts, such as truth/ untruth; presence/ absence; norm/deviation; inclusion/exclusion, etc., that can be deduced from our four cases.

## Greimas' semantic square applied to the Duomo prayer:

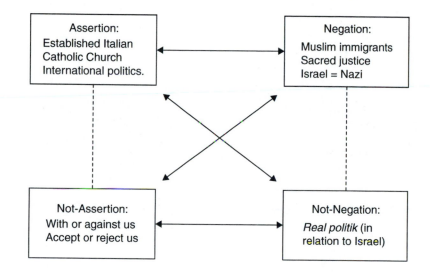

## Greimas' semantic square applied to Terry's pro-life manifestation:

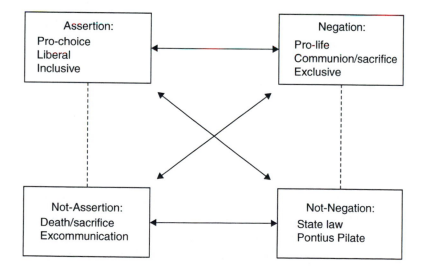

Greimas' semantic square applied to Mohammed Atta's self-sacrifice:

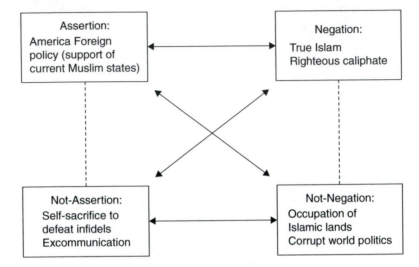

Greimas' semantic square applied to the prayer on Capitol Hill:

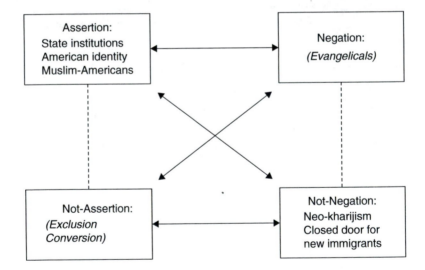

In the first three 'fundamentalist' cases the Non-Negation category tends to bring out the true contextual targets of the manifestations – the actual target of the group. Equally the Non-Assertion category brings out the message of inclusion and exclusion as the motivation of the actors.

However, in contrast to the three fundamentalist cases, it is not obvious what Negation or Not-Assertion can be read from the explicit words or actions of the organisers of the Capitol Hill prayer. Instead the religious and evangelical reaction (in the media and on the location) to the protest provides candidate concepts for these clauses. As such, this analysis suggests that although the praying Muslims on Capitol Hill did not express fundamentalist sentiment, such sentiment was voiced by those who reacted to it in that they resisted Muslims sanctifying national institutional sites. In a more recent case, the proposal for a mosque and community centre to be built near the site of the former World Trade Centre has met with similar public antagonism. However, in a fascinating twist, President Obama has supported the idea of a mosque and referred to the site as 'hallowed ground'. Thus Obama denied that the site was de-sanctified by the 9/11 self-sacrifice, in the same time as he (as embodiment of the state), together with New York's mayor Michael Bloomberg (as embodiment of the state, American business, and the media), sanctified it by enforcing the inclusive and non-excommunicating principle of freedom of religion for all American citizens (Batty 2010).

## Conclusion

In this paper we have examined four examples of public ritual performances 'played out' into the mass media. The fact that the rituals themselves are well established makes them easily understood in one way by members of groups who usually participate in them, while they provide a different meaning to the general public. The combination of these two perspectives makes the performances media-suitable even without being as spectacular as the 9/11 attack on the World Trade Centre. Through the media coverage itself some among the target audience are alerted to the fact of the event, and to the message about a confrontation or threat, while others in the audience receive the 'with or against us' message in terms which are emotionally and religiously laden due to their association with a common ritual. The analysis of these four cases also suggests that our combined model (of Rappaport-Jakobson-Greimas) allows us to understand both the theological/religious and the political/contextual levels of ritually communicated messages, and that when these two levels are combined, the implications of the political message appear considerably more complex than we might first have thought.

## Bibliography

Addario, Nicolò (2003) *Teoria dei sistemi sociali e modernità*. Roma: Carocci.

Almond, Gabriel A., Emmanuel Sivan and R. Scott Appleby (1995) 'Fundamentalism: genus and species'. In Marty, Martin E. and R. Scott Appleby (eds.) *Fundamentalisms Comprehended*. Vol. 5 of *The Fundamentalism Project*. Chicago: The University of Chicago Press, pp. 399–424.

Arjomand, Saïd Amir (1995) 'Unity and Diversity in Islamic Fundamentalism'. In Marty, Martin E. and Appleby, R. Scott (eds.) *Fundamentalisms comprehended*. Chicago: The University of Chicago Press, pp. 179–198.

Batty, David (2010) 'Barack Obama defends plans for Ground Zero mosque', *The Guardian*, 14 August 2010. At *http://www.guardian.co.uk/world/2010/aug/14/barack-obama-ground-zero-mosque*, accessed 15 August 2010.

Carey, James (1989) *Communication as Culture: Essays on Media and Society*. Boston: Unwin Hyman.

Chandler, Daniel (2003) *Semiotics for Beginners, Paradigmatic Analysis*. At *http://www.aber.ac.uk/media/Documents/S4B/sem05.html*, accessed 2 June 2009.

Clark, Andrew (2009) 'Anti-abortion protesters arrested as Barack Obama addresses Notre Dame', *The Guardian*, 17 May 2009. At *http://www.guardian.co.uk/world/2009/may/17/barack-obama-notre-dame-abortion*, accessed 1 June 2009.

Dobbs, Julian (Reverend Canon, Anglican Church) (2009) 'Time to Call Islam to Account'. At *http://www.churchandislam.com/Church_and_Islam/The_Time_has_Come.html*, accessed 8 August 2010.

Foschini, Paolo (2009) 'Gli islamici si scusano per la preghiera in piazza Duomo a Milano. Iniziativa del presidente della Casa della cultura islamica, Asfa Mahmoud', *Corriere della Sera*, 7 January 2009. At *www.corriere.it/cronache/09_gennaio_07/tettamanzi_duomo_islam_1cf662d4-dcf9–11dd-8a8f-00144f02aabc.shtml*, accessed 31 May 2009.

Greimas, Algirdas (1987): *On Meaning: Selected Writings in Semiotic Theory* (trans. Paul J Perron & Frank H Collins). London: Frances Pinter.

Grimes, Ronald (1992) 'Reinventing Ritual'. *Soundings*, 75(1), pp. 21–41.

—— (2006) *Rite out of place: ritual, media, and the arts*. New York: Oxford University Press.

Hebert, Louis (2006) *Tools for Text and Image Analysis: An Introduction to Applied Semiotics*, available at *http://www.revue-texto.net/Parutions/Livres-E/Hebert_AS/Hebert_Tools.html*, accessed 11 June 2009.

Hoover, Stewart (1998) *Religion in the News: Faith and Journalism in American Public Discourse*. London: Sage.

—— and Kaneva, Nadia (2009) *Fundamentalisms and the Media*. London: Continuum.

Hopper, John (2009) '"Eurabia" comes to Milan. Why was the reaction to Muslims praying in front of the city's Duomo so strong?' *The Guardian*, 10 January 2009 11.00. At *http://www.guardian.co.uk/commentisfree/2009/jan/10/islam-muslims-milan-duomo-prayers*, accessed 20 May 2009.

Iannaccone, Laurence and Introvigne, Massimo (2004) *Il Mercato dei Martiri. L'industria del terrorismo suicida*. Torino: Lindau.

Jakobson, Roman (1960) *Linguistics and Poetics*. In Sebeok Thomas (ed), *Style in Language*. Cambridge, Massachusetts: M.I.T. Press.

—— (1973) *Essais de linguistique générale, Volume 2: Rapports internes et externes du langage*, Paris: Les Editions de Minuit.

Jameson, Fredric (1972) *The Prison-House of Language*. Princeton, NJ: Princeton University Press.

Jones, James William (2008) *Blood that cries out from the earth: The Psychology of Religious Terrorism*. Oxford: Oxford University Press.

Kippenberg, Hans & Seidensticker, Tilmann (eds) (2006) *The 9/11 Handbook: Annotated Translation and Interpretation of the Attackers' Spiritual Manual*. London: Equinox.

Ling, John R. (2009) 'On Abortion, Civil Disobedience, the Execution of Paul J. Hill and the Downfall of Randall Terry', Dr. John R. Ling's website, at *http://users.aber.ac.uk/jrl/civildisobedience.htm*, accessed 31 May 2009.

McCormack, John and Brachear, Manya A. (2009) 'At Notre Dame, Obama tackles abortion debate', *Los Angeles Times*, 18 May 2009. At *http://www.latimes.com/news/nationworld/nation/la-na-obama-notre18–2009may18,0,4343910,full.story*, accessed 31 May 2009.

Makarenko, Tamara (2007) 'International terrorism and the UK: assessing the threat'. In Wilkinson, Paul (ed.) *Homeland security in the UK: future preparedness for terrorist attack since 9/11*. New York: Routledge. pp. 37–56.

O'Brien, Patrick (2009) 'The Gaza War's Italian Front', *PostGlobal*, 12 February 2009. At *http://newsweek.washingtonpost.com/postglobal/sais/nexteurope/2009/02/the_gaza_wars_italian_front.html*, accessed 16 June 2009.

Owen, Richard. (2009) 'Vatican alarmed by Muslims burning Israeli flags outside cathedrals in Rome', *The Sunday Times*, 6 January 2009, at *www.timesonline.co.uk/tol/comment/faith/article5461114.ece*, accessed 10 June 2009.

Powell, Michael (2004) 'Family Values: Randall Terry Fights Gay Unions. His Son No Longer Will', *Washington Post*, 22 April 2004. At *www.washingtonpost.com/ac2/wp-dyn/A32934–2004Apr21?language=printer*, accessed 10 May 2009.

Preiss, R. W., Gayle, B. M., Burrell, N., Allen, M., & Bryant, J. (eds.) (2007) *Mass media effects research: Advances through meta-analysis*. Mahwah, New Jersey: Erlbaum.

Radler, Christopher (2009) 'Suicide Attacks Driven by Islamic Fundamentalism as Rituals of Modernity', *DIAS-Analysis* No. 40, April 2009, DIAS (Duesseldorf Institute for Foreign and Security Policy). At *www.dias-online. org/fileadmin/templates/downloads/DIAS_Analysen/DIAS_Analysis_No_40_ Radler_Suicide_Attacks_090421.pdf*, accessed 16 June 2009.

Terry, Randall (2004) 'My prodigal son, the homosexual', *World Net Daily*, 9 April 2004. At *www.wnd.com/news/article.asp?ARTICLE_ID=37979*, accessed 17 May 2009.

—— (2009a) 'Arrested at Notre Dame; personal statement', *Christian News Wire*, 4 May 2009. At *http://www.christiannewswire.com/news/3318410260.html*, accessed 17 May 2009.

—— (2009b) 'Archbishop Burke, Prefect, Apostolic Signatura, Interviewed by Randall Terry', 2 March 2009, at *http://www.ahumbleplea.com/Docs/ ArchbishopBurkeTranscript.pdf*, accessed 10 June 2009.

Randy, Sly (2009) 'Randall Terry Arrested at Notre Dame', *Catholic Online*, 5 January 2009. At *http://www.catholic.org/politics/story.php?id=33423*, accessed 17 May 2009.

Rappaport, Roy (1999) *Ritual and Religion in the Making of Humanity*. Cambridge: Cambridge University Press.

—— (1984) *Pigs for the Ancestors: Ritual in the Ecology of a New Guinea People*. New Haven: Yale University Press.

Robbins, Joel (2001) 'Ritual Communication and Linguistic Ideology: A Reading and Partial Reformulation of Rappaport's Theory of Ritual', *Current Anthropology*, 42(5):2001, pp. 589–612.

Rosenberg, Joel C. (2009) '"Islam on capitol hill" event attracts far less than expected: Evangelical Christians use opportunity to share gospel with thousands of Muslims', 25 September 2009. At *http://flashtrafficblog.wordpress. com/2009/09/25/muslim-event-on-capitol-hill-attracts-far-less-than-expected- evangelical-christians-use-event-to-share-gospel*, accessed 15 August 2010.

Sageman, Marc (2004) *Understanding Terror Networks*. Philadelphia: University of Pennsylvania Press.

Salmon, Jacqueline L. and Wan, William (2009a) 'Muslim Prayers at Capitol Stir Protests', *The Washington Post*, 24 September 2009, at *http://www. washingtonpost.com/wp-dyn/content/article/2009/09/24/AR2009092404600. html?sid=ST2009092502033*, accessed 8 August 2010.

—— (2009b). 'At Capitol, a Day of Muslim Prayer and Unity', *http://www. washingtonpost.com/wp-dyn/content/story/2009/09/25/ST2009092502033. html?sid=ST2009092502033*, accessed 8 August 2010.

Sheikyermami (2009) 'Pseudo-prayers by Muslims in public have nothing to do with religion – they are threatening and intimidatory acts towards the Italian people', 21 January 2009. At *http://www.sheikyermami.com/2009/01/21/ italy-pseudo-prayers-by-muslims-in-public-have-nothing-to-do-with-religion- they-are-threatening-and-intimidatory-acts-towards-the-italian-people*, accessed 18 June 2009.

Squires, Nick (2009) 'Muslim apology over prayers outside Milan Cathedral', *The Telegraph*, 9 January 2009. At *www.telegraph.co.uk/news/worldnews/europe/italy/4208395/Muslim-apology-over-prayers-outside-Milan-Cathedral.html*, accessed 31 May 2009.

Vecchi, Gian Guido (2009) 'Il Vaticano e la piazza islamica "Turbamento per quella preghiera". Il cardinal Martino: infastidito da quelle bandiere di Israele bruciate', *Corriere della Sera*, 6 January 2009 . At *www.corriere.it/cronache/09_gennaio_06/vaticano_piazza_islamica_vecchi_34aae708-dbcb-11dd-8581-00144f02aabc.shtml?fr=correlati*, accessed 31 May 2009.

Von Grunebaum, Gustave E. (1970) *Classical Islam: A History 600–1258*. London: Allen and Unwin.

# CHAPTER 4

# THE GOLD STANDARD OF FUNDAMENTALIST METHODOLOGIES

## Lionel Sacks

### Introduction and background

This chapter explores the methodologies of two movements with fundamentalist profiles by examining their use of the 'gold standard' idea. Here, 'methodology' means a way of arriving, from evidence, advice and theories, at beliefs or conclusions; and then of communicating them. One aspect of fundamentalist methodology is typified by 'return to source', where the source may be scripture or original writings, often augmented with considerations by significant authorities, for example the authors of the sources and their associates. Such a methodology stands in contrast to modern scientific approaches, which tend to be evidence- and theory-based. Recognising what methodology is being used can help in analysing a movement's attitude to modern values and its positioning relative to existing political and social structures. Here, this positioning is explored in the context of numismatics – the study and collection of coins, but more broadly, the study of the economics of currency. This context is informative as modern economics, now a modern science, and the free market is – despite the credit crunch of 2008 – a totem of modern liberal societies. As such, modern economics serves as a point of contrast for those wishing to set themselves apart. This study of numismatics complements earlier studies of the economics of fundamentalists, such as (Kuran 1996b; Iannaccone 1996; 1998).

Here, it is assumed that the roles of methodologies in public communication are: to show the strength of the 'truths' being communicated; to show the corresponding weakness of the ideas being opposed; and to help in separating the various communities of discourse. Thus, methodologies play a role in differentiating communities in public debate, thereby contributing to community formation. As an illustration, adhering to a literal belief in the Old Testament's creation myths defines a broad community of discourse and enables distinctions to be made between truths derived from the Bible and truths derived from empirical scientific research. In this way, many of the characteristics defined for fundamentalists by Marty and Appleby are reflected in fundamentalists' methodology, particularly: the selective use of tradition and modernity; absolutism and inerrancy of essential texts; elect membership; sharp boundaries; and authoritarian organisation. That is, strategies which 'preserve their distinct identity as a people or group ... fortified by selective retrieval of doctrines, beliefs and practices from a sacred past' (Marty and Appleby 1996: 835). Here it is suggested that these strategies apply to both religious and secular movements, including those who consider the 'deeds of the founding fathers' of the US (Kuran 1996a: 299) and its Constitution, as points of foundational tradition.

The ability of individuals to obtain money and fulfil their material needs gives them an impression of how things are in their world, and a comparison of incomes provides a metric for how they are doing in society. As such, local and globalised economics are often central topics of debate in the public sphere, and are considered by religious, political and social movements. At the time of writing, both the 'credit crunch' and the economic consequences of climate change have impacted on people across the world, highlighting the global nature of the worlds' economic systems. Individuals are often aware of the influences which both governments and supra-national organisations have on money, and it is therefore natural for any social movement developing concepts of a future society to consider how the money and economy of that society would work. This might be done by appeal to the best theories and practices of economics; however, since such theories can contain ideological policies, a social movement which looks to communicate an ideology might select a suitable theory of money for that purpose. The idea of money based on gold conveys a feeling of ancient authenticity – a golden era of 'gold standard' excellence and fundamental truth. Exploring the use of the idea of the gold standard reveals a semiotic sign used to communicate feelings of authenticity, separateness and a return to basics, positioning a group's contribution in the discourse in the public sphere.

This chapter explores how two selected groupings of fundamentalists use the notion of the gold standard in communicating their ideas and attitudes. The first grouping consists of two pan-Islamic movements promulgating the resurrection of the Islamic Caliphate, with the legal and social structure defined by selective use of the Quran and the Prophetic traditions. These two movements are Hizb ut-Tahrir (HT) and al-Murabitun. Both consider the gold standard to be part of the envisioned caliphate, but otherwise their activities and modes of communication differ. The second grouping consists of American right-wing libertarians, who envisage the USA as a polity with 'small government' and minimal foreign policy, and above all as being circumscribed by the American Constitution. Here the gold standard is both a technical means of relieving the US dollar of its role as a reserve currency – and thereby of the international responsibility that entails – and of relieving the federal government of power over citizens' money. These two groupings – one American and one Islamic – share a vision of a future state (a federation or a caliphate) which is different from a nation state, and which isolates its citizens from globalisation, global institutions and norms, to permit, respectively, a libertarian or an Islamic fundamentalist society.

The character assigned to money concerns its management or control, and can thus be referred to Jürgen Habermas's discussion of the relationship between the sphere of public authority, that of public opinion, and the public sphere in which opinion is discussed and formed (Habermas 1963). It is argued here that the ideologists and activists of the above two groupings take on the role of presumptive

state authorities or, in Habermas's terms, 'the sphere of public authority' – 'presumptive' as they do not have any significant power at present
and 'public authority' as they envisage states ruled by neither lords nor
dictators. There are two levels on which messages are communicated.
First, there is the level of communication *within* the public sphere,
where the two groupings are using statements about their theories
of money, gold and economics to send messages within today's public sphere, which express the groupings' concerns about 'authenticity',
'tradition', 'separateness' or 'ethics'. Secondly, this public communication indicates how, in the future, envisioned state, the sphere of authority will communicate *into* the public sphere. Statements about how
money will be managed are thus part of a broader message about how
that future state would communicate with its public, along with other
policies such as the control of the media, foreign affairs or welfare. For
this purpose, the groupings considered here have put out extensive
material concerning the gold standard in the media, through books,
articles, videos and the internet, and have even attempted to redeploy
gold as money. For the most part, this is presented in opposition to
established political and national organisations – i.e. in opposition to
today's national and global spheres of authority.

## The medium of money and the message of the gold standard

'Money' is a technology which can fulfil a number of functions, such
as accounting production, a medium of exchange and a means of meas-
uring and storing value. How a society defines and manages money
reflects many of its institutions and external relationships. At this
time, in most countries, the management of money is done by using
a common set of principles and tools derived from economics, according to which 'money' is taken to be an abstract notion (*fiat* money), its
value stemming from legislation, common agreement and trust networks, along with the individual country's economic productivity and
trading activity.

Money provides a medium of communication, in many ways on a
par with other media, whether mass media such as television, radio or

newspapers, narrow media such as telephone and email, or 'new' media such as blogs or social-network sites. This was identified by Marshall McLuhan in his observation that money, like languages, '[a]part from common participation ... is meaningless' (1964: 133), where such participation is between individuals, within institutions and, critically, between national institutions, politics and the public – including the common understandings and shared beliefs that are a prerequisite for the '*fiat money*' injunction to work. McLuhan identifies parallels between the language of conventional media and money. Money acts as a 'translator and transmitter' of 'stored work and experience'. The relationship between money and society is reciprocal, so that: 'Money as a social medium or extension of an inner wish and motive creates social and spiritual values' (ibid: 135). McLuhan's analysis is thus a commentary on the media, while also reflecting that the role of money defined by economics and the form of money as a medium are part of its message.

As a store of value, money is used as a common denominator to equate the value of different things, whether hours of labour, necessary or luxury goods, justice (fines) or social engagement (charity and tax). How these values are established depends on factors involved in how the society works. Some aspects are controlled centrally, if there are price or wage constraints, others are controlled by external influences such as the cost of imports; but the dominant mechanism is the free market – the consensus of how individuals value goods and services. The economic policies of government consist of two parts: how the government raises and spends money (its fiscal policies) and how it manages the quality of the country's money. Political dialogue most often focuses on fiscal policies, such as taxation or public services, while a government's influence on the quality of money is more problematic. At one level this depends on such matters as how productivity, savings and investment in a country are managed. At another level the quality of a country's money depends on the institutions which define it. In the West today these are, principally, the banking systems – determining how much money costs (interest rates), how much currencies are worth comparatively (exchange rates) and how stable a currency is (reserves) – the regulatory policies of governments and global institutions such as the IMF, World Bank or G20.

Money has evolved from being represented by goods or commodities (e.g. beads, tobacco, gold, silver) to being representational (paper money), and is now becoming notional (digital money). For commodity money, the commodity can be traded (e.g. silver bullion) or can be used as a value store (e.g. the 'pound sterling', originally made of silver). In between *fiat* and commodity money are convertible instruments, where some contract or document has value because it is, or is believed to be, convertible into a commodity. The history of money across many of the world's civilisations varies greatly in detail, but little in principle – it has mostly followed the journey from barter through to a notional entity. The variation concerns issues such as: just what is meant by a gold coin; how much money is commodity-based and how much based on a promise; who manages the quality of money; and other economic and fiscal issues. For the most part, money based on precious metals in general, and gold in particular, is often considered to have a very special place historically. Although there have been times when coins were made of gold or silver, or when representative money was backed by gold reserves, in reality there were very few moments when these situations were simple – in the sense of a unit of money equating to a precisely-specified quantity of gold. The gold in coins was never 24-carat, and was often highly adulterated when a king's or a government's needs were pressing. Equally, when there was a gold standard, there were seldom times when the amount of currency in circulation exactly equalled the value of the gold in banks.

Of particular interest here is the history of money in the USA and Middle East. The background to American attitudes to banking and money is informed, to a large extent, by British history. From the Middle Ages through to early modern times, the English currency was controlled by the monarchy, and often debased through re-minting or re-defined (Davis 2002: 113–233). There were two reasons for this: first, the currency provided the monarch with income, as coins were re-minted with higher levels of adulteration or less gold by weight, thus providing more currency for the same amount of precious metal; secondly, there was a need to increase the quantity of coin, since there were limited stocks of precious metal and economic growth demands an increase in the quantity of money circulating. This illustrates an intrinsic problem with commodity money when a society is expanding economically. For example, the Roman Empire, which often paid its solders in gold, was forced to expand and conquer territory where gold was to be found, if for no other reason than to continue paying its huge and powerful army. The impact of debasement depends on where one looks; Davis observes that:

> On average all the devaluations in England over the whole of the previous two centuries [up to the 1400s] amounted to only one-fifth of 1 percent per annum, which was hardly more than the ordinary losses of weight through normal circulation ... in short, debasement was not really a problem in England before the sixteenth century. (ibid: 171)

However, in the mid-1500s Henry VIII managed to devalue sterling by up to 150 per cent, in the 'Great Debasement', and stability in British coinage was not restored until late in the rule of Queen Elizabeth I (ibid: 201). Part of this stabilisation was due to the (broadly fiscal) actions of Sir Thomas Gresham, from whom we inherit 'Gresham's Law' (that 'bad money drives out good') and the focus on the quality of money. It took Britain a further 100 years to establish the use of paper money, with which there were equally substantial problems of quality and devaluation.

The history of money in North America includes the use of foreign coins (from a range of European and South American countries), goods such as tobacco or wampum (beads), and paper money provided by the state or private banking enterprises. The US Constitution established the federal government as the power in charge of managing money, and the Coinage Act of 1792 established the definition of the dollar and the cent as the sole form of money, its value (subsequently adjusted to fall into line with European coins) in terms of a combination of gold and silver (bimetallic), its appearance, and how its quality was to be controlled. By 1862, with the Legal Tender Act, America gained a paper currency which was not convertible into gold coins. Although intended to be a temporary measure, for use only in paying customs duties and government interest, these so called 'greenbacks' formed the start of the *fiat* money system in the US. Over subsequent years, America went through a number of changes in the monetary and banking systems, adopting a policy of guaranteed conversion to bimetallic currency and then the gold standard, as well as establishing a banking sector. Money issues have never been stable, as Davis observes:

> Following the severe bank panics of 1873 and 1893 this lesson was finally underlined in unmistakable clarity by the crisis of 1907, which demonstrated that just being on the gold standard was no guarantee of either monetary stability or of the safety of the banking system. (ibid: 500).

Since the end of World War Two and the advent of the Bretton-Woods agreement, the US dollar has been the world's reserve currency, a benchmark of (relative) stability; and when it has not been stable, the rest of the world has felt the effects. As owner of the dominant world currency, the US government has often had to make economic and fiscal decisions, taking into account their impact on other countries and economies. Equally, decisions of other countries can have marked economic impacts on the US economy, for example when a country decides to stockpile US dollars – as China has recently been accused of doing; this highlights the interlocking nature of how the US dollar and global finance must be managed.

That money is rarely a single stable entity was no less true at the time of the founding of Islam than at any other time or place; and the development of coinage in Islamic countries was equally complicated. Siegfried has explored the origins of the Muslim currencies – gold (*dinar*, 661–97), silver (*dirham*, 639), or copper (*fals*, 1405), pointing out that: 'Byzantine coins were accepted until the monetary reform of Abd al-Malik Ibn Marwan in 694 or 695AD' and that the 'quality of coin striking was poor, and weight varied. Therefore, coins were treated like raw metal: people continued to weigh rather than count them' (2001: 320).

The Arabian Peninsula was a major gold-mining region in medieval times, and still holds significant gold reserves (Heck 1999), so that it might be possible to support a gold-based system even with economic growth. At the time Islam was founded, Arabia was a substantial gold producer, many tribal leaders had dealings in gold production and the early Muslims, including the Prophet Muhammad, were reported to have raided trade caravans carrying gold (ibid: 369). This abundance of gold enabled a trade- and import-based economy to flourish, and the early Muslim world gained from voluntary or obligatory *zakat* ('charitable contributions') from gold-mining (ibid: 372). The development of metallic money continued throughout the evolution of the Islamic caliphates, not only in its composition and value but in adding another dimension to the theme of money as media, in the use of engraved inscriptions (of the Islamic creed) to convey messages about Islamic imperial hegemony over Christian Byzantium (El-Hibri 1993). Regarding the theory of economics and money, a number of thinkers in the medieval Muslim world supported gold-based currency, for example al-Ghazzali (d. 1111) pre-empts Gresham's law:

> It is a great injustice to place counterfeited money in circulation ... Circulation of one bad dirham is worse than stealing a thousand dirhams, for the act of stealing is one sin and it finishes once committed but circulating bad money is bad "innovation" which affects many who use it in transactions. (cited in Islahi 2005: 49)

For a very detailed analysis of variation in the make-up of Near East coins, see Ehrenkreutz (1963). By 1405, 'copper money with little intrinsic value, struck by the Mamluk Government (ca. 1250–1500), superseded silver coins in long-distance trade' (Siegfried 2001: 321). Even at this time, letters of credit (issued by money changers) were also used for long-distance trade – to reduce the weight of material being transported and, possibly, to reduce the risk of theft. The legal discussions of and decrees on how money should work were complicated, but by the 1300–1400s it was eventually established that the legality of money was an agreed and symbolic value of coins and contracts, as opposed to value by weight of metal. This brings us to a point where in the Islamic world, as in Europe and North America, the issues with money concern as much how it is managed, and the state of the economy, as what it is made of.

## Pan-Islamic movements; the golden era of the Caliphate

Some 'pan-Islamic' fundamentalist movements have incorporated the notion of returning to a metallic currency – the *dinar, dirham* and *fals* – into their doctrines, along with some sharia-based economic ideas, such as the prohibition of usury (Wegerif 1999). Among these, the perspectives of al-Murabitun and HT will be used here as case studies. HT is a political organisation which has the declared aim of resurrecting the erstwhile Caliphate into, what effectively appears to be, an Islamic federation. HT was developed between 1928 and 1953 by Taqiuddin al-Nabhani, the author of most of HT's doctrinal writings (Taji-Farouki 1996: 7; Hizb ut-Tahrir 2006), the central one being the 'Draft Constitution', which is included in Nabhani's *The Islamic State* (1953a) and defines the future caliphate. *The Economic System of Islam* (1953b) elaborates on Nabhani's concept of Islamic econmics in general including the Gold Standard and international trade. These documents are referred to on the internet by HT itself, by associated organisations and by its opponents (e.g. British National Party 2009) as a means of explaining aspects of the envisioned caliphate. As an example of its own contribution, the HT website goes through many details of the caliphate's structure, using the Draft Constitution as a primary source (*Khilafah.com*, 2007a). For an example of the opposition, see the anti-Islamic website Morga (2007):

> An 186-point draft 'constitution' which appeared on a Hizb website claimed in its Article 7, clause c that 'Those who are guilty of apostasy (*murtadd*) from Islam are to be executed according to the rule of apostasy, provided they have by themselves renounced Islam'. This constitution ... 'disappeared' when it drew negative attention.

This quotation illustrates the ways in which HT's own material is used by members of the public to generate hostility towards it. However, from the viewpoint of 'spreading the message', even hostile communication is useful, as it draws the 'sharp boundaries' between HT and others. It is not only Western commentators who find material to worry about in HT's draft constitution. Among other provisions, Article 129 implies that the Arabian Peninsula constitutes the 'heart-land' of the Islamic state, so several existing nations might be concerned at such claims.

The core statement regarding money and the state is contained in Article 163:

> The currency of the State is to be restricted to gold and silver, whether minted or not. No other form of currency for the State is permitted. The State can issue coinage not of gold or silver provided that the treasury of the State (*bayt al-mal*) has the equivalent amount of gold and silver to cover the issued coinage. Thus, the State may issue coinage in its name [in the form of] brass, bronze or paper notes etc. as long as it is covered completely by gold and silver. (Abdul-Kareem 2008)

This is a clear statement of position supporting both metallic and representational money. Recent articles on how the currency should work are also included on HT's website (ibid) as an addition to the constitution of the caliphate. There are also publications which mirror the belief that gold intrinsically prevents devaluation: 'In 1507, 58 silver aspers, the Ottoman unit of currency, could buy one gold coin. 82 years later, in 1589, 1 gold coin cost 62 silver aspers, an inflation rate of only 7% over eight decades' (*khilafah.com* 2007b). Yet other publications use the 'credit crunch' and the financial crisis to attack globalised institutions and capitalism as well as to promote the gold standard and the caliphate (*khilafah.com* 2008b).

HT has never achieved political legitimacy. Following the peak of its power in Jordan in 1968–69 (Taji-Farouki 1996: 27), it has tended to operate openly or through front organisations in Central and South Asia, Europe and the Middle East, and has often been banned or placed on lists of proscribed organisations (Hamid 2007: 147). Members of HT have, on occasion, split off and formed more radical groups, such as al-Muhajiroun (Byers 2009). The exact relations between HT and such splinter groups has made it difficult clearly to distinguish how radical a stance HT takes (Hamid 2007: 155). HT has generated interest amongst Islamist-inclined youth, whose most common activity is to form groups in universities and colleges; organised activism in the occupied Palestinian West Bank has also occasionally occurred (Spyer 2007).

As an Islamic fundamentalist movement, al-Murabitun is less conspicuous than HT. Founded by European converts to Islam, it focuses on evolving ideology, policy and local activism. Al-Murabitun was developed through the 1980s as the 'Murabitun European Muslim Movement' (Clark 2006) by Ian Dallas, who converted to Sufi Islam in Morocco in 1967, took the name Abd al-Qadir al-Sufi al-Darqawi (Westerlund 2004: 9), and now practises as a Sufi *sheikh* in South Africa. Followers of Abd al-Qadir call themselves al-Murabitun – approximately 'the confederates' or 'a confederation with a leader'.

Groups of Murabitun appear world-wide, but their heartland is in Spain where Abd al-Qadir went after leaving Morocco, and where they are associated with the Mosque of Granada. Although they were one of the first Muslim organisations in (post re-conquest) Spain, their position has changed as immigrant workers from Morocco and other Muslim countries have also become organised (Arigita 2006). Compared to other Spanish Muslims, the writings of Abd al-Qadir and the activities of his followers express a particular interest in political, economic and social issues (Westerlund 2004: 22).

Although Murabitun and HT are quite different in their organisational form and in their relationships with other Islamic organisations, they have some important similarities. First, both promote a 'federated Islamic state' or caliphate, with laws based on sharia. Thus, according to the Murabitun member Umar Ibrahim Vadillo:

[We will make] a path through these dark ages into a new day on which we can celebrate once more the Khalifate, and we can see again one nation – not 27 – with one flag, and one Shahada [testimony of faith]. One nation gathered for the sake of Allah, subhanahu wa ta'ala [swt], for the fulfilment of His Shari'at. (2004a)

In Nabhani's analysis of Muslim history, which forms the background to HT's draft constitution, it is argued that Islam was a single unified state up to 1924, when the Caliphate was abolished by Kemal Atatürk, and that this establishes the concept of a single, united, Islamic state:

> The point at hand is not establishing several states, but one single state over the entire Muslim world. And not establishing just any state, nor a state that calls itself Islamic while ruling by other than what Allah [swt] has decreed ... (Nabhani 1953: 2)

Insofar as HT and Murabitun share a concept of returning to an original 'true' state, and claim that knowledge of that state is to be derived from sacred scripture (the Quran, the Prophetic traditions), both can be considered 'fundamentalist'. Further, given that this structure of a governmentally-unified federation coincides with the structure of the *umma* (the community of Islam), then both HT and Murabitun match the concept of 'neo-fundamentalism' as described by Olivier Roy (2004: 2, 232–89).

The discussion on the gold dinar and silver dirham, developed by Vadillo (2004b), spans three main perspectives. First, there is the idea that a gold-based currency carries 'authenticity' for Muslims. Second, there is a broad political and ethical stance against dominance of world affairs by the USA. Third, there are ideas on how the gold dinar can be used now, both between individuals and by Islamic countries.

Anti-globalisation, anti-capitalist (McCallum 2003) and anti-Western sentiments are apparent in writings associated with Murabitun. The following article was posted on the Mosque of Granada website, which was founded by *sheikh* Abd al-Qadir:

> Apart from the debt-traps of the IMF and WTO ... what would happen if capitalism, which economically encapsulates democracy, were to penetrate all of that system's political institutions so deeply that its own purported political form no longer offered any kind of democratic correction to it? The problem, therefore,

is not democracy; the problem is radically intolerant capitalism. (Rieger 2008)

Abu Bakr Rieger edits the online *Globalia* magazine (www. globaliamagazine.com), which contains articles on Islam in the globalised world and on the importance of the gold dinar; it links directly to the Mosque of Granada websites. Arguments for the gold dinar and against global institutions are woven together, around the theme of 'good' and 'bad' money, to attack key organisations such as the WTO (Vadillo n.d.) for promoting monopoly, and the IMF as protector of the US dollar. Indeed, the 'problem' with the IMF is particularly interesting in the context of this discussion. The IMF's sole purpose is to eliminate any competition to the dollar. The competition is gold. Under IMF rules, all nation States can settle their balance of payments by any currency or commodity with only one exception: gold' (Vadillo 2004c). Consequently, the adoption of the gold standard is set up in opposition to 'Western' global institutions.

The Muslim world has found a novel way to strike back at the West – or at least at those Western bankers who rule the world's currencies – introducing a gold coin (Vadillo 2002). Members of Murabitun have seen the gold dinar as sufficiently important to attempt to introduce it as a currency, by trying to persuade the government of Malaysia to adopt it. The initiative was promoted by the then Malaysian prime minister, Dr Mahathir bin Mohamad in 2002, shortly before resigning from office; he has continued to promote the cause since that time (Al Jazeera 2004; *Globalia* 2008: 6). Murabitun members are also part of the e-Dinar company (Dibbel 2002) which facilitates financial transactions in virtual gold dinars; Umar Vadillo is a founder partner (see *www.e-dinar.com*) and *Globalia* strongly supports it.

## The American way: 'gold, guns and grub'

Using issues around the soundness of currency as a mode of argument to criticise the Western economic system is not the sole preserve of Islamic fundamentalist movements. The following, entitled 'The case for the gold standard', is taken from a private individual's blog site: 'While historically seen as solid and desirable, the dollar today is worth 4% of its original value, and continues to decrease. Foreign markets are now abandoning the dollar in favour of stronger currencies such as the Euro.' How can it be that a currency once considered 'as good as gold' has become worth less than the paper it is printed upon? The answer to this question lies in the understanding of *fiat* currency (Connor 2008).

The blog quoted above echoes many of the concerns of the Islamic movements, but with regard to the dollar. Meanwhile, at the top of the website the blogger proclaims his political allegiance to the 'Ron Paul Revolution'. United States Congressman and 2008 Republican presidential candidate in 2008 Dr Ron Paul is a long standing advocate of returning the US dollar to the gold standard. Paul is part of an American political and economic movement which supports a strong libertarian stance, small federal government, and adherence to the American Constitution as the basis for all law in the USA. Paul has used this stance to criticise many laws and many aspects of the federal government's functioning, including its management of money, the basis for which is Article 1, Section 10 of the American Constitution: 'No state shall ... make anything but gold & silver coin a tender in payment of debts'. This is reflected, in part, in Article 163 of the HT's draft constitution.

Within this movement the core economic perspective is often provided by followers of the Austrian School, such as Eugen Von Mises and Murray Rothbard. The Austrian School economists are strongly anti-totalitarian government, as typified by Friedrich August von Hayek (Hayek 1944), and they see liberalisation of the banking system as an important factor in reducing the strength of central government. There are also those who argue the case for the gold standard from a legal perspective, such as Henry Mark Holzer: their arguments concern these issues: what should underpin money; how to achieve a fully liberal banking system not controlled by the federal government; and what the character of the currency should be, as determined by the US constitution.

The crux of the first issue is the use of a commodity-based monetary system as a means of limiting inflation. However, some part of the argument for the use of gold or silver to underpin the currency reflects a more popular view – that these commodites possess some more essential quality. For example, Rothbard argues that:

> Mises showed as far back as 1912 that since no one will accept any entity as money unless it had been demanded and exchanged earlier, we must therefore logically go back (regress) to the first day when a commodity became used as money, a medium of exchange. (1992: 4)

From this Rothbard concludes that only a commodity which has been exchanged as a highly-valued good could be used, so that: 'In practice precious metals such as gold or silver, metals in stable and high demand per unit weight, have won out over all other commodities as moneys.' Here Rothbard demonstrates the fundamentalist methodology of 'selective retrieval of the past', i.e. referring to the historical 'Great Debasement' as if debasement only happened slowly, whereas in reality it has sometimes occurred instantaneously:

> Debasement was a relatively slow process. Kings could not easily have explained continuous changes in their solemnly defined standards. Traditionally, a new king ordered a recoinage with his own likeness stamped on the coins and, in the process, often redefined the unit so as to divert some much needed revenue into his own coffers. But this variety of increased money supply did not usually occur more than once in a generation. Since paper currency did not yet exist, kings had to be content with debasement and its hidden taxation of their subjects. (2008: 43)

The presence of the Rothbard material on the web is widely used, not only by American commentators but also, for example, by Muslim content-providers such as Globia (*Globalia* 2009: 25). Holzer, on the other hand, argues principally from a legal viewpoint, providing a different example of the fundamentalist methodology of relying on an original text and the beliefs of its author(s) for authority. Holzer's legal approach provides a contrast to those of practising economists such as von Mises, Rothbard and Hayek. The arguments of Holzer (and others, such as Vieira 1997) concern the legality of the actions of the American federal government and its agencies, in their role as managers of the dollar. These arguments are based primarily on the American constitution, secondarily on deliberations regarding the true intent of the writers of the constitution, and, finally, on history. Through print and on-line media Holzer (1981; also Holzer online) and Ron Paul (2008: 41–69; 2009) argue that the constitution gives the federal government power to raise money by credit (and therefore to issue credit notes), to mint money and to manage it (determine its value, prosecute counterfeiters); and that these powers do not include starting a federal bank or printing paper money. The discussion then focuses on an argument between two 'founding fathers', Hamilton and Jefferson, concerning whether a general purpose clause – the "Necessary and Proper Clause" in the constitution (United States Constitution: Article 1, section 8, clause 18) which gives powers to the federal government to pass any 'necessary and proper' laws required to execute its prescribed powers, such as establishing a federal reserve bank – has granted the federal government too much power.

Ron Paul uses this line of argument over a range of issues, including foreign policy – calling for minimum intervention, including no foreign wars and no foreign aid. Quoting Washington and Jefferson, Paul reveals a literalist attitude to the Constitution:

> If the Founders' advice is acknowledged at all, it is dismissed on the ground that we no longer live in their times. The same hackneyed argument could be used against any of the principles the Founders gave us. Should we give up the First Amendment because times have changed? (2008: 9)

Such statements share the fundamentalist methodology of using founding texts, which underlies Ron Paul's argument for constraining the federal government and re-shaping the US as a small-government, libertarian polity; the gold standard plays the role of both removing fiscal power from the federal level and circumscribing international economic, as well as political, relations.

Use of the American Constitution in this way is applied to a range of other 'Amendment rights', such as the Second Amendment – the right to keep and bear arms – appropriated by the American National Rifle Association. It is also used by Ron Paul in claiming a negative impact on the part of supra-national organisations such as the UN, and in support of his argument for the defence of individuals against the federal government, in parallel with the gold standard argument:

The United Nations is holding a conference beginning this week in New York that ironically coincides with our national 4th of July holiday. It's ironic because those attending the conference want to do away with one of our most fundamental constitutional freedoms – the right to bear arms. (Paul 2006)

The above quotation from Paul is to be found on the *lewrockwell. com* website, which is run by Llewellyn Rockwell, chairman of the Ludwig von Mises Institute, which publishes the Rothbard material used above, and whose banner proclaims 'anti-state, anti-war, pro-market'. This is one example of a range of mainstream, libertarian, web-based media, which includes websites such as *campaignforliberty. com* and *dailypaul.com*, and YouTube channels such as *eLIB3RTY*, the channel of *eliberty.us* or *campaignforliberty*. The methodology of these channels is to weave together material from various authors, including Ron Paul who himself reaches back to key libertarians such as Ayn Rand, directly and by quoting the article by Alan Greenspan which she published (Greenspan 1966). This produces a feeling of a ground swell within the public sphere supporting policies which 'defend the great American principles of individual liberty, constitutional government, sound money, free markets, and a non-interventionist foreign policy' (see *campaignforliberty*). This material is also used, in parallel with *e-dinar.com*, to support commercial gold-trading operations such as *gold-eagle.com* (Fekete 2002).

Ron Paul is often the focus of radical movements further to the right. An example of this is his standing with the White Supremacists and, so far as communications in the public sphere are concerned, he is frequently the subject of debate on websites such as *Stormfront.org* – a 'web-based hate entity' (Perry 2003: 336). A Google site-search shows that on *Stormfront.org* 'Ron Paul' gets 17,200 hits, compared with the 2008 Republican presidential candidate's 'John McCain' at 3,100 and the current president 'Obama' at 41,300 hits. Search results for the whole web give 32 million, 21 million and 200 million hits respectively, showing a disproportionate interest in Ron Paul on that website. Among Paul's policies discussed on *Stormfront.org*, the gold standard is the basis of a number of bulletin-board 'thread' discussions although these are not always in favour, especially when the notion is linked to Jewish financial practices. For example one post suggests: 'Auditing the **Jewish run Federal Reserve System** is fine, but the gold standard is a Jewish banker scam from the Middle Ages' (*Stormfront.org/1*). The associative relationship between *Stormfront.org* and Paul goes deeper than discussions on a bulletin board. As reported both in the mainstream press (e.g. msnbc) and on blog sites (e.g. *blogs4conservatives*, *MarkH*), Ron Paul has received at least one donation from *Stormfront. org* founder, Don Black, and has appeared at the same political rallies. Although Paul does not hold a strong position in the GOP (the Grand Old Party, but also 'God's Own Party' (Phillips 2006), i.e. the Republican Party), his message works with other members of the public sphere:

> America gets what it deserves. Anyone with a brain would know that Ron Paul was the last hope for America. As for me I am loading up on gold, guns, and grub. The rest of you can fight over who will be your master. As for me I will continue to support the Constitution, especially the 2nd Amendment. (Beowulf 2009)

## Conclusions

The above discussion has not explored the contrasts between the pan-Islamic and American libertarian movements, which take opposite stances on a range of issues. For example, the pan-Islamic caliphate is envisioned as a form of non-dynastic monarchy with a strict legal system based on *sharia*, and is anti-capitalistic; whereas for the American libertarians, the concept of a monarchy was rejected during the constitutional convention; the law has a minimal impact on the day-to-day lives of its citizens; and they believe in free-market capitalism. These differences notwithstanding, there are several common themes in the form and method of their arguments. The appeal to the gold standard, or a gold coinage, is based on an appeal to the authority of foundational documents and their authors, which were located in a time when things where 'right'. This notion of an almost literal 'golden age' is used to criticise modern globalised institutions, such as the IMF and the World Bank, the banking systems and the UN. The complexities of the actual history of money and the recurrent pattern that it is the state, its institutions and the economy which give value to money, are, if not overlooked, put aside in favour of the ideological message.

The material provided by key activists and writers is picked up by a range of agents in the public sphere, through blogs and popular writings, who continue to propagate the 'gold standard' objectives. These objectives involve a common view of a supra-national state delineated by 'sharp boundaries' and within which the citizens are united by a common ideology, while externally the interaction between this state and others is limited to a bare minimum. Such a state is constrained neither by global institutions nor by agreements – and especially not international agreements on values in general or the value of its money in particular. This future state is set in contrast to the failures of the modern world and we are given a view of how to change a base society into a golden one.

## Bibliography

Abdul-Kareem (2008) 'The currency of the Khilafah'. *khilafah.com*, at *khilafah.com/index.php/the-khilafah/economy/3322-currency-of-the-khilafah*, accessed 10 April 2008.

Al Jazeera (2004) 'Mahathir: sell oil for gold, not dollars'. At *english.aljazeera.net/archive/2004/01/200841013171181781.html*, accessed 10 October 2009.

Arigita, E. (2006) 'Representing Islam in Spain: Muslim identities and the contestation of leadership'. *Muslim World*, Vol. 69, No. 4 (October), pp. 563–84.

Beowulf (2009) at *features.csmonitor.com/politics/2009/09/20/huckabee-beats-romney-palin-in-soon-to-be-forgotten-poll/*, accessed 20 October 2009.

blogs4conservatives    (2007)    at    *blogs4conservatives.wordpress.com/2007/10/26/ stormfront-founder-enthusiastic-about-ron-paul/*, accessed 20 October 2009.

British National Party (2009) 'Thousands of Muslims gather in London to demand a caliphate'. At *bnp.org.uk/2009/07/thousands-of-muslims-gather-in-london-to-demand-a-caliphate/*, accessed 20 October 2009.

Byers, D. (2009) 'In depth: al-Muhajiroun'. *TimesOnline*, 11 March, at *www.timesonline.co.uk/tol/news/uk/article5889411.ece*, accessed 23 October 2009.

Campaignforliberty,    at    *www.youtube.com/user/campaignforliberty*,    accessed 23 October 2009.

Clark, P.B. (2006) *New Religions in Global Perspective: A Study of Religious Change in the Modern World*. London: Routledge.

Dibbel, J. (2002) 'In gold we trust'. *Wired Magazine*, No. 10.01 (January), at *www.wired.com/wired/archive/10.01/egold.html*, accessed 10 January 2009.

Ehrenkreutz, A.S. (1963) 'Studies in the monetary history of the Near East in the Middle Ages: the standard of fineness of Western and Eastern dinars before the Crusades'. *Journal of the Economic and Social History of the Orient*, Vol. 6, No. 3, pp. 243–77.

El-Hibri, T. (1993) 'Coinage reform under the Abbasid Caliph Al-Ma'mun'. *Journal of the Economic and Social History of the Orient*, Vol. 36, pp. 58–83.

Fekete, A.E. (2002) 'Gold-eagle university'. At www.gold-eagle.com/gold_digest_02/fekete070102.html, accessed 10 January 2009.

Taji-Farouki, S. (1996) *A Fundamental Quest: Hizb al Tahrir and the Search for the Islamic Caliphate*. London: Grey Seal.

*Globalia* (2008) 'Far from retiring'. *www.globaliamagazine.com/*, No. 1, at *www.scribd.com/doc/9655324/Globalia-01*, accessed 20 March 2009.

—— (2009) 'The end of coercion'. *www.globaliamagazine.com/*, No. 6, at *issuu.com/izmedien/docs/globalia6*, accessed 20 March 2009.

Greenspan, A. (1966) 'Gold and economic freedom'. Originally from Ayn Rand, (ed.) *The Objectivist*. Reprinted in Ayn Rand: *Capitalism: The Unknown Ideal*, New York, NY, New American Library 1986, pp. 101–108.

Habermas, J. (2nd edn. 1992) *The Structural Transformation of the Public Sphere: An Inquiry into a Category of Bourgeois Society*. Cambridge: Polity.

Hamid, S. (2007) 'Islamic political radicalism in Britain: the case of Hizb-ut-Tahir'. In Abbas, Tahir (ed). *Islamic Political Radicalism: A European Perspective*. Edinburgh: Edinburgh University Press, pp. 145–59.

Heck, G.W. (1999) 'Gold mining in Arabia and the rise of the Islamic state'. *Journal of the Economic and Social History of the Orient*, Vol. 42, No. 3, pp. 364–95.

Holzer, H.M. (2008) at *henrymarkholzer.blogspot.com/2008/11/ben-bernanke-henry-paulson-and.html,* accessed 10 October 2009.

Holzer, H.M. (1981) 'Government's money monopoly'. San Jose, New Your, Lincoln, Shanghai: iUniverse.com.

Hizb ut-Tahir (2006) 'Who is Hizb ut-Tahir?' at *www.hizb.org.uk/hizb/who-is-ht.html,* accessed 10 October 2009.

Iannaccone, L.R. (1996) 'Heirs to the Protestant ethic? The economics of American fundamentalists'. In Marty, Martin E. and R. Scott Appleby (eds.) *Fundamentalisms and the State: Politics, Economies, and Militance*, Vol. 3 of Marty and Appleby (eds.) *The Fundamentalism Project*. Chicago: The University of Chicago Press, pp. 346–66.

—— (1998) 'Introduction to the Economics of Religion'. *Journal of Economic Literature*, Vol. XXXVI, No. 3 (September), pp. 1465–96.

Islahi, A.A. (2005) 'Contributions of Muslim scholars to economic thought and analysis (11–905 a.h./632–1500 a.d.)'. Jeddah: Scientific Publishing Centre, King Abdulaziz University.

*khilafah.com* (2007a) 'The Khilafah is not a totalitarian state'. At *www.khilafah. com/index.php/the-khilafah/issues/1175-the-khilafah-is-not-a-totalitarian-state*, accessed 20 January 2008.

—— (2007b) 'Part two: the Khilafah, investment and the economy'. At *www. khilafah.com/kcom/the-khilafah/economy/part-two-the-khilafah-investment-and-the-economy.html*, accessed 20 January 2008.

*khilafah.com* (2008b) 'There are alternatives to free market capitalism!' At *www. khilafah.com/index.php/the-khilafah/economy/3919-there-are-alternatives-to-free-market-capitalism*, accessed 23 October 2009.

Kuran, Timur (1996a) 'Fundamentalists and the economy'. In Marty and Appleby (eds.) *Fundamentalisms and the State*, pp. 289–301.

—— (1996b) 'The economic impact of Islamic fundamentalism'. In ibid, pp. 302–335.

Marty, Martin E. and R. Scott Appleby (eds.) (1996) *Fundamentalisms and the State: Remaking Politics, Economies, and Militance*, Vol. 3 of Marty and Appleby (eds.) *The Fundamentalism Project*. Chicago: The University of Chicago Press.

MarkH (2007) 'Values, voters and neo-Nazis'. At *scienceblogs.com/denialism/2007/12/ values_voters_and_neo_nazis.php*, accessed 23 October 2009.

McCallum, M. (2003) 'Muslim call to thwart capitalism'. *BBC News*, at *news.bbc. co.uk/2/hi/europe/3061833.stm*, accessed 1 April 2008.

McLuhan, M. (1964) *Understanding Media: The Extensions of Man*. London: Routledge.

msnbc (2009) at *www.msnbc.msn.com/id/22331091/*, accessed 10 October 2009.

Morga, A. (2007) 'Islamism: Hizb ut-Tahrir – a danger to the West?' at *www. westernresistance.com/blog/archives/003859.html*, 18 September, accessed 1 April 2009.

an-Nabhani, Taqiuddin (1953a) *The Islamic State*. London: Al-Khilafah Publications, available at *http://www.hizb-ut-tahrir.org/PDF/EN/en_books_ pdf/IslamicState.pdf*, accessed 20 January 2008.

—— (1953b) *The Economic System in Islam*. London: Al-Khilafah Publications, available at *http://www.hizb-ut-tahrir.org/PDF/EN/en_books_pdf/ economic_system.pdf*, accessed 20 January 2008.

Paul, R. (2008) *The Revolution: A Manifesto*. New York, NY: Grand Central Publishing.

—— (2006) 'The worldwide gun-control movement'. At *www.lewrockwell.com/ paul/paul330.html* and *www.lewrockwell.com/paul/paul73.html*, accessed 23 October 2009.

—— (2009) 'The Federal Reserve vs the Constitution'. At *www.tenthamendmentcenter.com/2009/09/24/the-federal-reserve-vs-the-constitution/?rta*, accessed 23 October 2009.

Perry, P. (2003) *Hate and Bias Crime*. London: Routledge.

Phillips, K. (2006) 'How the GOP became God's Own Party'. *Washington Post*, 2 April, at *www.washingtonpost.com/wp-dyn/content/article/2006/04/01/ AR2006040100004.html*, accessed 1 April 2009.

Roy, O. (2004) *Globalized Islam: The Search of a new Ummah*. New York, NY: Columbia University Press.

Rothbard, M. (1992) 'The case for a genuine gold dollar'. In Rockwell, Llewellyn H., Jr. (ed.) *The Gold Standard: Perspectives in the Austrian School*. Auburn, Ala: Ludwig von Mises Institute, Auburn University.

—— (2008) *The Mystery of Banking*. Auburn, Ala: Ludwig von Mises Institute, Auburn University.

Siegfried, N.A. (2001) 'Concepts of paper money in Islamic legal thought'. *Arab Law Quarterly*, Vol. 16, No. 4, pp. 319–32.

Spyer, J. (2007) 'The rise and rise of Hizb ut-Tahrir'. *Guardian*, 9 October 2007, at *www.guardian.co.uk/commentisfree/2007/oct/09/theriseandriseofhizbuttahrir*, accessed 1 April 2008.

Rieger, A.B. (2008) 'Debate: Islam and modern politics. The political consequences of terrorism are especially devastating for the Islamic community – but also for non-Muslims'. At *www.granadamosque.com/resources/articles/ islammodernpolitics.html*, accessed 20 January 2008.

Vadillo, U.I. (2004a) 'The future of Islam'. At *www.shaykhabdalqadir.com/content/ articles/Art021_03072004.html*, accessed 1 February 2008.

—— (2004b) 'Paper money: a legal judgement'. At *www.shaykhabdalqadir.com/ content/articles/Art029_04112004.html*, accessed 30 January 2008.

—— (2004c) 'Discussion'. *muslimvillage.com*, at *muslimvillage.com/forums/index. php?showtopic=8098&st=60*, accessed 30 January 2008

—— (n.d.) 'Guidelines on the use of the Islamic dinar'. At *www.granadamosque. com/gold/index.html*, accessed 2 December 2007.

—— (2002) 'Return of the dinar'. At *www.beautifulislam.net/finance/return_dinar. htm*, accessed 2 December 2007.

Vieira, E. (1997) 'The forgotten role of the Constitution in monetary law'. *Texas Review of Law & Politics*, Vol. 2, No. 1, pp. 77–128.

Westerlund, D. (2004) *Sufism in Europe and North America*. London: Routledge.

# CHAPTER 5

# THE CARTOON CONTROVERSY IN NORWAY: THE NEW CHRISTIAN RIGHT AND LIBERAL FUNDAMENTALISM CONFRONTING ISLAM?

## Oddbjørn Leirvik

The controversy over the cartoons of the Prophet Muhammad in 2005–06 was seen by many as a conflict related to freedom of expression, more specifically as a universal value currently 'threatened by Islamists' (Selbekk 2006). Both the Danish daily newspaper *Jyllands-Posten* and the Norwegian monthly *Magazinet* (which made an issue of republishing the cartoons in Norway) insisted that the publication of the Muhammad cartoons was a necessary defence of liberal values, faced with mounting Islamic influence in Europe and the perceived illiberal attitudes associated with it.

In the perception of many 'public debaters', the ensuing protests from Muslims all over the world were due to the fact that, according to Islam, depictions of the Prophet Muhammad are forbidden. There is, however, no universal ban in the Muslim world on depicting Muhammad in drawing or painting. Persian tradition in particular has a strong tradition of pious, artistic representations of the Prophet (Flaskerud 2002).[1] Thus the controversy was clearly about something other than the legitimacy of making pictures of Muhammad. The issue was rather about *caricatures*, that were taken by Muslims as a deliberate attack on Islam.

The most controversial cartoons reproduced well-known stereotypes of Islam as a patriarchal, oppressive and violent religion; others appeared to be utterly harmless. In hindsight, it might be difficult for an innocent observer to comprehend why the cartoons created so much havoc. However, in order to understand Muslim reactions to them, one will have to take a much broader approach.[2] With regard to established stereotypes, the image of 'the violent Muslim' has probably become as widespread in Western culture as previous images of 'the greedy Jew'. The cartoons – and the way they were presented, as a provocative test of Muslim attitudes towards freedom of expression – contributed also to a climate of mutual confrontation between groups of Westerners and groups of Muslims, who already see themselves in a state of cultural war.

Despite a common framing of the controversy as a perceived clash between 'freedom of expression' and 'oppressive Islam', the cartoon affair took very different turns in the two neighbouring Nordic countries of Denmark and Norway. In Denmark, the controversy's country of origin, the affair could be seen as a clash between a peculiar form of secularised Christian nationalism on the one hand and a (partly radicalised) Muslim community, suffering under the pressure of mounting Islamophobia, on the other.[3]

Presenting his reasons for commissioning and publishing the cartoons, Flemming Rose (the cultural editor of *Jyllands-Posten*) claimed that many artists, authors, cartoonists and theatre people fail to tackle 'the most important cultural encounter of our time that takes place between Islam and the secular, Western societies which have their roots in Christianity.'[4]

The depiction of Islam over against secularised Christianity is a typical feature of mainstream Danish discourses about immigration and integration, but may also reflect a globalised, neo-conservative rhetoric. The aspect of neo-conservatism in focus here is its uncompromising attitude towards values thought to be alien to 'the West', and its readiness for global confrontation with those perceived as ideological and military enemies of the USA or the West. As noted by Peter Hervik, *Jyllands-Posten's* discourse on Islam as an imminent threat to the fundamental values of the secular-and-Christian West drew heavily on neo-conservative discourses, as reflected in Flemming Rose's close association with neo-conservative ideologues such as Daniel Pipes in the USA, and the newspaper's numerous interviews during 2006 with thinkers who in the name of freedom have taken uncompromising stances towards Islam and Muslims (Hervik 2008).

In Norway, the controversy took on a different shape. Whereas in Denmark it was one of the country's largest newspapers that had published the cartoons, in Norway it was a relatively small Christian magazine (*Magazinet*) that made it a political issue to reprint them – in order to affirm freedom of expression which, as expressed by editor Vebjørn Selbekk, 'in our part of the world is threatened by a religion that is not alien to resorting to violence'.[5] (The cartoons were also reprinted by some other newspapers in Norway, but only as illustrations to a news item and without the Islam-critical slant of *Magazinet*.)

Although there are obvious affinities in the ways that Rose and Selbekk vilify 'Islam' (as expressed by the editors when the cartoons were published in *Jyllands-Posten* on 30 September 2005 and in *Magazinet* on 10 January 2006), I shall argue that the action taken by *Magazinet* reflects not only mounting Islamophobia in general society but more specifically the increased influence of the New Christian Right (NCR) in Norway.

The action taken by *Magazinet* coincided in the public sphere with an increase in the influence of secular-minded critics of Islam who portray Islamic faith and Muslim culture as inherently patriarchal and violent. *Magazinet*'s action coincided also with the growing influence of the populist right-wing Fremskrittspartiet (Progress Party), which since the mid-1990s has repeatedly played the anti-Islamic card in its electoral campaigns, as part of an identity politics which according to Torkel Brekke could be characterised as 'ethno-religious nationalism' (2004: 120–2). Although the party's electoral turnout has not exceeded 20 per cent, in 2006 (the year of the cartoon controversy) more than 30 per cent of Norwegian voters expressed their sympathy with the Progress Party.

In what follows, I will analyse the *political* alliance that has evolved between the NCR and the Progress Party, as well as the *rhetorical* alliance that has developed between the former and secular intellectuals who share the anti-Islamic rhetoric of Christian fundamentalists, though not necessarily their neo-conservative leaning in politics. Apart from the perception of 'Islam' as an ideological and demographic threat to European values, secular intellectuals harbouring such apprehensions tend also to see freedom of expression as a sacred value that should not be confused by moral deliberations.

The rhetoric alliance between Christian and secular fundamentalists exposed by the cartoon affair in Norway represent, however, only half the picture. Contrary to what happened in Denmark, a strong political majority in Norway supported the joint action taken by Muslim and Christian leaders to resolve the conflict through respectful dialogue. This was symbolised by a public act of reconciliation between the Islamic Council of Norway and the editor of *Magazinet*, initiated by the Christian Democrats and presided over by the ruling Social Democratic (Labour) Party. Whereas in Denmark the government refused to speak to the Muslim organisations, in Norway the government (as part of their crisis management) financed trips by joint Muslim-Christian delegations to the Middle East and Pakistan, organised by the Islamic Council.

In the following analysis, I will discuss the competing influence of the NCR and secular critics of Islam on the one hand, and on the other what could be termed 'the dialogue movement' in Norwegian society. In this connection, possible tensions between dialogical and confrontational tendencies among Norwegian Muslims will also be considered. My analysis is based on a critical reading of news items and newspaper articles published during the crisis.[6] It relates also to a discursive analysis of the cartoon crisis by the media researchers Risto Kunelius and Elisabeth Eide, in which they distinguish between background discourses informed by liberal fundamentalism, liberal pragmatism, religious-ethnic fundamentalism and dialogical multiculturalism respectively (Kunelius et al 2007).

As one can see from the discursive matrix applied by Kunelius and Eide, their use of the notion 'fundamentalist' applies to religious as well as secular lines of argument. Their notion 'liberal fundamentalism' is used to characterise a secular discourse in which freedom of speech is treated as 'the primary value to defend and uphold' – in this case, against Islam as the dangerous 'other' (Kunelius et al 2007: 17).

Kunelius and Eide's extended use of the concept 'fundamentalism' is debatable, but is also found in those leading sociologists of religion who argue that the phenomenon of fundamentalism extends well beyond the religious sphere. One example is Grace Davie, who identifies types of secular reactions to resurgent religion that display some family similarities (for instance the tendency to think in black-and-white terms, and a desire to shock) with religious fundamentalism: '... religious movements are not the only ones to succumb to fundamentalist tendencies, a situation greatly exacerbated by the uncertainties of the late or postmodern world; a world in which the reassertion of certainty or truth becomes inherently attractive' (Davie 2007: 199).

Following Kunelius/Eide and Davie, I will use the notion of liberal fundamentalism to characterise a secular type of discourse that sees no compromise between freedom of expression and other considerations – with a particular slant against Islam as a religious 'other' which must be vigorously confronted.

### The NCR and the Progress Party: in *political* alliance against Islam?

When *Magazinet* republished the cartoons in January 2006, the newspaper was located in Oslo and owned by the charismatic (neo-Pentecostal) 'Living Word' movement in Sweden, whose leader Ulf Ekman did in fact dissociate himself from the action taken by editor Selbekk. As for Living Word connections, the movement's most famous offspring in Norway has been the congregation of 'Levende Ord', located in Bergen, the country's second-largest city. In January 2008, *Magazinet* merged with the larger Christian daily *Dagen*, also published in Bergen. Whereas *Magazinet* has had its stronghold in charismatic and (neo-)Pentecostal circles, *Dagen* has traditionally served more old-fashioned, pietistic Christianity on the Norwegian west coast. *Dagen* has also been known for its strong pro-Israeli stance and for a critical approach to Islam.

Trying to understand the action taken by *Magazinet* in January 2006, I have previously suggested that the composite agenda of *Magazinet* seemed first to resemble that of the New Christian Right in the USA, and second to reflect the cultural and religious rhetoric of the Progress Party in Norway (Leirvik 2006: 151–3). When challenged by the media, editor Selbekk readily admitted that 'ideologically, *Magazinet* is quite close to the New Christian Right in the USA'. He also confirmed that politically, he would like to see the Progress Party in government together with the conservative parties in Norway.[7] Correspondingly, in his book *Truet av islamister* ('Threatened by Islamists') (Selbekk 2006) he praises the support he received from the Progress Party during the crisis, in contrast with how he felt betrayed by the Labour Party and the ruling red-green coalition who (in Selbekk's perception) made him a scapegoat for the conflict and repeatedly emphasised the marginality of *Magazinet* in Norwegian society.

Along with their uncritical support for Israel, both *Magazinet* and *Dagen* have stood out as fervent supporters of conservative family values, another defining feature of the NCR. Analyses from the early 1990s (Casanova 1994: 135–66; Beyer 1994: 114–34) trace the NCR movement back to Jerry Falwell's 'Moral Majority' and identify the following amalgam of defining issues: resistance to abortion, to homosexuality, to feminist policies and to children's rights (i.e. conservative family issues); defence of private enterprise, and resistance to the expanding state (defining issues also for the Norwegian Progress Party); a dichotomisation of good and evil in international politics; and spiritual war against domestic or global enemies such as secular humanism and communism.

After the fall of communism, and more particularly after 9/11, both the NCR and neo-conservatism have placed Islam (in more nuanced versions, 'Islamism') in communism's previous position as the main global enemy of the USA and the West. In the same period, pro-Israel lobbying has increasingly become another defining element of NCR agendas, as expressed by John Hagee and others who see 'radical Islam' as the prime enemy of both Israel and 'Judeo-Christian civilization today' (Berkowitz 2006).

The combination of anti-Islamic and pro-Israel stances in NCR circles is strikingly revealed in Hagee's *Jerusalem Countdown* (2006), a book that combines apocalyptic visions of an Israel threatened by its enemies with the 'unveiling' of Islam as an inherently violent religion. The main source of Hagee's attack on Islam appears to be the books of the convert Mark A. Gabriel, in particular *Islam and Terrorism: What the Qur'an Really Teaches about Christianity, Violence and the Goals of the Islamic Jihad* (2002) and *Islam and the Jews: The Unfinished Battle* (2003). Like Hagee's book, Gabriel's are published by Front Line and Charisma House – both publishing houses under the Strang Communications Company in Florida.[8]

Behind these publishers one will find the international movement Youth With A Mission (YWAM), to which Mark A. Gabriel has been attached since his conversion from Islam to Christianity. Correspondingly in Norway, Gabriel's books are published by Prokla Media, the publishing house of YWAM's national branch 'Ungdom i Oppdrag' which must probably be regarded as an important contributor to the anti-Islamic rhetoric of NCR groups in Norway.

In *Islam and Terrorism* Gabriel puts forward the argument, conventional in NCR circles, about Islam as an inherently violent religion. He insists that militant Muslims' interpretation of the Quran is the most authentic one, characterises Islamic history as 'a river of blood', and warns Christians against dialogue-seeking Muslims who must be suspected of hiding their real agenda, which is to take control of the West.

In YWAM's perspective, their spiritual-war approach to Islam is linked with fervent support of Israel, sometimes in the apocalyptic perspective also to be found in Hagee's book referred to above. In a 2003 newsletter from YWAM Norway, put out in connection with the launch of the Norwegian edition of Gabriel's *Islam and the Jews*, their leader Alv Magnus offers the following perspective: 'Islam is a spiritual power. It keeps millions as captives in spiritual darkness, denies Christ and opposes God's plans for Israel and the Jews'.[9]

The Norwegian translation of Gabriel's *Islam and Terrorism* has been one of the best-selling books on Islam during the last few years. When published in 2003, it was also distributed free to all members of the Norwegian parliament. Indicative of an emerging alliance between NCR and the Progress Party, its chairman Carl I. Hagen, in a televised debate in November 2004, pointed to Gabriel's book as one of most reliable sources on Islam.[10] Some months before, Hagen made headlines after his visit to the charismatic Living Word congregation in Bergen, which was already known for the connections between some of its members and the Progress Party in Bergen. In his Living Word address in the summer of 2004, Hagen was applauded by his Christian audience when praising Israel and characterising Muhammad as a warlord.[11] In his autobiography, he repeats this characterisation: a 'warlord, assailant and abuser of women ... who murdered and accepted rape as a means of conquest' (2007: 539).[12] Hagen's speech in Living Word was probably the first example of his use of the expression 'we Christians', as a mature expression of his growing insistence that 'Christian values and culture are challenged by Islam' (as stated in a parliamentary document of 1999–2000; Brekke 2004: 121).

What about *Magazinet* and its editor Vebjørn Selbekk – in this larger picture of a growing alliance between the NCR and the Progress Party in Norway, fuelled by Gabriel's and YWAM's anti-Islamic rhetoric? In his book *Truet av Islamister* ('Threatened by Islamists'), which was published towards the end of 2006, Selbekk makes no direct references to Gabriel's books. Instead, he cites Ibn Warraq and Ayaan Hirsi Ali (Selbekk 2006: 215) and their harsh critique of Islam, their former religion. The critique is more or less identical with that of Gabriel and the NCR (only with a stronger focus among secularised critics on the oppression of women in Islam) and also has neo-conservative affinities (particularly in the case of Ayaan Hirsi Ali).

It should be noted, however, that Selbekk's critique of 'Islamist' tendencies is slightly more nuanced than the wholesale condemnation of Islam as a religion in Gabriel's books. In Selbekk's book, one will also find a number of positive references to the moderate position taken by Norwegian Muslim leaders during the cartoon crisis, and their willingness to reconcile with Selbekk (cf. below). In his book, Selbekk also repeatedly distances himself from xenophobic attitudes and from those who oppose immigration from the Muslim world.

One might wonder whether the observed tension between Selbekk's harsh and generalising critique of Islam on the one hand and his more reconciliatory approach to Muslims on the other reflects also a similar ambivalence towards Islam and Muslims in the NCR. As Jennifer S. Butler has noticed in her book *Born Again: The Christian Right Globalized* (2006), in recent years several efforts have been made in international forums to forge interreligious alliances between Muslims and conservative Christians on the basis of 'family values'.

Butler notes also a growing convergence between the NCR's agenda and that of slightly more secularised neo-conservatives, centred around what she calls 'a moralist foreign policy' in which conservative family values are seen not as a defensive issue but 'nothing less than as an integral component of a process of American empire-building that will help America save and democratise the world' (2006: 135). A related convergence can be found in NCR and neo-conservative support for right-wing politics in Israel (ibid: 139), whereas in the case of Islam ideological rhetoric against it competes with realistic assessments of (groups of) Muslims as potential allies in a global struggle for conservative values.

## A *rhetorical* alliance between the populist-Christian right and liberal fundamentalists?

In a larger perspective, it is interesting to note that, parallel in time to the cartoon controversy, a number of bloggers and website editors with a hypercritical approach to immigration and Islam (such as *rights.no*, *honestthinking.org* and *document.no*) made their voices heard more loudly than before by the Norwegian public. Aided by alarmist books from 2006–7, such as *While Europe Slept: How Radical Islam Is Destroying the West from Within* by Bruce Bawer (an American journalist and writer resident in Norway) and *Amerikabrevet: Europa i fare* ('A letter to America: Europe in danger') by Hallgrim Berg (an former Member of Parliament from Høyre, the Conservative Party), neo-conservative bloggers and activists have claimed that totalitarian Islamism is the dominant tendency within European Islam, warned against a demographic takeover of Europe by Muslims in the course of this century, and appealed to the overwhelming power of the USA to protect the fundamental freedoms of the West. Added to these core issues, among secular critics of Islam one will also find either a feminist agenda (which is also shared by more nuanced critics of Islam as well as by reformist Muslims), or a pro-Israeli agenda in which Israel is conventionally portrayed as the only democracy in the Middle East.

The picture is not, however, that of a uniform alliance between *Magazinet*, the NCR and more secularised and neo-conservative critics of Islam. For instance, Jens Tomas Anfindsen, who in 2006 worked with *honestthinking.org*, did not support *Jyllands-Posten* and *Magazinet*'s publication of the cartoons.[13] However from the vantage point of Norwegian Muslims it is clear that the action taken by *Magazinet* was perceived as a further intensification of the pressure put upon them by the combined weight of mounting anti-Islamic rhetoric, from more or less secular neo-conservatives and from representatives of the NCR and the Progress Party, who in consort depict not only Islamism (or 'radical Islam') but Islam itself as an almost endemic danger to European identity and Western values.

In addition during the cartoon affair, many secular-minded liberals with no particular neo-conservative leanings voiced their support for what they perceived as *Magazinet*'s brave defence of freedom of expression. In October 2006, on the anniversary of *Jyllands-Posten*'s caricatures, the main national TV-channels in Norway (NRK and TV2) published rather uncritical portraits of Selbekk as a hero of freedom of expression.[14] The most prominent example of traditional liberals backing *Magazinet* was probably Per Edgar Kokkvold, of the Norwegian Press Association, who strongly supported *Magazinet*'s action and also wrote a laudatory preface to Selbekk's 'Threatened by Islamists'. Kokkvold's preface demonstrates that not only does he regard freedom of expression as an absolute right that trumps all other values. He also shares the perception that in Europe it is in danger of being stifled by radical Muslims, thus endorsing alarmist discourses on Europe and Islam. In his preface, the only example Kokkvold gives of Muslim activism in Europe is an extremist demonstration in London during the cartoon crisis, staged by a relatively small group of radical Muslims who are identified (and generalised?) as 'Islamists' (Kokkvold 2006: 18ff).

In their analysis of competing background discourses during the cartoon crisis, Kunelius and Eide characterise the position 'where freedom of speech is seen as the primary value to defend and uphold' as liberal fundamentalism (Kunelius et al 2007: 17). They suggest that this position also implies a purely formal understanding of tolerance, as merely tolerating opposing views, and the view that deliberate provocations can actually nurture a culture of tolerance in this (limited) sense. However, deliberate provocations in the name of freedom of expression may also contribute to a culture of intolerance by the 'othering' of groups perceived as a threat to the freedom values of the West, and should therefore be circumscribed.

If fundamentalism means that there is something absolute and untouchable in one's convictions which is not open to discussion, it makes sense to speak not only about 'religious or ethnic fundamentalism' (another category in Kunelius and Eide's paradigm) but also about 'liberal fundamentalism'. For instance in a 2006 'op-ed' in connection with a media discussion about liberalism and neo-conservatism in 2006, Knut Olav Åmås of the Norwegian newspaper *Aftenposten* referred to 'freedom of expression' as the only form of 'fundamentalism' that he – representing a position that he termed 'radical-liberal' – would subscribe to.[15]

In the liberal-fundamentalist paradigm, in which freedom of expression stands out not only as an inviolable right but also as an absolute value, there is not always room for pragmatic considerations of what is wise (such as those actually carried out on a daily basis in any editorial office) or for moral deliberations focused on the responsibility of the more powerful in relation to vulnerable groups in society.

## The dialogue movement in Norway

The above scenario – a *political* alliance between (parts of) the NCR and the Progress Party, and a *rhetorical* alliance between right-wing forces and secular intellectuals of a liberal orientation – was not the entire picture of the cartoon affair in Norway. Equally striking was the firm action jointly taken by mainstream Christian and Muslim leaders who opposed the confrontational approach of *Magazinet*, and the

Norwegian government's use of the Islamic Council Norway as a partner in crisis management (especially after Norwegian interests were threatened abroad, as exemplified by the burning of the Norwegian embassy in Damascus and attacks on the Norwegian mobile-telephone company Telenor in Pakistan).

Before the cartoon crisis erupted, institutionalised trust-building dialogue between Muslims and Christian leaders had been going on in Norway for more than 15 years (Leirvik 2003). An important part of the dialogue movement in Norway is the national Christian-Muslim Contact Group – between the Church of Norway and the Islamic Council – established in 1993. In this forum, Christian and Muslim leaders have been able to address a wide range of controversial questions (such as religion in school, the situation of religious minorities and the question of conversion) in an atmosphere of relative calm and trust. On several occasions, mainstream church leaders involved in dialogue with Muslims have also warned against the mounting anti-Islamic rhetoric of the political right and religiously-tinted xenophobia in Christian circles.[16]

When the cartoon crisis began in Norway, Christian and Muslim leaders quickly came together, formulating a joint appeal in which they supported freedom of expression, deplored the fact that religious feelings had been hurt, warned against violent reactions to provocative utterances, and called for moral responsibility in the way freedom of expression was exercised.[17]

During the crisis, leading politicians from the ruling red-green coalition (such as the Prime Minister and the Minister of Foreign Affairs, both members of the Labour Party) made several references in public to the long-standing dialogue work of the Christian-Muslim Contact Group, on which the government could lean when the conflict erupted.

In contrast, during the 1990s it was rather difficult for dialogue activists in Norway to attract any serious interest from the politicians. The situation gradually changed towards the end of that decade, during the centrist government led by the Prime Minister, Kjell Magne Bondevik, a Christian Democrat. Himself an ordained minister in the Church of Norway, he was susceptible to more than average sensitivity with respect to the critical role that religious leaders can play in either aggravating or appeasing inter-group conflicts in society.

## Empowerment of Muslims, or radical protest?

For the Muslims' part, there are good reasons to suggest that Muslim leaders' involvement in interreligious dialogue has contributed to the empowerment of the Muslim community in Norway, particularly as represented by their umbrella organisation, the Islamic Council. The introduction of a 'politics of recognition' on the part of the government was symbolised by Kjell Magne Bondevik's first visit to a Norwegian mosque, in 1999, followed up in 2007 by the first financial contribution by the (red-green) government to the Islamic Council.

What can be said about the concrete role of Norwegian Muslims in the cartoon crisis, and how were they seen by the media during the crisis? Acting in a quite different fashion to the Danish government, who simply refused to speak with the Muslims during the crisis, the Norwegian government invited the Islamic Council to be their partner in managing the crisis. On the initiative of the Council, and financed by the Ministry Foreign Affairs, Muslim-Christian delegations went to the Middle East and to Pakistan in order to appease Muslim reactions internationally, by explaining the Norwegian position and demonstrating Norway's culture of dialogue.[18] In terms of Kunelius and Eide's paradigm, the Islamic Council could clearly be seen as representing a form of 'dialogical multiculturalism', in tune with the government's politics of recognition.[19]

Mediated by Christian Democrat politicians and presided over by the Labour Party's Minister of Labour and Inclusion, a public reconciliation was also reached between Vebjørn Selbekk, the editor of *Magazinet*, and the Islamic Council, represented by its chairman Mohammad Hamdan. After Selbekk had apologised for having hurt Muslim feelings (but not for having exercised his freedom of expression), Hamdan publicly 'forgave' Selbekk and promised to 'protect' him.

It was probably at this point that some liberal authors and media people in Norway decided that they had already had their fill of

Islamic influence in this country. Who do the Muslims think they are? As TV2's editor Kåre Valebrokk phrased it: 'Have Norwegian newspapers now got the Islamic Council as an additional editor on their shoulders, to decide what should be printed or not and (if Muslim feelings have been hurt) who should be forgiven or not?[20] In addition, both press people and the general public felt offended by a remark made to the Arab television channel Al-Jazeera by the chairman of the Islamic Council, right after the public reconciliation with editor Selbekk: 'Unfortunately, freedom of expression is their religion'.[21]

To the extent that the cartoon crisis contributed to the empowerment of Norwegian Muslims, this was clearly seen by many as controversial. In response to the Norwegian government's public recognition of the role that interreligious dialogue might play in conflict resolution, neo-conservatives as well as some liberals in the media sector took a much more critical approach to the very idea of dialogue – on the (mistaken) assumption that interfaith dialogue implies a harmonising approach and is unable to tackle real conflict. During the crisis, both neo-conservatives and liberals criticised the joint Muslim-Christian delegation that went to the Middle East. In particular, they targeted the delegation's visit to Yusuf al-Qaradawi, a Qatar-based Muslim Brother who runs the influential *islamonline.net* website and is also a member of the European Council for Fatwa and Research. Why do Christian leaders, it was asked, bow their necks and travel with their Muslim counterparts to visit Yusuf al-Qaradawi, as if his voice and the opinion of international Islamists deserve to be heard in a national controversy? In response, the delegation members emphasised the need to explain the path of reconciliation taken in Norway to influential Muslim leaders in the more conflict-ridden region of the Middle East.

The background to the delegation's trips was of course the violent attacks on Scandinavian embassies and companies in parts of the Muslim world, incidents that contributed strongly to the dramatic perception of the cartoon crisis in the Norwegian public. On the domestic scene, the Islamic Council worked hard to prevent angry demonstrations in the streets of Oslo. Although no less than 46 imams joined the Islamic Council in warning against demonstrations, some 1,000 people took to the streets, with a rather troubling combination of slogans proclaiming 'Freedom of expression is telling the truth' and 'Islam is the truth'. Although carried through in a peaceful way and without any call for jihad, the demonstration might seem to reflect more radical attitudes than the 'responsibility approach' typical of the Islamic Council. With missionary-type slogans and a separate section for women at the rear, the demonstration could on a whole be taken as a sign of more confrontational attitudes among some younger Muslims in Norway.

In comparison with the demonstration in Oslo, a demonstration outside the Danish embassy in London on 3 February 2006 (organised by the extremist group al-Ghuraba) created international reaction because of its call for violent responses to the cartoons, under slogans such as 'Slay those who insult Islam', 'Europe you will pay, Bin Laden is on his way' or 'Britain you will pay: 7/7 on its way'.[22] This is the demonstration referred to by Kokkvold in the preface to Selbekk's book, there generalised as an expression of 'Islamism'. Kokkvold fails to note, however, that whereas the demonstration, with its violent slogans, attracted about 100 participants, while a much larger demonstration of some 10,000 people two weeks later did not call for any kind of violent responses, although angrily protesting against the cartoons.[23]

Obviously, in the British context Islamic radicalism is a very real phenomenon, as most dramatically demonstrated by the 7/7 London bombings. As for enemy images and hate speech, one can also see that the vicious depiction of Islam spread by the NCR and in neo-conservative literature are reciprocated by hate speech against Christians and Jews in books and booklets spread through some mosques. Although the soundness of the report on extremist literature published in 2007 by the (neo-conservative) think-tank Policy Exchange (MacEion 2007) has been challenged,[24] there is little doubt that the type of confrontational literature targeted in this report has an influence on the minds of many.

Returning to Norway, a poll carried out in 2006 regarding the attitudes of Norwegian Muslims does not indicate the same amount of radicalisation among young Muslims as indicated by British polls in the aftermath of 7/7 and the cartoon affair (Leirvik 2007). Nevertheless, the soft approach taken by the Islamic Council Norway during the cartoon controversy might not be representative of all Muslim groups in Norway. It could in fact be that the dialogical approach of the Islamic Council and its conspicuous cooperation with the government was out of tune with the frustrated feelings of young Muslims who (rightly or wrongly) feel that public debates about Islam in Norway are becoming as much infected by Islamophobia as those heard in Denmark and some other European countries in recent years.

With regard to Kunelius and Eide's matrix of different discourses in the cartoon affair, both the Muslim demonstration and attitudes expressed by some representatives of the Christian Right (not necessarily by Selbekk himself) might seem to reflect a form of 'religious or ethnic fundamentalism' which 'does not look for consensus, compromises or moments of learning in its encounters with other' (Kunelius et al 2007: 18).

## Critical dialogue on powerful majorities, vulnerable minorities and ethical responsibility

A striking feature of liberal-fundamentalist discourses during the cartoon crisis was the absence of any ethical reflection on the relation between legal and moral aspects of freedom of expression. Conversely, the question of moral responsibility was a pivotal argument in the type of discourses that Eide and Kunelius characterise as representative of 'dialogical multiculturalism'.

Moral questioning of the action taken by *Jyllands-Posten* and *Magazinet* was typically interpreted by liberal fundamentalists as a questioning of the legal right to blasphemous utterances.[25] Some of those who criticised the two publications referred to the responsibility to prevent hate speech (if necessary, by legal means) that rests with the state, as set out in article 20 of the UN Convention on Civil and Political Rights. The legal argument was not, however, a dominant feature of dialogical discourses in the Norwegian context: the focus was instead upon moral responsibility. For instance, the joint 'Statement on the Caricatures of the Prophet Muhammad' issued by Christian and Muslim leaders in Norway on 2 February 2006 emphasised that: 'Freedom of expression is a fundamental right which must be respected, but it must be exercised with responsibility and wisdom.'[26]

Some 'dialogical' participants in public debates also emphasised that moral responsibility for how freedom of expression is used increases in step with the right's legal enlargement. Those following this line of argument often have a perspective on power as a factor, suggesting that it makes a great deal of difference in moral terms whether a provocative (even blasphemous) statement is uttered by dissidents who are challenging the religious power in their own community from below, or whether freedom of expression is used by the cultural majority as a satirical weapon from above – against vulnerable religious minorities.[27]

Kunelius and Eide seem to associate the discourse of dialogical multiculturalism with cultural relativism: 'In the cartoon case, a typical argument from this position would claim that all people, groups and cultures have various kinds of censorship related to manners, beliefs, taste and power structures' (Kunelius et al 2007: 18). This does not quite fit with the power-critical reasoning of dialogically-oriented actors in the Norwegian case. Dialogical approaches that focus on the protection of vulnerable minorities are far more controversial, and could more aptly be termed 'critical dialogue'. Whether defending the Muslim minority in Norway against Islamophobia and ridiculing stereotypes, or Christian and Muslim minorities in Pakistan against discrimination and frequent charges of blasphemy, critical dialogue challenges asymmetrical power relations between cultural and religious groups. Such critical dialogue is not culturally relativist: in defence of vulnerable groups, it calls instead for interreligious solidarity against the oppressive language of power.

However, the question of who is strong and who weak in any given cultural conflict is debatable. In his preface to Selbekk's book, Per Edgar Kokkvold depicts illiberal political and religious leaders as the stronger party, against which 'the West' will have to defend itself – if necessary by 'ridiculing the powerful ones'. By juxtaposing the image of powerful religious leaders, Muslims who oppose any challenge to their dogmas, and radical Islamists who intimidate not only the West but even 'peaceful Muslims' (Kokkvold 2006: 18ff), Kokkvold paints a picture which is perfectly in tune with the general outlook of editor Selbekk, who (as part of the West) felt 'threatened by Islamists'.

By many religious leaders, the cartoons were taken as a disrespectful assault on believers' religious feelings, as also by Christian and Muslim leaders in Norway in their joint statement: 'The caricatures of the Prophet Muhammed published in Danish and Norwegian newspapers offend Muslims' religious feelings. Our sympathies go out to Muslims in Norway and the rest of the world who feel hurt by this unnecessary show of disrespect. When that which is sacred to one religion is attacked, all religions suffer.'[28]

In an ethical perspective, this joint Christian-Muslim statement on respect for religious feelings should also be critically examined, since the call for inter-faith solidarity against attacks on religion seems actually to blur the distinction between powerful actors and more vulnerable groups in society. The statement's reference to religions under attack seems more in tune with the (obsolete) blasphemy paragraph in the Norwegian penal code, which aims at protecting religious teachings from offence,[29] whereas their references to 'religious feelings' might be more in tune with the so-called racism paragraph of the same penal code, which protects vulnerable members of society against hate speech related to their ethnic origin, religion or sexual orientation.[30]

As noted, the religious leaders did not call for any legal steps against *Magazinet*, in either paragraph of their statement, but focused instead on ethical responsibility. This does not primarily relate to religious teachings but rather to the vulnerability of cultural and/or religious groups (whether in Norway, Pakistan or the Middle East) who feel that they are constantly under attack by the cultural and/or religious majority. This was clearly how Muslims in Norway, Denmark and elsewhere perceived the cartoons: as another Islamophobic assault against (immigrant) Muslims whose religion is constantly being criticised for being oppressive and violent.

The Muslims are not, however, a homogenous group. Any given Muslim group may suffer under Islamophobic attack from a secular or Christian majority, and simultaneously exercise oppressive power against vulnerable groups within its own ranks (whether women, gay people, or Muslims with 'deviant' beliefs). Liberal fundamentalists may argue that attacking Islam as an oppressive religion is effectively the same as supporting Muslim dissidents or Muslim women repressed by a male-dominated religion. However, this was not how the cartoons were seen by those who identified themselves as Muslims. With the exception of self-proclaimed apostates from Islam, it seems rather that the cartoons reinforced Muslim group identity across the liberal-conservative or patriarchal-feminist spectrum. If so, it illustrates the fact that believing Muslims of *different* inclinations feel increasingly under siege from an Islamophobic majority whose anti-Islamic feelings are fuelled by confrontational actors on the religious and political scene.

## Conclusion

In my analysis of the cartoon controversy, I have identified three different tendencies that can be identified in the Norwegian public sphere, as reflected in competing media discourses:

- A *dialogical* tendency that has fostered a climate of trust between mainstream religious leaders and, more recently, between religious leaders and politicians from all parties, with the exception only of the Progress Party. In the wake of the cartoon affair, those who identify with the culture of dialogue have increasingly felt that they have to defend it against religious fundamentalists, neo-conservatives and hard-core liberals who see 'dialogue' as a sign of weakness.
- The *confrontational* approach taken by the NCR – in *political* alliance with the Progress Party and in *rhetorical* alliance with secular neo-conservatives – is applauded by a growing number of citizens, who voice their anger towards Muslims through blogs and other media that invite confrontation. This confrontational approach is shared by estranged Muslims and radical Islamists who want a tougher rhetoric against the Christian West. These tendencies, antagonistic as they are, seem to feed on each other.
- As for the *liberal forces* in society, those who (differing from 'liberal fundamentalists') take a more pragmatic approach, warning

against the dangers inherent in the politics of religious identity, not only in the form of Islamism but also in that of Christian nationalism informed by the NCR or by neo-conservatism. In contrast to liberal fundamentalists and their sometimes aggressive secularism, pragmatic liberals as well as dialogue activists with a liberal agenda would be expected to support the forces of liberal reform *within* the religions.

## Notes

1. When the cartoon controversy erupted in Norway, the University of Bergen temporarily removed a website related to a project on popular Muslim iconography (including pious pictures of Muhammad from contemporary Iran – see at *http://www.hf.uib.no/i/religion/popularikonografi/utstill02.html*), apparently on the mistaken assumption that the controversy was simply over depictions of Muhammad rather than about caricatures more specifically.

2. A contextual analysis of how the cartoon crisis took a different form in different countries can be found in Kunelius et al 2007.

3. A summary report on Islamophobia in the EU noted 'widespread Islamophobic and xenophobic attitudes' in Danish society and politics (Allen and Nielsen 2002: 16).

4. *Jyllands-Posten*, 5 September 2005, cited with approval in *Magazinet* 6 January 2006 (Selbekk 2006: 128ff, my translation).

5. Ibid.

6. A comprehensive collection of media items from the cartoon affair in Norway can be found in the following section of the present author's homepage, at *http://folk.uio.no/leirvik/Interrelnytt2005–2006.html*.

   As can be seen from some of the references, the author of this article (who has co-founded a number of interfaith dialogue initiatives in Norway), was personally engaged in the media debate over the cartoons in Norway.

7. *Aftenposten* (2006) 'Ønsket konflikt med islam' (my translation), 6 January.

8. More recent titles from Gabriel include *Journey into the Mind of an Islamic Terrorist* (2006) and *Culture Clash: Islam's War on the West* (2007).

9. *Mot målet* 5, 2003 (my translation).

10. Leirvik, Oddbjørn (2004) 'Boka Hagen har lest'. *Dagbladet*, 4 November.

11. Hagen, Carl I. (2004) 'Lovpriste Israel, angrep islam'. *Bergens Tidende*, 14 July; cf. Hagen 2007: 466–70.

12. My translation.

13. *honestthinking.org* 8 and 14 January 2006.

14. See interview with NRK by Anders Magnus in *Dagsrevyen* 7 January 2006, and the TV2 documentary by Per-Christian Magnus entitled 'Truet til taushet' ('Threatened into silence') which was broadcast 2 October 2006 (cf. presentation of the *Document 2* programme on TV2's webpages, at *http://www.tv2.no/magasiner/dokument2/article755879.ece*).
15. 'Radikal-liberalt, ikke nykonservativt', *Aftenposten* 6 October 2006. Cf. Thune, Henrik (2006) 'Nykonservatisme på norsk', *Aftenposten* 3 October.
16. See the Contact Group's homepage, at *http://folk.uio.no/leirvik/Kontaktgruppa.htm*.
17. See the English version of the statement, at *http://folk.uio.no/leirvik/tekster/IRN-MKR-uttalelse.htm*.
18. See reports on the Contact Group's homepage.
19. 'Dialogical multiculturalism shares with pragmatism the attitude that conversation and dialogue are the essence of the human condition. They see dialogue and intercultural conversation potentially as ways of learning, and since this is the 'highest' form of human activity, dialogue should be prioritized over the absolutization of freedom speech.' (Kunelius and Eide 2007: 17f.).
20. Valebrokk, Kåre (2006) 'Islamsk Råd som redaktør' ('The Islamic Council as editor'), *Aftenposten* 12 February.
21. 'Ytringsfrihet er religion i Vesten' (NRK, 10 February 2006).
22. 'Arrest extremist marchers, police told'. *The Guardian*, 6 February 2006.
23. 'Muslims march in cartoons protest'. *BBC News*, 18 February 2006.
24. See for instance the internet article by Gabriele Marranci, posted on 31 October 2007, 'Policy Exchange hijacks professional research', at *http://marranci.wordpress.com/2007/10/31/policy-exchange-hijacks-professional-research/*.
25. See Rønning, Helge (2006) 'Et forsvar for blasfemien', *Dagbladet*, 4 February.
26. At *http://folk.uio.no/leirvik/tekster/IRN-MKR-uttalelse.htm*.
27. See Leirvik, Oddbjørn (2006) 'Fridom under ansvar', *Dagbladet*, 4 February.
28. At *http://folk.uio.no/leirvik/tekster/IRN-MKR-uttalelse.htm*.
29. Paragraph 142 of the Norwegian Penal Code.
30. Paragraph 135a of the Norwegian Penal Code.

# Bibliography

Allen, Christopher and Jørgen S. Nielsen (2002) *Summary Report on Islamophobia in the EU after 11 September 2001*. Vienna: European Monitoring Centre on Racism and Xenophobia.

Berkowitz, Bill (27 July 2006) 'Christian Right Steps Up Pro-Israel Lobbying'. At *http://www.antiwar.com/ips/berkowitz.php?articleid=9419*, accessed 4 January 2008.

Beyer, Peter (1994) 'The New Christian Right in the United States'. In *Religion and Globalization*. London, Thousands Oak, CA, and New Dehli: Sage.

Brekke, Torkel (2004) 'Religious nationalism in contemporary Norway'. In Stålsett, S. and O. Leirvik (eds.) *The Power of Faiths in Global Politics*. Oslo: Novus.

Butler, Jennifer S. (2006) *Born Again: The Christian Right Globalized*. London and Ann Arbor, MI: Pluto.

Casanova, José (1994) 'Evangelical Protestantism: from civil religion to fundamentalist sect to New Christian Right'. In Casanova: *Public Religions in the Modern World*. Chicago: The University of Chicago Press.

Davie, Grace (2007) *The Sociology of Religion*. London: Sage.

Flaskerud, Ingvild (2002) 'Det kontroversielle bildet: Profeten Muhammed i islamsk billedkunst.' *Din. Tidsskrift for religion og kultur*, Vol. 3, No. 2–3, pp. 56–63.

Gabriel, Mark (2002) *Islam and Terrorism: What the Qur'an Really Teaches about Christianity, Violence and the Goals of the Islamic Jihad*. Lake Mary, FL: Creation House.

_____ (2003) *Islam and the Jews: The Unfinished Battle*. Lake Mary, FL: Creation House. Hagee, John (2006) *Jerusalem Countdown: A Warning to the World*. Lake Mary, FL: FrontLine.

Hagen, Carl I. (2007) *Ærlig talt: Memoarer 1944–2007*. Oslo: Cappelen.

Hervik, Peter (2008) 'Original spin and its side effects: freedom speech as Danish news management'. In Eide, Elisabeth, Risto Kunelius and Angela Phillips (eds.) *Transnational Media Events: The Mohammed Cartoons and the Imagined Clash of Civilizations*. Göteborg: Nordicom.

Kokkvold, Per Edgar (2006) ' "Ytringsfrihed bør finde Sted" '. In Selbekk, V. (ed.) *Truet av Islamister*. Oslo: Genesis.

Kunelius, Risto, Elisabeth Eide, Oliver Hahn and Roland Schroeder (eds.) (2007) *Reading the Mohammed Cartoons Controversy: An International Analysis of Press Discourses on Free Speech and Political Spin*. Arbeitshefte Internationaler Journalismus/Working Papers in International Journalism. Bochum: ProjektVerlag.

Leirvik, Oddbjørn (2003) '15 år med kristen-muslimsk dialog i Norge'. *Norsk Tidsskrift for Misjon*, Vol. 57, No. 3, pp. 131–45.

—— (2006) 'Kvar var karikatursaka eit bilete på?' *Kirke og Kultur*, Vol. 111, No. 2, pp. 147–59.

—— (June 2007) 'Muslimske meiningar anno 2006: Norge, Danmark, Storbritannia'. At *http://folk.uio.no/leirvik/tekster/MuslimskeMeiningar.htm*.

MacEion, Denis (2007) *The Hijacking of British Islam: How Extremist Literature Is Subverting Mosques in the UK*. London: Policy Exchange. At *http://www.policyexchange.org.uk/images/libimages/307.pdf*.

Selbekk, Vebjørn (2006) *Truet av Islamister*. Oslo: Genesis.

# CHAPTER 6

# AMERICAN CONSERVATIVE PROTESTANTS AND EMBEDDED LITERACY

## Jennifer L. Bailey

Americans live in a modern, formally secular and highly diverse society where secular and religious groups actively market their beliefs. In addition, the US liberal political and economic creeds emphasise freedom and individualism. This might be thought poor soil for the growth of conservative religions, but the USA is home to a conservative Protestant movement that is unusual in its strength compared to other industrialised Western countries.

How can we account for the success of conservative Protestantism in such a setting? The answer seems to hinge on the concept of individual choice, which is celebrated by both Protestantism and the USA. The former's individualism, stemming from its emphasis on the individual's relationship with God and the Bible, was a contributing factor to the eventual emergence of liberal democracy and capitalism, both of which rely on individual choice. The USA is a liberal democracy where the individual's freedom to choose is celebrated. One explanation, then, for the success of conservative Protestantism is that strict churches are chosen rationally: they are attractive precisely because of their exclusivity and strictness (Finke and Stark 2005; Iannaccone 1994). This chapter, however, shifts the focus from the rational-choice approach to the social and political features that can condition choice, in society and within these churches. It argues that to the extent to which conservative Protestants have built enclave communities in the USA, these condition individual choice. Such enclaves may be physically isolated communities or private institutions that parallel secular public institutions. These entities create virtual societies, with their own frames of reference that exist beyond the 'mainstream'. We can access this effect through the concept of literacy. Conservative Protestantism encourages literacy in order to access scripture; literacy in turn has the potential to enhance individual choice, and thus to promote freedom. But enclaves 'embed' literacy. Instead of enhancing freedom, embedded literacy becomes a way of conditioning it. The potential liberating effect of Protestantism's emphasis on individual choice is accordingly curbed by distance from the public sphere and close supervision of the individual's engagement with the authoritative text (the Bible).

The political success of the religious right in the USA over the past decades owes much to the ability of conservative Christians to operate out of sheltered spaces to engage with the broader community. While their political power has for the moment declined, the continued existence of these enclaves will ensure that conservative Protestants and the religious right remain a vibrant force in the USA.

## American conservative Protestants

The term 'fundamentalism' was born in an American context: the title of a series of pamphlets issued in the USA, under the name 'The Fundamentals', between 1910 and 1915. The term soon came into general use, designating those who rejected the modernisation of the church and sought a return to the 'fundamentals' of their faith. 'Fundamentalist' is often used interchangeably with the term 'Evangelical'. However, most scholars are careful to distinguish between the two.

Walter Russell Mead (2006) distinguishes Fundamentalist and Evangelical Protestants by their relationship to politics and the state: Fundamentalists are separatists, Evangelicals are politically engaged. But Fundamentalists also isolate themselves from a society which they hold to be impure and a source of danger. Ammerman (1987) suggests that Fundamentalists are best understood as separatists, unwilling to compromise on matters of doctrine or to cooperate with churches that do not share their particular interpretation of Christianity. Mead (2006: 27–8) agrees that they are more doctrinal, with a 'consistent and all-embracing "Christian world view" and ... systematically applying it to the world'. They are 'deeply pessimistic about human nature and the prospects of world order and they see an unbridgeable divide between believers and non-believers'. Evangelicals are more hopeful and more engaged with the world, less concerned with doctrinal purity, and able to cooperate with others.

This chapter acknowledges the distinction between Fundamentalists and Evangelicals, but argues that they share many common traits. The University of Chicago's *Fundamentalism Project* directed by Martin Marty and Scott Appleby (1991–95) posited nine interrelated features that characterise Fundamentalists:

> 1) a reaction against the marginalisation of religion; 2) the selective use of tradition and modernity; 3) moral dualism; 4) absolutism and inerrancy of essential texts; 5) millennialism and messianism; 6) elect, chosen membership; 7) sharp boundaries; 8) authoritarian organisation; and 9) strict behavioural requirements. (Almond et al 1995: 405–8)

Both Fundamentalists and Evangelicals accept the Bible as the direct and inerrant word of God. Both evince a strong sense of moral dualism, embrace millennialism and messianism and divide the world sharply between those who are saved and those who are not. Their differences lie in their degree of isolation from society, stemming in part from the sharpness of their boundaries and the strictness of their behavioral requirements. Evangelicals have varying tendencies towards separation, although this seldom manifests itself as physical isolation from others. The USA, with a famously large private sphere, has a particularly permissive environment for constructing parallel institutions: US Evangelicals have accordingly constructed relatively sheltered, *ersatz* enclave communities, somewhat diminishing the distinction between Fundamentalists and Evangelicals. Key statistical studies do

not distinguish the two (Pew Forum 2008), and a key actor like Jerry
Falwell can move between the Fundamentalist and Evangelical communities. This chapter will accordingly discuss both Fundamentalists
and Evangelicals as 'conservative Protestants'.

### Protestant Christianity and literacy

Protestantism has traditionally been associated by many scholars
with the historical origins of democracy (Nichols 1951; Woodberry
and Shah 2004). Of the reasons given for this, the importance of the
printed Bible, the use of vernacular languages and the emphasis that
Protestants placed on encouraging believers to read the Bible for themselves have been central. These elements broke down the Church's
authority and encouraged the individualism and 'intellectual independence' that were critical for the eventual emergence of liberalism,
the ideological cornerstone of capitalism and democracy (Katz 2004:
43; Bruce 2004; Woodberry and Shah 2004; Daniel 1994; Berger
2004).[1]

Literacy was central to Protestantism. The printing press and
public literacy were prerequisites for Luther's and Calvin's admoni-
tion of *sola scriptura* (scripture alone): Everyman cannot directly access
the Bible if the Bible is inaccessible. The printing press also contributed to the remarkable spread of Luther's ideas: the number of tracts,
broadsheets, pamphlets and engravings exploded. Publication, literacy
and Protestantism went hand-in-hand, and in turn drove diversity
by opening the door to ever-new interpretations of the text (Simpson
2007; Katz 2004).

Modern conservative Protestants share Luther's and Calvin's admo-
nition of *sola scriptura*: the core belief that the Bible is the direct word of
God, and the call for a literal reading of the text. The ordinary believer
can and must access its meaning directly on his or her own (Garvey
1993). Accordingly, the conservative Protestant encourages the believer
to have direct, personal and intimate knowledge of the Bible.

To use the Bible in this way requires literacy. But literacy poses
dilemmas for the believer. Literate believers are potentially greatly
empowered – they have in their hands the power to read and interpret

the Bible at will. Yet they are confronted by a bewildering variety of Bibles and commentaries about the Bible: today's Bible does not derive from a single undisputed text. Different versions call upon different source texts, and these vary, while 'authoritative' interpretations of the text abound, and disagree with each other. Commentaries may challenge the believer's core beliefs, or even ridicule religion itself. Advances in communications technology, from radio to the internet, have magnified the problem. Falling into error is a persistent danger.

At the same time, there are few formal barriers to inhibit the believer's choice. The US setting facilitates the 'exit' option: the lack of backing by the state or an established church for any favoured interpretation maximises the individual's ability to 'shop' for a church that feels right, or to break away and establish a rival church – or even to leave religion behind. As a result, the USA is home to a highly diverse religious community. The World Christian Database (WCD 2004) reports 635 Christian denominations in the USA. The number of individual Christian sects or independent churches within the conservative Christian community is more difficult to determine: many conservative Christian congregations are organised as independent churches. Gallup reports 2000 different denominations of all kinds, not counting independent churches and faith communities (Gallup 1996/2009). How does the conservative Protestant deal with this range of choice?

### Containing diversity

Conservative Protestants can deal with potentially autonomous, empowered individuals in four ways, it is suggested here. Evangelicals and Fundamentalists differ in the extent to which and the way in which they avail themselves of these strategies. One way is to maximise the attractiveness of the message. Evangelical mega-churches are good examples of this strategy, with their huge congregations, upbeat messages, charismatic leaders, clear and absolute answers to life's questions, and use of media and sophisticated stagecraft (Bishop 2008; Warren 1995). This is a positive strategy: to attract believers by providing support and fellowship. Here, doctrine is often de-emphasised (and boundaries are correspondingly more porous). Even so, as Finke and Stark (2005) and Iannaccone (1994) argue, strict churches have attractions of their own. The Fundamentalist message is usually much less upbeat and production values less important: its stricter codes of behaviour and narrower range of interpretation create more sharply-defined boundaries and closed communities which are attractive on their own merits.

This chapter, however, focuses on other solutions. Because conservative Protestants in the US exist within a society and a secular state that places limits on the enforcement of orthodoxy in a more substantial way, barriers to exit must be built elsewhere, such as within the family and within the church itself. One way to do this is by guiding the believer in his or her reading of the text to the correct interpretation. Here the setting is important. Begun at an early age within the family or within an isolated setting, choice can be effectively conditioned. This is related to a third strategy, the separatist tendencies shown by Fundamentalists and to a lesser degree by Evangelicals. Here, believers limit contact with the external world. Choice is limited by narrowing the range of choices to which the believer is exposed. Here there is a fine line to be walked, for the idea of free will, although always problematic, remains important. The difficulties of ensuring correct choices on the part of individuals ultimately propel some conservatives towards the fourth strategy: to reach beyond the community of believers to narrow the range of choices available in general in society. In what follows, these four strategies will be explored in more detail.

## Guiding the believer

The insistence on the Bible as the literal word of God would seem simple enough. The central idea of fundamentalist Protestantism is that there is one Truth, and that Truth is to be found in the Bible. Believers are encouraged, nay, pressed, to read and study the Bible for themselves. As Herman C. Hanko, professor in the Protestant Reformed Seminary in Grandville, Michigan, puts it:

> It has always been a principle of the Protestant Reformation over against Roman Catholicism that Scripture is easy to

understand ... Scripture is ... clear and understandable by anyone who is able to read ... It makes no difference what his age, education or station in life is, he can know what the Spirit says to the Church. (1990: 39)

While this remains a guiding principle for both Fundamentalists and Evangelicals, it has not proved to be so simple in practice. While the Bible is held to be literally true, it is broadly acknowledged that its meaning may not always be immediately apparent. Tim LaHaye (1998) co-founder of the Moral Majority and author of the best-selling *Left Behind* series, outlines a three-year study plan that includes reading books of the Bible in succession, 30 or more times each. To judge by the internet, he is hardly alone in such a study plan.

Given the acknowledged effort required to master a text the meaning of which is supposedly 'easy to understand', and the high stakes involved (millennialism), conservative Protestants provide a good deal of guidance to the believer. The first step is to select the text itself. Many Fundamentalists use the Authorised Version of the King James Bible (KJV) from 1611 (Ammerman 1987). Others accept a range of Bibles to be the real, inspired word of God. LaHaye (1998), for example, recommends the New King James Bible and a number of others. But this remains a hot topic, and there are clearly translations of the Bible that are not acceptable. As Rev. Steven Houck of the Protestant Reformed Churches[2] puts it, 'it is ... imperative that every child of God takes great care that the Bible version which he uses, defends, and promotes in the world is a faithful translation of the Word of God' (Houck 2000: 1).

Despite the effort actually required to understand the Bible, Fundamentalists and Evangelicals reject absolutely the idea that understanding the Bible requires the academic-based Higher Criticism against which Fundamentalists rebelled at the turn of the 20th century. LaHaye advises the believer to '[f]ollow the golden rule of interpretation: When the plain sense of Scripture makes common sense, seek no other sense; therefore, take every word at its primary, ordinary, usual, literal meaning ...' (1999: 17). But this approach does not resolve the difficulties of interpretation. The continuation of the quoted passage from LaHaye demonstrates the difficulties faced by those who seek a clear, unambiguous message: ' ... unless the facts of the immediate text, studied in the *light of related passages and axiomatic and fundamental truths clearly indicate otherwise*' (emphasis added). Which passages are 'clearly related' and which are 'the axiomatic and fundamental truths'?

There are many other aspects of the Bible that must be considered. LaHaye (1998), for example, stresses the importance of Biblical hermeneutics which includes understanding the use of terms in the context of the times in which the texts were recorded. The 'Believers' Web' stresses the importance of the historical background of the texts, understanding the culture of the time and place the books of the Bible were written, placing Scripture in context, and understanding the meaning of words. LaHaye, the Believers' Web and Bob Jones University all acknowledge that the Bible employs different literary styles, including five–six kinds of figures of speech (Believers' Web 2006; Bob Jones University 2006a; LaHaye 1998).

The Bible books of Revelation and Daniel raise particularly important issues. The distinctive premillenarian beliefs shared by many Conservative Christians about the 'End Times', the rapture, and the imminent second coming of Christ are rooted in these apocalyptic texts, which abound in allegorical symbolism. Interestingly, it is precisely these texts that produce some of the most significant theological differences between many conservative Christians on the one hand and mainline Protestant Churches on the other.

In recognition of these difficulties, there is plenty of help on offer. Ammerman writes that the Fundamentalist church which she observed relies very heavily on the *Scofield Reference Bible* and the *Ryrie Reference Bible* (1987: 5, 44). The former (in its 1917 edition) is in wide circulation today, and its reference notes incorporate the dispensationalism and premillennialism that are keynotes of American Fundamentalism. LaHaye (1998: 143–50) recommends many books as good guides to the Bible, including the *New Scofield Reference Bible, Halley's Bible Handbook* (for children), *Strong's Exhaustive Concordance, Cruden's Complete Concordance, Unger's* or *Holman's Bible Dictionary, Matthew Henry's Commentary, The Wycliffe Bible Commentary, Gaebelein's Concise*

*Commentary on the Whole Bible*, and *The Bible Has the Answer*. Many of these are published by the Moody Bible Institute or the Institute for Creation Research. LaHaye himself claims authorship of 37 books providing guidance for the believer, with a total of some ten million copies in print (1998: 45).

Even so, the deeper study of the Bible remains risky. Here, the orientation of the student is all important. Writing in the famous 'Fundamentals' pamphlets (1910/1917: 1–2), Canon Dyson Hague warned that 'the Bible...has no revelation to make to unbiblical minds'. This guidance takes on greater importance given conservative Protestants' tendency towards separatism. In the books growing out of the *Fundamentalism Project*, the 'enclave' character of Fundamentalism and its sharp boundaries are stressed. In addition, they note the fundamentalist tendency towards charismatic and authoritarian leaders (Almond et al 1995: 405–8). Ammerman's (1987) portrayal of a Fundamentalist church suggests that attitudes towards the authority of the pastor and the structure of worship play an important role in how the individual believer relates to the Bible. The pastor's guidance in helping believers interpret the text can be critical, and serves to reinforce the preferred Fundamentalist understanding of the Bible. The authority structure within the church is replicated in other institutions throughout the Fundamentalist world, and to some extent also within that of the Evangelicals, who – while generally less authoritarian and less isolated – share the tendencies to charismatic leadership and separatism, and are committed to a single truth. Within conservative Protestant schools, discipline is strict and students are taught to respect authority; within the family, children are taught submission, and wives acceptance of their husbands' authority. One of the most influential conservative Protestant organisations in the US today, Focus on the Family, emphasises the importance of establishing the authority of parents: founder James Dobson's book, *Dare to Discipline*, has become a central text for conservative Protestants (see also Dobson 2006). The position of authority figures is held to be prescribed by the Bible, and they in turn teach the authority of their interpretation of the Bible.

In conditions of enclave, strong guidance combines with the absence of contending authoritative interpretations to condition choice.

Education for submissiveness intends to diminish the autonomous character of the individual, and sometimes succeeds in doing so.

## The USA and enclave communities

The permissive US environment has long allowed enclave communities of various kinds to flourish within its boundaries. Historically, separatists of all kinds fled to the USA, including the famous Puritans as well as Mennonites, Pietists and Anabaptists, each group seeking to found a pure community isolated from external corruption. This turned out to be an endemic impulse in what became the United States of America, where the founding of separate communities, many of a religious character, became common. These have ranged from the Shakers to the Mormons to a temperance community – the Union Colony – in Greeley, Colorado. In addition, the USA developed many ethnic enclaves, particularly within urban settings. Ethnicity combined with religion to produce enclave communities such as the Amana community in Iowa (German Pietists) and the Amish (Swiss-German Mennonites) of Pennsylvania (Hayden 1979; Nordhoff (1875/1993). An impulse to separation continues today: the Christian Exodus movement hopes to build a 'Christian nation' based in South Carolina (Christian Exodus 2009), and the town of Ave Maria, Florida – founded by pizza magnate Tom Monaghan – is to be a home for conservative Catholics. The impulse is not limited to religion: Bishop (2008) has documented what he calls the 'Big Sort', a tendency evident since approximately 1976 for Americans to segregate themselves according to lifestyle, religion and politics, producing clusters of similar, like-thinking people at the county level.

Fundamentalism works best in the true enclave, whose isolation is the concrete expression of an abstract notion – a sharp boundary between believer and non-believers. The private sphere in the USA is today famously larger than it is in other industrial democracies, but for the Fundamentalist it cannot be large enough. With family and church at the centre of the Fundamentalist view of life, these institutions must be protected at all costs. This means keeping the state's authority out of them. It also means that anything that might weaken their authority must also be avoided. Some Fundamentalist Christians are able to withdraw entirely from society and do so, living in closed communities away from distractions such as radio, TV and the internet, and sharply – and sometimes militantly – limiting contact with outsiders. Contemporary examples of strict enclaves include the fundamentalist Branch Davidians of Waco, Texas, and the Latter Day Saints (Mormons) of Colorado City, Arizona and Hildale, Utah. Federal, state and local authorities are often reluctant to intervene in such communities, in part on principle but in part in order to avoid tragedies such as the fire that killed many members of the Branch Dividian sect in Waco, Texas, when their compound was raided by Federal authorities.

## Embedding literacy

There are forms of separatism that are less extreme than physical isolation, and the US setting has made these relatively easy. Some fundamentalists withdraw individually; the more outgoing Evangelicals are less physically isolated from society around them but have built a broad range of institutions that parallel the public provision, allowing them, to varying extents, to minimise contact with others. Christians frequently have no need to connect to secular media: Christian broadcasters have long made extensive use of radio, and today there are approximately 200 Christian television channels and 1,500 Christian radio stations in the USA, reaching an audience of roughly 61 million people. Pat Robertson's Christian Broadcasting Network (CBN) has its own comprehensive news reporting, with reporters in the field covering, for example, events in the Middle East (see *cbn.com*); it is the fifth-largest cable network in the country, claiming 30 million subscribers (Micklethwait and Wooldridge 2004: 84). There are alternative publishers, bookshops and bestseller lists. The Christian *Yellow Pages* allows believers to source goods and services from like-minded people, so that they can isolate themselves to the fullest possible degree from potential sources of corruption. Of these parallel institutions, those devoted to education have been especially important.

### Conservative Protestant educational institutions

Education is today one of the key battlefields in American politics, a high priority for conservative Protestants of all kinds. As elsewhere, many educational institutions have religious roots. Efforts in the 1960s and 1970s finally to expel the 'church' from education at all levels ignited a movement for conservative Christian education in the USA (ibid: 83; Rose 1993: 469).

The creation of Christian elementary and secondary schools is an important part of the conservative Protestant agenda. According to the Department of Education's Institute of Education Sciences, 27 per cent of all elementary and secondary school students were enrolled in private institutions in 2003–04 (Institute of Education Sciences 2009a). In 2008, Conservative Christians of all kinds accounted for 15.2 per cent (or about 772,951) of students in private schools, and for 15.1 per cent of private schools themselves. Religious schools of all kinds accounted for about 80 per cent of all students in private elementary and secondary schools (2009b: 6).

Conservative Protestants have also been active in the growing home-schooling movement in the USA: the 2007 National Education Surveys Program reported that 1.5 million American students were being home-schooled in 2007. This was 2.9 percent of the school-age population, up from 1.7 percent in 1999. The survey found that providing 'religious or moral education' was a factor in the decision of fully 83 per cent of respondents (Institute of Education Sciences 2008: 1).

However, these figures do not tell us about Fundamentalists per se. They can only give us a rough idea of the degree to which these separatists have truly withdrawn from society at large, and of how significant this is for the nation as a whole. Religious separatists are not always eager to register their schools or home-schooling with the government. The figure for home-schooling claimed by many Fundamentalists is closer to two million, a figure to which some studies have given credence (McDowell and Ray 2000; Lines 2000, both cited by Bauman 2001). All sources agree that the home-schooling movement is growing, and most probably represents the most significant change in educational patterns, in terms of the number of students involved, to have taken place in recent years (Bauman 2001: 2).

We must conclude from the available statistics that both home-schoolers and Christian schools are a small but still significant (and growing) minority. James Dobson (Focus on the Family), Robert Simmons (Citizens for Excellence in Education) and D. James Kennedy (Coral Ridge Ministries) have called for all Christian parents to with-draw their children from public schools; they are supported by radio personalities such as Dr. Laura Schlessinger and by politicians such as Representative Tom Tancredo (Republican, Colorado) (People for the American Way 2006: 1).

Conservative Protestants support each other in their educational efforts, linked in associations and over the internet. This is extremely important in a society that is as large and mobile as the USA. The National Christian School Association provides a long list of accept-able elementary and secondary schools; the National Association of Evangelicals has its own National Christian Education Association (2006; Encyclopædia Britannica Online 2006). The Wholesome Words website provides a directory of 'Fundamental Baptist ministries in the United States and Canada that take a stand for the Authorized King James Version', with listings for 14 colleges that use that version of the Bible, and/or the preferred *Textus Receptus* for Greek transla-tion classes and the Masoretic Text of the Old Testament for Hebrew classes (Wholesome Words 2009).

These associations do more than guide the believer from one com-munity of like-minded individuals to the next. They provide assist-ance in setting up and maintaining educational institutions, including legal advice and teaching/learning materials. They also provide a net-work for marketing such materials. Bob Jones University (BJU), for example, offers an extensive range for Christian schools and home-schoolers at all levels (Bob Jones University 2006b). BJU publishes books, recommends curricula, works out lesson plans and provides checklists for students.

Unsurprisingly, the educational materials supplied by these sources are written specifically to support the world view of the believ-ers who purchase them. Frances Patterson (2002) has examined the social-studies textbooks published by A Beka Press (grades 4 to 12), by BJU (grades 3 to 12) and 84 texts published or distributed by the School of Tomorrow/Accelerated Christian Education. These texts include US history, civics and government, social studies and world studies. Patterson finds that:

> the materials are biased toward an overwhelmingly conservative point of view on social, political, and religious matters. Shorn of the text that makes them uniquely 'textbooks' — long passages about the influence of Prince Metternich, descriptions of Thailand's geography, and explanations of the Religious Right — the materials are indistinguishable from the literature of the Religious Right. On matters of religion, the texts adhere to a literal interpretation of the Bible, and are rife with stereotypes and distortions of not only non-Christian religions but of the Roman Catholic Church. (2002: 1)

The School of Tomorrow/Accelerated Christian Education history booklets explicitly teach that Social Security and other government anti-poverty programmes are contrary to the Bible. An eighth-grade US history text published by A Beka states that unemployment is caused by personal weakness or by actions of the government, with the market the best solution for the unemployed. A Beka texts in general are hostile to taxation, and connect the progressive income tax to Communism. Another (School of Tomorrow/Accelerated American) history booklet for high-school seniors states flatly: 'It was wrong for outlaw Robin Hood to steal from the rich and give to the poor, and it is wrong for governments to do it. U.S. law needs to be changed' (Patterson 2002: 4–5).

Beyond the curriculum, these schools tend to emphasise discipline and respect for authority. According to Rose (1988: 185):

> The goal is for their young people to grow into disciples of Christ, being obedient to His Higher Authority and spreading His Word. To prepare them for this ultimate submission, they teach their children to obey their parents, teachers, spiritual leader, and civil authorities ... (1988: 185)

This is not an environment in which children are encouraged to ask questions. On the other hand, they are taught to be sceptical of authorities who do not embrace the beliefs of their own community. As Rose goes on to say, 'they warn against those who are not saved and who therefore are not considered legitimate authorities.'

Higher education has been another important area of expansion. In general, conservative Christian higher educational institutions vary as to just how engaged they are with US society as a whole. BJU has emerged as the premier Fundamentalist university in the country (Schultze 1993: 503). It sought from its beginnings to model itself after the liberal-arts colleges that flourish in the USA, and has a wide variety of courses, including a highly-ranked film programme and a focus on art (ibid: 490). But it retains a strong streak of separatism: it rejects the Federal funding that would bring with it the obligation to meet a broad array of Federal standards (such as racial integration), and it has not sought accreditation from the usual regional accreditation bodies for similar reasons. BJU does not participate in the inter-collegiate sports typical of many colleges and universities in the USA, or allow 'outside' organisations such as sororities, fraternities and honour societies on campus. It recruits its teaching staff on the basis of their religious views, rather than (primarily) their academic credentials. This means that 'BJU is one of the most academically incestuous colleges or universities in the country' (ibid: 501). Finally, the University is run in a highly autocratic manner, today under the leadership of Bob Jones III. According to Schultze: 'BJU represents as close to a religious monarchy as one finds in fundamentalist higher education, and the monarch is vested with political as well as ceremonial authority (ibid).'

This sort of insulation in turn promotes separatism by inhibiting the ability of the BJU graduate to find a job beyond the religious community – competition in the US job market requires credentials. A glance at the accreditation list maintained by the US Department of Education (DOE) illustrates the problem: its interactive webpage allows searching for schools and colleges accredited by a broad range of associations. Many of the religiously-oriented educational institutions listed are not accredited by professional associations, or offer only a few, limited, programmes that have been accredited. BJU is not accredited by any secular-oriented national or regional accrediting agency. Only the music programme of the Moody Bible Institute is accredited (by the National Association of Schools of Music, Commission on Non-Degree-Granting Accreditation, Commission on Community/Junior College Accreditation) (DOE 2009).[3]

Evangelical Jerry Falwell's Liberty University and Charismatic Christian Pat Robertson's Regent University have taken a different path. Both have sought to establish themselves as broadly accepted academic institutions. Regent University is accredited by the Southern Association of Colleges and Schools (SACS), its law school by the American Bar Association, its clinical psychology programme by the American Psychological Association and its theology programme by the Association of Theological Studies in the United States and Canada. Relevant Liberty University programmes are accredited by the American Bar Association, the Commission on Collegiate Nursing Education and the National Council for Accreditation of Teacher Education (ibid). In contrast to BJU, Liberty University boasts that its faculty members collectively hold degrees from over 400 colleges and universities; it offers 60 areas of study, including business, education and aviation, in addition to biblical studies; and unlike BJU, Liberty University has a tenure system. Both Liberty and Regent are far more open to external influences than is BJU, and both are criticised for it by more strict segments of conservative Christianity. Even so, Liberty University strives to maintain a clear Christian profile and to provide a distinctively Christian educational experience. It claims to incorporate the Bible into every subject area it offers, and faculty members are only hired after they satisfy the university that they have a personal relationship with Christ and that they are committed to the university's purpose and aims (Liberty University 2006).

## Beyond isolation

Despite the construction of parallel institutions, it remains difficult for those believers who do not live in genuine enclave communities to insulate themselves from their environment; pursuing business or a career often requires reaching out beyond a narrow community. For this and other reasons, conservative Christians have of late been on the offensive, and there has been an effort to make isolation itself easier and more acceptable. More ambitiously, a thrust has been made to improve the character of American society itself. It is these activities that recently have made conservative Protestantism so very visible in the US.

A key tactic in changing society is to win converts by spreading the message and by personal example: true change has to come individual by individual. This of course means bringing the repentant sinner into the Christian community. Secular society as a whole may be unredeemable, because people who are not saved cannot produce a society that is positively good, but some of the worst behavior might be curbed or stopped – such as abortion. In line with such thinking, conservative Protestants have taken the offensive in politics at the national, state and local levels. Lindsay's study (2007) clearly showed the large number of Evangelicals active in significant power centres such as Washington, DC. The active participation of conservative Protestants (and other religious groups) in the US presidential elections of 2000, 2004 and 2008 has been widely noted. Conservative Protestants also exercise their power as consumers and voters over issues having to do with family, sexuality, more generally ethics and science. The struggle over public school curricula – from Shakespeare to Darwin – is a case in point (Rose 1993: 470). The battle remains active and acrimonious and is fought on several fronts: in the local school boards, at the state and federal level and in the market-place.

The Fundamentalist approach to the Bible as comprehensive guidance for the believer means that all topics in life merit concern from the fundamentalist Christian. Because Fundamentalists and Evangelicals frequently accord the USA a special status, this extends to views about the nation's place in the world; capitalism is also similarly given special status (Ammerman 1987; Frank 2004). Conservative Protestants have accordingly objected to school texts that are even marginally critical of the USA or its economic system.

But another effect of the conservative Christian movement has been to make separation from corrupt society easier and more acceptable.

This means that the movement's members have retained and perhaps expanded their safe havens, within which their culture is preserved and from which they can launch forays into secular politics. As a result of these efforts, home-schooling is increasingly supported by state law, making it progressively easier for parents of all sorts of persuasions to make this choice (Bauman 2001: 2). In addition, the home-schooling choice is supported by the increasing acceptance of home-schooled children in post-secondary educational institutions. These include explicitly conservative Christian colleges but also more 'mainstream' institutions. Reacting to lobbying and court cases, many states have removed barriers to admitting home-schooled children to state colleges and universities. Patrick Henry College (founded in 2000) became the first post-secondary institution established specifically to receive home-schooled students. The Bush administration openly supported this trend, as a part of its support of 'faith-based' institutions of all sorts (Kaplan 2005).

Since the public schools – and society in general – are ultimately unlikely to achieve standards that conservative Christians would consider acceptable, the agenda of many Fundamentalist Christians goes further than simply reforming these schools. People for the American Way quotes the late Jerry Falwell as having said: 'I hope I live to see the day when, as in the early days of our country, there won't be any public schools. The Churches will have taken them over again and Christians will be running them' (2006).

## Conclusion

Protestant Evangelicalism and Fundamentalism today contain key characteristics associated with the rise of liberal democracy and capitalism. These are the stress on an individual relationship with God and on believers reading the Bible for themselves. Literacy remains the prerequisite for this approach to Christianity, and is also supportive of democracy.

But literacy is a double-edged sword, and the nature of individual freedom a vexed question. Individuals must choose salvation, and therefore alternative paths must be discouraged. Genuine freedom in this context means freedom gained by submission to a single Truth: the stakes involved for the individual are considered too high (eternal salvation or damnation) to leave individuals to their own devices.

Embedded literacy works to constrain individual choice in the liberal, diverse, democratic society that is the USA. This strategy has had mixed results. Americans remain a remarkably religious people by Western standards. Only 1.6 per cent of Americans admit openly to being atheists. Even so, the number of people who claim affiliation with conservative Christian churches is in decline, and few denominations retain a lock on their members: Americans continue to shop around for a religion that suits them. Many change their religion at least once in their lives, and a significant percentage change it more than once (Pew 2008).

The embedded literacy of conservative Protestantism thus flourishes in a liberal democratic setting but is ultimately incompatible with it: it constrains rather than facilitates freedom of choice. The tendency to physical or virtual enclaves provides a sheltered space for fostering beliefs and attitudes that are highly incompatible with liberal democracy, and a closed site from which believers can engage with the public sphere even while rejecting the true commitment to dialogue that democracy requires.

## Notes

1. The Protestant relationship to democracy is most likely an unintended one, or as Bruce (2004: 6) puts it, 'the ironic (and often deeply regretted) by-product of actions promoted for quite different reasons. The Reformation contributed to the evolution of democracy but its supporters can hardly take credit.'
2. Protestant Reformed Churches in America (PRCA) claims 27 churches with almost 6,000 members in the USA and Canada. It was founded in 1924, parting ways with the Christian Reformed Church over the issue of 'common grace' (PRCA 1951; 2006).
3. Many of the institutions listed by the Fundamentalist ministries (KJV) are not listed as accredited by either the Association for Biblical Higher Education or the Transnational Association of Christian Colleges and Schools.

## Bibliography

Almond, Gabriel A., Emmanuel Sivan and R. Scott Appleby (1995) 'Fundamentalism: genus and species'. In Marty, Martin E. and R. Scott

Appleby (eds.) *Fundamentalisms Comprehended*, Vol. 5 in Marty and Appleby (eds.) *The Fundamentalism Project*. Chicago: The University of Chicago Press, pp. 399–424.

Ammerman, Nancy Tatom (1987) *Bible Believers: Fundamentalists in the Modern World*. New Brunswick, NJ: Rutgers University Press.

Bauman, Kurt J. (2001) 'Home schooling in the United States: Trends and characteristics'. Population Division, Working Paper No. 3. Washington, DC: US Census Bureau.

Berger, Peter (2004) 'The global picture'. *Journal of Democracy*, Vol. 15, No. 2, pp. 76–80.

Bishop, Jim (2008) *The Big Sort*. Boston, MA, and New York: Houghton Mifflin.

Bruce, Steve (2004) 'Did Protestantism create democracy?' *Democratization*, Vol. 11, No. 4, pp. 3–20.

Cole, Juan (2002) 'Fundamentalism in the contemporary U.S. Baha'i community'. *Review of Religious Research*, Vol. 43, No. 3, pp. 195–217.

Daniel, David (1994) *William Tyndale: A Biography*. New Haven, CT: Yale University Press.

Finke, Roger and Rodney Stark (2005) *The Churching of America 1776–2000: Winners and Losers in Our Religious Economy*. New Brunswick, NJ: Rutgers University Press.

Frank, Thomas (2004) *What's the Matter with Kansas?* New York: Metropolitan Books.

Gallup, George Jr. (1996/2009) 'Religion and civic virtue at home and abroad'. *Faith and International Affairs*, Vol. 7, No. 2, pp. 3–5.

Garvey, John H. (1993) 'Fundamentalism and American law'. In Marty, Martin E. and R. Scott Appleby (eds.) *Fundamentalism and the State: Remaking Polities, Economies, and Militance*, Vol. 3 of Marty and Appleby (eds.) *The Fundamentalism Project*. Chicago: The University of Chicago Press, pp. 13–27.

Hague, Canon Dyson (1910/1917) 'The history of higher criticism'. In Torrey, R.A. (ed.) *The Fundamentals: A Testimony to the Truth*, Vol. 1. At *http://www.xmission.com/~fidelis/volume1/chapter1/hague.php*, accessed 2 December 2009.

Hanko, Herman C. (1990) 'Issues in hermeneutics'. *Protestant Reformed Theological Journal*, Vol. 23, No. 2 (April), pp. 35–50.

Hayden, Dolores (1979) *Seven American Utopias: The Architecture of Communitarian Socialism 1790–1975*. Cambridge: MIT Press.

Iannaccone, Laurence (1994) 'Why strict churches are strong'. *American Journal of Sociology*, Vol. 99, No. 5, pp. 1180–211.

Institute of Education Sciences (2009a) 'Issue brief: 1.5 million students homeschooled in the United States in 2007'. National Center for Educational Statistics, Report 2009–30 (December). Washington, DC: National Center for Education Statistics.

Institute of Education Sciences (2009b) *Characteristics of Private Schools in the United States: Results from the 2007–08 Private School Universe Survey*. Washington, DC: National Center for Educational Statistics.

Kaplan, Esther (2005) *With God on Their Side: George W. Bush and the Christian Right*. New York: The New Press.

Katz, David S. (2004) *God's Last Words: Reading the English Bible from the Reformation to Fundamentalism*. New Haven, CT: Yale University Press.

LaHaye, Tim (1999) *Revelation Unveiled*. Grand Rapids, MI: Zondervan.

—— (1998) *How to Study the Bible for Yourself*. Eugene, OR: Harvest House.

Lindsay, Michael D. (2007) *Faith in the Halls of Power: How Evangelicals Joined the American Elite*. Oxford: Oxford University Press.

Lines, Patricia (2000) 'Homeschooling comes of age'. *The Public Interest*, Summer, pp. 74–85.

Marty, Martin E. and R. Scott Appleby (1991–95) *The Fundamentalism Project*. Chicago, IL: University of Chicago Press.

Mead, Walter Russell (2006) 'God's country?' *Foreign Affairs*, Vol. 85, No. 5, pp. 24–43.

McDowell, Susan A. and Brian D. Ray (2000) 'The home education movement in context, practice, and theory: editor's introduction'. *Peabody Journal of Education*, Vol. 75, Nos. 1–2, pp. 1–7.

Micklethwait, John and Adrian Wooldridge (2004) *The Right Nation: Conservative Power in America*. New York: Penguin.

Nichols, James Hastings (1951) *Democracy and the Churches*. Philadelphia, PA: Westminster.

Nordhoff, Charles (1875/1993) *American Utopias*. Stockbridge, MA: Berkshire House.

Pew Forum on Religion and Public Life (2008) *U.S. Religious Landscape Survey*. Washington, DC: Pew Research Center.

Rose, Susan D. (1988) *Keeping them Out of the Hands of Satan: Evangelical Schooling in America*. New York: Routledge.

—— (1993) 'Christian fundamentalism and education in the United States'. In Marty, Martin E. and R. Scott Appleby (eds.) *Fundamentals and Society: Reclaiming the Sciences, the Family, and Education*, Vol. 2 of Marty and Appleby (eds.) *The Fundamentalism Project*. Chicago: The University of Chicago Press, pp. 452–89.

Schultze, Quentin (1993) 'The two faces of fundamentalist higher education'. In Marty; Martin E and R. Scott Appleby (eds.) *Fundamentals and Society: Reclaiming the Sciences, the Family and Education*. Vol. 2. of Marty and Appleby (eds.). *The Fundamentalism Project,* Chicago: The University of Chicago Press, pp. 490–535.

Simpson, James (2007) *Burning to Read: English Fundamentalism and Its Reformation Opponents*. Cambridge, MA: Belknap/Harvard University Press.

Warren, Rick (1995) *The Purpose-Driven Church: Growth without Compromising Your Message and Mission*. Grand Rapids, MI: Zondervan.

Woodbury, Robert Dudley and Timothy S. Shah (2004) 'The pioneering Protestants'. *Journal of Democracy*, Vol. 15, No. 2, pp. 47–61.


### Internet sources

Believers' Web (2006) 'Hermeneutics'. At *http://www.beliversweb.org/view.cfm?ID= 833*, accessed 13 October 2006.

Bob Jones University (2006a) 'University creed'. At *http://www.bju.edu/about/creed/ inspir.html*, accessed 10 October 2006.

—— (2006b) 'Distance learning'. At *http://www.bju.edu/academics/distance/*, accessed 10 October 2006.

Christian Exodus (2009) 'About us: forsake the empire, seek the Kingdom'. *http:// christianexodus.org/index.php?option=com_content&view=article&id=9&Itemid= 37*, accessed 31 August 2009.

Department of Education (2009) 'US Department of Education database of accredited postsecondary institutions and programs'. At *http://ope.ed.gov/ accreditation/*, accessed 6 October 2006.

Dobson, James (2006) 'How to shape your child's will'. At *http://www.family.org/ parenting/A000001164.cfm*, accessed 6 November 2006.

Encyclopædia Britannica Online (2006) 'National Association of Evangelicals'. At *http://www.britannica.com/e/article-9054956/National-Assocation-of-Evangelicals*, accessed 9 October 2006.

Houck, Steven (2000) 'The King James Version of the Bible'. At *http://prca.org/ pamphlets/pamphlet_9.html*, accessed 9 October 2006.

Institute of Education Sciences (2009a) 'Fast facts'. At *http://nces.ed.gov/fastfacts/ display.asp?id=84*, accessed 19 August 2009.

Liberty University (2006) 'Liberty University'. At *http://liberty.edu/indes. cfm?PID=61*, accessed 12 November 2006.

National Christian School Association (NCSA) (2006) 'Directory'. At *http://www. nationalchristian.org/directory.htm,* accessed 9 October 2006.

Patterson, Frances (2002) 'With God on their side … '. *Rethinking Schools Online*, at *http://www.rethinkingschools.org/about/contact.shtml*, accessed 2 November 2006.

People for the American Way (PFAW) (2006) 'The continuing assault on public education' at *http://www.pfaw.org*, accessed 2 November 2006.

Protestant Reformed Churches in America (PRCA) (2006) 'History and government'. At *http://www.prca.org/prc.html*, accessed 9 October 2006.

—— (1951) 'A brief declaration of principles of the Protestant Reformed Churches in America'. At *http://www.prca.o/principles.html*, accessed 9 October 2006.

Wholesome Words (2009) 'Fundamentalist ministries (KJV)'. At *http://www. wholesomewords.org/direc.html*, accessed 19 August 2009.

World Christian Database (WCD) (2004) Center for the study of Global Christianity, Gordon-Conwell Theological Seminary. At *http://www. worldchristiandatabase.org/wcd/default.asp,* accessed 12 November 2009.

# CHAPTER 7

# THE QUEST FOR THE 'PERFECT TILE': FUNDAMENTALISM IN ROMAN CATHOLICISM

## Michael Trainor

As several essays in this book make clear, the universal phenomenon of fundamentalism must be situated within the broader social and cultural concerns of humanity. Fundamentalism is one response to concerns held by some who consider the emergence of liberal democratic ideals as problematic. The maturation of these ideals, as has been explored in the introduction to this present volume, requires robust public discourse and interaction amongst people as citizens and as members of social groupings and institutions. The most significant institutions that deeply influence peoples' sense of themselves and their relationship to others are religious. Church, synagogue and mosque are important religious institutions: they influence social behaviour and teach core ethical values that can influence the sense of well-being of a democratic society.

The present essay focuses on arguably one of the most stable religious institutions, the Roman Catholic Church. From a broader political and democratic perspective, this phenomenon is open to study, comment and analysis. The Catholic Church has had a powerful influence on all areas of social life over the past two thousand years, whatever historians, social commentators and theologians might make of this influence within particular cultural and historical settings. In recent decades Catholic fundamentalism has emerged and become more pronounced as a response to the perceived or interpreted values promulgated by Catholic leaders.[1] Within a theological setting, fundamentalism has been defined as:

> a tendency of some members of traditional religious communities to separate from fellow believers and to redefine the sacred community in terms of its disciplined opposition to nonbelievers and 'lukewarm' believers alike. 'Fundamentalists' within these historic religious traditions [of Christianity, Judaism, Islam, Hinduism, Sikhism, Buddhism and Confucianism], convinced of the conspiratorial nature of secularists and liberal religionists, adopted a set of strategies for fighting back against what is perceived as a concerted effort by secular states of elements within them to push people of religious consciousness and conscience to the margins of society. (Marty and Appleby 1995: 1)

Catholic fundamentalism coheres with this description, and represents a particular ideology within a religious, explicitly Christian, global institution. Catholic fundamentalism has features that come under a broader heading concerned with globalisation; it also has local manifestations. Catholic fundamentalists, borrowing from the Marty and Appleby description above, seek to redefine the religious (Catholic) community in 'disciplined opposition' and to interpret other Catholics as conspiratorial humanists. I shall explore this further in the pages ahead as I describe and identify the burgeoning fundamentalist phenomenon evident in some quarters of Roman Catholicism, and explore its global and local phenomena. Presuming the social democratic context outlined above, and the description of fundamentalism as defined by Marty and Appleby, I shall explicate the theological, religious and biblical dimensions of Catholic fundamentalism. While there are already some fine analyses of the phenomenon, the perspective I bring to this study is a little different.[2]

I will suggest that Catholic fundamentalism cannot be pinned down to one single, controlled expression, but has a multiplicity of facets that touch on every aspect of Catholic life, and on four in particular. Further, the only response possible for those within the Catholic community who seek to engage this phenomenon critically from a liberal democratic perspective is an educational one. This means rather than engaging in the combative response which seems most natural in the light of feeling under attack, education offers grounds for conversation, if ever this becomes possible, with those who hold a fundamentalist stance. I will argue that this educational response must be concerned with literacy and anthropology, that is, concerned with the deepest quest of human beings. I will say more about this in the final section of this essay.

As with Protestant fundamentalists, the nature of authoritative or sacred texts and their interpretation is also the concern of Catholic fundamentalists. However, the identity of these texts and their authoritative interpreters open up four expressions or 'types' of fundamentalism in Roman Catholicism: biblical, doctrinal, authoritarian and devotional. The first, biblical fundamentalism, reflects similarities with classical Protestant fundamentalism; the other three are uniquely Roman Catholic expressions.

With this background in mind, the following essay falls into three parts. In the first I look at the nature of Catholic fundamentalism as a response to modernity and a nostalgic search for an earlier age perceived as 'golden'. I begin by first locating Catholic fundamentalism against the backdrop of Protestant fundamentalism, especially in its adversarial claim to 'fight for the truth'. In the second section I describe and analyse four expressions of Catholic fundamentalism: biblical, doctrinal, authoritarian and devotional. In the final section I suggest ways of responding to Catholic fundamentalism. I first investigate the role which literacy plays in either encouraging or addressing fundamentalist attitudes. Finally, as already indicated, I advocate that a constructive response to Catholic fundamentalism, and indeed in addressing all forms of religious fundamentalism, must be an educational one.

A preliminary word about the context from which I write might be helpful. I am an Australian who teaches within a secular university and a Catholic school of theology. What I reflect upon here is local and personal; but it is a phenomenon in Roman Catholicism easily observable in other parts of the world. This is evident in the explicit emerging divide between the insights of contemporary Catholic scholars and their neo-conservative co-religionists who regard Catholic scholarship as inimical to true piety and devotion.[3] A visitor from another planet observing this debate within Catholicism might think that this is an internal issue, unique to a particular religious or theological tradition. However, it is symptomatic of a wider fundamentalist trend upon which this book reflects more broadly.

## The nature of Catholic fundamentalism

While fundamentalism is not new to the Catholic Church, in recent decades and particularly since the Second Vatican Council, it has shown signs of renewed vigour; the move towards theological and liturgical renewal has been perceived by some as a threat to Catholic orthodoxy. Catholic fundamentalism, like other forms of fundamentalism, is essentially a reaction to the perceived relative-truth claims of modernity. Catholic fundamentalists seek to mould theological and moral diversity into a rigid monolithic religious form where the voice of authority is unquestionable and the interpretation of selected texts definitive (Sanders 1994: 336). Their response to contemporary theological or liturgical renewal is often one of strong, almost militant opposition. Their hostile reaction parallels the response typical of Protestant fundamentalists.

George Marsden describes Protestant fundamentalism as a particular form of conservative Christianity that is 'militantly traditionalist'. He portrays a Christian fundamentalist as

> an evangelical who is militant in opposition to liberal theology
> in the churches or to changes in cultural values or mores, such as
> those associated with 'secular humanism' ... fundamentalists are a
> subtype of evangelicals and militancy is crucial to their outlook.
> Fundamentalists are not just religious conservatives, they are
> conservatives who are willing to take a stand and fight. (1991: 1)

Marsden's description of fundamentalists parallels earlier language first used in 1920 by Curtis Lee Laws, editor of the Baptist paper *The Watchman Examiner*. Laws reported the reactions of a vocal group of lobbyists in a Baptist Convention who opposed the perceived liberal biblical teachings of other Baptist members. They (and Laws) wanted

> the reinthronement of the fundamentals of our holy faith ... We here and now move that a new word be adopted to describe the men among us who insist that the landmarks shall not be removed ... We suggest that those who still cling to the great fundamentals and who mean to do battle royal for the Fundamentals shall be called 'Fundamentalists'. (Laws 1920: 834)

## Key aspects of fundamentalism

Laws' description highlights two key features of fundamentalism: its idelogical reaction to a perceived threat to traditional beliefs, and its intention to do 'battle royal' with those who hold a contrary position. Marsden's later definition echoes the essence of Laws' original description of fundamentalism: its opposition to what seems changeable, and its uncompromising position expressed in militant action.

Marsden's description concerns specifically Protestant fundamentalism, but the uncompromising aggressiveness of its proponents also finds an echo in Catholic fundamentalists. The reason for their antagonistic attitude comes from a resistance to the perceived theological and liturgical heresies encouraged by the Second Vatican Council. Like their Protestant colleagues, they crusade to wrest (Catholic) truth from cultural relativity and religious compromise. With the aggressive attitude typical of fundamentalists identified in the University of Chicago's *Fundamentalist Project*, they fight 'for,' 'with,' 'against' and 'under' (Marty and Appleby, 1991: ix).

### The combative nature of fundamentalists

- Fundamentalists fight *for* a world-view they inherited, believe in and seek to reinforce; it is comprehensive, strictly defining religion, morality, family life and public policy.

For Catholic fundamentalists this world-view was the experience of Catholic Christianity before the Second Vatican Council. They seek a return to Catholic religious practice and piety that existed from the 16th-century counter-reformation and continued into the mid-20th century. They look back to the Catholic Church that emerged from the Council of Trent (1545–63) and which they see as the 'golden age' of Catholic life: numbers in the pews were at their greatest, priests and religious were numerous, and all were bonded together by the mystery of the Latin Mass. From this perspective, the 'renewal' endorsed by the Second Vatican Council and the Council's explicit agenda were disastrous. This agenda and its theological compromise to the pressures of modernity are best expressed in the opening lines to the Council document *Lumen Gentium*:

> The joys and the hopes, the griefs and the anxieties of the people of this age, especially those who are poor or in any way afflicted, these are the joys and hopes, the griefs and anxieties of the followers of Christ. Indeed, nothing genuinely human fails to raise an echo in their hearts. (Flannery 1975: 903)

This statement spelt out a new agenda for future Catholic life in its commitment to the world; the explicit contemporary cultural and humanist engagement was, in the eyes of Catholic traditionalists, the cause of the church's demise. It encouraged them to fight for the truth and for a church reflective of a 'golden age,'

- Fundamentalists fight *with* the use of certain clearly defined resources, using the past (either real or imagined) selectively, and classified in ways that help them define the central truths for which they fight.

For Catholic fundamentalists these truths are found in the teachings of the Council of Trent, and in pious devotions which originated at that time and which continued into the mid-20th century. These teachings and devotions contributed to the formation of the influential 'little tradition' that I shall discuss below.

- Fundamentalists fight *against* those who do not share their belief in these central truths. These others become outsiders and the enemy. They may hold diametrically opposed views, or they may exhibit more moderate positions, open to dialogue and prepared to work towards a middle position. Such moderates are also the enemy, because there can be no moderation or compromise on what is judged as truth. In other words, fundamentalists hold a black-and-white view of their world.

This is made clear by Catholic fundamentalists who attack Catholic theologians and biblical scholars, and those whom they consider tainted by the modernist heresy.

* Fundamentalists fight *under* God or a transcendent reference who ensures victory. When fundamentalists believe that God has called them to wage war on those they regard as the enemy, the results, as history has shown, are devastating.

In Catholic fundamentalism the voice of God often comes mediated through charismatic authorities. The 'authorities' are those Church officials or seers who 'are instructed by the Holy Spirit on many topics and are given immediate and certain information apart from research and consultation' (O'Meara 1995: 548). They may be an emissary, seer or visionary who can reveal to 'true and faithful Catholics' messages sometimes from Jesus, sometimes from Mary. The seer's visions and teachings are absolute and assume an incontestably sacred status, more important than any biblical writing or church dogma. When this teaching is perceived directly from Mary, then these Marian apparitions offer teachings believed to be from God. They shape conduct and identify who are members of the true Catholic Church and determine personal identity.

### The search for the divine blue-print and 'true' Catholic teaching

Catholic fundamentalists consider true Catholic teaching to be that which is entirely and uncompromisingly consistent with their religious world-view (Marty and Appleby 1991: 816–20). In this view, truth is not culturally relative or historically conditioned, and their refusal to compromise with their fellow Catholics is consistent with their divinely-allotted crusade for truth. Their actions and unyielding extremism differentiate them from false believers or outsiders, whom they frequently demonise. Catholic fundamentalists are convinced they are enacting an eschatological drama established by God that will influence the future life of the Catholic Church and its influence on the corrupting influence of the world. For Protestant fundamentalists, the eschatological drama concerns no less than the history of the world; for Catholics, it is the salvation of the Church. This conviction about the historical significance of their conduct encourages fundamentalists to look for the divinely pre-orchestrated blue-print, which they find confirmed in sacred texts. For Protestants, this is the Bible; for Catholic fundamentalists, these are the teachings from God, Jesus or Mary, communicated by the visionary or found in the teachings of the Council of Trent.

The claim to impart 'true' Catholic teaching also allows Catholic fundamentalists to develop a counter-cultural orientation that establishes clear boundaries of community designation. These prescribed boundaries preserve Catholic fundamentalists from assault, contamination or corruption. This concern for pure Catholic truth uncontaminated by modernity demonstrates a yearning for the past. It connects to the nine characteristics of fundamentalism identified in the *Fundamentalism Project* and summarised in the Introduction to this book: responding to religion's social marginalisation; selective use of tradition and modernity; moral dualism; absolutism and inerrancy of essential texts; millennialism; elect membership; sharp boundaries; authoritarian organisation; strict behavioural requirements (Marty and Appleby 1991: vii-xiv, 814–40). All these elements have their Catholic expression.

### A return to the 'Golden Age', and the pursuit of the 'perfect Tile'

In summary, Catholic fundamentalism is a response to the theological and liturgical changes that occurred in the Catholic Church and were defined in the Second Vatican Council of the 1960s. This response is expressed in a return to 'traditional' Catholic teaching and devotion, reinforced by Marian piety, the teachings of seers and the earlier catechetical documents that emerged from the Council of Trent. Behind this lies a deeper social, intellectual and psychological need. In a time of transition, change or turmoil, an experience that is global and not unique to people who are explicitly religious, there lies a deep desire for stability and control. In this yearning for protection and security, Catholic fundamentalists seek a 'golden age' which they see in a return to the religion of the past, as the panacea for life's turmoil and for the ills they perceive as befalling the institutional Church. In other words, Catholic fundamentalism looks like a religious movement within the Catholic Church; rather, it is a human response in a changing world to cultural and social concerns that are deeper and more universal.

A pertinent example of such a response – but from a different context – is provided by an Australian social commentator, Hugh Mackay. He considers that Australians respond to their contemporary cultural situation in four ways: with ambiguity, uncertainty, paradox and diversity (2007: 25–160). These reactions, Mackay observes, are best located in the domestic, in our passion for household renovations and in the 'search for the perfect tile' (ibid: 263–8). This is the ceramic tile used in bathrooms, kitchens, passage-ways and balconies. The search for the 'perfect tile' exemplifies a focused preoccupation with domestic renovations that is controllable, local and secure. It offers certainty when other, more menacing, international matters could dominate. Mackay's recognition of the Australian quest for the 'perfect tile' approach to life is reflected in Roman Catholicism. This is the search by some for a 'true' Catholic Church characterised by a strict orthodoxy; it explains the attraction of Catholic fundamentalism that guarantees religious truth and divine favour in a time of apparent relativism and uncertainty. To borrow Mackay's analogy, for some the certainty provided by the fundamentalists' approach to Catholic belief and practice is their 'perfect tile'.

## Catholic expressions of fundamentalism

As we now move to explore the unique expressions of the Catholic fundamentalist phenomenon, we see how these cohere with the earlier insights of Marty and Appleby. Catholic fundamentalism offers what might seem to its adherents a certain security and a distinct boundary of religious practice, defined over and against those Catholics who seem to them to be more secular and humanist. This is Mackay's 'perfect tile' phenomenon. It is identified through selected teachers of Catholic orthodoxy and their interpretation of designated sacred texts, one of which, though not exclusively, is the Bible. I shall explore the various expressions of Catholic fundamentalism in terms of the way the Bible is interpreted (biblical), doctrine taught (doctrinal), authority exercised (authoritarian) and devotions practised (devotional).

### Catholic biblical fundamentalism

Those who hold a fundamentalist position accept certain texts as sacred and interpret them in a way that offers direction and purpose in a fragmented world. This approach is also found amongst Roman Catholics who can be identified as biblical fundamentalists (Wood 2005: 183). Although currently there are few studies of Catholic biblical fundamentalism it is this form that has been most clearly identified by Catholic leaders.[4] Their concerns can be found in two official statements.

The first emerged from the Catholic bishops in the US in 1987 as they became aware of the growth of biblical fundamentalism (National Conference of Catholic Bishops Ad Hoc Committee on Biblical Fundamentalism 1987). The bishops recognised that Catholic biblical fundamentalists

> present the Bible, God's inspired word, as the only source for teaching about Christ and Christian living ... the Bible alone is sufficient. There is no place for the universal teaching church – including its wisdom, its teachings, its creeds and other doctrinal formulations, its liturgical and devotional traditions (ibid).

The bishops acknowledged that some Catholics use the Bible in a particular way and regard it as without error, even in scientific and historical matters. More critically, they acknowledged that the Bible assumes an authority through a literal interpretation devoid of critical scholarship. This perception of the Bible as the sole authority on doctrinal or moral matters rules out the role of the interpreting community, especially the bishops as teachers within the Catholic community.

The second formal document that explicitly addressed biblical fundamentalism was the statement in 1993 by the Vatican's Pontifical Biblical Commission (PBC),[5] *The Interpretation of the Bible in the Church* (1996). This endorsed the newer approaches to biblical exegesis and hermeneutics developed in recent decades, including structuralist, materialistic, psychoanalytic and liberationist approaches.

At a formal and public level, the Vatican statement represented a high point in Roman Catholic appropriation of contemporary methods of biblical interpretation. It was the fruit of a gradual and painful assimilation of modern methods of biblical interpretation by the Church.

### The official Catholic position on fundamentalism

Exegetical methods developed by European and North American scholars became more acceptable in Catholic circles, and received Papal endorsement from 1943 onwards. Key moments of official approval can be identified with Pius XII (1876–1958), John XXIII (1881–1963), Paul VI (1897–1978) and John Paul II (1920–2005). Pius XII's 1943 encyclical *Divino Afflante Spiritu* ('Under the Influence of the Holy Spirit') encouraged interpreters to be aware of the times and culture out of which the Bible had emerged. His letter launched a biblical renaissance in Catholic scholarship. Paul VI continued this spirit of openness and critical biblical engagement through his endorsement of the Second Vatican Council's 1965 Constitution, *Dei Verbum* ('The Word of God'). This document confirmed, *inter alia*, the revelatory nature of the Word of God acting in history, the centrality of the Bible to the life of the Church and the importance of the Catholic Community in reclaiming the Bible in its life of faith and worship. The year before the proclamation of *Dei Verbum*, the Pontifical Biblical Commission issued an 'Instruction on the Historical Truth of the Gospels' which also encouraged the use of modern methods of biblical interpretation for understanding the Bible. In summary, towards the end of the 20th century the Catholic Church was formally distancing itself from any form of literalist and fundamentalist interpretation of the Bible. A section on fundamentalism in the PBC's 1993 *Interpretation of the Bible in the Church* clearly articulated this divorce:

> The fundamentalist approach is dangerous, for it is attractive to people who look to the Bible for ready answers to the problems of life. It can deceive these people, offering them interpretations that are pious but illusory, instead of telling them that the Bible does not necessarily contain an immediate answer to each and every problem. Without saying as much in so many words, fundamentalism actually invites people to a kind of intellectual suicide. (ibid: Sect. F)

Here, the Vatican clearly and unambiguously named the deep-seated cognitive problem associated with biblical fundamentalism.

### Catholic doctrinal fundamentalism

The US bishops recognised in their statement a second form of fundamentalism, which they called 'doctrinal' (ibid). According to the bishops, those who advocate doctrinal fundamentalism seek definitive answers to life's uncertainties. The roots of doctrinal fundamentalism lie in an ideological rigidity which the Pontifical Biblical Commission does not address and at which the US Bishops only hint. Although, as L.J. White argues, 'doctrinal fundamentalism and biblical fundamentalism may be so intimately connected that just as one breeds the other, one cannot be addressed without addressing the other (1988: 50).

Doctrinal fundamentalism is found in those particular Catholic movements where its adherents strongly or sometimes, as mentioned above, militantly object to any critical study of Catholic faith, beliefs, church documents or papal teaching (Allik 1993: 432). They stress instead the unchanging literalness of their own nominated sacred canon of divinely-inspired texts, especially the teachings of the Council of Trent and the anti-modernist *Syllabus of Errors,* a document issued by Pope Pius IX in 1864 condemning certain propositions considered to undermine Catholic teaching.

Some doctrinal fundamentalists were also encouraged by the stance taken by Archbishop Marcel Lefebvre (1906–91). He unambiguously rejected the liturgical renewal of the Second Vatican Council and established, in his seminary at Ecône in Switzerland, his own 'Fraternity of Pius X' for neo-traditionalist priests. Lefebvre offers the clearest expression of Catholic doctrinal fundamentalism. In his 1974 *Profession of Faith* he proclaimed:

> [W]e refuse and always have refused to follow the Rome of neo-modernist and neo-Protestant tendencies which clearly manifested themselves in the Second Vatican Council and after the Council in all the reforms which issued from it ... This reform, the fruit of liberalism and modernism, is completely and utterly poisoned; it starts from heresy and ends with heresy, even if not all its acts are formally heretical. It is accordingly impossible for any aware and faithful Catholic to adopt this reform and to submit to it in any way whatsoever. (Congar 1976: 77–8)

Lefebvre's association of the Council's reforms with modernism, Protestantism and heresy demonstrates an attitude that totally rejects any form of dialogue or compromise. It is this which leads the Catholic theologian T.F. O'Meara to consider doctrinal fundamentalism as an important dimension of Catholic fundamentalism. Doctrinal fundamentalism is less centred on the role of the sacred text than on the importance of an authoritative and charismatic leader who offers to a select, elite group divine certitude in a changing church perceived as inimical to truth; this form of fundamentalism is 'an interpretation of Christianity in which a charismatic leader locates with easy certitude in chosen words, doctrines and practices the miraculous actions of a strict God saving an elite from an evil world' (O'Meara 1990: 18).

The charismatic interpreter teaches frequently without formal theological training, ignorant of contemporary theological, biblical approaches or the cultural and historical conditioning of biblical or ecclesial texts. The approach of such teachers reveals a third form of Catholic fundamentalism, authoritarian fundamentalism (ibid: 548).

## Catholic authoritarian fundamentalism

Authoritarian fundamentalism is found across the whole spectrum of Catholic Church life. It expresses itself in a style of censorship that stifles theological dialogue or debate, encourages particular expressions of piety, offers a monolithic understanding of biblical interpretation, predominantly employs a 'proof-text' approach in securing biblical authority to support religious views, doctrinal points of theology and devotional practice, and prevents any expression of difference in theological matters.

Authoritarian fundamentalists are not open to historical consciousness, a recognition of the development of doctrine within the Catholic Church, the diversity and complexity in the Bible and the various understandings of church life or portraits of Jesus that emerge from the New Testament. Authoritarianism is especially threatened by any form of doctrinal acculturation. O'Meara offers a summary portrait of Catholic fundamentalism especially reflective of authoritarianism:

> [It is based on a fundamentalist personality] usually ignorant of Catholicism's diverse, rich, and complex traditions. Fundamentalism of any sort is opposed to basic facets of the Catholic understanding of Christianity: a variety of traditions in theology, liturgy, and the spiritual life; a theology of grace that focuses on the presence and image of God in each human being; the absence of an angry God or an apocalyptic future; the importance of the local church; and Church authority. (ibid: 548)

For those with this world-view, theological dialogue is impossible and unnecessary: an apodictic claim on truth defies any need for conversation. This spirit of rigid authoritarian fundamentalism seeks an entrenched critical viewpoint on modernity and secularism, rejects pluralism and encourages polarisation (O'Donnell 1996: 184).

A further expression of authoritarian fundamentalism is assigned to official Catholic teachers, especially the Pope. As a result of the Reformation, the Catholic Church replaced one form of authority (that of the Bible) with another (the Bishop of Rome). Up until the Second

Vatican Council, when the theological balance was restored and the role of the Bible reclaimed as central to Catholic life, Church members were consequently governed not by the expert interpretation of the Bible, but by the teaching of the bishops, especially the Pope: one form of obedience was replaced by another. For many traditionalists, the touchstone of orthodoxy is one's obedience to the Pope and his teaching, as it is interpreted by Catholic fundamentalists. In other words, papal teaching has become the Catholic 'sacred text', regarded as incontestable, sacred and without need of cultural adaptation, assimilation or interpretation. It has been called by one Catholic bishop 'creeping' or 'gradual' papal infallibility (Robinson 2007: 120–1).

White offers a helpful analysis of the growth of authoritarian fundamentalism in Catholicism. He contends that authoritarianism grows in a time of conflict over literacy, which can only be addressed by education. White's primary thesis is that 'the virus that explains fundamentalism is literacy; but a more complex literacy critically informed is also an antidote to the ideological rigidity we call fundamentalism' (1988: 51). For White, those who live in a literate society develop fixed formulas that help them understand social meaning; those from non-literate societies depend upon codes and rites. Those codes and rites expressed in terms of the sacramental life of the church supplemented by devotional popular piety expressed what White calls 'the little tradition', which, once respected, trusted and formative, strengthened in the wake of the Protestant reformation. It sustained those non-literate Catholics as the heartbeat of public Catholic life, while the rise of literacy over the 19th and 20th centuries articulated the 'great tradition' of Catholic faith, but also created a crisis for those from a non-literate context. It changed the manner by which non-literate people come to faith.

White considers that the Catholic hierarchy underestimated the impact of the Friday fast and of abstinence, a powerful symbolic expression of the 'little tradition'. It is a non-literate, practical example of devotional conduct and identity in a non-literate 'word' (ibid: 55). This expression became slowly overtaken by the 'great tradition', the literate word of Biblical texts, doctrinal formulations, dogmatic expressions, papal announcements and decrees, episcopal pastoral letters, and theological and philosophical enquiry.

As White interprets history, the ability of Catholicism to blend these two traditions, literate and non-literate, has enabled the Catholic Church to appeal to a wide cross-section of various peoples, attracted to either tradition. Formed in the 'little tradition', they can embrace the 'great tradition' to which the 'little tradition' and its attendant practices bear witness.

White sees that the contemporary fundamentalist phenomena in the aftermath of the Second Vatican Council are symbolic of the tensions and reactions by those formed essentially in the 'little tradition' and unable to engage the 'great tradition'. They are now exposed to a literate Catholicism which seeks to offer a complementary faith tradition and are unable to integrate it. In other words, those formed in the 'little tradition' find themselves encouraged to initiate their own education, to embrace the literacy emphasis of faith education, practice and learning, especially its emphasis on the Bible, and to seek personal guidance in situations of difficulty. But this invitation to engage the 'great tradition' comes at a cost. Unformed and unable to personalise individually the implications of this tradition for the life and growth of faith, some Catholics have found themselves in a theological and spiritual wilderness. One response has been to embrace a certain and defined future; Catholic fundamentalism in its traditionalist and authoritarian expressions provides them with a panacea (ibid: 56).

From a global perspective, this struggle between those schooled in the 'little tradition' and those comfortable in the 'great tradition' is a microcosm of the universal struggle amongst human beings. The encouragement found in the documents of the Second Vatican Council for the Catholic Church to engage people's human aspirations reflects a more universal openness to truth and goodness evident in all cultures and religious traditions, Christian and non-Christian. Thus the Catholic fundamentalist phenomenon is a mirror of what happens globally when those schooled in different literate traditions encounter each other.

### Catholic devotional fundamentalism

As indicated earlier, Catholic fundamentalism in reality concerns the quest for the 'perfect tile.' This is about control, and at its heart lies the desire to claim access to the transcendent. Certain objects and specified actions that concern Catholic devotional life can become the tools for such access. This leads us to a brief discussion of the fourth and final expression of Catholic fundamentalism, devotional fundamentalism.

A particular feature of fundamentalism is that it 'tends to isolate and control the divine objects, to claim special and direct access to God, to encourage the miraculous, and to hold an apocalyptic and elitist stance toward humanity' (O'Meara 1995: 548). Catholic fundamentalists imbued with an overwhelming desire to control and access God focus on objects and actions. They regard some things – medals, water, relics, cards and images of saints – as invested with an exaggerated degree of intrinsic divine powers. The use of the statue of St Joseph is a case in point for the New York real-estate industry:

> With the housing market at its worst in recent years, St Joseph is enjoying a flurry of attention. Some vendors of religious supplies say St Joseph statues are flying off the shelves as an increasing number...look for some saintly intervention to help them sell their houses. (Schaefer Muñoz 2007: 6)

Certain devotional practices are also invested with quasi-magic power to dispose God to respond to the petitioner's request. Catholic fundamentalists consider the acquisition of certain religious objects and the performance of set devotional practices a guarantee of divine protection and favour. The 'novena' was a popular devotional practice,[6] and for some the undertaking of the novena and its nine sequential actions would lead unfailingly to divine favour. For others, a 'miraculous medal' worn around the neck would ensure divine protection. An obsession with these objects and actions can further dispose Catholic fundamentalists to sensory auditions and visions of persons or objects, which of course cannot be subject to question.

## Catholic responses to fundamentalism

Catholic fundamentalism and its four neo-traditionalist expressions are an attractive alternative for those who struggle with life and are not nurtured by the literate emphasis placed on the 'great tradition.' The phenomenon can be engaged in a critical, open and realistic manner. A study of the present situation suggests that extreme expressions of Catholic fundamentalism may not survive – at least within the Catholic mainstream. New Catholic fundamentalist movements purporting to be reformist are emerging and growing outside the mainstream. As we have noted, these movements are reverting to past traditional practices considered idyllic. They identify more strongly with the 'little tradition', tend to be sectarian and are intolerant of ecumenism, religious difference, and contemporary Catholic theology and biblical scholarship. This Catholic fundamentalist phenomenon raises the need for mass literacy:

> For a church tradition that has prided itself on the exclusivity across classes and across the globe, the darker prospect is the likelihood that once again, as in the centuries following the protestant reformation, mass literacy will coincide with the development of new ecclesial bodies outside the catholic communion and/or drift of catholics to existing denominations. (White 1988: 57)

White's analysis of literacy suggests another response to the growth in fundamentalism in the Catholic Church, with its various biblical, doctrinal, authoritarian and devotional expressions. In essence, the best response to fundamentalism is educational. As White suggests, this must be in terms of a literacy that underpins the formational importance played by the 'little tradition' in Catholic history and that is intentionally linked with the 'great tradition'. Providing this educational link would recognise how Catholics schooled or formed in the 'little tradition' have tried to seek answers and responses to their world in the light of the faith that they once knew. The desire for simple, coherent and accessible responses has made devotional practices, Catholic seers, and easy-to-use handbooks of faith (especially the Catechism) attractive.

### The desire for spirituality

While Catholic fundamentalism purports to be concerned about truth rooted in a way of traditional Catholic teaching and devotional

life, it is really reflective of a deeper search: a search for a spirituality that addresses the deep longings of the human spirit, a theology
that helps articulate the transcendent dimension of human experience,
an anthropology that honours the existential struggles of humanity, and a community that offers support and nurture in a world of
upheaval, seeming chaos and meaninglessness. Each of these elements
requires a specific Roman Catholic response. But this response must
take into consideration the diversity of Catholic fundamentalism and
the complexity of its origins. More broadly, each aspect also suggests
the future educational agenda for dealing with the global phenomena
of fundamentalism in all its various forms. Let me explore how these
might look within a specifically Roman Catholic context.

Many spiritual writers in Australia have recognised that, despite
obsessive materialism, greed and xenophobia among Australians,
there exists a desire for an experience of the transcendent, however
this is expressed (Tacey 2003; 2000; 1998). There is an observable
largeness of spirit revealed in the many extraordinary acts of kind-
ness performed by ordinary people. Such acts demonstrate another
side frequently unnoticed or articulated – that many are obviously
led by values of a deeply spiritual nature. They seek a simpler form
of living, are conscious of their use of the world's resources, and desire
to live with integrity, justice and a concern for others. In theological
discourse, they live guided by the spirit. In other words, there exists
a deep religious and theological sensibility that permeates the lives of
human beings. This response is the obverse of our apparent cultural
secularity and agnosticism. The groaning of this religious spirit cannot be stifled within a culture that appears banal and rootless. Human
beings seek something more than what appears to be. That which is
superficial and material simply does not quench the deep spiritual
yearning within. Ironically Catholic fundamentalism reflects this spiritual quest – the desire to seek meaningful answers to life's questions.

### The 'problem' with contemporary, critical Catholic scholarship

Some Catholics are attracted to fundamentalism because of their difficulties with modern, critical, theological and biblical scholarship. This

scepticism is reinforced by an anti-intellectual attitude they pick up from some Catholic leaders cynical of recent scholarship. The Catholic biblical scholar Sandra Schneiders described as follows the theological problem that has attracted Catholics to fundamentalism:

> Modern critical scholarship seems often to be so complicated on the one hand, and so spiritually empty and dry on the other, that the non-professional student of Scripture is driven either to conclude that the Bible, after all, was not meant for ordinary Christians, or else that God must have made the biblical message plain and the scholars are complicating it for purposes of blunting its demanding message. (1982: 102)

These words express a critical issue with theological and biblical scholarship in the Catholic Church. Essentially it is an educational problem: contemporary theological and biblical scholarship cannot remain the exclusive domain of academics, but must speak in a way which Catholics schooled in the 'little tradition' will hear.

Fundamentalism can appear to offer security and a sense of community to people experiencing isolation, loneliness and personal abandonment. Precisely because of their relatively small size, Catholic fundamentalist and traditionalist movements are able to offer community to people at a time when they are lonely. The experience of Catholic fundamentalism therefore raises theological and organisational questions about ecclesiology – how the Catholic Church expresses and organises itself as church. The large size of church communities with their impersonal structures will continue to make smaller, traditionalist church communities seem attractive.

One of the unique features common to all forms of fundamentalism is its combative nature. Confrontational aggression and transparent aversion to dialogue reinforce one of the clearest issues which fundamentalism reveals: an anti-intellectualism born out of fear. This fear is, in essence, concerned with what it means to be human, and is essentially anthropological in nature. Catholic fundamentalism and devotional nostalgia are sometimes embraced by those who seek an escape from personal or social suffering. In such times, the desire to shut out the world or put off decision-making is stronger than the search for the wisdom of authentic theological scholarship.

## Conclusion: recognition of our humanity

This leads to a final anthropological note. The most important response that those in positions of leadership and education in the Catholic community must make to those who are attracted to the various expressions of fundamentalism is one of recognition – recognition of the very humanness of those who are attracted to the simple answers that Catholic fundamentalism seems to offer. A specifically future 'Catholic' curriculum in addressing fundamentalism would need to focus on finding ways of enabling Catholics to become biblically literate, theologically educated and devotionally sensitive. From a broader, more global perspective, a future educational curriculum in addressing fundamentalism, whether this fundamentalism is in Roman Catholicism, Protestantism or other monotheistic religious traditions, must be anthropological. It must be related to the spiritual quest and global concerns of human beings in a way that is socially constructive and relevant (Tacey 1998; 2000; 2003). Somehow it must recognise the universal desire for the religious 'perfect tile' and offer a global vision of what is possible.

## Notes

1. Though Catholic fundamentalism as described in the following pages is a recognisable and growing phenomenon, there is currently no hard data on how widespread it is within the Catholic community. Such data would be near impossible to calculate.
2. Two helpful studies of Catholic fundamentalism are Weaver and Appleby's *Being Right: Conservative Catholics in America*, and O'Meara's *Fundamentalism: A Roman Catholic Perspective*.
3. A note about the terminology I use to identify Catholic fundamentalists in the pages ahead might be helpful. Within the context of the discussion on fundamentalism from a Roman Catholic perspective, my use of the terms 'neo-conservative,' 'traditionalist' and 'neo-traditionalist' are interchangeable with 'fundamentalist'. Each term, however, highlights a particular aspect of

Catholic fundamentalism. 'Neo-conservative' emphasises the recent trend by some Catholics to move towards a rigid theological, biblical, devotional and liturgical position. 'Traditionalist' emphasises the claim which some Catholics hold that their doctrinal position is more in keeping with what they consider the Catholic Church teaches than any other position, especially one held by a contemporary Catholic theologian, educator or biblical scholar. The 'neo' of 'neo-traditionalist' stresses the recent nature of this position.

4. Besides other explicit Catholic studies on fundamentalism referenced in this article, a helpful earlier analysis of the growth in Catholic conservatism is Weaver and Appleby's *Being Right*.

5. The Pontifical Biblical Commission (PBC) was established in the late 19th century. Study of its writings is regarded as essential to gauge the level of authority with which positions about the Bible are held within the Catholic Church.

6. 'Novena' is a distinct Roman Catholic expression derived from 'nine' and meaning the nine days of devotion. Rigidly 'performing' some action for nine days – for example the 'nine first Fridays' on which pious Catholic attend Catholic Mass on the first Friday of each month for nine months—would guarantee God's positive disposition towards the devotee. Therefore the devotee could confidently expect God to grant some favour requested because of the faithful *performance* of the novena.

## Bibliography

Allik, Tiina (1993) 'Fundamentalism'. *The New Dictionary of Catholic Spirituality*. Collegeville, MN: Liturgical Press, pp. 431–2.

Congar, Yves (1976) *Challenge to the Church: The Case of Archbishop Lefebvre*. London: Collins, and Dublin: Veritas.

Flannery, Austin (ed.) (1975) *Vatican Council II: The Conciliar and Post-Conciliar Documents*. Collegeville, MN: Liturgical Press.

Laws, Curtis Lee (1920) *Watchman-Examiner*, 1 July, p. 834.

Mackay, Hugh (2007) *Advance Australia ... Where? How We've Changed, Why We've Changed, and What Will Happen Next*. Sydney: Hachette Australia.

Marsden, George (1991) *Understanding Fundamentalism and Evangelicalism*. Grand Rapids, MI: Eerdmans.

Marty, Martin E. and R. Scott Appleby (1991) *Fundamentalism Observed*. Chicago: The University of Chicago Press.

—— (1995) *Fundamentalism Comprehended*. Chicago: The University of Chicago Press.

National Conference of Catholic Bishops Ad Hoc Committee on Biblical Fundamentalism (1987) 'Pastoral statement for Catholics on biblical fundamentalism'. Washington, DC: US Catholic Conference of Bishops. In *Origins: NC Documentary Service*, Vol. 17, No. 21, pp. 376–7.

O'Donnell, Christopher (1996) 'Fundamentalism'. In O'Donnell, Christopher (ed.) *Ecclesia: A Theological Encyclopedia of the Church*. Collegeville, MN: Liturgical Press, pp. 183–4.

O'Meara, Thomas F. (1990) *Fundamentalism: A Roman Catholic Perspective*. New York: Paulist.

—— (1995) 'Fundamentalism, Catholic'. In McBrien, Richard P. (ed.) *The HarperCollins Encyclopedia of Catholicism*. San Francisco, CA: Harper SanFrancisco, p. 548.

Pontifical Biblical Commission (1996) *The Interpretation of the Bible in the Church*. New York: St Paul.

Robinson, Geoffrey (2007) *Confronting Power and Sex in the Catholic Church: Reclaiming the Spirit of Jesus*. Melbourne: Garratt.

Sanders, Therese (1994) 'Fundamentalism'. In Glazier, Michael and Monika K. Hellwig (eds.) *The Modern Catholic Encyclopedia*. Collegeville, MN: Liturgical Press, pp. 335–6.

Schaefer Muñoz, Sara (2007) 'Sellers without a prayer turn to buying St Joseph'. *The Weekend Australian: Primespace*, 17–18 November, p. 6.

Schneiders, Sandra (1982) 'God's Word for God's People'. *The Bible Today*, Vol. 22, pp. 100–6.

Tacey, David (1998) 'Spirituality and the common good'. *South Pacific Journal of Mission Studies*, Vol. 20, pp. 3–6.

—— (2000) *Re-enchantment: The New Australian Spirituality*. Sydney: HarperCollins.

—— (2003) *The Spirituality Revolution: The Emergence of Contemporary Spirituality*. Sydney: HarperCollins.

Weaver, Mary J. and R. Scott Appleby (eds.) (1995) *Being Right: Conservative Catholics in America*. Bloomington, IN: Indiana University Press.

White, Leland J. (1988) 'Fundamentalism and "fullness of Christianity": Catholicism's double challenge'. *Biblical Theology Bulletin*, Vol. 18 No. 2, pp. 50–9.

Wood, Ralph C. (2005) *Flannery O'Connor and the Christ-Haunted South*. Grand Rapids, MI: Eerdmans.

# CHAPTER 8

# HIZB UT-TAHRIR AND THE PUBLIC SPHERE IN BANGLADESH: CONFRONTING THE CRISIS

## Ahmed Abidur Razzaque Khan

### Introduction

The rise of Islamic extremist movements and militant groups, and a 'trans-nationalist' Islamic political culture, has been evident in Bangladesh – the third-largest Muslim country in the world – since the early 1990s. At present, besides the well-established Jamaat-i Islami[1] and its activist student network Islami Chatra Shibir, there are other organisations that have as their goal the establishment of a state based on the principles of *sharia* (Hossain and Siddiquee 2004: 384). The transnational organisation Hizb ut-Tahrir's Bangladeshi branch (HTB) is one such group, which has gained a foothold in Bangladesh and created a well-established local network. It has been particularly successful in its activities in universities throughout Bangladesh: Chartra Mukti, the student wing of HTB, has grown steadily more popular among students at both private and public universities. However, as this paper was being completed, the Bangladeshi government declared HTB illegal, on the grounds that it threatens 'public security in the country' (*bdnews24.com*, 23 October 2009).

This chapter has three objectives (defined before the banning of HTB): to describe HTB's use of information technology (IT) and new media to create a 'pseudo public sphere' in Bangladesh; to explore the extent to which HTB poses a threat to human security; and to suggest the best possible policy to respond to HTB's activities. The data in the study comes from HTB's own press releases, and from news reports, newspaper articles and electronic sources.

Before proceeding, the question of whether HTB is a fundamentalist organisation should be addressed. Fundamentalism is a complex phenomenon which has been defined and analysed in various ways. Noorani, for example, suggests that: 'Fundamentalism is a response to the challenges of modernity which were perceived by the zealous as threats to the integrity and survival of their faith' (2002: 66). Marty and Appleby's *Fundamentalism Project* posits the existence of a universally recognisable notion of fundamentalism, mainly involving religion, and displaying most of the following nine characteristics:

1) a reaction against the marginalization of religion in society; 2) the selective use of tradition and modernity; 3) moral dualism; 4) absolutism and inerrancy of essential texts; 5) millennialism; 6) elect, chosen membership; 7) sharp boundaries; 8) authoritarian organization, and 9) strict behavioural requirements. (Almond et al 1995: 402–14)

With respect to Islamic fundamentalism, two further characteristics have been added to this list of traits: resistance to a scientific worldview and to the application of scientific principles to religion and religious texts; and opposition to a secular state (Cole 2002: 195–217). While most of these characteristics can be seen in HTB, this chapter will focus specifically on its views of the secular nation state, which have immediate implications for the issue of human security. The analysis will take into account two levels of action on HTB's part: on one level, it seems to embrace the secular state by claiming to be a political party, and accordingly also claiming the right to operate within a secular democratic setting. However, on another level, the party advocates the end of the secular nation state, the resurrection of the Islamic caliphate, and the adoption of *sharia* in all areas of society and government, which effectively rules out the conditions that allow the HTB to function.

According to the Bangladeshi media (Ahsan: 2005), and to the economist Barkat (2007), the HTB is one of seven main militant Islamic front organisations in Bangladesh. By 'militant' is here meant that the organisation is committed *on principle* to a non-pacifist struggle for their objectives, even though the practical methods it espouses may be non-violent. HTB is committed to toppling current Muslim governments for the sake of resurrecting the caliphate, but believes the change must come through a popular uprising, which cannot be directed from above (Saeed 2006: 149).

Others have used the term 'Islamist' to define organisations such as HTB. Noorani, for example, argues that:

Islamism describes the 'ideologization' of Islam at the political level, the construction of a political ideology using some symbols culled from the historical repertoire of Islam, to the exclusion of others. This ideology, sometimes referred to as 'Islamic fundamentalism' is better described as Islamism ... Islamism is not Islam. (2002: 68)

Noorani's concept of 'Islamism' is applicable to HTB, in the sense that HTB has indeed transformed the religion of Islam into a project for a political objective, the establishment of a caliphate. However, Roy's term 'neo-fundamentalism' is even more useful in the context of this chapter; Roy distinguishes between 'Islamists' – fundamentalists who accept the nation-state model and seek to 'Islamise' it through Islamic government based on the principles of *sharia* – and 'neo-fundamentalists' – those who reject the nation-state structure and focus on reforming the universal Islamic community (the *umma*), which for some of them includes resurrecting the caliphate. Some neo-fundamentalists are entirely pacifist (Tablighi Jamaat), others are militants espousing non-violent methods (Hizb ut-Tahrir), and yet others (the Islamic Jihad and al-Qaeda) are violent extremists (Roy 2004: 247–57). In this chapter, HTB will thus be referred to as Islamist to distinguish it from secular political parties and 'ordinary Islam', and as neo-fundamentalist with respect to its rejection of the nation state. (The term 'transnational' is sometimes used synonymously with 'neo-fundamentalism', to refer to the fact that neo-fundamentalism rejects both nation states and national identities, in favour of 'Muslim' as a 'transnational' identity based on the universal religious community.)

The concept of 'human security' also requires examination. After the end of World War Two, the idea of people-centred security emerged around the world, commonly understood as prioritising the security of people, or as Amartya Sen (1999) put it, providing 'freedom from want and freedom from fear'. More specifically, it means protecting people from critical and pervasive threats to human dignity, such as disease, hunger, unemployment, social conflict and political repression. This chapter argues that the HTB potentially aggravates social conflict in Bangladesh, undermining the goal of 'freedom from fear'.

## The rise of Islamic fundamentalism in Bangladesh

Bangladesh experienced a painful birth in separating from Pakistan in 1971: the Pakistani military junta had used harsh and terrifying measures to try to extinguish the drive for independence, including mass killing, rape, the systematic destruction of property and forced exile (Karlekar 2005: 47). In the newly-independent Bangladesh, 97.8 per cent of the population were ethnic Bengalis, of whom 88.3 per cent were Muslims (Government of Bangladesh 1999).

Since the separation from Pakistan was partially motivated by that country's adoption of a religious-based nationalism, the new state emerged as a secular polity with a constitutional embargo on religion in politics. The preamble to the first constitution (adopted in 1972) emphasised secularism as one of the state's fundamental principles. This secular state is now being challenged. In recent years, the popular and humanist Islam that once dominated Bangladesh has given way to 'Islamism'. Attacks by Islamist militants are now commonplace, and politicians, scholars, journalists, members of the judiciary, religious minorities – including members of the Islamic Ahmadiyya sect – have been targeted (Ganguly 2006: 1–6). The world began to notice this trend in 2004, when grenades were thrown at a political rally, there was an assassination attempt on a British diplomat, and a country-wide bombing campaign claimed many lives.

The election of October 2001 showed that Islamism had gained a foothold in Bangladesh. This development has roots in the country's political history: the first President, Sheikh Mujibur Rahman, was assassinated in 1975 during a military coup, which was followed by three military regimes. The first step towards the introduction of religion into the state came when Ziaur Rahman added the 5th amendment to the constitution in 1977 under martial law. Among other things, it added the phrase *Bismillah–ar-Rahman-ar-Rahim* ('in the name of God, the Merciful, the Compassionate') and also paved the way for Jamaat-i Islami and other Islamist parties to enter national politics. In June 1988 the second military junta – the government of Hussain Muhammad Ershad – passed the Eighth Amendment to the constitution, which declared Islam to be the state religion of Bangladesh. Finally, the Bangladesh Nationalist Party (BNP) formed a coalition government with Jamaat-i Islami (2001–06). This made Jamaat-i Islami much more active in the public sector, including banking, education and health. However, the mass corruption and political–economic criminal charges against the BNP-Jamaat coalition resulted in a political deadlock in late 2006, which culminated in the postponement of planned elections, the imposition of a state of emergency, and on 11 January 2007 the installation of a new military-backed interim government.

It could be argued that once Islamist political parties were established, with their public discourse about Islamic government, *sharia* and social justice, the ground was prepared for the emergence of Islamist militancy. But there were also socio-economic and political factors which contributed to the development of militancy. According to Barkat these factors are associated with:

> the emergence of 'the religious doctrine-based Pakistan State' (in 1947), failure in punishing the 'war criminals' (in the 1971 War of Independence), and legitimizing communalism by replacing 'secularism' by 'Islam as state religion' in the Constitution (eighth amendment 1988). The failure of the State in satisfying

basic needs of the people (in line with Constitutional obliga-
tions), growing criminalization of the economy and politics,
growing inequality in society, increasing youth unemployment,
communalization of culture and education, lack of people's confidence in mainstream political (democratic) leadership, external
environment – all contributed to the growth of Islamist extremism in Bangladesh. (Barkat 2006: 2)

According to Barkat, of the three major types of Islamist organisations that exist in Bangladesh, the first operates openly, like Jamaat-i
Islami. The second and third types operate secretly. Of the second
type – the militants – Barkat estimates that there are some 125
groups. Of the third type there are 231 non-government organisations (NGOs) that are Islamist in ideology or promote Islamist
militant activities (Barkat 2007: 23). Barkat places HTB in the second category because it is militant or supportive of militancy and it
carries out its activities clandestinely (see also Samir 2008). We shall
see below, however, that HTB is perhaps more public than clandes-
tine, as it indeed propagates its presence, ideology and objectives as
widely as possible.

Public universities and their students have played a strong role
in Bangladeshi politics since the early twentieth century. Students
have often led major political movements, including the Language
Movement of 1950, the people's appraisal of 1969, and the drive
towards independence in 1971. During the 1980s, the anti-
Ershad student movement helped to (temporarily) oust the military
regime. Religion-based student politics were introduced with the
emergence of Islamism, and are thus a part of the nation's higher-
education institutions. HTB has targeted a particular section of students, those in the private universities. Its success in recruiting student
supporters is mainly due to its message, which targets the misdeeds
of corrupt politicians and offers 'Islamic solutions' to such problems
through a changed popular conscience and a new form of Islamic government, the caliphate.

The successes of HBT and other Islamist groups and organisations
to establish themselves politically has led to the creation of an Islamist

political culture as mainstream political parties have sought to respond to the challenge (Samad 1998).

## Hizb ut-Tahrir and Bangladesh's 'pseudo public sphere'

Hizb ut-Tahrir (HT) is today an influential international neo-fundamentalist movement. Its founder, Taqi al-Din al-Nabhani (d. 1978), was a Palestinian judge and former member of the Muslim Brotherhood. He founded HT in Jerusalem in 1953, with the avowed objective of resurrecting the Islamic caliphate that had been abolished by Kemal Atatürk in 1924.

HT's Bangladeshi chapter, HTB, was launched on 17 November 2001, just two months after 9/11, in the wake of a rising tide of anti-Americanism. At present, HTB has established six divisional head-quarters and centres in four major cities: Dhaka, Chittagong, Comilla and Sylhet. HTB is very active, but keeps a low profile. Its goal is to become a political third force, an alternative to the Islamist Jamaat-i Islami and the dominant right-wing parties, the BNP and the Awami League.[2] Like its parent organisation, HTB uses the internet and new media to conduct its mission, and runs a well-managed official web site (at *www.khilafat.org*).

HTB recently published its 'Islamic Manifesto' for the country. Here it outlines the goal of establishing the caliphate gradually and by spreading *sharia* 'completely to all Islamic lands'. It also supports the removal of all foreign ownership of the country's resources. Moreover, HTB does not legitimise the transfer of power through democratic elections, because they are the hallmark of the nation state that HT rejects on principle; in the caliphate, other processes of selecting the right caliph will be followed (Rahman 2007: 14). The Manifesto threatens human security by encouraging social conflict around the national constitution and the nation state itself. In a free public sphere, such a threat would be reduced because the argument would be submitted to critical counter-arguments. However, Bangladesh lacks a vibrant public sphere, and is therefore vulnerable to the potential social disruptiveness of this message. Habermas defines the 'public sphere' thus:

> A realm of our social life in which something approaching pub-
> lic opinion can be formed ... Citizens behave as a public body
> when they confer in an unrestricted fashion – that is, with the
> guarantee of freedom of assembly and association and the free-
> dom to express and publish their opinions ... about matters of
> general interest. (Habermas et al 1974: 49)

The Bangladeshi public sphere lacks most of these traits which means
there is no national arena where real argumentation can be take place.
In the words of Majumder:

> A non-partisan civil society, one of the foremost pre-conditions
> of the success of liberal democracy, which is able to [create pres-
> sure] and bargain and negotiate with the state without the influ-
> ence of political parties in favour of the citizen, is yet to flourish
> in Bangladesh. (Majumder 2006: 150)

Bangladeshi civil society is in fact divided into two political blocks,
the more secularly-minded pro-Awami League and the more religious-
ly-Islamist-inclined pro-BNP-Jamaat alliance (Sobhan 2002: 18).

The press in Bangladesh is not free. The ruling party has always
controlled it, using methods such as nationalsecurity legislation and
criminaldefamation laws. Although the Constitution provides for freedom of expression, journalists are constantly subjected to assaults and
death threats from local politicians because of their reporting on corruption and other misdeeds. Self-censorship and other types of restrictions on the media are therefore common, and were particularly so
during the last state of emergency (2006–08). Given this situation,
it is easy for Islamist groups and their allies to attack the press. In
September 2007, cartoonist Arifur Rahman was jailed for supposedly
insulting Islam in a cartoon depicting a cat named Mohammad. The
newspaper *Prothom Alo,* which published the cartoon, was temporarily
suspended and its editors were forced to issue an apology. Rahman himself remained in prison until February 2008 (Freedom House 2008).

The absence of a vibrant public sphere creates a vacuum, of which HTB has taken advantage. Claiming to be the voice of the voiceless 'Muslim masses', it has created its own set of networks, knowledge-based institutions and arenas of debate. In a recent interview in *Khilafah* magazine (May 2009), its chief coordinator, Mohiuddin Ahmed, reported that the HTB is engaged in various political activities, including demonstrations and protest rallies, and is making contact with professional people such as teachers, doctors and imams, in the first instance by visiting their work-places and organisations. It also organises round-table discussions with influential people, tackling critical national issues (*Khilafah*, 26 June 2009b). It produces publications on various issues and places them on its web-site, thus helping to form opinion and cre-ate specifically 'Muslim' views – all with the aim of influenc-ing public political discourse and consciousness. By addressing national crises and championing demands for social justice, HTB has managed to set the tone for the other Islamist groups and organisations hungry for direction and eager to become a centre of public attention.

These activities on the part of HTB may appear to be consistent with activities in a democratic public sphere. Yet, as the next sec-tions will show, HTB uses its networks and forums and its IT and digital technology in ways that run counter to Habermas's notion of a public sphere: it is not open to true dialogue and has no intention of developing democracy and a free public sphere. While it enjoys the democratic rights of assembly and freedom of expression – in so far as they apply in Bangladesh – HTB opposes them on prin-ciple. For these reasons, it is suggested here that HTB has both *created* and is *operating within* a 'pseudo-public sphere'. It uses the public media and other forums for debate to discuss issues of public national concern, but rephrases these issues in terms of an objective (the caliphate) which it is not prepared to submit to public critical scrutiny and debate. Moreover, the restricted nature of Bangladesh's public sphere more broadly means that no other actors are able to raise the controversial issues that HTB raises and to present alternative approaches.

## Activities and influence

HTB has advantages compared to other political parties, notably the fact that it has student wings in both public and private universities, including the women's sections.

With regard to private universities, HTB currently has groups at the American International University Bangladesh, City University, East/West University, Independent University Bangladesh, Southeast University, the leading public university (Dhaka University) and the leading private university (North/South University in Bangladesh) (Sadique 2005). It has targeted young people, especially non-practising Muslim students marginalised from mainstream politics. These young people would like to discuss their views on issues of daily life, like politics, philosophy, economy, culture and lifestyle, but students at private universities do not have direct access to politics, and their various social clubs do not address this need. HTB has taken advantage of these politically marginalised students by providing forums for political discussions. They organise dialogues with both individual students and student political groups, through numerous seminars, discussion sessions and study circles. The topics covered include the existence of God, the blind faith of atheism, cloning, globalisation, imperialism, and economic systems. Even sensitive issues are discussed: pre-marital sex, drugs, alcohol, communism and US imperialism. In fact there is effectively no other place where students can discuss such matters; correspondingly, these forums are extremely appealing to young people (Ibid).

This connection with universities allows HTB to organise regular discussions, debates and symposiums around the country, as part of its broader strategy. In an interview published in *Probe* news magazine (3 August 2007), Mohiuddin Ahmed, the head and chief coordinator of the party in Bangladesh, claimed that:

In Bangladesh *Hizb ut-Tahrir* is working in four steps: a) earning people's confidence through a continuous political process; b) mobilizing people's movement in a disciplined way; c) toppling the existing system of governance along with the people with it;

and d) electing Khalifa following the Khelafat system through the participation of the people. At present *Hizb ut-Tahrir* is concentrating on the first two steps. (Rahman 2007:14)

In the following, a few examples of HTB's work towards these objectives are given. For example, on 17 April 2008, during the state of emergency, HTB organised a round-table on the 'Post-9/11 scenario and regional geo-politics – the way to protect Bangladesh from imperialist intervention'. The Former Chief of the Bangladesh Rifles (BDR), a former Energy Minister, two editors of daily newspapers, a columnist, a former MP of the Bangladesh Nationalist Party and three senior leaders of different Islamic parties, all participated in this seminar, during which HTB's chief spokesman accused the government of collusion with India and acts of treachery against the Bangladeshi people. Thus, the seminar, although superficially appearing a public space for discussion, was really a pseudo public space, used to exploit public fears about India rather than to submit these fears to critical examination. Previous examples of how HTB spreads such talk of malicious foreign plots against Islam include its response to the massive bombing attack on 17 August 2005, when it accused India of a campaign to destabilise Bangladesh. Later investigations revealed that the bombing had in fact been carried out by another extremist Islamist organisation, *Jamaat-ul Mujahiden*. The most recent example of this strategy came during the BDR mutiny of February 2009: HTB posted an 18-page booklet, in Bengali, entitled 'BDR massacre: Indian conspiracy to destroy Bangladesh defence forces' (*Hizb ut- Tahrir*, Bangladesh 2009: 16–17).[3]

On 20 June 2009, HTB responded to a Bangladesh Rural Advancement Committee (BRAC) seminar entitled '*Fatwa*, illegal arbitration, inhumane punishment: where is the rule of law?' by holding a seminar of its own. BRAC lawyers and human-rights activists had urged the government to take immediate steps to stop the issuing of *fatwa*s (religious legal edicts), the number of which had increased alarmingly in recent months. The main objective of HTB's seminar was to convince the public that 'so-called human rights organisations' were agents of imperialism who sought to discredit the *hudud*[4] and sharia;

HTB clearly indicated that no compromise was possible on sharia or the caliphate. This seminar was thus not an open debate but an example of a limited, closed network with the clear objective of pressuring government and policy-makers by bolstering public support.

Mohiuddin Ahmed (HTB coordinator) insists that HTB does not believe in violence (Sadique 2005); he claims that they have condemned all terrorist activity in the country and abroad. But HTB rhetoric explicitly stirs up deep-seated fears and the emotions it deliberately provokes can easily lead to violence. As Coady argues – in reference to Johan Galtung – the definition of violence should be based on a broader concept than the merely physical: thus he distinguishes between physical and psychological violence, giving as examples of the latter lies, brainwashing, indoctrination and threats (2008: 25). From this point of view, some of HTB's activities – notably its attempts to convince its audiences through emotional appeals to defend Islam and sharia from 'imperialists' who seek to harm Muslims and Islamic countries for no other reason than that they are Muslim – constitute psychological violence. Other examples of practices which may incite violence are the public processions, gatherings and angry rallies which HTB stages as a response to current, sensitive political and Islamic issues, usually in front of the national mosque after the weekly Friday prayers. These activities end up in clashes with the police. In this manner, the campaign and activities aim at restructuring the affairs of state around 'Islamic issues' and reorganising social relations according to Islamic principles.

At times, HTB demonstrations challenge state laws. In 2008, it organised a march to the office of *Prothom Alo*, a national daily in Dhaka, demanding the newspaper's closure for publishing the 'blasphemous' cartoon about the Prophet Mohammad. This march occurred during the state of emergency, when protests of this type were supposedly banned. Similarly, it organised a protest outside the Danish Embassy in Bangladesh for the publishing of cartoons depicting the Prophet Mohammad in a daily newspaper in Denmark in 2005 and 2006. Similarly, in 2007 HTB campaigned for the right for women to wear the *hijab* ('headscarf', which covers a key biometric feature, the ears) when photographed for ID cards.

## IT, new media and their uses

In addition to direct actions and meetings, HTB makes extensive use of information technology and new media. As previously mentioned, it has a well-organised English-language website (*www.khilafat.org*) with 17 different interlinked sections. The organisation's website carries a banner that reads: 'Khilafat.org ... then there will be *Khilafah Rashida* ['rightly-guided caliphate'] on the method of Prophethood ... '. The site describes itself as the 'Official website of Hizb ut-Tahrir Bangladesh'. Although the website's main language is English, it posts items in both English and Bengali, along with Arabic versions of quotations from the Quran. There are no external links.

The website's 'press-room' and 'leaflets' sections are routinely updated with the latest information in Bengali and English, while the 'events' section offers a comprehensive up-to-date record of HTB activities and events. The 'media coverage' section of the site is also well-maintained: it posts news accounts of HTB found in local newspapers, again in both languages. The 'multimedia' section contains video clips of HTB activities like seminars, demonstrations and rallies, and of members being arrested. The 'articles' page offers seminar papers or articles on current state issues. The 'circle information' section provides information about six circles in different parts of Dhaka, including a sisters' circle in Dhanmondi, Dhaka. For each circle, an address and meeting time, and in some cases mobile-phone contact numbers, are listed. The Hizb ut-Tahrir section provides information about the organisation – its rationale, aim, membership, work and methods. Finally, the feedback section allows visitors to the site to post comments along with their name, email address and country. The site is notably reader-friendly and better focused than the websites of the two other major political parties, Jamaat-i Islami (*http://jamaat-e-islami.org*) and the Bangladesh Nationalist Party (*http://bnp-bd.com*).

Anyone can download documents from the HTB website and post comments on the feedback page (provided they are accepted by a monitor). This makes the site interactive and a 'virtual treasure trove' for young educated Muslims around the world. The remarks in the feedback section reveal that users are not only from Bangladesh: many are from the UK and other countries. One posting from the UK includes the words: '...I read this website very often, I enjoy reading this site and recommend people to do that...', and one Islam Richards from Venezuela writes:

> Salam to my muslim brothers. I've known hizb [HT] from london UK. what you doing in bangladesh is amazing inshaalah, you must be very brave inshaalah, knowing the politics in bangladesh...please keep the work the blood around the world need end for good inshaallah. wsalam your brother Islam. (*Khilafah*, 16 March 2009a)

The website has become a platform for Bangladeshis, including those in the Bangladeshi diaspora in UK and elsewhere in the world. But it is not a site for genuine debate: no negative comments are posted on the feedback page, nor are any contradictory political thoughts shared on the site. The site shows that HTB is connected with like-minded people in the UK and other countries, and that it organises support for its Bangladesh-based activities in the UK and around the world. Cronem (2005: 59) reports that the organisation is quite active in – among other places – the Tower Hamlets area of London, where it has tried to influence local religious and political institutions. Thus information technology allows HTB to induce young British- and Bangladesh-based Bengalis to identify with each other, express mutual solidarity and form a web-based social network. Knowing that British Bangladeshis are also engaged with the movement has encouraged young people in Bangladesh, and vice versa.

HTB also uses Facebook for its networking and other activities. The author found three groups under the name of *Hizb ut-tahrir* Bangladesh on Facebook in March 2009. Another Facebook group called 'Release the leaders and activists of *Hizb ut- Tahrir* immediately' has 236 members; the site publicises news on 27 activists arrested by police. The creators and administrators of this group are Bangladeshi, including one from North-South University. The group information indicates that most of those arrested had academic backgrounds. Of those who post on 'the wall', most are university teachers, while others include engineering and medical students (Facebook, 16 March 2009). This suggests that a specific group of academics and young students in private universities are involved with the movement. One of the group members wrote on the wall:

> O Muslim army of Pakistan what is the use of your nuclear bombs if those can not save the lives of your Palestinian brothers. O Muslim army of Sirya [*sic*], Jordan, Egypt, Libya, Bangladesh, Iran: When will you fight back? You have the highest number of army in the world. No other has such a large army of 65, 00,000[*sic*]. You have nuclear bombs, you have the most of natural resources in your lands. You have the manpower. Why you are silent???' (Facebook, 16 March 2009)

Facebook allows HTB to invite people to join its university circles, circulate telephone contact numbers, provide web addresses, and publish weekly schedules for local mosques. It also reveals that at the North South-University, HTB members are known as *Ly Gen*, 'Liberated Generation'. A few members of '*Hizb ut-Tahrir* Bangladesh' are also members of 'I'm aware of *Hizb ut-Tahrir* Bangladesh'. They post videos on Facebook about their activities and on Islamic issues. The press section postings reveal that the women's section of *Hizb ut-Tahrir* is quite active and uses IT for its discussions.

Other new media which HTB uses extensively are YouTube and other video sites. In August 2009, a search of Google video produced 54 items within 0.04 seconds. Most of these are high-quality videos on HTB activities, and some have been viewed more than a thousand times. One video is that of the protest held a fortnight after the August 2005 bombing: it shows that most of the people in the demonstration are young men wearing skull-caps or orange forehead bands with *shahadatain* (Arabic, 'two testimonies of faith') written on them. In March 2009, *Hizb ut Tahrir* UK posted a video on the BDR mutiny, entitled 'Philkhana Massacre – Bangladesh security in Danger' (Google Videos, 16 March 2009).

Thus when young men join the party they can find its views, programme updates and activities on the internet, and they can network with other members via social-networking groups like Facebook and 'Ly Gen'. As the internet allows them to post and share their ideas, it also makes them feel empowered and part of the process of 'liberation' (Arabic *tahrir*). Typical comments on Facebook concern the oppressive character of society and the distortions of mass media, e.g. 'where is our freedom to express the truth ... ?' or 'we believe that our Bangladeshi media is always active in portraying the people who work for Islam as terrorists'. There are obvious parallels with how other disgruntled groups to both the left and right of the political mainstream view the mass media and public debates.

All this is particularly interesting, as the present government is about to create a 'Digital Bangladesh'. With the landslide victory of the Awami League in the recent general election (December 2008), the making in Bangladesh of a society driven by ICT (information and communication technology) has become a real possibility. Digitalisation means that a broad range of government activities will take place via computers and the internet. This raises the question of whether such a 'digital Bangladesh' will be conducive to a broader liberalisation of the public sphere and of the conditions for public debate which, it is argued here, is the only democratically acceptable way of defusing the attraction of HTB's messages. To answer that question, HTB's potential to engender social unrest and conflict needs to be assessed.

## A critical assessment

The 1971 liberation struggle for Bangladesh was a struggle against injustice and about establishing the national rights of the Bengali people, but these grand goals have subsequently been forgotten. Although successive Bangladeshi governments have declared their intention of meeting the United Nation's Millennium Development Goals (MDG) and thus ensuring human development and security, they have rarely met their targets. None of the major political parties, including the current government, has made human security part of its agenda, even though the country suffers from frequent natural calamities and nearly half the population lives in poverty. The reality is that an unhealthy political environment and the confrontational politics of both major rightist parties have not only accelerated the growth of militant and extremist religious groups (World Bank 2006) but have also blocked the achievement of human security in Bangladesh. There are six points that can be made regarding HTB and threats to human security.

First, HTB has thrived in this atmosphere of political division. HTB claims to stand for social justice, which seems like a positive political stand. However, because it rejects national, secular states and seeks to establish a single Islamic state covering all Muslim countries, it has a militant and radical agenda. According to Mayer:

> *Hizb-ut Tahrir* has been calling with mounting intensity for the eradication of Israel by *Jihad* since the early 1980s, but this means calling for action by Muslim states, the Muslim masses and the armies of Muslim countries and not the party itself organizing the jihad. In fact they call on them to re-establish the *Caliphate* so that jihad can be launched. (2004: 18)

Thus HTB, according to its own stated objectives, is now at the stage of creating popular awareness, as a necessary phase in the move towards the envisioned broader uprising.

Second, HTB openly engages in the politics of hatred, particularly towards Jews, India and the USA. This is in line with Mayer's observation, that HTB's statements are fiery and deliberately provocative (2004: 13). It has accused previous governments in Bangladesh of being the tools of foreign imperialists and denounced the democratic system as a failure. It regularly seizes the opportunity presented by national crises to accuse the current government of collusion with India. Therefore, while the HTB may not directly engage in violence, it certainly encourages violence and creates confusion and suspicion about the intentions of its opponents by accusing them of being crypto Indians, Jews or Americans.

Third, HTB is attempting to instil a virtual monolithic transnational identity in the minds of young, educated people. It offers the romantic dream vision that HTB can lead the country into a 'new Golden Age', recapturing past Islamic glory. But this transnational Islamic identity has no cultural context. There is thus a conflict between HTB's goal of creating an identity based on religious faith, and the identity of most young citizens of Bangladesh. A language-based national identity is much more firmly established for the people of Bangladesh, who in fact rejected the religion-based nationalism of the Pakistani era (1947–71). Moreover, as Amartya Sen has pointed out, Bangladeshi national identity is complex and consists of many more important factors than religion:

> A Bangladeshi Muslim is not only Muslim but also a Bengali and a Bangladeshi, typically quite proud of Bengali language, literature, and music, not to mention the other identities he or she may have connected with class, gender, occupation, politics, aesthetics, taste, and so on. (2006: 15)

The election of December 2008 demonstrated the enduring strength of this language-based Bangladeshi identity: the voters rejected the pro-religious BNP-Jamaat coalition. HTB, however, remains outside that coalition, and continues to campaign for its transnational Muslim identity, which clashes with the Bangladeshi identity precisely over language and cultural factors: Bangladeshis speak Bengali (*Bangla*), not Arabic or Urdu (the two 'Islamic' languages), and their culture is quite different from those of the Arab countries, which are still the focal point for HTB's envisioned caliphate. Thus the attempt to supplant the dominant Bangladeshi national identity by a transnational Islamic one has the potential of being socially disruptive, both because of the entrenched nature of Bangladeshi national identity, and because of the intrinsically divisive character of revolutionary transnationalism.

Fourth, HTB's idea of sharia is also incompatible with the modern nation-state, as it does not (in theory) accept man-made law. Regarding HTB's positions on legal matters, one may note that it does not accept the idea of equal rights for women, and particularly where political office is concerned. Commins quotes al-Nabhani, the founder and chief ideologue of HT, to the effect that the HTB forbids women from holding ruling positions in the state, such as caliph (1991: 207). This would be a giant step backwards, considering that the head of the Bangladeshi state currently is a woman.

Fifth, HTB's rhetoric about jihad attracts supporters precisely through the notion of violent struggle implied by the term jihad, and ever popular among young people aspiring to be radicals, of whatever creed or nationality. As Roy points out, 'The Hizb ut-Tahrir ... believes that the time has not come for jihad, but that jihad is the compulsory duty for any individual Muslim' (2004: 256). Mayer's research supports this, and also shows that it is a view shared by al-Qaeda on the issue. In contrast, the dominant position among Muslim scholars is that only heads of states can declare jihad, and that it is a collective duty for which some professionals are appointed (Mayer 2004: 18). However, HT also differs from al-Qaeda, in that only when the caliph is restored as head of all Muslims will jihad be incumbent on all individuals, whereas al-Qaeda holds that jihad must be waged by every Muslim *in order to* resurrect the caliphate. Thus, HTB does not actively call for jihad but rather uses it as a 'carrot', promising that once the caliphate is in place jihad will indeed be launched against the enemies of Islam. Again, this message is socially divisive – because it calls for the abolishing of the existing nation state, and is preoccupied with identifying 'enemies' (of Islam).

The main conclusion from these five points is that HTB seeks to fulfil a romantic dream about the resurrected caliphate as the 'rule of God', and uses the younger generation to achieve this goal. As HT does in other countries, HTB specifically targets university students. In Bangladesh this has the additional advantage that university students play an important part in Bangladeshi government and politics. Moreover, these young people are Bangladesh's IT generation, mostly from the middle and upper-middle classes. Consequently, to have large numbers of IT-literate supporters appears to give HTB a strategic advantage when Bangladesh, as mentioned above, enters the digital age and computerises government agencies.

## Concluding analysis

The UNDP Human Development Report (1994) states that Human Security should be viewed in terms of threats and rights. The HTB website, *www.khilafat.org*, explicitly renounces 'violence, force and militancy'. However, its rejection of the secular political system and the nation state, its frequent and conspiratorial accusations of intervention by Western imperialists or Indian authorities, its claims that Islam is therefore in danger, and its views of women and religious minorities are all factors which threaten to engender social unrest in Bangladesh. Consequently, the HTB constitutes a threat to human security even though the organisation does not advocate violent methods.

By using IT and new media to market its Islam-based transnational identity and its programme to resurrect the caliphate, HTB has created a 'pseudo public sphere' where the threat is perpetuated. 'Pseudo' refers to the fact that this public sphere is limited to those who share the HTB's objectives, and thus it represents neither the nation as a whole nor differing opinions. This HTB 'pseudo public sphere' is now well-established, particularly in the private universities of Bangladesh. The risks of a pseudo public sphere are clear: no critical counter-arguments are heard, which makes it harder to see alternatives to the propagated ideology. Here the Bangladeshi national media have an important role to play – they should be able to challenge any and all campaigns of 'misinformation', whether this comes from the secular and Islamic parties or the HTB. If, however, the government fails to ensure the freedom of the media, no genuine public sphere can emerge, and no convincing counter-arguments to claims about international conspiracies against Islam and Bangladeshi Muslims can be heard. However, the government is aware that liberating the media and public debate will direct criticism towards its own policies and practices, and is therefore unwilling to make the necessary reforms. Still, reforms are the only way to defuse the popular discontent that also contributes to radicalising young people and to making messages such as those preached by HTB sound viable.

Consequently, even though fundamentalists such as HTB find shelter within a democratic civil society through the rights granted to all citizens and residents, such a society also presents fundamentalist movements with their greatest challenge: contestation. In a 'real' public sphere, other actors could freely challenge HTB and contest its pseudo public sphere. As Johan Galtung writes: 'A violent structure leaves marks not only on the human body but also on the mind and spirit' (1990: 4). A free public sphere will foster critical minds among the young IT generation of Bangladesh, and that is the best protection against militant visionaries such as HTB, as well as against bad national government. The recent ban against HTB does not, as such, solve these problems.

Post Script: As this article goes to press, there have been key developments in the struggle between secularists and Islamists in Bangladesh. In early February 2010 the Supreme Court of Bangladesh confirmed earlier court rulings that declared the 5th Amendment to the constitution to be illegal. The ruling sparked a violent reaction by Jamaat-i Islami and its student wing Islami Chatra Shibir. A Rajshahi University student, Faruk Hossain, was brutally killed and this was followed by clashes between the Bangladesh Chatra League (the student wing of the ruling Awami League) and Shibir that claimed more lives. Lawmakers from the Awami League then demanded the banning of both Jamaat and Shibir (The Daily Star, 11 Feb 2010). There has now been a crackdown on both: thousands of cases have been filed against Jamaat- and Shibir activists, and hundreds have been arrested. The court ruling may pave the way for the restoration of secularism and a ban on religion-based politics (The New Age, 3 February 2010) but this outcome is not certain. It could instead provoke the unification of all Islamic fronts in attempts to derail the government's ban against religion-based politics.

### Acknowledgements

The author gratefully acknowledges the editing support, encouragement and constructive criticism of Perry Whalley, Jennifer Bailey, Ulrika Mårtensson, Melinda MacDonald and Michael Miner.

### Notes

1. Organised by Ghulam Azam in December 2002, it is the largest and most active political party in Bangladesh. In the 2001 election it won 17 seats and became a part of the BNP-led coalition government, holding two ministries.

2. From a leaflet dated January 2004, available at *www.khilafat.org*.
3. Original title *Plikhana Hottakando: Bangladesher Protirokkha Babostha Dhongser Varotio Sarojontro*, trans. HTB.
4. Literally, 'limit' or 'restriction'. The word is often used in Islamic literature in describing the bounds of acceptable behaviour and the punishments for serious crimes. In Islamic law (sharia) *hudud* usually refers to the class of punishments fixed for certain crimes considered to be 'claims of God'.

# Bibliography

Ahsan, Zayadul (2005) 'Inside the militant Groups-7: profiles show them interlinked'. *Daily Star*, 28 August, p. 1.

Almond, Gabriel A., Emmanuel Sivan and R. Scott Appleby (1995) 'Fundamentalism: genus and species'. In Marty, Martin E. and R. Scott Appleby (eds.) *Fundamentalisms Comprehended*, Vol. 5 of Marty and Appleby (eds.) *The Fundamentalism Project*. Chicago: The University of Chicago Press, pp. 399–424.

Barkat, Abul (2007) 'Islamic militants in Bangladesh: an analysis on the basis of 30 case studies'. In Berger, Maurits S. and Abul Barkat (eds.) *Radical Islam and Development Aid in Bangladesh: Preliminary Study*. The Hague: The Clingendael Institute, Netherlands Institute for International Relations, pp. 23–32.

_____ (2006) 'Economics of Fundamentalism and the Growth of Political Islam in Bangladesh'. *Social Science Review*. Dhaka University Studies, Part-D, Vol. 23, No. 2, pp. 1–32.

Commins, David (1991) 'Taqi- Al-Din Al-Nabhani and the Islamic Liberation Party'. *The Muslim World*, Vol. LXXXI, Nos. 3–4, pp. 194–211.

Coady, C.A.J. (2008) *Morality and Political Violence*. Cambridge: Cambridge University Press.

Cole, Juan (2002) 'Fundamentalism in the contemporary U.S. Baha'i community'. *Review of Religious Research*, Vol. 43, No. 3, pp. 195–217.

Cronem, David G. (2005) 'Bangladeshi diaspora in the UK: some observations on socio-cultural dynamics, religious trends and transnational politics'. Paper presented at a Conference on Human Rights and Bangladesh, 17 June, SOAS, University of London.

Escobar, Pablo (2005) 'A very peaceful jihad'. *Index on Censorship*, Vol. 34, No. 1, pp. 164–9.

Ganguly, Sumit (2006) *The Rise of Islamist Militancy in Bangladesh*. Special Report No. 171 (August). Washington, DC: United States Institute of Peace.

Galtung, Johan (1990) 'Culture of violence'. *Journal of Peace Research*, Vol. 27, No. 3, pp. 291–305.

Guillaume, Alfred (1956) *Islam*. Harmondsworth:Penguin.

Government of the People's Republic of Bangladesh (1999) *Statistical Yearbook: Bangladesh 98*. Dacca: Bangladesh Bureau of Statistics.

Habermas, Jurgen, Sara Lennox and Frank Lennox (1974) 'The Public Sphere: An Encyclopedia Article [1964]'. *New German Critique*, Vol. 3, (Autumn,1974), p. 49.

Hibz ut-Tahrir, Bangladesh (2009) 'BDR massacre: Indian conspiracy to destroy Bangladesh defence forces' (*Plikhana Hottakando: Bangladesher Protirokkha Babostha Dhongser Varotio Sarojontro*), 2nd draft (23 March). Dhaka: HTB, pp. 1–18.

Hossain, Ishtiaq and Noore Alam Siddiquee (2004) 'Islam in Bangladesh politics: the role of Ghulam Azam of Jamaat-I-Islami'. *Inter-Asia Cultural Studies*, Vol. 5, No. 3, pp. 384–99.

Karlekar, Hiranmay (2005) *Bangladesh: the next Afghanistan?* New Delhi: Sage.

Majumder, Shantanu (2006) 'NGO-Donors Partnership and Decaying of the Traditional Civil Society: The Experience of Civil Society in the Post-Military Era'. *Identity, Culture & Politics: An Afro-Asian Dialogue*. Vol. 7, Nos. 1–2, pp. 150–58.

Marty, Martin E. and R. Scott Appleby (eds.) (1991–95) *The Fundamentalism Project*. Chicago: The University of Chicago Press.

Mayer, J. François (2004) *Hizb ut-Tahrir- The Next Al-Qaida, Really?* Programme for the Study of International Organisations, Occasional Paper No. 4/2004. Geneva: Graduate Institute of International Studies, pp. 1–24 .

Noorani, A.G. (2002) *Islam and Jihad: Prejudice versus Reality*. London and New York: Zed Books.

Rahman, Shafiq (2007) 'Hizb-ut-Tahrir does not believe in transfer of power through elections'. *The Probe*, 3 August, p.14

Roy, Olivier (2004) *Globalized Islam: The Search for a New Ummah*. London: Hurst.

Sadique, Mahfuz (2005) 'Islam's new face?' *The New Age*. Eid Special, 2 November, pp. 26–8.

Saeed, Abdullah (2006) *Islamic Thought: An Introduction*. New York: Routledge.

Samad, Saleem (1998) 'State of Minorities in Bangladesh: From Secular to Islamic Hegemony'. Paper presented at a conference on 'Regional Consultation on Minority Rights in South Asia', 20–2 August, Kathmandu, organised by South Asia Forum for Human Rights.

Sen, Amayrta (2006) *Identity and Violence: The Illusion of Destiny*. London: Allen Lane.

_____ (1999) *Development as Freedom*. New York: Oxford University Press.

Samir, K.D. (2008) '125 militant organisations active' (*125 Jongi Songothon Sokriyo*). *The Daily Shamokal*, 19 November, p. 1.

Sardar, Ziauddin (2006) 'The long history of violence behind Hizb ut-Tahrir'. *Daily Star*, January 28, p. 610.

Sobhan, Rehman (2002) *The Political Economy of the State and Market in Bangladesh*. Dhaka: Centre for Policy Dialogue.

Sullivan, Daniel P. (2007) 'Tinder, spark, oxygen and fuel: the mysterious rise of the Taliban'. *Journal of Peace Research*, Vol. 44, No. 1, pp. 93–108.

United Nations Development Programme (1994) *Human Development Report.* New York: Oxford University Press.

World Bank (2006) *Bangladesh: Country Assistance Strategy 2006–2009.* Washington, DC: World Bank.

Zakaria, Farid (1997) 'The rise of illiberal democracy'. *Foreign Affairs*, Vol.76,No.6 (November-December), pp. 22–43.

## Internet sources

*bdnews24.com* (2009) 'Hizb ut Tahrir banned in Bangladesh'. At *http://www. bdnews24.com/mhc/rb/ans/sh/zr/2330h*, 23 October, accessed 23 October 2009.

Freedom House (2008) At *http://www.freedomhouse.org/template.cfm?page=251&year= 2008*, accessed 29 June 2009.

Facebook (2009) 'Release the leaders and activists of Hizb ut-Tahrir immedi-ately', 16 March. At *http://www.facebook.com/s.php?q=hizb+ut+tahrir+&init=q &sid=950891e7aeddef90a8e8*, accessed 16 March 2009.

Google Videos (2009) at *http://video.google.com/videosearch?q=Philkhana+Massac re+%E2%80%93+Bangladesh+security+in+Danger&hl=en&emb=0&aq=f#*, 16 March, accessed 16 March 2009.

*Khilafah* (2009a) 'Feedback/Islam Richards, Venezuela'. At *http://www.khilafat. org/newPages/Feedback/feedback.php?pageNum_results= 2*, 16 March, accessed 16 March 2009.

*Khilafah* (2009b) 'The Bangladesh army massacre'. At *http://www.khilafah.eu/ kmag/article/the-bangladesh-army-massacre*, 26 June, accessed 26 June 2009.

*The New Age* (2010) '5th amendment to constitution illegal' At *http://www. newagebd.com/2010/feb/03/front.html#1*, 3 February, accessed 12 February 2010.

*The Daily Star* (2010) 'Ban politics of Jamaat, Shibir Demand AL lawmakers at JS' At *http://www.thedailystar.net/story.php?nid=125816*, 11 Feb 2010, accessed 14 February 2010.

# CHAPTER 9

# CYBER-BUDDHISM: FUNDAMENTALISM, THE INTERNET AND THE PUBLIC SPHERE IN THAILAND

## Soraj Hongladarom and Krisadawan Hongladarom

### Introduction

Buddhism is practised by over 90 per cent of the Thai population. It is so fully integrated into the fabric of the mainstream Thai culture that it is difficult for some Thais to realise that the religion in fact originated in India, and that the Buddha himself was originally a Nepali prince. This shows that Buddhism has long been co-opted by the Thais as part of their culture and their identity. The Buddhism practised by most Thais is in the *Theravada* tradition, but there are also pockets of practices in the *Mahayana* tradition among Thais of Chinese descent.

In this paper we look at the contemporary Buddhist scene in Thailand, focusing on how the new technology of the internet is being employed to propagate different versions of Buddhism and to facilitate intense discussions about the religion amongst the population. We treat the phenomenon of emerging online discourses about Buddhism in Thailand. The internet has even penetrated the arcane and tranquil world of Buddhism itself – religious or spiritual websites regularly spring up to serve the growing needs of the public. Some belong to established religious institutions, such as temples or Buddhist universities, while others are home-based and driven by their own members. Since the websites of the established institutions tend to be rather staid and uninteresting, it is the 'home-grown' ones that merit close attention. We contend that these websites can tell us a lot about the role of religious discourse in constructing knowledge and belief and in shaping contemporary Thai society and culture.

The topic of this chapter is the lengthy and acrimonious online debate about whether or not Buddhism should be officially recognised as the national religion. This debate took place over several months in 2007, when the new (and current) constitution was being deliberated. The discussion, taken up on many websites in Thailand around this time, is interesting because it shows clear 'fundamentalist' traces. It might seem rather odd that fundamentalism should have a place in Buddhism at all, especially since the media focus is almost exclusively on fundamentalism within Christianity and Islam. However, we will argue that fundamentalist ideas are alive and clearly discernable even within Buddhism itself. Commonly, fundamentalism is associated with religious zealots who often resort to violence to achieve their aims. On the face of it, this image is incongruous when associated with Buddhism, given the religion's core teachings on non-violence and compassion. However, as we shall show with respect to incidents in Thailand in 2007, fundamentalist behaviour can be attributed to Buddhism. During this period, certain Buddhist groups felt that their religion was being threatened by outside forces, against which, they believed, the government was failing to give Buddhism the support it deserved. They showed their discontent by protesting in significant numbers, in particular demanding that the Constitution Drafting Assembly recognise the importance of Buddhism by inserting a clause in the Constitution specifying that Buddhism was to be recognised as the national religion of Thailand. Their efforts failed in the end, since the majority of the members of the Constitution Drafting Assembly felt that to formalise Buddhism as the official national religion would do more harm than good. Nonetheless, these efforts, as well as the content of the debates that took place online, provide much insight into how Buddhism is faring in the contemporary globalised world. Furthermore, we shall also show that the Thai Buddhist group that is commonly associated with fundamentalism, namely the *Santi Asoke*, does not mix religion and politics in the way fundamentalists usually do. Thus the idea implicit in this paper is that fundamentalism has more to do with the merging of religion and politics than simply with the nature of religious beliefs and doctrine.

The website used as source material here is *larndham.net*, which has more than 11,000 members, many of whom are very active (exchanging two or three hundred messages a day). This site was formed by a group of practitioners who were formerly members of *www.pantip.com*, another very popular website which contains discussion forums on a large variety of topics. On the other hand, *larndham.net* focuses exclusively on discussions about Buddhism; it is the most visited and largest site about Buddhism in Thailand, among the hundreds that have sprung up in the country. We call this phenomenon of using the medium of the internet to communicate Buddhist teachings 'Cyber-Buddhism' (Taylor 1993).

The main online debates have revolved around the issue of whether a clause recognising Buddhism as the national religion of the Kingdom should be introduced in the Constitution. The proponents of such a clause tend to perceive Buddhism as threatened by a variety of outside forces and seek to have it protected by the Constitution. Their opponents, however, believe that such a legal measure would be unfair to other religions and would violate the principle of separation between church and state. The ferocity of those who argue for the inclusion of the clause may be seen as indicative of the emergence of what could be termed 'fundamentalist Buddhism', a phenomenon which is significantly different from the movements previously described as such by Keyes (1996) and Swearer (1991). In arguing for the existence of such a phenomenon, we will discuss the following questions: what do the online discourses and debates relating to Buddhism as the putative state religion tell us about fundamentalism, the state and religion? What theoretical principles could best illuminate the issue? What are the status and role of Buddhism in Thai society in the early

21st century? How is Cyber-Buddhism possible at all? And how is
Buddhism adapting itself so that its central message can reach the
public in the modern era?

## Fundamentalism and Buddhism

Since Buddhism is commonly associated with the principle of non-
violence, it is not often discussed in the context of fundamentalism.
The doctrinal emphasis on releasing oneself from the bondage of *sam-
sara* (reincarnation), as well as on the notion that the material world is
impermanent and insubstantial, means that Buddhists rarely attempt
to change that world on the basis of beliefs and doctrines. After all, the
main emphasis in Buddhism is on the mind of the practitioner, and
not so much on the world outside. Nonetheless, as we will see, there are
numerous scholars who consider many contemporary Buddhist movements to be 'fundamentalist' in one way or another. Perhaps the most
visible form of Buddhist fundamentalism can be found in Sri Lanka,
where there have been repeated calls for the recognition of Buddhism as
the national religion, and where it is used as a pretext for the preservation
of the perceived identity and cultural integrity of the majority Sinhalese,
as opposed to the Hindu Tamils (Bartholomeusz and de Silva 1998;
Berkwitz 2003). Bartholomeusz and de Silva describe this Buddhist-
Sinhala fundamentalism as a call for the preservation or (perhaps more
accurately) the continued dominance of the Sinhalese, as opposed to other
ethnic groups in Sri Lanka (1998: 8). What emerges from their study is
that Buddhism in Sri Lanka is linked to political power, since Sinhalese
politicians repeatedly evoke the religion to justify their activities. In this
context, Buddhist fundamentalism is understood as a strategy which
employs Buddhism as a means of realising political power within a context where an overwhelmingly Buddhist majority feel that they and their
religion are being threatened by outside forces. Here Bartholomeusz and
de Silva follow the lead of Marty and Appleby in defining fundamentalism as the creation of a boundary between 'us' (inside the religion) and
'them' (outside the religion), as well as linking religion with political
and ethnic identity (Marty and Appleby 1991–95; 2002; Tambiah 1992;
Riesebrodt 2000; Schalk, in volume one of this book).

However, Susantha Goonatilake sharply criticises those academics who argue that there are any fundamentalist traits in Buddhism (Goonatilake 2001). Goonatilake states that the Judaeo-Christian religions and Buddhism are vastly different in that the former rely on the revelation of God recorded in Holy Scriptures as the ultimate source of authority, while Buddhism (although maintaining a scriptural tradition of its own) lays much less emphasis on the literal interpretation of the text. This difference stems from these religions' differing attitudes toward the scriptures. In the Judaeo-Christian and Islamic traditions, the scriptures are believed to be the revealed words of God and are thus to be accorded great respect. The Buddhist scripture, on the other hand, is regarded as the teachings of the Buddha and his immediate disciples, but the Buddha is not a god and Buddhism typically allows for a wide range of interpretations, since the sole authority is a practitioner's own understanding and not any external source. Goonatilake then equates fundamentalism with any system that puts the primary emphasis on the text of the scripture as the revealed words of God – thus ruling out from the start any possibility of Buddhism being a fundamentalist religion.

Nonetheless, as the case of the Sinhalese Buddhist oppression of the Tamils in the name of Buddhism shows, we would argue that it is meaningful to maintain that there is fundamentalism even in Buddhism. For even though Buddhism rejects violence and segregation as a matter of principle, when people use Buddhism for their own purposes the original teaching can be distorted. In this context, fundamentalism must be understood not as a theological but as a sociological and political phenomenon, where religious teachings are used by a group of practitioners to gain political advantage, often at the expense of other groups.

There have also been a number of studies on the role of Buddhism in contemporary Thailand. Suwanna Satha-Anand reviews the major groupings of new Buddhist movements in Thailand that have arisen as a result of modernisation and as a response to the inadequacies of the traditional Buddhist establishment (Satha-Anand 1990). She mentions three major such movements, namely, *Buddhadasa Bhikkhu*, the *Dhammakaya* Temple and *Santi Asoke* (ibid). What these movements share is their divergence from the traditional Thai *sangha*, or monastic establishment, which has been a constant fixture in the Thai polity for centuries. These movements can be understood as responses, on the part of modern Thais, to the old-established form of the religion, as well as attempts by contemporary Buddhists to gain relevance (McCargo 2004). However, none of these three movements are, strictly speaking, fundamentalist. Even though *Santi Asoke* had some political clout in the early 1990s, thanks to its charismatic leader, Chamlong Srimuang (McCargo 1997), the group was not successful in using its political power to create divisions within Thai society, and failed to hold on to that power. The majority of Thais who do not belong to the group certainly feel that the members of *Santi Asoke* are different from them, and in fact the group is viewed with some suspicion, especially as it conflicts with the traditional *sangha* establishment. The situation cannot, moreover, be equated to the one in Sri Lanka, where political oppression of 'the other' is justified in the name of religion. The *Santi Asoke* movement never managed to gain total political power, and they failed to use the power they did have to create any form of division between Buddhists and non-Buddhists. We would thus argue that if we consider the *Santi Asoke* movement against the criteria provided by Marty and Appleby, it does not seem to qualify as a fundamentalist group.

This view is not shared by other scholars of Thai studies, however. Charles Keyes and Donald Swearer consider the movement to represent a form of religious fundamentalism in Thailand, on the basis that the movement clearly mixes religion and politics (Keyes 1996; Swearer 1991; see also Haynes, accessed 5 June 2009. Nonetheless, they also concede that this claim is difficult to uphold. According to Haynes:

> Reflecting the impact of modernisation, Thailand's new Buddhist movements are part of a global pattern of religious resurgence – a development which cannot wholly be correlated with country-specific patterns of socio-economic change and which, in some contexts, has seen the emergence of religious fundamentalist groups. (2009: 93–94)

This is related to the individual-centred nature of Buddhism. Given that the *Santi Asoke* hold on political power was in the end no more than partial, and more importantly, that they did not create divisions between Buddhists and non-Buddhists, it would be quite difficult to classify them as fundamentalists. Perhaps they could be conceived as fundamentalist in the weak sense of advocating a return to the 'fundamental principle' of living close to nature and rejecting consumerism. But since they do not advocate any divisive or identity politics, it would be more useful *not* to classify them as such, especially as there is a new group emerging in Thailand that clearly does seek to link Buddhism to nationalism, ethnicity and identity politics, in a way which recalls the situation in Sri Lanka. If there is anything resembling Buddhist fundamentalism in Thailand today, then it is this newly-emergent group that should be so characterised. Since the emergence of *Santi Asoke* roughly coincided with that of the online form of Buddhism, it would be useful to compare it to the online one, which we discuss in detail in the next section, in order to assess whether there is any correlation between them.

## Buddhism and the internet in Thailand

The internet first came to Thailand around 1991, when a group of academics at Prince of Songkhla University in the south of the country hooked up their network to the global network based in Australia; however, the connection was not a permanent one. Soon afterwards, in 1992, Chulalongkorn University created the first permanent, leased-line connection with the internet, and following this, the newly-established National Center for Electronics and Computer Technology Center (NECTEC) created another pipeline, assuming the function of the main national gateway to the internet. This period was closely followed by a boom in internet use, not only by academics but also, increasingly, by the growing middle class. Due to efforts by successive governments to bridge the digital divide between the urban middle class and rural villagers, more and more of the latter are using the connection, and there is a scheme in place to instal an 'e-village internet centre' in each village in the Kingdom in the near future.

It is not surprising, then, that Buddhism finds itself on the internet. In fact, there have already been many studies of the online emergence of religion, including several focusing on Asia. In the case of Singapore, Randy Kluver found that the more educated a user is, the more likely it is that he or she will use the Internet for religious purposes (Kluver, accessed 5 June 2009). Another study by Kluver and Cheong (2007) shows that Singaporeans fully embrace information technology in their daily lives, including their religious lives. Research on the online Buddhist community in Korea also found it to be very active (Kim 2005). As more people become familiar with the internet and use it in their daily lives, more and more websites devoted to Buddhism spring up. Given the nature of the internet, it is difficult to obtain an exact number of Buddhist websites in Thailand, but a directory compiled by *www.dhammajak.net*, a well-known Buddhist portal site, lists 197. *Sanook.com*, Thailand's largest and most popular web portal site, lists 477 websites directly related to Buddhism. In addition, there are 131 websites based in temples outside Thailand; 363 sites in Thai temples; and five centred on important religious holidays (*http://webindex.sanook. com/social_and_people/religion/bhuda/*, accessed 24 February 2008). This number does not, however, include blogs, a growing category of websites which allows for easy updating and a more personal style of writing.

Perhaps the most interesting of the Buddhist websites in Thailand is *larndham.net*, whose web pages provide a history of the website itself (*http://larndham.net/larndham/history.html*, accessed 24 February 2008), stating that it was founded in 1999, when a group of young Buddhist practitioners broke away from the religious section of *www.pantip.com*, a large web-based discussion site containing a large variety of topics, which was and still is among the most visited websites in Thailand. There was a doctrinal dispute between this protest group and the dominant group in the religious section of *pantip.com*, with the result that the dissident group split off and formed its own website. After setting this up, and trying several versions of the web discussion programs, the group finally settled on the *www.larndham.net* domain name. From its beginning as a closed forum for close- knit members, the site has now expanded into a forum for serious practitioners of Buddhism, and is still attracting new members on a daily basis.

The website itself is divided into several sections. Members can post a new topic or reply to previously posted topics; they can post private messages to other members; and they are provided with an amount of disc space to keep the messages. There is also a calendar where members can post announcements of events and activities. Other posts are about questions concerning the practice and understanding of Buddhism. What is quite remarkable is the degree of helpfulness that members show towards one another, and that the people who maintain and administer the site work very hard to ensure that it is kept free from advertisements and from the acrimonious disputes that often flare up in free discussion websites. It is not uncommon for posts to be censored or members to be rejected, which, surprisingly, is helpful in filtering out messages that are not consonant with the teachings of Buddhism. The administrators of the site, who are all close to the core group that founded it, work on a purely voluntary basis.

One characteristic of the website is that the administrators readily amend or reject posts which are deemed to be out of line with core Buddhist teachings. This is to ensure that those who enter the site receive 'genuine' answers, representing the 'true' teaching of the Buddha. However, this line of action is very controversial, with the administrators defending their stance by saying that those who would like to advocate other interpretations of the teachings can go elsewhere. This policy is specified in the rules for members, which are posted in the 'sticky post' section within the 'News & Announcements' area (*http://larndham.net/index.php?showtopic=23674*, accessed 24 February 2008). Basically the line of interpretation maintained by the administrators is in line with the traditional teachings of forest monks, whose lineage goes back to the highly-respected monks Luang Pu Sao Kantasilo and Luang Pu Man Purithattresp, who stayed in the forests of north-eastern Thailand and practised the *Dharma*, as opposed to those who 'merely' stayed in temples and studied Bhuddist texts (cf. Kamala Tiyavanich 1997). The rather authoritative stance of the website administrators can perhaps be explained by the history of the website itself, which originated as a protest against the dominant line of teaching propagated by the *Dhammakaya* movement and the

*Dhammakaya* Temple, which commands a very large following but is seen by many from outside the movement as a distortion of the Buddha's original teaching.

## The call for Buddhism to become Thailand's national religion

After the coup d'état on 19 September 2006, the ruling junta decreed that a new constitution should be drafted within one year of the promulgation of the temporary constitution. The task of drafting the new constitution, for consideration by the National Legislative Assembly, was given to the newly appointed Constitution Drafting Assembly. The plan was that there would be a general election and an elected government after the new constitution became law. It was during the first half of 2007 that the group of Buddhists mentioned above launched their campaign to demand that the Constitution Drafting Assembly add a clause to the new constitution specifying that Buddhism was to be recognised as the national religion of the Kingdom.

This campaign for Buddhism to be declared the national religion was not unprecedented; a similar effort was mounted in 1997, when the previous constitution was being considered. The protests on this earlier occasion were louder than in 2007, and although no real violence took place they were more aggressive in tone. Nonetheless, the second, more recent campaign gained more momentum because many Buddhists felt that their religion was under even greater threat, since the leader of the ruling junta, General Sonthi Boonyaratkalin, was a Muslim; and such feelings were deepened by the continuing unrest in the Muslim-dominated south of the country. As a result, the protesters saw a need for a formal legal provision that would recognise Buddhism's status and guarantee its support by the state. What distinguished this second protest was that a large number of Buddhist monks took part in the demonstrations, camping for many weeks in the grounds in front of the Parliament building, and effectively turning them into a temple – the monks carried on their monastic routines there, and some even went as far as fasting and sleeping inside a coffin, saying that they would keep on doing so until the clause was voted into the newly-drafted constitution.

In the end, however, the Constitution Drafting Assembly decided not to accept the draft motion to recognise Buddhism as the national religion, citing national unity and the need for tolerance towards all religions. Once this statement was released, the monks and their lay followers called off the demonstration, claiming that they respected the parliamentary vote; it appeared they were willing to suspend the campaign until the next round of drafting the constitution and of deliberating on it. However, as a concession to the protesting monks, another clause was added to the constitution guaranteeing support for Buddhism and all other religions in the kingdom.

What the campaigning group actually wanted was formal recognition of Buddhism as an integral part of the Thai state, and a statement to the effect that the state was legally bound to support, defend and protect Buddhism. Pathompong Poprasitthinand, a Buddhist scholar at the forefront of the campaign, argued that one of the main reasons why Buddhism needed to be officially proclaimed as the national religion was that there would then be a basis for instigating legal sanctions against monks who disobeyed the *Vinaya* rules or the monastic codes – laid down by the Buddha to regulate monks' behaviour (Bodhiprasiddhinand, accessed 10 December 2008). The campaign's demands included a clear call for the integration of specifically Buddhist laws and codes of behaviour into the constitution. Even though there has always been a clause in all previous constitutions specifying that the King is a Buddhist and a defender of all religions, this statement was not considered sufficient by the protesters.

Those who oppose the move to recognise Buddhism as the official national religion argue that this is already, *de facto*, the case, since the Thai (or Siamese) kingdom has always been Buddhist and the King has always performed all the important Buddhist rites on behalf of the entire nation. They therefore see no need to include a specific clause in the constitution. For the protesters, however, it was important for the state's relation with Buddhism to be formalised, especially since, in their opinion, many concessions had been made to the Muslim population while Buddhists' needs were simply set aside.

## Online debates

One of the most interesting aspects of the debate was the activities that took place online. The *larndham.net* site was very active where issues surrounding the constitution controversy was concerned. One discussion thread on the topic, entitled 'What Do You Think about Buddhism as the National Religion?' received as many as 479 posts between 12 February and 15 June 2007, when it was closed by the administrators (*http://larndham.net/index.php?showtopic=24724&st=0*, accessed 25 February 2008) A poll of respondents in this thread came up with the following result:

| Answers | Percentages |
|---|---|
| The constitution should recognise Buddhism as the national religion; meanwhile, all other religions should also be protected. | 53.11 |
| There is no need to put include the new clause, but the Sangha Act needs to be revised so that the King is given back his power to appoint a Supreme Patriarch. | 9.94 |
| The constitution should not specify any religion as the national religion, but the clause stating that the King is a Buddhist should be retained. | 17.70 |
| Anything goes, because whether or not Buddhism degenerates depends on its practitioners; constitutions will be torn up again anyway. | 18.63 |
| The clause should be put in, but indirectly, so as not to offend the other religions. | 0.62 |

It is clear from this vote that the majority of surfers who responded to the poll were in favour of including the clause recognising Buddhism as the national religion, and a similar outcome is also reflected in the content of the 479 posts – in which there were also attempts to mobilise people to join the demonstration in front of Parliament, as well as attacks on various personalities who disagreed with them.

The debate in the thread was between those who thought that Buddhism should be legally recognised and given official state support, and those who believed that Buddhism was a private matter, and that any support for Buddhists should come privately from the faithful rather than as a result of legal formalities. As an illustration of the debate, the following is a post by Dabaswanee, who was resolutely in favour of Buddhism being recognised as the state religion:

> Almost all other Buddhist countries in Asia say this [that Buddhism is their national religion], because there are facts about which percentage of the population professes which religion. Islamic countries have gone further, since they actually bar other religions [from proselytizing].
>
> We are not barring other religions; we are only defending ourselves. The clause has consequences for budgets and for the requirement of the content of the national curriculum, since the former Minister of Education [a Catholic] took the course on morality and Buddhism out of the national school curriculum.
>
> Today mosques are expanding all over the place; there is news that they [Muslims] want to marry Buddhists so that they can recruit more people. Please study the extinction of Buddhism in India. I am not being pessimistic, but I happened to get hold of some data.
>
> Thai people, including politicians and academics, do not know much about religions. They have copied the idea [of separation between Church and State] from America. But there are a lot of problems relating to ethnicity and religions there. Their culture is that of a 'melting pot'. So it is not possible for them to have a national religion because otherwise their people would fight with each other. (*http://larndham.net/index.php?showtopic=24724*, accessed 25 February 2008)

The writer of this post has many ideas in common with the Sri Lankan fundamentalists mentioned earlier in this chapter. She senses that Buddhism is under threat from other religions, such as Christianity and Islam, and feels that Buddhism should be recognised as the national religion so that the legal and political mechanisms of state can be harnessed to support it. This idea harks back to the ancient practice of those kings and emperors of Siam/Thailand who defended and propagated the Buddhist religion, just as Emperor Asoka did in India more than two millennia ago. Thailand is perhaps unique in Asia in that freedom of religion in one form or another has been practised for centuries. Christian missionaries have been relatively free to propagate their faith since they first arrived in the sixteenth century. There have been no religious wars between Buddhists and other religions in the kingdom. However, even though Christian missionaries were given the freedom to preach to Thai people, relatively few Thais, as a proportion of the population, actually converted to Christianity. So the question is, why did the participants of this discussion thread suddenly feel that Buddhism was being threatened and that there was now a need for legal protection and support for the religion? After all, Christians and Muslims were given freedom to practise their faiths, and such freedoms are a well-known hallmark of Thai culture.

Meanwhile, there were also dissenting voices in the thread. Representing the minority, another discussant, Tiberium115, feels that the constitution should not proclaim Buddhism as the state religion. He reasons as follows:

> I don't quite know what good it would do if Buddhism were promulgated as the national religion. I thought it would be a good thing because it would get more support. However, I fear that this support would be in vain and would be like giving royal titles to elephants or monks [this is a Thai idiom meaning giving things to those who have no need of them]. If this were indeed the case, then it would be no use at all. Actually I want Buddhism to be the religion within peoples' hearts. As for the nation, it can go either way because there are many other religions in our land. Many of those who profess other religions are benefiting the country too. Another thing – I suspect that if Buddhism were to be declared the national religion, some groups might take the opportunity to divide Thailand. (*http://larndham. net/index.php?showtopic=24724*, accessed 25 February 2008)

The demarcation line here is between those who want Buddhism to be officially sanctioned and those who fear that such an action would violate the principle of freedom of faith, and cause other religions to feel threatened. Voices such as Tiberium115's were in the minority, as the poll results above indicate. Many respondents in the thread felt that Buddhism was taken for granted and not given the official support it deserved. They compared the situation of Buddhism with that of Islam in Thailand, perceiving the latter to benefit from more official recognition and support. Many Buddhists considered that the establishment of an Islamic bank in Thailand, and the provision of prayer rooms for Muslims, but not Buddhists, in Thai airports, were grounds for arguing that Buddhism was being threatened and therefore needed official protection. They referred back to the time when the King was the defender and supporter of the religion, and felt that contemporary democracy called for the politicians and the constitution to take over that responsibility.

Another respondent in the thread, Pajjekabukkon, voiced the following view:

> We have conceded too much already. Nobody loves Buddhism as much as Buddhists. People of other religions also love their religion and try to propagate their faith. I used to talk with somebody who said that those who did not believe in God would go to hell. I asked if this applied also to the Buddha, and he said that according to this law it had to be that way. I hit him so much that his head fell backwards because he had insulted the Founder of my religion. How dare he say something like that. Today we are being taken advantage of by other religions too much. Beware. We will be taken over and dissolved. If I have to choose between praying to the Buddha and praying to Mecca five times a day, or going to church every Sunday, I won't choose the latter two at all. Believe me. No other religion is as broad-minded as ours. (*http://larndham.net/index.php?showtopic=24724*, accessed 25 February 2008)

The strong feelings expressed in the post result from the author's perception that Buddhism is being taken advantage of – and in this is similar to the calls by some Sri Lankan Buddhists for their religion to be defended against the forces of [colonialism and of non-Buddhist ethnic groups. This post, as well as the first one quoted above, exemplify a new movement emerging in Thailand, which aims at protecting Buddhism through *external* means. As has been pointed out, Thailand has always been open to all other religions, which are free to propagate and practise their faith in the Kingdom, as a Buddhist country. For this newly emerging group, however, matters have been taken too far – the liberal attitude of the previous Thai kings and regimes seems to them to have resulted in Buddhism itself being endangered; they consider it to be in a state of decline, and believe this situation has to be rectified. But instead of examining this decline from inside the workings of the Buddhist establishment or as an effect of the concrete and social expressions of Buddhism, they look towards the outside, as if seeking an external force on which to lay the blame.

## Buddhist fundamentalism and the public sphere

Previous studies of so-called 'fundamentalist' Buddhism in Thailand have typically focused their attention on the emergence of new movements, such as *Santi Asoke*, which criticises modernity and consumerism and aspires to an alternative way of life. This movement responds to the needs of the modern, urban middle classes, who are disillusioned with globalised economic competition and instead want to find a simpler and more tranquil way of living. For some scholars, *Santi Asoke's* temporary involvement in politics and the political career of its former leader, Major General Chamlong Srimuang, warranted labelling the movement fundamentalist. Like *Santi Asoke*, the *Dhammakaya* movement also responds to the needs of the middle classes, but it does so in a different way, by catering to the material desires of the populace rather than by seeking to avoid them. So whereas the *Santi Asoke* asks their followers to eschew consumerism, the *Dhammakaya*, in propagating its version, in effect incorporates consumerism and materialism in its teaching (Satha-Anand 1990).

The new and emerging group which has been calling for Buddhism to be proclaimed as the national religion differs considerably from *Santi Asoke* and the *Dhammakaya*. In the first instance, they represent a very conservative section of Thai Buddhism. One notable fact relating to the protests and demonstrations in front of the Thai Parliament in the first half of 2007 was that the *Santi Asoke* movement was not involved at all. This new campaigning movement was led exclusively by traditional establishment Buddhists. They had always been a privileged group, which enjoyed the extensive support and patronage of the royal family and of the traditional, bureaucracy-dominated political machine. More recently, however, the rapid democratisation of Thailand, which has now trickled down to village level, has led to the decline of this royal-patronage form of Buddhism. Another issue relevant to this whole controversy relates to the appointment of the 'Chairperson of the Group of Those Acting on Behalf of the Supreme Patriarch', a totally new position given to Somdej Phra Putthajarn, the second most senior monk in the Kingdom in terms of ecclesiastical rank, after that of the Supreme Patriarch himself. Since the latter is now over 95 years old and is barely able to talk, let alone rule over the more than 200,000 monks in the country, the Thaksin administration issued a decree appointing Somdej Phra Puttajarn – who at 81 years of age (in 2009) is still relatively 'young' – to act on behalf of the Supreme Patriarch. This created a huge controversy: several groups of the Supreme Patriarch's former students protested at the appointment, charging the Thaksin government with foul play (since traditionally it is the King who appoints the Supreme Patriarch). Those who challenged the government's decision to appoint Somdej Phra Puttajarn are closely related to the group who instigated the movement calling for Buddhism to be recognised as the national religion.

Thus this latter group was close to the traditional centre of power, and also to the current Supreme Patriarch, who was the King's personal attendant-teacher when he was ordained as a monk at Wat Bovornnives during the 1950s. What links the two groups together is their perception that Buddhism is being threatened by outside forces; they felt very strongly about the fact that the power to appoint a new Supreme Patriarch had been taken away from the King, and believed that the non-proclamation of Buddhism as the national religion would be an act of negligence that would endanger it. So when they call for Buddhism to be the national religion, they are simultaneously calling for a return to the King's traditional right to appoint the Supreme Patriarch, on the basis solely of his own judgement. The same people also refer to the traditional Thai political arrangement whereby the King both defends and provides material support for Buddhism. In 2007, sensing that this material support was slipping away as a result of the propagation of liberal ideas about freedom for all faiths, they protested by assembling in front of the Parliament. This group cannot be compared to the *Santi Asoke* movement, a group which has been marginalised, driven away from the centre of Thai Buddhism by the Sangha Council, the very epitome of the traditional Buddhist establishment. This time, however, it was the establishment itself that was feeling insecure, and needed to protect itself by means of the proposed clause in the draft constitution.

Thus it could be argued that the establishment is turning itself into a fundamentalist group, in the sense that it seeks to protect its interests in the context of social changes arising from globalisation. By campaigning for Buddhism to be the national religion, the demonstrators were in effect calling for the integration of *Sangha* and state, given that they planned to use the new clause and, by extension, the law, as grounds for punishing violations of Buddhism's internal code of conduct. This would not be so remarkable if the violations of the code were to constitute violations of a national law, such as the killing of another human being. But this is not the case, since acts such as consensual sexual relations between a monk and an adult woman, which are currently not illegal, would be considered as crimes under the new proposal.

## Conclusion

In the case of contemporary Thai Buddhism, we have seen how fundamentalism and democracy are connected to each other, and also how the public sphere, mediated by the new technology of the internet, has a role to play in these relations. We have seen how groups such as the *Santi Asoke* are succeeding despite the absence of any support from the political authorities, and how this has made the traditional Buddhist establishment feel insecure. According to Marty and Appleby, fundamentalism is understood as an attempt to divide 'us' from 'them' through shared traditions and beliefs. In the case of Thailand, this divisive attitude is a modern phenomenon arising from dissatisfaction with the contemporary economy and with globalisation, which appear threatening to the most conservative members of the *Sangha*. In this sense, it is ironic that the austere and anti-capitalist *Santi Asoke* is less fundamentalist than the traditional Buddhist establishment.

Perhaps all this actually depends on how we define fundamentalism. On the one hand, Keyes and Swearer view Buddhist fundamentalism as a reaction against the encroachment of Western values and of the globalised economy into Thailand, prompting Buddhists to react in a defensive manner. However, as the case of the call for Buddhism to be the national religion of Thailand shows, it is the group at the very core of the traditional source of power, the monarchy and the *Sangha* establishment, that has responded most vehemently to the impact of globalisation, organising protest movements to demand an increase of the state's level of support and for the strengthening of relations between Buddhism and the state. So if fundamentalism is related to the strengthening of ties between religion and state, then it can be said that the traditional establishment has become more fundamentalist. The increase in the number of websites and other online activities related to Buddhism bears witness to a real popularisation of Buddhism in Thailand, where Buddhists in general now appear to take matters into their own hands and no longer feel a need to depend on the *Sangha* order or even on the state for support in their religious activities. This seems to have alarmed the traditionalists and turned them into fundamentalists. Viewed from this perspective, and considering their demands for state law to incorporate Sangha regulations, Buddhist fundamentalism looks like an attempt to subvert not only the dissociation between state and religion but also the notion of liberal individual freedoms, at least as applied to monks and nuns. Thus they appear to be defending 'the fundamentals of Buddhism', that is, the *Sangha* rules.

## Bibliography

Bartholomeusz, Tessa J. and Chandra R. de Silva (eds.) (1998) *Buddhist Fundamentalism and Minority Identities in Sri Lanka.* Albany, NY: State University of New York Press.

Berkwitz, Stephen C. (2003) 'Recent trends in Sri Lankan Buddhism'. *Religion*, Vol. 33, No. 1, pp. 57–72.

Goonatilake, Susantha (2001) *Anthropologizing Sri Lanka: A Eurocentric Misadventure*. Bloomington, IN: Indiana University Press.

Keyes, Charles F. (1996) 'Buddhist economics and Buddhist fundamentalism in Burma and Thailand'. In Marty, Martin E. and R. Scott Appleby (eds.) *Fundamentalisms and the State: Remaking Politics, Economies, and Militance*. Chicago: The University of Chicago Press, pp. 367–410.

Kim, Mun-Cho (2005) 'Online Buddhist community: an alternative religious organization in the information age'. In Hojsgard, Morten T. and Margit Warburg (eds.) *Religion and Cyberspace*. Oxford: Routledge, pp. 139–48.

Kluver, Randolph and Pauline Hope Cheong (2007) 'Technological modernization, the internet, and religion in Singapore'. *Journal of Computer-Mediated Communication*, Vol. 12, No. 3, pp. 1122–42.

Marty, Martin E. and R. Scott Appleby (2002) 'Fundamentalism'. *Foreign Policy*, Vol. 128, pp. 16–22.

—— (1991–95) *The Fundamentalism Project*, five vols. Chicago: The University of Chicago Press.

McCargo, Duncan (2004) 'Buddhism, democracy and identity in Thailand'. *Democratization*, Vol. 11, No. 4, pp. 155–70.

—— (1997) *Chamlong Srimuang and the New Thai Politics*. London: Hurst.

Riesebrodt, Martin (2000) 'Fundamentalism and the resurgence of religion'. *Numen*, Vol. 47, No. 3, pp. 266–87.

Satha-Anand, Suwanna (1990) 'Religious movements in contemporary Thailand: Buddhist struggles for modern relevance'. *Asian Survey*, Vol. 30, No. 4, pp. 395–408.

Schalk, Peter (2011) 'Fundamentalism, ultimate truth, absolutism, inerrancy, and armed conflict in Sri Lanka'. In Mårtensson, Ulrika *et. al.* (eds.) *Fundamentalism in the Modern World. Volume 1: Fundamentalism, Politics and History: The State, Globalisation and Political Ideologies*. London: I.B.Tauris, pp. 53–74.

Swearer, Donald (1991) 'Fundamentalistic movements in Theravada Buddhism'. In Marty, Martin E. and R. Scott Appleby (eds.) *Fundamentalisms Observed*. Chicago: The University of Chicago Press, pp. 594–627.

Tambiah, Stanley (1992) *Buddhism Betrayed? Buddhism, Politics and Violence in Sri Lanka*. Chicago: The University of Chicago Press.

Taylor, Jim (1993) 'Cyber-Buddhism and changing urban space in Thailand'. *Space and Culture*, Vol. 6, No. 3, pp. 292–308.

Tiyavanich, Kamala (1997) *Forest Recollections: Wandering Monks in Twentieth-Century Thailand*. Honolulu, HI: University of Hawaii Press.

## Internet sources

Haynes, Jeff, at *http://www.law.emory.edu/ihr/worddocs/haynes5.doc*, accessed 5 June 2009.

Kluver, Randy, Benjamin H. Detenber, Lee Waipeng, Shahiraa Sahul Hameed, and Pauline Hope Cheong, at *http://www.ntu.edu.sg/sci/sirc/workingpapers/IR%20report%20–26%20Sept%202005.pdf*, accessed 5 June 2009.
Bodhiprasiddhinand, Pathompong, at *http://www.bodhinanda.com/index.php?tpid=0025*, accessed 10 November 2009.

# CHAPTER 10

# THE QUEST FOR ORTHODOXY AND TRADITION IN ISLAM: ḤANBALĪ RESPONSES TO SUFISM

## Gavin N. Picken

> Nowhere in the history of religion is the danger of interpretative generalization becoming reductionist or simplistic more acute than in the study of Islamic religion. No tradition, not even the Buddhist or Christian, has manifested itself in such widely varied geographical, historical, and cultural milieux with such diversity of particular manifestations and simultaneous continuity of generic social, religious, cultural, and political traits.[1]

Few could readily dispute the sentiments expressed by Graham in the above quotation, as Islam has indeed, despite its historical genesis and geographical spread, produced a 'unity in diversity' that is admirable. Nevertheless, there have been numerous tensions between particular trends, schools of thought and sectarian groups throughout Islam's history. In this regard, the very terms 'Ḥanbalism' and 'Sufism' are seemingly antagonistic, especially when examining contemporary Islamist discourse. This chapter therefore discusses how historical Ḥanbalī responses influence and shape this debate, with special reference to Wahhābism and in turn, how such attitudes define the relationship of this contemporary manifestation of 'fundamentalist' Islam and the seemingly more quietist yet activist Sufi tradition.

Despite such apparent disputes, perhaps one of the major contributory factors to the commonality found in Islam, alluded to by Graham above, is the preservation of a tradition perceived to be divinely inspired. Thus, it is the sacred texts of Islam – the Qur'ān and ḥadīth – that in many ways provide not only the 'foundation' but also the 'cement' for the notion of 'tradition' in Islam. One may select numerous textual examples from these sources to illustrate this point but here it will suffice to quote a single narration attributed to the Prophet. The text in question is a relatively popular one, deemed 'rigorously authenticated' (ṣaḥīḥ) by Muslim scholarship and commonly referred to as the 'Gabriel ḥadīth' (ḥadīth Jibrīl). It concerns the visit to the Prophet and his companions of a mysterious stranger who questions him regarding various facets of theological and religious life, namely practical religion (islām), faith (īmān) and what may be referred to as 'spiritual excellence' (iḥsān). The Prophet replies to these three questions by elaborating on 'the five pillars of Islam' in answer the question on islām, explicates the six basic creedal points of Islamic faith in reply to the question on īmān and goes on to define iḥsān: 'It is to worship God as though you see Him and while you cannot see Him He sees you' (Muslim 1998: 24–5). The Prophet goes on to explain that the mysterious stranger who posed these questions was none other than the angel of revelation, Gabriel (Jibrīl) who came with a pedagogical purpose: 'to teach you your religion' (ibid).

This narration, although brief in purport, was considered to be paradigmatic by some in classical Muslim scholarship, since it defines three major areas and consequently, creates a tripartite division of religious life.[2] The notion of islām was considered to be primarily concerned with praxis and hence it is suggested that the field of Islamic jurisprudence (fiqh) was developed as a discipline to study and regulate this practical aspect of religious life. Equally, the concept of īmān as referred to in the narration is said to underpin the development of Islam's theological tradition, manifested primarily in the form of creed ('aqīda) and later, with the more sophisticated articulation of scholastic theology ('ilm al-kalām). Having dealt with the religion's practical and theological facets, the narration continues with an elaboration of the religion's spiritual element and it is here that one of the problems seems to arise, as Islam's mystics – the Sufis – would make the claim that Sufism was developed as a discipline specifically to actualise *iḥsān*. As a consequence, it would be argued by many in later times that it is necessary for all practitioners of religion to follow a juristic school (*madhhab*), a specific methodology in theology and adopt a specific Sufi fraternity (*ṭarīqa*) to fulfil their spiritual purification. In contradistinction to this, another perspective would posit that the acquisition of *iḥsān* is achieved by the application of *islām* and *īmān* as described in the *ḥadīth* and hence would negate the necessity for a separate discipline such as Sufism, since 'spiritual excellence' may be achieved by merely 'practising Islam' in its every aspect.

Thus, despite the source text being accepted by all, its interpretation creates a dichotomy that becomes virtually impossible to reconcile. Moreover, the dispute over the interpretation of the *ḥadīth* may also be viewed as representative of the often antagonistic relationship between Ḥanbalism and Sufism. It would be disingenuous, however, to suggest that this relationship has always been so 'black and white' and there have in fact been a variety of Ḥanbalī responses to Sufism. This chapter will therefore attempt to explore the complex and often tendentious relationship between Ḥanbalism and Sufism. Prior to this, however, we need to examine the evolution of classical Ḥanbalism to see how the past continues to influence the present.

## Ibn Ḥanbal and classical Ḥanbalism

The term 'Ḥanbalism' originates with the personage of Aḥmad b. Ḥanbal (d. 241/855) who was representative of the traditionist trend that began to take precedence in Islamic learning from the beginning of the second/eighth century onwards. This trend was characterised by an erudite approach to the authentication of *ḥadīth* narrations, and the verification of their chains of transmission. Moreover, it was characterised by a strict and uncompromising outlook to both the interpretation and the application of such texts, that constituted the notion of 'Prophetic practice' (*sunna*) (Melchert 2006: 19–33).

In addition to this, however, Ibn Ḥanbal was a unique scholar in his own right, with his own specific approach. For example, with respect to the composition of books his strict traditionist nature comes through in the following quotation from Ibn al-Jawzī (d. 597/1201), who states that Ibn Ḥanbal said: 'Do not look at the books of Abū 'Ubayd, nor that which Isḥāq wrote, nor that of Sufyān, or al-Shāfi'ī, or Mālik; you yourself should go to the source ('alayka bi 'l-aṣl)' (Ibn al-Jawzī 1979: 249–50). Thus, even the opinions of the foremost scholars were to be discarded when compared to the scriptural sources and indeed, one should not even consult them but only refer to the primary texts. Similarly, this scripturalist attitude was not only applied to other scholars but also by Ibn Ḥanbal to himself, in the sense he would forbid that even his own statements be recorded (ibid: 251–2). In this vein, it is suggested that he did not write any original works of his own but rather – like many of his peers in the nascent traditionalist movement – only compiled ḥadīth. It is worthy of note, however, that his particular compendium of Prophetic narrations is one of the most voluminous, further indicating his commitment to the textual sources of Islam (Melchert 2005: 32–51; 2006: 33–48).

It is then quite surprising that, despite forbidding his own opinions to be recorded and confining himself to compilation, an entire legal methodology and consequent school of Islamic jurisprudence (mad-hhab) is also associated with him.[3] Since it seems that Ibn Ḥanbal left little more than a voluminous compilation of ḥadīth, it was left to his successors to formulate his jurisprudential worldview. In this regard both his sons, Ṣāliḥ (d. 266/880) and 'Abd Allāh (d. 290/903), are important; along with his faithful 'student' Abū Bakr al-Khallāl (d. 311/923), they are said to have compiled Ibn Ḥanbal's responses to jurisprudential questions, which are commonly referred to as the Masā'il (Melchert 1997a: 136–55; Al-Matroudi 2006a: 11–13). These textual references to Ibn Ḥanbal's juristic thought and methodology provide the basis for the development of a fully-fledged school which, although it would never attain the popular appeal of the other juristic schools, provided Islamic history with a number of luminaries, such as Ibn 'Aqīl (d. 488/1119), Ibn Qudāma al-Maqdisī (d. 620/1223) and Ibn

Rajab al-Ḥanbalī (d. 795/1392), among many others (Makdisi 1962: ix–xxvi; 1970: 88–96; 1997; al-Najdī 1996: 2, 474–6; Leder 1997: 279–304).

Another factor that requires consideration is the reverence that Ibn Ḥanbal enjoys within the Sunni hagiographical sources, due not only to his immense knowledge but also, because he was persecuted during the 'inquisition' (miḥna)[4] for his insistence on the belief that the Qurʾān was non-created.[5] Consequently, in addition to a jurisprudential connotation there also exists a theological inference to the term 'Ḥanbalism' and in fact Ibn Ḥanbal, due to his sacrifices in this regard, was referred to as the 'Imam of the Sunni community' (ahl al-sunna wa 'l-jamāʿa). This, no doubt, is a rank which Ibn Ḥanbal probably deserved, given his forbearance, patience and certitude during the tribulation that personally afflicted him but at the same time, his position has been somewhat exaggerated in consequent generations. This has led to what Cooperson terms 'the cult of sanctity' surrounding the personality of Ibn Ḥanbal in the hagiographical sources generally and specifically in those dealing with the Ḥanbalites (2000: 138–151). The essential notion that this posits is the idea that due to his closeness to the original sources and his application of them, as well as his experiences during the miḥna, Ibn Ḥanbal becomes almost 'untouchable' and 'infallible', so much so that the precedent he sets is considered to be the standard by which religious belief and practice is judged.

Perhaps the best samples of the exaggerated reports used to enhance the status given to Ibn Ḥanbal are manifested in Ibn al-Jawzī's Manāqib al-imām Aḥmad. For example, Ibn al-Jawzī relates a spurious narration regarding a man whose boat is damaged when travelling on the Indian Ocean; consequently, this individual encounters two people who inform him that he would be saved if he simply relayed the greeting of salām to Ibn Ḥanbal. The significance of this incident is further embellished by the first of these two individuals being the angel entrusted with the welfare of the oceans and the second being the prophet Elias (Ilyās) (Ibn al-Jawzī 1979: 186–7). Such fabrications are clearly hagiographic devices to further augment Ibn Ḥanbal's already considerable status and as such, almost place him in a position where his views are beyond reproach.

In a less esoteric but equally exaggerated account the Ḥanbalite biographer Ibn Abū Yaʿlā (d. 526/1132) relates in his *Ṭabaqāt al-Ḥanābila* that al-Shāfiʿī (d. 204/820) stated Ibn Ḥanbal was an imam in eight qualities: Prophetic narration (*al-ḥadīth*), jurisprudence (*al-fiqh*), language (*al-lugha*), the Qurʾān, poverty (*al-faqr*), abstinence (*al-zuhd*), scrupulousness (*al-waraʿ*) and Prophetic practice (*al-sunna*) (Al-Farrāʾ 1931: 3). Ibn Abū Yaʿlā then goes on to elucidate these various facets of Ibn Ḥanbal's personality but by far the most interesting for us here is his exposition of the last quality, 'imam concerning Prophetic practice (*al-sunna*)'. Not satisfied with al-Shāfiʿī's appraisal, Ibn Abū Yaʿlā then adds another eight qualities, which he claims were unique to the personality of Ibn Ḥanbal but in reality they are little more than a pastiche of the points raised by al-Shāfiʿī (ibid: 8–11).

Nevertheless, two of the issues raised by Ibn Abū Yaʿlā further illustrate the exaggerated status given to Ibn Ḥanbal and will therefore, be discussed briefly here. The first of these is the contention that the principles of faith (*al-uṣūl*) that Ibn Ḥanbal derived and believed in personally have reached the status of consensus (*al-ijmāʿ*). For example Ibn Abū Yaʿlā states: 'If anyone deviated from such a principle (*al-aṣl*) they would attribute disbelief to him, warn others regarding him and repudiate him, as all proof leads back to him [Ibn Ḥanbal]' (ibid: 8). In a later, related point Ibn Abū Yaʿlā also suggests that concerning the issue of innovators (*ahl al-bidʿa*), Ibn Ḥanbal's opinion regarding them is final, such that, 'If anyone manifested rejection of his [Ibn Ḥanbal's] view or wished to change one of his beliefs, then the attribution of disbelief to such a person is confirmed' (ibid: 9).

Thus, the image of Ibn Ḥanbal portrayed to us in the later tradition of Sunni hagiography – at least according to Ibn Abū Yaʿlā – is one of religious perfection, such that his opinions, beliefs and praxis are the criteria by which all issues in Islamic thought and law should be judged. Therefore, the very delicate issues of belief and disbelief are no longer to be judged according to the revelatory sources but rather to the faith and practice of Ibn Ḥanbal, given his physical and moral representation of the essence of Islam. Consequently, Ibn Ḥanbal appeared as a Sunni paragon of virtue and his views, whether related to theology, jurisprudence, morals or ethics, became paradigmatic.

Furthermore, what is also clear from the above discussion is that the term 'Ḥanbalism' proves quite difficult to define, as it is used to denote both the theological stances adopted by Ibn Ḥanbal and the jurisprudential school affiliated with him.[6] In addition, this is further complicated by the fact that the term is also used to infer an uncompromising and rigid position on religious matters and perhaps, a dogmatic and obdurate 'attitude' that accompanied it amongst his followers (Abū Zahra: 356–65; Laoust 1969: 158–62). This combination of characteristics, along with the exemplary personality of Ibn Ḥanbal, provided a complete model of early Sunni piety that was followed rigorously by a number of succeeding scholars. Therefore, although the initial affiliation with Ibn Ḥanbal and Ḥanbalism is jurisprudential, these later generations often emulated their forebear in each of the connotations that the term Ḥanbalism implies.

## Ḥanbalī responses to Sufism

Bearing in mind the 'mystical' and 'esoteric' nature of Sufism vis-à-vis the 'exoteric' and 'scripturalist' nature of Ḥanbalism, it is not surprising then that a number of later Ḥanbalīs – in terms either of jurisprudence or of theology – exhibited considerable anti-Sufi tendencies. There are numerous examples that one may quote but it will suffice here to mention the case of Abū 'l-Faraj 'Abd al-Raḥmān b. 'Alī Ibn al-Jawzī (d. 597/1201). Ibn al-Jawzī was a prolific author, who, as one might expect, wrote extensively on the traditional Islamic sciences but also authored works on a number of 'non-religious' subjects, indicating his sophistication of thought and his eloquence.[7] He put these skills to the service of jurisprudential Ḥanbalism and his allegiance to this juristic school is also well documented and is further witnessed by his dedicated biographical work concerning Ibn Ḥanbal – the *Manāqib* – quoted above (Ibn Rajab 1952: 1, 399–432).

Although we may be tempted to place Ibn al-Jawzī squarely in the corner of traditional Ḥanbalism, it is worthy of note that his theological views tended towards the more rational approach of Ash'arism and on occasion, even of Mu'tazilism, than representing the traditional views of Ibn Ḥanbal.[8] This egalitarian attitude towards theology was not, however, a courtesy that was extended to Sufism and he maintained an uncompromising stance towards what he considered Sufi innovations.[9] Although it has been suggested that Ibn al-Jawzī was exposed to Sufism in early life he seems to have rejected it in favour of a primordial asceticism much like that of the eponym of his school.[10]

This negative attitude towards Sufism is most tangible in his work *Talbīs Iblīs* ('the devil's deception'), which is dedicated to the discussion of how Satan has deceived various types of religious practitioners into adopting a variety of misguided beliefs and practices. More specifically, more than half the text of *Talbīs Iblīs* is devoted to a devastating attack on Sufism, critiquing not only its practices but also some of its major scholarly figures (Ibn al-Jawzī 1999: 166–398).[11] In addition Ibn al-Jawzī also produced an abridged version of the classic Sufi biographical work *Ḥilyat al-Awliyā* by Abū Nuʿaym al-Aṣfahānī (d. 430/1038). In the introduction to this version, entitled *Ṣifat al-Ṣafwa*, he elaborates ten points as to why he set out to shorten this voluminous work, suggesting that in addition simply to reducing its length, he undertook the task because much of what is related in the original is flawed in terms of transmission and because it contains much of the innovative practices of Sufis (Ibn al-Jawzī 2001: 1, 5–9). Furthermore, *Ṣifat al-Ṣafwa* was not the only classic Sufi text that Ibn al-Jawzī abridged: he also summarised the *Iḥyā Ulūm al-Dīn* of al-Ghazzālī (d. 505/1111), entitling it *Minhāj al-Qāṣidīn*. It is equally worthy of note that in the introduction to this text he again heavily criticises Sufism, referring to many Sufi practices as 'corruptions' (*mafāsid*), which he critiqued at length in his *Talbīs Iblīs* and which he makes further reference to in *Minhāj al-Qāṣidīn* (al-Maqdisī 1994: 14–15). Thus, although Ibn al-Jawzī only qualifies as a Ḥanbalī in jurisprudential terms, he displays an uncompromising attitude towards Sufism and in many respects is a quintessential Ḥanbalī anti-Sufi.[12]

Although one may confidently anticipate a negative response from many adherents of Ḥanbalism a much less expected phenomenon may be the fact that a number of Ḥanbalīs were also Sufis. In many respects, one of the most interesting personalities in this regard is Abū Ismaīl ʿAbd Allāh Anṣārī (d. 480/1088). Born in Herat in modern-day Afghanistan, Anṣārī displayed considerable talent as a child and grew into a precocious teenager who mastered many traditional fields of learning. Although originally an adherent of the Shāfiʿī school common to the region, he later changed his juristic affiliation to the Ḥanbalī school, which is illustrated by his play on words, 'The way of Aḥmad is the best of ways' (madhhab Aḥmad, aḥmad madhhab) (Ibn Rajab 1952: 1, 51). His association with Ḥanbalism was not merely jurisprudential, however, but also extended to the theological dogmatism exhibited by his forebear. This was demonstrated by his refutations of the rationalising trend in scholastic theology (ʿilm al-kalām) of both the Ashʿarites and Muʿtazilites, which caused him considerable consternation since the Ashʿarites in particular were very much in the ascendancy in the Eastern province of Khurasān during this period (Ibn Rajab 1952: 1, 50–68; Thackston 1979: 168–71; de Beaurecueil 1985: 13–31; 1988: 11–21; Farhadi 1996: 4–13; Knysh 2000: 136–7).[13]

Despite Anṣārī's commitment to both theological and jurispruden-tial Ḥanbalism, he was also very much dedicated to Sufism, which he learned from a number of masters but specifically and perhaps most surprisingly, under the tutelage of the 'ecstatic' mystic al-Kharaqānī (d. 481/1089) (Thackston 1979: 172; de Beaurecueil 1985: 18–20; 1988: 13–14; Farhadi 1996: 13–15; Knysh 2000: 136). This is also indi-cated by the fact that he authored a number of works, in both Arabic and Persian, devoted to a variety of mystical subjects. In Arabic he wrote primarily on the stages of the path to God, authoring the 'Illal al-Maqāmāt ('the defects of spiritual stations') and Manāzil al-Sāʾirīn ('resting places of the wayfarers'). This latter work is of particular inter-est, since although he treats many of the same subjects discussed in the 'spiritual state/station' (ḥāl/maqām) system of classical Sufism, he reinvents these notions using the term 'manzila' ('resting place') and provides a sophisticated interpretation of their sequence and realisa-tion (Thackston 1979: 174; de Beaurecueil 1985: 45–79; Farhadi 1996: 75–97; Knysh 2000: 137). In Persian, he supplied a Sufi biographical work in the same vein and with the same name (Ṭabaqāt al-Ṣūfiyya) as that of his predecessor Abū ʿAbd al-Raḥmān al-Sulamī (d. 412/1021) and provided another treatise on spiritual wayfaring similar to those already mentioned (Ṣad Maydān), as well as composing a series of inti-mate invocations of the divine (Munājāt) (Thackston 1979: 174–9;

Godlas 1985: 87 and 93–8; de Beaurecueil 1985: 40–5; Farhadi 1996: 43–72, 115–35; 1999: 1: 385–99; Knysh 2000: 138). Thus, although Anṣārī was heavily influenced by the exotericism of Ḥanbalism, this did not prevent him from exploring the mysteries of the esoteric world of Sufism and in this sense he becomes an exemplary practitioner of the paradigmatic concepts of *islām*, *īmān* and *iḥsān*, related in the Gabriel *ḥadīth* mentioned earlier.

In addition to Ḥanbalī Sufis and anti-Sufis a third category may be posited – Ḥanbalī reformers of Sufism, which is exemplified by figures such as Ibn Taymiyya (d. 728/1328). Many will be surprised by the inclusion of Ibn Taymiyya here since he is commonly associated with anti-Sufi trends within Islamic intellectual history but there is sufficient evidence to suggest that in fact he was not necessarily opposed to Sufism. Aḥmad b. ʿAbd al-Ḥalīm Ibn Taymiyya, was a native of Harran, in contemporary Turkey but later migrated to Damascus due to the unrelenting invasion of the Mongols. Born into a scholarly family he adopted the Ḥanbalī school of jurisprudence under the influence of his immediate relatives and in addition, mastered a variety of scholarly fields at a young age.[14] Maturing into a formidable scholar, Ibn Taymiyya utilised his considerable talents to critique and refute a number of disciplines common to the era, including philosophy and logic.[15] Like Anṣārī he continued this approach with theology and was highly critical of those advocating scholastic theology (*ʿilm al-kalām*) – in particular of the Ashʿarites, who were the most powerful theological faction in Damascus at the time.[16] Thus in addition to his adherence to Ḥanbalī jurisprudence, he was also faithful to the tradition of Ḥanbalī theology, writing a number of works on the subject, including the creedal treatises *al-ʿAqīda al-Ḥamawiyya* and *al-ʿAqīda al-Wāsiṭiyya*. It was this later association that was to dictate much of the remainder of this career, due to the fact that he was accused of anthropomorphism and as a consequence, was imprisoned at various times and in various places until his death (Little 1973: 311–37; Al-Matroudi 2006a: 13–30).

We have already seen that despite dedication to both jurisprudential and theological Ḥanbalism, scholars chose both the path of Sufism and its antithesis. In fact both positions are attributed to Ibn

Taymiyya. The vast majority view him as a Ḥanbalī anti-Sufi, in much the same vein as Ibn al-Jawzī, due to his considerable critique of certain Sufi practices. There is also, however, a minority view promoted by George Makdisi that Ibn Taymiyya was a Sufi disciple of the Qādirī fraternity (1974: 118–29). Although Makdisi's position is not easy to defend, the opposing view is also debatable and hence, I place Ibn Taymiyya in this third category – that of Ḥanbalī Sufi reformers.[17] I base this notion on his own writing on the subject since we have an excellent source in his fatwa on Sufism collected in the celebrated *Majmūʿat al-Fatāwā*.[18] The *fatwa* itself, like much of his writing, is well-structured and well-informed, displaying not only his own considerable knowledge of the subject but also the fact that he reached his conclusions entirely through personal endeavour. The fatwa commences – as one might expect – in response to a question on the nature of Sufism and the related term 'indigent' (*faqīr*). Ibn Taymiyya begins by giving an exposition of the etymology of the term 'Sufism' (*taṣawwuf*) and its historical origin. He concludes that the term is derived from the Arabic word '*ṣūf*, meaning 'wool', and was used to refer to a number of ascetics, in the southern Iraqi city of Basra, known for the wearing of wool. Ibn Taymiyya seems to dislike this 'wool-wearing', since he quotes early authorities denouncing this practice. He does not, however, necessarily dislike the practice of otherworldliness and renunciation that accompanies the wearing of wool, on condition that it is done sincerely for Allah's sake (Ibn Taymiyya 1998: 11, 5–6).

Ibn Taymiyya continues his juristically structured discussion of Sufism by turning his attention to technical definitions of Sufism provided by Sufis themselves. His selection seems significant, as he quotes some of the most articulate and eloquent examples of such statements, further indicating his familiarity with them. Perhaps more significant, however, is that he equates such meanings with the Qurʾānic laudatory epithet 'true believer' (*ṣiddīq*), which in Ibn Taymiyya's own words are, 'The best of people after the prophets' (ibid: 11, 9–10).[19] What is equally interesting is that when discussing Sufism Ibn Taymiyya describes Sufis as exercising independent opinion (*ijtihād*) to arrive at their teachings. By this Ibn Taymiyya seems to imply that the whole subject area under discussion is an issue of independent reasoning and personal judgement (*ijtihād*) and hence interpretation, which by its very nature is open to disputation that is not only permissible but which, to some extent, is to be anticipated. As such, the scholar capable of *ijtihād*, the *mujtahid*, is often regarded as the most elite scholar in Islamic learning who, even if he errs, is rewarded due to his elevated status as described in a Prophetic narration (al-Bukhārī 1999: 1264; Muslim 1998: 761).

Ibn Taymiyya notes, however, that the success of Sufis in expressing their *itjihād* varies considerably. In addition, due to the sensitive nature of the subject – it concerns the spiritual and mystical facet of religion – to err has extremely serious consequences and may lead to innovative practices or beliefs that are the real subject of his rejection. He gives a specific case of this in quoting the example of al-Ḥallāj (d. 309/922) noting at the same time that many of the major figures of Sufism also rejected him, including his own teacher and the eponym of the 'sober' school of Sufism in Baghdad, al-Junayd (d. 298/910). In quoting this example Ibn Taymiyya relies on the *Ṭabaqāt al-Ṣūfiyya* of al-Sulamī (d. 412/1021), which once again shows his familiarity with the tradition and that he studied it first-hand, rather than relying on the opinions of others. Ibn Taymiyya concludes his discussion of Sufism by describing the state of Islam's mystical dimension in his own era, by classifying Sufis into three categories: 'true Sufis' (*ṣūfiyyat al-ḥaqāʾiq*); 'worldly Sufis' (*ṣūfiyyat al-arzāq*) and 'superficial Sufis' (*ṣūfiyyat al-rasm*). Although Ibn Taymiyya clearly considers the last two categories in a pejorative light, it is interesting to note that he also concedes that there were Sufis who had truly experienced the realities of faith and by inference were successful in exercising their *ijtihād* (Ibn Taymiyya 1998: 10–11).

Thus we may deduce a number of issues from Ibn Taymiyya's own words: first, he studied Sufism from its own classical sources and drew his own independent and unique conclusions; secondly, he recognised that there were Sufis who not only exercised *ijtihād* but also did so successfully and as a consequence, reached the mystical and spiritual realities of faith; and finally, his rejection of certain aspects of Sufism, like his rejection of many other issues, was due to the fact he considered them innovative matters with no basis in religion. In conclusion, it is clear that Ibn Taymiyya did not reject Sufism outright but rather objected to certain practices and beliefs that he believed required rectifying and hence, we may consider him a Ḥanbalī reformer of Sufism.[20]

## Contemporary Ḥanbalism

Regardless of the debate surrounding its relationship with Sufism, Ḥanbalism remained the most marginalised of the extant juristic schools in terms of adherents, perhaps in some respects due to the multifarious inferences that accompany the term. This was of course until the advent of a religious movement in the Arabian Peninsula commonly referred to as 'Wahhābism'.[21] An 'ultra-orthodox' revivalist movement, Wahhābism is named after its founder Muḥammad b. ʿAbd al-Wahhāb (d. 1206/1792). Ibn ʿAbd al-Wahhāb was born in ʿUyayna in Najd and after extensive travelling for the purpose of study he defined his own articulation of Islam and its revival. He was a devout adherent of Ḥanbalism and is said to have been heavily influenced by Ibn Taymiyya.[22] Consequently, his teachings placed considerable emphasis on the correct understanding of divine unity (tawḥīd), on strict adherence to the Islamic Law (sharīʿa) and on the eradication of beliefs and actions considered, in a pejorative sense, as innovative (bidʿa). Thus he targeted practices such as celebrating the Prophet's birthday (mawlid), visiting graves/tombs (ziyāra), seeking the intercession of the pious (tawassul) and using rosaries (subḥa), which were not only part of popular religion but specifically identified with Sufism (Ende 1969: X, 39–47; Sirriyeh 1989: 123–32; Peskes 1999: 145–61; Algar 2002: 5–37; DeLong-Bas 2004: 14–40, 63–75, 83–91).

After varied success Ibn ʿAbd al-Wahhāb fortuitously gained the support of a tribal chieftain in the town of Dirʿiyya, Muḥammad b. Suʿūd, who supported his views and aided him in their propagation. From this point onward the fates of the ruling family and the scholarly elite were firmly intertwined, each gaining authority from the other.[23] Long after the death of Ibn ʿAbd al-Wahhāb and after considerable changes in fortunes, a descendant of Ibn Suʿūd, ʿAbd al-ʿAzīz

(r. 1932–53) took charge of a large part of the Arabian Peninsula by force of arms, establishing the state of Saudi Arabia in 1932. With the discovery, production and export of oil later in the same decade this provided huge state revenues, which to some extent were used to propagate the revivalist message of Wahhābism, providing the movement with a platform to spread its ideas and this in turn, has ensured its spread across the world (Ende 1969: X, 39–47; Farsy 1990: 12–22; Peskes 1999: 157–61; Algar 2002: 37–46).

The promulgation of Wahhābī Islam has used a multi-faceted approach. In terms of education, universities such as the International Islamic University in Medina and the Imam Muḥammad b. Suʿūd Islamic University have been established and particularly, in the case of the former institution, attract students from all over the globe. Moreover, seminaries (madāris), usually for the memorisation of the Qurʾān and Islamic centres (marākiz) have been heavily sponsored by the Saudi state in other countries. International organisations such as the World Assembly of Muslim Youth and the Muslim World League have also been set up, to provide yet further global links and in most cases, also supply a variety of free literature.[24] In addition, the establishment of the King Fahd Holy Quran Printing Complex in Medina has ensured that there is a copy of the Qurʾān (muṣḥaf) in virtually every Muslim home in the world. Moreover, the Qurʾān has been translated into numerous languages and in many cases, the translation is accompanied by the Arabic text (Algar 2002: 47–54).[25]

With the advent of a variety of contemporary technologies a number of further advances have been made. With regard to television, for example, satellite channels have been established, either within Saudi Arabia such as al-Majd,[26] or with funding from it, such as al-Resalah.[27] Although such channels are entirely in Arabic, they can still reach an enormous audience especially since they can also be viewed online and can thus, reach viewers all over global. Consequently, this 'religious' message – which would otherwise have been often subject to considerable state censorship – is able to transcend state boundaries and restrictions to reach an even larger audience.

In addition to broadcasting satellite-television channels, the internet of course has the more mundane function of hosting websites and the relative simplicity of maintaining a webpage makes them too innumerable to track. However, one such website will be mentioned here to illustrate the utility of the worldwide web in this regard: the website in question is *Islam QA*, hosted by the Saudi scholar Muḥammed Ṣāliḥ al-Munajjid.[28] This site is essentially a database of *fatwas* arranged according to a variety of categories and available in ten languages. The *fatwas* are not necessarily by Al-Munajjid himself, but are supervised by him.[29] In many cases, however, the sources are Saudi scholars, in particular the late mufti of Saudi Arabia, ʿAbd al-ʿAzīz b. Bāz (d. 1420/1999) and another of the major Saudi scholars of his generation, Muḥammad Ṣāliḥ al-ʿUthaymīn (d. 1421/2001). Perhaps the most commonly quoted source, however, is the 'Permanent Council for Research and Fatwa' (*al-Lajna al-Dāʾima li 'l-Buḥūth wa 'l-Iftā*), which is one of the state bodies charged with issuing legal rulings and consisting of the leading jurists in the country.[30]

Thus we can conclude that despite the fact that both the jurisprudential and theological implications of Ḥanbalism originated over a millennium ago, in the person of Aḥmad b. Ḥanbal, they are also still well represented in the twenty-first century, via a variety of media and albeit under the guise of state-sponsored Wahhābism.

## Conclusion

As we saw in the quotation at the head of this chapter, Graham quite rightly celebrates the 'unity in diversity' of the Muslim community but it is also telling that he astutely observes:

> It is a truism to say that there is no single entity called 'Islam', only the various 'Islams' of local contexts: to speak of Islamic society or civilization is to speak of myriad local or regional traditions of sharply differing forms and often rapidly changing historical circumstances.[31]

It was also observed that despite there being a canon of 'sacred' material that underpins religious life, it is often the interpretation of this material that becomes paramount in deciding the course of 'tradition' and 'orthodoxy'. For example, another paradigmatic theological concept provided by a number of Prophetic narrations is the idea of the 'saved sect' (*al-firqa al-nājiya*). In these narrations, which according to Muslim scholars vary considerably in authenticity, the Prophet informs that the Muslim community will be divided into 73 sects and that only one of these will be saved.[32] Although the majority consider this to be the main body of the Muslim community, others have claimed that deliverance was to found only among their ranks. Thus, a variety of 'fundamentalist' doctrinal positions have resulted, since such groups protest the absolutism and inerrancy of their position, being lured by the 'Seductiveness of Certainty'.[33] Basing their stance heavily on scriptural authority and with little attention paid to interpretation, such groups claim salvation can only be achieved by their particular method of religious praxis. Thus, it is they and they alone, who are the guardians of religious 'purity', defending 'orthodoxy' and 'tradition' from the dangers of 'heresy' and 'innovation'.

Furthermore, the memory of colonialism and the experience of modernity have seemingly put pressure on some Muslims, who feel a need to identify openly with a specific form of religious practice and hence, in many cases, to reject others. This is not merely an 'assertion of identity' but also a definitive mind-set. Moreover, for the practitioner of faith, his/her fate in the hereafter is also at stake and so the need to identify with the 'correct' position is a compelling one. Such polarised perspectives naturally lead to a polemical relationship with other co-religionists and the current tendentious relationship between Ḥanbalism and Sufism would seem representative of this trend.

From its inception, theological Ḥanbalism has had an authoritarian flavour, which often rejected competing interpretations and its contemporary manifestation – Wahhābism – has continued this trend with its pursuit of a 'correct' creed (*al-ʿaqida al-saḥīḥa*). Thus, if we were to apply the tri-partite division suggested by the Gabriel *hadīth* to this perspective, we would find in fact that there are only two components – rigorous theology and strict jurisprudence, which in combination deliver the third component of *iḥsān*. Therefore, the recognition of a distinctive third facet would be deemed entirely extraneous, since the spiritual dimension is achieved by the actualisation of its binary prerequisites. Consequently, the development of Sufism as this third part of the paradigm would be an unnecessary addition to a model already deemed complete and pristine. Although Ḥanbalīs have had different perspectives on Sufism, the advent of Wahhābism with its particular anti-Sufi flavour and the revival of a 'primordial Ḥanbalism', suggest that the existence of Ḥanbalī Sufis such as ʿAbd Allāh Anṣārī are most definitely a thing of the past.

Indeed, what is fascinating to observe is that these centuries-old debates do not take place only in traditional Muslim lands of the Orient but rather also in the liberal democracies of the Occident. The migration of Muslims from their homelands throughout the twentieth century brought not only a new 'faith community' to these Western societies but also the diverse sectarian views identified with traditional Muslim countries. This, combined with the personal freedoms normally enjoyed in the West, allowed a public space for the articulation of these multifarious doctrinal positions. Moreover, with the passage of time the usual channels for such views have been augmented – the traditional public lectures and publication of literature have been joined by the World Wide Web, internet chat-rooms, MP3/4 recordings, podcasts, You Tube and satellite television. Thus, competing Islamic discourses and their historical contexts are 'relived' in the modern era and are articulated via the most advanced technology, not only to influence the global public sphere but also, to promulgate various competing notions of 'orthodoxy' and 'tradition'.

## Notes

1. Graham 1993: 495.
2. It is interesting to note that Chittick and Murata also adopted this model in their *Vision of Islam* (Chittick and Murata 1994: xxv–xxxix).
3. For a detailed discussion of Ibn Ḥanbal's juristic school see Laoust 1969: 158–62; Makdisi 1981: 216–74; Melchert 1997a: 137–55; 2006: 59–81; Hurvitz 2000: 37–64; 2002: 73–112; Al-Matroudi 2006a: 4–191; 2006b: 203–60).

4. For a detailed discussion of this religio-political event see Patton 1897: 1–194; Hinds 1996: 232–45; Nawas 1994: 615–29; 1996: 698–708; Cooperson 2000: 33–40, 117–38; Hurvitz 2001: 93–111; 2002: 115–57).

5. Ibn Ḥanbal's uncompromising attitude in religious matters did not only cause him to fall into dispute with the ruling authorities but also caused friction with his scholarly contemporaries (Melchert 1997b: 234–53: Picken 2008: 337–61).

6. With regard to theology, Ibn Ḥanbal's dogmatism and scripturalism on points of creed are so pronounced that they were often perceived to verge on corporealism and anthropomorphism (Williams 2002: 441–63).

7. Although estimates vary, it is often suggested that the number of works he composed was in the hundreds. It is not just the sheer volume, however, that is impressive but also Ibn al-Jawzī's 'Jāḥiẓesque' quality of writing literary treatises on opposing themes, examples of which would be his *Akhbār al-Ḥamqā᾽ wa'l-Mughaffalīn* and the *Kitāb al-Adhkiyā᾽*. Despite demonstrating considerable admiration, al-Dhahabī comments in his *Tadhkirat al-Ḥuffāẓ* that Ibn al-Jawzī is the most prolific author that he encountered, but also observes, however, that Ibn al-Jawzī's writing also displays numerous contradictions, which al-Dhahabī's suggests is due to his lack of revision of his writing and the fact that he would often write a number of texts simultaneously. Thus, both the volume of the material and the contradictions within them make Ibn al-Jawzī a particularly difficult scholar to assess (al-Dhahabī 1998: 4, 92–6; Swartz 1971: 36–7; 2002: 30–1; and cf. Ibn Rajab 1952: 1, 399–432).

8. Swartz suggests that Ibn al-Jawzī was influenced by a variety of theologians but was especially affected by the writings of his Ḥanbalī predecessor Ibn ῾Aqīl (d. 488/1119), who, despite being dedicated to the pursuit of scholastic theology for a considerable period, distanced himself from this position in later life. This was not the case with Ibn al-Jawzī, however, who it seems remained committed to the 'reformation' of Ḥanbalism towards a more 'rational' theology, which in turn raised the ire of his fellow Ḥanbalites, who did not hesitate in castigating him and refuting his views (Swartz 1971: 34; 2002: 20–7, 46–7 (nn. 3–4), 62–4, and cf. Makdisi 1997: 28–43).

9. Makdisi attempts to argue that Ibn al-Jawzī was not necessarily a Ḥanbalī anti-Sufi but was merely averse to certain Sufi practices, as was his later Ḥanbalī colleague Ibn Taymiyya (Makdisi 1979: 120–5). Consequently, he would qualify as a Ḥanbalī reformer of Sufism according to our categorisation here. As I have mentioned, however, on examining the quantity, content and nature of Ibn al-Jawzī's critique in his *Talbīs Iblīs*, this is a particularly difficult position to maintain. In addition, Makdisi claims that because Ibn al-Jawzī wrote biographies of many proto-Sufi personalities he was not

necessarily an opponent of Sufism (ibid: 124–5). One may comment, however, that the vast majority of these personalities – perhaps with the exception of Rābiʿa al-ʿAdawiyya – were representative of the ascetic trend in the early period, with which Ḥanbalism had little problem as Ibn Ḥanbal himself was well known for acts of otherworldliness and renunciation. One may even argue that Ibn al-Jawzī wrote such biographies to counter Sufi claims to the spiritual dimensions of Islam and in this regard it is telling that Makdisi does not see the need to distinguish between the terms 'Sufi' and 'ascetic' (ibid: 117). Perhaps the most significant indictment of Ibn al-Jawzī's anti-Sufi tendency is his refutation of his Ḥanbalī contemporary ʿAbd al-Qādir al-Jīlānī – a fact that Makdisi merely glosses over (ibid: 124–5; 1981: 242).

10. Swartz's assertion that Ibn al-Jawzī was a dedicated ascetic rather than a committed Sufi appears equally problematic. If the goal of asceticism is the inculcation of 'otherworldliness' then Ibn al-Jawzī may have been dedicated to it as an ideal but in reality it seems to have had little effect on him since, by Swartz's own admission, Ibn al-Jawzī was prone to conceit, tendentiousness and antagonism (Swartz 2002: 27–32). Moreover, seemingly following Makdisi, Swartz does not distinguish sufficiently between asceticism and Sufism and the transition that takes place from a rudimentary asceticism in the post-Prophetic period to a nascent mysticism sometime in the mid-third/ninth century (Swartz 1971: 23–5; 2002: 27–32; and cf. Melchert 1996: 51–70). In addition, following Makdisi again, Swartz supports the notion that Ibn al-Jawzī was not necessarily opposed to Sufism, but rather merely wished to rid it of its innovative excesses. To this end he suggests the evidence that Makdisi provides is 'unequivocal' and adds to this that his son was endowed with a Sufi patched cloak (al-khirqa) by his close confidant Ibn Sukayna (Swartz 2002: 14–16, 29). It is worthy of note, however, that the Sufi khirqa has various categories, such as 'the cloak of aspiration' (khirqat al-irāda), 'the cloak of blessing' (khirqat al-tabarruk) and 'the cloak of succession' (khirqat al-khilāfa) (Ernst 1997: 143–5). Therefore, the gift of a Sufi patched cloak, especially from a close friend, is not necessarily indicative of commitment, which was certainly the case with Ibn al-Jawzī's son. Thus it would seem that the evidence is not as 'unequivocal' as Swartz suggests.

11. Once again Swartz merely glosses over the anti-Sufi nature of Talbīs Iblīs. In addition to describing Sufism as 'unique' and 'innovative', Ibn al-Jawzī also asserts that the origin of the term derives from a pre-Islamic tribe known for their asceticism in Mecca. This not only clearly places Sufism in a negative light but is also a view that Ibn Taymiyya categorically rejects. Ibn al-Jawzī does show minimal admiration for certain early proto-Sufi figures but again this is only really in terms of their ascetical ideals rather than their mystical

articulations. On the contrary, when the discussion turns to the mystical aspects of their teachings, Ibn al-Jawzī's critique begins in earnest. Quite significantly he focuses his attention on the major authors of the Sufi apologetic works, such as Abū Naṣr al-Sarrāj (d. 378/988), Abū Ṭālib al-Makkī (d. 386/996), Abū 'Abd al-Raḥmān al-Sulamī (d. 412/1021), Abū Nu'aym al-Aṣfahānī (d. 430/1038) and Abū al-Qāsim al-Qushayrī (d. 465/1074). Ibn al-Jawzī's aim seems clear: he is attempting to undermine Sufism's claim to 'orthodoxy' by discrediting the very works that are Sufism's most articulate response to anti-Sufi critique (Swartz 1971: 25; 2002: 15–16; Ibn al-Jawzī 1999: 166–74).

12. This conclusion is based on the discussions presented primarily in these notes but one may add here two further observations: first, Ibn al-Jawzī's anti-Sufism, in addition to being exceedingly direct on most occasions, could be extremely subtle and nuanced on others. This may be illustrated by his continual mention – in negative contexts – of major figures associated with Sufism, such as al-Muḥāsibī (d. 243/857), al-Junayd (d. 297/910), al-Makkī and al-Ghazzālī (d. 505/1111). Since these personalities are not only seen as major figures within Sufism but are often held in high regard outside Sufi circles, in many ways they represent the 'acceptable' face of Sufism. Moreover, their 'sober' and pietistic articulations of Islamic spirituality and mysticism are often viewed as Sufism's major claim to a place within the realms of traditional 'orthodoxy' and so to attack their professionalism and understanding as Muslim scholars completely undermines the credibility of any such claim. Quite paradoxically, Ibn al-Jawzī does not hesitate to include the same figures in his works, seemingly as illustrations of renunciation and otherworldliness and thus, utilises them in the construction of an ascetic ideal, while at the same time rejecting any semblance of practices that he deemed 'unorthodox.'

Secondly, the difference between the anti-Sufism of Ibn al-Jawzī and the reformatory character of the approach adopted by Ibn Taymiyya may be illustrated by the way in which both scholars approach the issue of the sincerity of certain individuals who would faint or be otherwise overcome on hearing the an emotive passage of the Qur'ān that, for example, mentions the events of the hereafter. Ibn al-Jawzī completely rejects this kind of behaviour, which was associated with Sufism in the formative period and quotes the censure of this practice by the early authority Muḥammad b. Sīrīn (d. 110/728) and further supplements this view with the opinions of his 'mentor' Ibn 'Aqīl (Ibn al-Jawzī 1971: 96–7). Ibn Taymiyya, on the other hand, while discussing the very same issue, not only exhibits a more extensive knowledge of the topic but also a difference in approach: he quotes exactly the same statement made by Ibn Sīrīn but introduces a considerably more nuanced argument, even claiming that Ibn Ḥanbal was also be susceptible to this type of experience, and suggesting that, when sincere, such behaviour is entirely acceptable (Ibn Taymiyya 1998: 11, 5–6). Thus, Ibn Taymiyya differentiates between actions that are merely associated with Sufism and hence are held to be reprehensible by certain sections of the scholarly community, like Ibn al-Jawzī and the value of such actions in the context of Islamic law as a whole.

13. His dogmatic affiliation to Ḥanbalism is illustrated in samples of poetry that he composed; he states for example, while refuting the scholastic theologians: 'Our God is seen and rises above the throne; His speech is eternal and His prophet is an Arab; anyone who states other than this is an Ashʿarite; our way is the Ḥanbalī way.' On another occasion, he exhorts his peers to join him, saying: 'I am a Ḥanbalī as long as I live and if I were to die then my last will and testament to people would be that they be Ḥanbalī too' (Ibn Rajab 1952: 1, 52–3).

14. Whether Ibn Taymiyya remained a Ḥanbalī jurisconsult all his life is debatable since many consider him to have transcended this association and to have became an entirely independent jurist (mujtahid) (Al-Matroudi 2006a: 50–5).

15. See for example (Hallaq 1993: xi–lii).

16. For an exposition of Ibn Taymiyya's views on this, see Makdisi 1981: 256–62.

17. Makdisi's position is difficult to defend because he bases his opinion primarily on the notion that Ibn Taymiyya is mentioned in an initiatic chain of transmission (al-silsila) provided for the wearing of a Sufi patched cloak (al-khirqa) (Makdisi 1974: 118–29; 1979: 120–3; 1981: 249–50). Although Makdisi goes to great lengths in attempting to corroborate this evidence, he rarely discusses Ibn Taymiyya's actual views on Sufism as represented in his extant works, and when does do so he seems to base his views on the findings of Laoust (ibid: 128–9). Ibn Taymiyya's own writings on Sufism are clearly far more informative than circumstantial evidence from secondary sources and hence it is a discussion of Ibn Taymiyya's actual fatwa on Sufism that is provided here. In addition, there are two main criticisms of Makdisi's perspective that may be posited: first, he relies entirely on sources dedicated to the subject being discussed. Therefore it is not really surprising that Ibn Taymiyya, or anyone else for that matter, is mentioned in a chain for the wearing of a Sufi patched cloak, when the likely purpose of such texts is to prove the 'orthodoxy' of such practices and hence the mention of a number of renowned Ḥanbalī jurists would certainly fulfil this task. Secondly, even

if we were to accept that Ibn Taymiyya accepted such a symbolic garment, one may suggest that if any cloak was bestowed on Ibn Taymiyya it would have been this second type mentioned above (note 10), since it is done purely for the acquisition of divine blessing (*baraka*) and does not necessarily indicate commitment (cf. van Ess 1999: 30–1). Similar comments may be put forward with respect to Makdisi's assertion that Ibn Qudāma was also a committed Sufi (Makdisi 1970; 88–96; 1974: 123–6; 1979: 118–19, 122; 1981: 250). Ibn Qudāma's lack of Sufi credentials is further substantiated by the fact that he summarises the sanitised version of the al-Ghazzālī's *Iḥyā' 'Ulūm al-Dīn*, entitling it *Mukhtaṣar Minhāj al-Qāṣidīn*, clearly indicating his approval of the 'cleansing' of the text by Ibn al-Jawzī of inauthentic traditions and Sufi anomalies.

18. Homerin has provided an effective translation and commentary on the fatwa (1985: 219–44).

19. This, quite significantly, was also a laudatory epithet bestowed upon none other than Abū Bakr (d. 13/634), the Prophet's closest companion and the first caliph in the post-Prophetic era.

20. I would equally consider his student Ibn al-Qayyim al-Jawziyya (d. 751/1350) in the same vein, since although he did not accept certain beliefs and practices within Sufism, he also wrote an eloquent exposition of Anṣārī's *Manāzil al-Sā'irīn* entitled *Madārij al-Sālikīn*, adding his own corrective glosses on the traditional Sufi text of his Ḥanbalī forebear.

21. I prefer to refer to Wahhābism as a 'religious movement' rather than a 'sect' as some writers do, since it is essentially a revivalist interpretation of Islamic sources that has not necessarily produced new beliefs or practices but rather has revived a form of piety that is considered 'pristine' and 'unadulterated'. In this sense, it represents a form of 'Ḥanbalism' in every sense of the word.

22. Having examined the fatwa above, however, Ibn 'Abd al-'Wahhāb seems to have been selective in his application of Ibn Taymiyya's views, especially with regard to Sufism.

23. For the role of Ḥanbalism, Wahhābism and the scholarly elite (*al-'ulamā'*) in Saudi Arabia, see Bligh 1985: 37–50; Kechichian 1986: 53–71; Layish 1987: 279–92; Sedgwick 1997: 349–68.

24. In many cases these are often translations of the works of Ibn'Abd al-Wahhāb or works by the State mufti, which in most cases relate to some fundamental creedal point or other.

25. I am not suggesting for a moment here that there is such a thing as a 'Wahhābī Qur'ān', but rather that the free distribution of printed copies of the Qur'ān, combined with the fact that Saudi Arabia is home to the two holiest places in the Muslim world and hence the venue of pilgrimages, gives

the country considerable kudos for the average practitioner of religion. The doctrinal aspect of Wahhābī proselytising is tangible in the accompanying translations: to take the English version, for example, there is an appendix included with the volume that deals almost exclusively with Islamic mono-theism (*tawḥīd*) and its antithesis – polytheistic association with the divine (*shirk*) (al-Hilali and Khan 1417 A.H.: 891–913).

26. See at *http://www.almajdtv.net/site/*.

27. See at *http://www.alresalah.net/*.

28. See at *http://www.islam-qa.com/en*.

29. Quite telling are the discussions on the *fatwas* posted for the questions, 'What is the place of Sufism in Islam?' and 'Is it permissible for a Muslim to marry a Sufi woman?' See at *http://www.islam-qa.com/en/ref/4983/sufism* and *http://www.islam-qa.com/en/ref/85370/sufism* respectively.

30. One might assume that this is a purely Ḥanbalī juristic apparatus, or per-haps that it may even display a tendency towards the 'neo-*ijtihād*' stance of many reformist Salafī groups; but in reality it is neither. In fact, the coun-cil's scholars distil opinions from a variety of jurisprudential perspectives and thus, do not necessarily restrict themselves to the Ḥanbalī school but often choose the opinions of non-Ḥanbalī jurists, if the latter's evidence is perceived to be more convincing. Therefore they remain within the realms of the classical paradigm of school-based jurisprudence, and consequently maintain the traditional structures of legal hermeneutics. Although theoret-ically they may be engaged in a form of *ijtihād*, in reality they are applying a process of selection (*ikhtiyār*) from the myriad of legal opinions that exist both within and outside the Ḥanbalī school. Despite the focus not neces-sarily being on jurisprudential Ḥanbalism, theological Ḥanbalism remains clearly tangible in a variety of fatwas that deal with the topic of Sufism. See for example at *http://www.alifta.net/Fatawa/FatawaSubjects.aspx?View=Tree&NodeID=10392&PageNo=1&SectionID=3*.

31. Graham 1993: 495.

32. For an in depth discussion of such narrations, their authenticity and purport, see al-Judayʿ 2007: 7–105.

33. See Albertini 2003: 455–70.

# Bibliography

Abū Zahra, Muḥammad (1949) *Ibn Ḥanbal – Ḥayātuhu wa ʿAṣruhu wa Ārāʾuhu wa Fiqhuhu*. Cairo: Dār al-Fikr al-ʿArabī.

Al-Aṣfahānī, Aḥmad b. ʿAbd Allāh (2001) *Ḥilyat al-Awliyāʾ*, ed. Saʿīd Saʿd al-Dīn al-Iskandarī. 10 vols. Beirut: Dār Iḥyāʾ al-Turāth al-ʿArabī.

Albertini, Tamara (2003) 'Seductiveness of certainty: the destruction of Islam's intellectual legacy by the fundamentalists'. *Philosophy East and West*, Vol. 53, No. 4, pp. 455–70.

Algar, Hamid (2002) *Wahhabism: A Critical Essay*. Oneonta, NY: Islamic Publications International.

Al-Matroudi, Abdul Hakim I. (2006a) *The Ḥanbalī School of Law and Ibn Taymiyyah: Conflict or Conciliation*. Culture and Civilization in the Middle East Series, No. 5. London: RoutledgeCurzon.

—— (2006b) 'The Ḥanbalī school of law in the light of contemporary Western studies'. *Journal of Qur'anic Studies*, Vol. 8, No. 2, pp. 203–60.

Bligh, Alexander (1985) 'The Saudi religious elite (*ulama*) as participant in the political system of the Kingdom'. *International Journal of Middle East Studies*, Vol. 17, No. 1, pp. 37–50.

al-Bukhārī, Muḥammad b. Ismāʿīl (1999) *Ṣaḥīḥ al-Bukhārī*. Riyadh: Dār al-Salām.

Chittick, W.C. and Murata, S. (1994) *The Vision of Islam*. New York: Paragon House.

Cooperson, Michael (2000) *Classical Arabic Biography – the Heirs of the Prophets in the Age of al-Maʾmūn*. Cambridge Studies in Islamic Civilisation. Cambridge: Cambridge University Press.

de Beaurecueil, Serge (1985) *Chemin de Dieu: trois traités spirituels: les cent terrains, les etapes itinérants vers Dieu, les déficiences des demeures*. Paris: Sindbad.

—— (1988) *Cris du Coeur: Munâjât traduit du person*. Paris: Sindbad.

DeLong-Bas, Natana J. (2004) *Wahhabi Islam: From Revival and Reform to Global Jihad*. New York: Oxford University Press.

al-Dhahabī, Muḥammad b. Aḥmad (1998) *Tadhkirat al-Ḥuffāẓ*. 3 vols. Beirut: Dār al-Kutub al-ʿIlmiyya.

Ernst, Carl W. (1997) *The Shambhala Guide to Sufism*. Boston, MA: Shambhala.

Farhadi, A.G. Ravân (1996) *ʿAbdullah Anṣārī of Herāt (1006–1089 C.E.): An Early Ṣūfī Master*. Richmond: Curzon Press.

—— (1999) 'The hundred grounds of ʿAbdullah Anṣārī of Herat (d. 448/1056): the earliest mnemonic Sufi manual in Persian'. In Lewisohn, Leonard (ed.) *The Heritage of Sufism*. Oxford: Oneworld.

al-Farrāʾ, Muḥammad b. al-Qāḍī Abū Yaʿlā (1931) *Ṭabaqāt al-Ḥanābila*, abridged Muḥammad b. ʿAbd al-Qādir al-Nābulūsī, ed. Aḥmad ʿUbayd. Damascus: al-Maktaba al-ʿArabiyya.

Farsy, Fouad (1990) *Modernity and Tradition: The Saudi Equation*. London: Kegan Paul International.

Godlas, Alan (1985) 'Stations of wisdom and battlefields of love: introduction and translation'. *Alif: Journal of Comparative Poetics*, No. 5, pp. 87–98.

Graham, William A. (1993) 'Traditionalism in Islam: an essay in interpretation'. *Journal of Interdisciplinary History*, Vol. 23, No. 3, pp. 495–522.

Hallaq, Wael B. (1993) *Ibn Taymiyya Against the Greek Logicians*. Oxford: Oxford University Press.

Hinds, Martin (1996) *Studies in Early Islamic History*. Studies in Late Antiquity and Early Islam. Princeton, NJ: Darwin, pp. 232–45.

Homerin, Thomas Emil (1985) 'Ibn Taimīya's al-Ṣūfiyah wa-al-Fuqarā''. *Arabica*, Vol. 32, No. 2, pp. 219–44.

Hurvitz, Nimrod (2000) 'Schools of law and historical context: re-examining the formation of the Hanbali Madhhab'. *Islamic Law and Society*, Vol. 7, No. 1, pp. 37–64.

—— (2001) 'Miḥna as self-defense'. *Studia Islamica*, No. 92, pp. 93–111.

—— (2002) *The Formation of Hanbalism: Piety into Power*. London and New York: RoutledgeCurzon.

Ibn al-Jawzī, 'Abd al-Raḥmān b. 'Alī (1971) *Kitāb al-Quṣāṣ wa'l-Mudhakkirīn*, ed. Merlin Swartz. Beirut: Dar El-Machreq Éditeurs.

—— (1979) *Manāqib al-Imām Aḥmad b. Ḥanbal*, ed. 'Abd Allāh b. 'Abd al-Muḥ sin al-Turkī and 'Alī Muḥammad 'Umar. Cairo: Maktabat al-Khānjī.

—— (1999) *Talbīs Iblīs*, ed. Ayman Ṣāliḥ. Cairo: Dār al-Ḥadīth.

—— (2001) *Ṣifat al-Ṣafwa*, ed. 'Abd al-Raḥmān and Ḥayāt al-Lādiqī. 4 vols. Beirut: Dār al-Maʿrifa.

Ibn Rajab, 'Abd al-Raḥmān b. Shihāb (1952) *Kitāb al-Dhayl 'alā Ṭabaqāt al-Ḥanābila*. 2 vols. Cairo: Maṭbaʿat al-Sunna al-Muḥammadiyya.

Ibn Taymiyya, Aḥmad b. 'Abd al-Halīm (1998) *Majmūʿat al-Fatāwā*, ed. 'Āmir al-Jazzār and Anwār al-Bāz. 20 vols. 2nd edn., Riyadh: Maktabat 'Ubaykān.

al-Judayʿ, 'Abd 'Allāh (2007) *Aḍwāʾ 'alā Ḥadīth Iftirāq al-Umma*. Beirut: Muʾassasat al-Rayyān.

Kechichian, Joseph A. (1986) 'The role of the ulama in the politics of an Islamic state: the case of Saudi Arabia'. *International Journal of Middle East Studies*, Vol. 18, No. 1, pp. 53–71.

Laoust, H. (1969) 'Ḥanābila.' In *Encyclopaedia of Islam*. 2nd edn., Leiden: Brill, pp. 158–62.

Layish, Aharon (1987) 'Saudi Arabian legal reform as a mechanism to moderate Wahhābī doctrine'. *Journal of the American Oriental Society*, Vol. 107, No. 2, pp. 279–92.

Leder, Stefan (1997) 'Charismatic scripturalism: the Hanbalī Maqdisīs of Damascus'. *Der Islam*, Vol. 74, No. 2, 279–304.

Little, Donald P. (1973) 'The historical and historiographical significance of the detention of Ibn Taymiyya'. *International Journal of Middle Eastern Studies*, Vol. 4, No. 3, pp. 311–37.

Makdisi, George (1962) *Censure of Speculative Theology: An Edition and Translation of Ibn Qudama's 'Tahrim an-nazar fi kutub ahl alkalem'*. Norfolk: Thetford.

—— (1970) 'L'isnād initiatique soufi de Muwaffaq ad-Dīn Ibn Qudāma'. In Six, Jean-François (ed.) *Cahiers de l'Herne: Louis Massignon*. Paris: Editions de l'Herne, pp. 88–96.

—— (1973) 'Ibn Taymīya: a Ṣūfī of the Qādiriya order'. *American Journal of Arabic Studies*, No. 1, pp. 118–29.

Makdisi, George (1979) 'The Hanbali School and Sufism'. *Boletín de la Asociación Espanola de Orientalistas*, Vol. XV, pp. 115–26.

—— (1981) 'Hanbalite Islam'. In Swartz, Merlin (ed.) *Studies on Islam*. Oxford and New York: Oxford University Press, pp. 216–74.

—— (1997) *Ibn 'Aqīl: Religion and Culture in Classical Islam*. Edinburgh: Edinburgh University Press.

al-Maqdisī, Aḥmad b. Muḥammad Ibn Qudāma (1994) *Mukhtaṣar Minhāj al-Qāṣidīn*, ed. Muḥammad Wahbī Sulaymān and 'Alī 'Abd al-Ḥamīd Balaṭjī. Beirut: Dār al-Khayr.

Melchert, Christopher (1996) 'The transition from asceticism to mysticism at the middle of the ninth century C.E.'. *Studia Islamica*, No. 83, pp. 51–70.

—— (1997a) *The Formation of the Sunni Schools of Law, 9th–10th Centuries C.E.* Studies in Islamic Law and Society, Vol. 4, Leiden: Brill.

—— (1997b) 'The adversaries of Aḥmad b. Ḥanbal'. *Arabica*, Vol. 44, No. 2, pp. 234–53.

—— (2001) 'The Hanābila and the early Sufis'. *Arabica*, Vol. 48, No. 3, pp. 352–67.

—— (2005) 'The *Musnad* of Ahmad ibn Hanbal: how it was composed and what distinguishes it from the Six Books'. *Der Islam*, Vol. 82, No. 1, pp. 32–51.

—— (2006) *Ahmad ibn Hanbal*. Makers of the Muslim World Series. Oxford: Oneworld.

al-Najdī, Muḥammad b. 'Abd Allāh (1996) *al-Suḥub al-Wābila 'alā Ṣarā'iḥ al-Ḥanābila*, ed. Bakr Abū Zayd and 'Abd al-Raḥmān al-'Uthaymīn. Beirut: Mu'assasat al-Risāla.

Nawas, John A. (1994) 'A reexamination of three current explanations for al-Ma'mūn's introduction of the Miḥna'. *International Journal of Middle East Studies*, Vol. 26, No. 4, pp. 615–29.

—— (1996) 'The Miḥna of 218 A.H./833 A.D. revisited: an empirical study'. *Journal of the American Oriental Society*, Vol. 116, No. 4, pp. 698–708.

Patton, Walter M. (1897) *Aḥmad b. Ḥanbal and the Miḥna*. Leiden: Brill.

Peskes, Esther (1999) 'The Wahhābiyya and Sufism in the eighteenth century'. In De Jong, Frederick and Bernd Radtke (eds.) *Islamic Mysticism Contested: Thirteen Centuries of Controversies and Polemics*. Leiden: Brill, pp. 145–61.

—— and Werner Ende (1969) 'Wahhābiyya'. *Encyclopaedia of Islam*. 2nd edn., Leiden: Brill, Vol. X, pp. 39–47.

Picken, Gavin (2008) 'Ibn Ḥanbal and al-Muḥāsibī: a study of early conflicting scholarly methodologies'. *Arabica*, Vol. 55, No. 3, pp. 337–61.

al-Qushayrī, Muslim b. al-Ḥajjāj (1998) *Ṣaḥīḥ Muslim*, ed. Muḥammad Fu'ād 'Abd al-Bāqī. Riyadh: Dār al-Salām.

Sedgwick, Mark J.R. (1997) 'Saudi Sufis: compromise in the Hijaz, 1925–40'. *Die Welt des Islams*, Vol. 37, No. 3, pp. 349–68.

Sirriyeh, Elizabeth (1989) 'Wahhābīs, unbelievers and the problem of exclusivism'. *Bulletin of the British Society of Middle Eastern Studies*, Vol. 16, No. 2, pp. 123–32.

—— (1999) *Sufis and Anti-Sufis – the Defence, Rethinking and Rejection of Sufism in the Modern World*. Richmond: Curzon.

Swartz, Merlin (1971) *Ibn al-Jawzī's Kitāb al-Quṣāṣ wa'l-Mudhakkirīn*. Beirut: Dar El-Machreq Éditeurs.

—— (2002) *A Medieval Critique of Anthropomorphism: Ibn al-Jawzī's Kitab Akhbār aṣ-Ṣifat*. Leiden: Brill.

Thackston, W.M. (1979) *Intimate Conversations*. Classics of Western Spirituality. London: SPCK.

van Ess, Josef (1999) 'Sufism and its opponents: reflections on topoi, tribulations and transformations'. In De Jong and Radtke (eds.) *Islamic Mysticism Contested*, pp. 22–44.

Williams, Wesley (2002) 'Aspects of the creed of Imam Ahmad ibn Hanbal: a study of anthropomorphism in early Islamic discourse'. *International Journal of Middle East Studies*, Vol. 34, No. 3, pp. 441–63.

# CHAPTER 11

# ISLAMIC FUNDAMENTALISM IN ARAB TELEVISION: ISLAMISM AND SALAFISM IN COMPETITION

## Jakob Skovgaard-Petersen

Television in the Arab World is evolving dramatically. Since its introduction in the early 1990s, and particularly since 2002–03, satellite TV has completely altered the way programmes are designed, prepared, marketed and launched. Within less than 20 years, the number of Arabic-language satellite channels has risen from zero to more than 500, including channels financed by the US, Russia, China, the UK and France. Some 50 of these channels label themselves as Islamic (and a handful are Christian), but Islamic programming is also present in many of the other channels, whether state-run or private. This massive proliferation of Islamic programming has also given rise to specifically Islamist and Salafist channels and programmes. This chapter will describe these developments and discuss their implications.

### The Salafist print public, Islamism and Salafism

Mass media and Islamic fundamentalism go back a long way in the Arab World. The introduction of printing, and the establishment of independent privately-owned printing-houses in the second half of the 19th century led to the discovery and spread of older religious texts which had hitherto been extant in only a few copies. Printing not only made many more copies of a text available, and affordable, but it also made it much more readable, introducing paragraphs, punctuation and indexing. The emergence of a market for printed books led to a market-driven selection of parts of the medieval corpus, and the neglect of other parts, such as *tafsir* (Schulze 1993: 56–8). What were to become the stable classics of Salafism – the works of the medieval Damascene thinkers Ibn Taymiyya, Ibn al-Qayyim al-Jawziya and Ibn Kathir – were also selected for printing, in Baghdad and later Cairo (Weismann 2003–4). But perhaps the enhanced accessibility of the major *hadith* collections, and their most famous commentators, are of equal significance for the development of a new scripturalism.

By the early 20th century, a distinction could be drawn between on the one hand a modernist current, interested in developing interpretations of Islam that would enable Muslims to take advantage of the opportunities offered by European civilisation, and on the other hand a much more puritan tendency, concerned with preserving the true *sunna* of the Prophet and cleansing it from later accretions (Schulze 1982: 103–6). Opposite in many ways, both these tendencies argued that the traditional stress of the Islamic law schools (the *madhahib*) on the unquestioning imitation of the schools' early masters (*taqlid*) was against the teaching of Islam; instead, Muslims had to approach the Quran and the *sunna* anew to establish the true rulings of Islam. Confusingly, both currents are being referred to as Salafist, due to the fact that both of them aim to re-establish the true, but long-forgotten Islam of the first generations of Muslims (*al-salaf*). This fixation on the earliest Islam was, of course, only possible through a close scrutiny of the available texts (the historians, the Prophet's biography, or *sira*, and the *hadith*), and this text-oriented approach, in turn, favoured not just the reading but also the scrutiny and the editing of the relevant texts. The introduction of the printing press may not have been a prerequisite of Islamic fundamentalism in the form of Salafism – opposition to the law schools and stress on the religion of the *salaf* has a long pedigree – but it certainly facilitated a revival of this position in scholarly circles in the early 20th century. As a basis for a broader social movement, fundamentalism in the sense of scripturalism (that is, referring back to the Scriptures for guidance in individual and social life) is to a considerable degree dependent on the availability of those Scriptures, and of laymen who can read. Even today, the book trade is clearly the part of Arab media most dominated by Islamists and conservative Salafists.

After World War One, in a political arena dominated by the struggle between the colonial powers and local, nationalist elites, Islamism emerged as an oppositional, and socially conservative movement – though not necessarily an anti-modernist one. Generally, this movement was more inspired by the modernist *salafi*s than the conservative ones; the latter's stress on dogmatic issues was of secondary importance to the new social classes who became its core activists. In Egypt, this turn towards Islamism gave rise to societies such as the Young Muslim Men's Association (1927) and the Muslim Brotherhood (1928), both of which were modernist in organisational culture and in their general understanding of Islam; their main aim was to mobilise especially young Muslims to build a modern society in conformity with the progressive teachings of Islam and its Prophet. Each of these societies had its own publication, which warned against secularisation and the adoption of Western lifestyles. A similar tendency could be observed in Syria, Iraq, Palestine and elsewhere.

But conservative Salafism, with its strong emphasis on dogma and unrelenting attacks on Sufism, found its own organisational expressions, in Egypt in the Ansar al-Sunna al-Muhammadiya (1926); and in the newly-established (1932) kingdom of Saudi Arabia, Wahhabism as a distinct and anti-modernist variety of Salafism became an established official ideology. By the 1930s and 1940s, tendencies towards conservative Salafism were visible in several Arabic-language journals. A turn towards more conservative scripturalism, e.g. on the issue of women, is evident in the last issues of *al-Manar*, the famous modernist magazine and Quran commentary (which published only one more issue after the death of its founder, Rashid Rida, in 1935). But the centre of this development was the Salafist printing press in Cairo whose proprietor, Muhyi ad-Din al-Khatib was also the editor of *al-Fath* (1926–48). Contrary to Hasan al-Banna (the founder and leader of the Muslim Brotherhood), al-Khatib was a staunch opponent of the attempts at Sunni-Shiite rapprochement initiated in the 1930s and 1940s (Brunner 2004: 257–60). Attitudes towards the rapprochement (*taqrib*) between Sunnis and Shiites is still an important dividing line between Islamists and conservative Salafis. Apart from this and other divisions over dogma, the Salafis also took a much more categorical stand against many contemporary issues, such as smoking, performing arts and women's role in society. These issues of Salafist-Islamist disagreement have resurfaced today in a new medium: television.

## The new Arab public sphere

The significance and role of the Arab media changed dramatically during the 1950s and 1960s, when more Arab countries became fully independent. The growth of literacy, and of the new states' interest in their citizens' ideological formation, led them to pursue a much more ambitious and state-centred policy on information. Serving as an inspiration to other countries, Egypt set up a news agency and a Ministry of Information, and in 1960 nationalised its press. Equally importantly, the new states began to develop radio and television, almost invariably as state monopolies. While both radio and television would broadcast Friday sermons and carry programmes where leading *ulama* would talk about religion, Islamist groups such as the Muslim Brotherhood in Egypt and Syria were banned, and their point of view could not reach the airwaves. The exception was Saudi Arabia, where Islamist activists fleeing from the modernist and secularist republics were welcomed, and allowed to assist in developing the kingdom's media.

The Islamic awakening of the 1970s and 1980s put pressure on states to open far more Islamic programming on radio and television. This they did, but it was closely supervised, as most regimes came to consider the Islamist movements their main political opponent. Countries such as Syria and Iraq did not allow any opposition publications. Others, such as Jordan and Egypt, did allow the publication of minor Islamic magazines where at least Islamist-leaning *ulama* could voice their opinions, but overtly Islamist activists were not given access to mass-circulation newspapers, radio or television.

The period of strong state control and state direction of the media seems to be nearing an end in most Arab countries. This is due above all to the development of satellite technology and the Internet, which has made it increasingly difficult for states to control what their citizens watch, read or listen to. Along with technological developments, migration and higher levels of education and technical competence have ensured that significant groups of Arab citizens were ready to take advantage of this new situation. Finally, since the late 1980s most Arab countries have embarked on a policy of economic liberalisation and bureaucratic de-regulation, which have also helped in opening the way for the establishment of new media.

After initial resistance to the Internet and the prohibition of satellite dishes, most Arab regimes have come to accept the presence of this new trans-national Arab public sphere (Lynch 2006: 29–49). This does not mean, of course, that they have given up any idea of controlling, or at least influencing, the media. The states are still major actors: as legislators, regulators and owners, or through various forms of pressure – from funding (or withdrawal of it) to control of trade unions, or in some countries to threatening journalists and editors (Sakr 2001: 64–5). In most countries private TV companies rely so heavily on the good will of the state that they are as politically loyal as the state channels; but the private channels still sharpen commercial competition. Meanwhile, almost all countries have invested in satellite channels of their own, and most have elaborate strategies for IT in public administration and for the development of an IT sector.

In the 21st century, then, citizens in most Arab countries can have access to information and entertainment from a variety of sources, and the most important medium of all, television, is the arena of a fierce competition between literally hundreds of channels, the majority of which had not even been planned ten years ago. This competition is consumer-controlled in the sense that the individual viewer can sit at home and decide what to watch by means of the remote control. At the same time, the proliferation of channels is not the result of consumption, but of politics. In the 2000s, says Naomi Sakr, 'the region did see the rise of a new form of patronage, geared to producing something akin to public-service television, at least in the field of information'

(2007: 200). Almost all channels are loss-making, economically speaking, but those who set them up hope to influence viewers, or perhaps benefit from their leverage with consumers and advertisers in other ways. To many state and non-state actors, this is not a business investment, but an attempt to influence Arab public opinion. Even non-Arab states such as the US, Russia, Iran, Britain and China have set up Arabic-language channels.

## Islam on TV

Much has been made of Islam as the religion of recitation and audition. Although radios have received their share of *fatwa*s from believers who were unsure about the legality of aspects of its use – for instance whether it is lawful to listen to the Friday sermon at home without having made ablutions – radio as such has not met with significant resistance. Television, on the other hand, has been controversial from the outset. With its images and close-ups, its power to distract and engage, it has often been seen as transgressing propriety and turning people away from religion. Saudi-Arabia, in particular, has a long history of opposition to television, from its inception in the 1960s to threats against owners of satellite channels today. However, puritans who do not want to watch or engage in television in any way are but a small minority. The classic Islamist position, going back to Hasan al-Banna's embrace of film and theatre (Talima 2008), is that all media must be approached as venues of *dawa* (Islamic mission). Salafi-Wahhabis have been more hesitant, but today they are also involved in TV production. Even militant Salafists such as al-Qaeda have been actively engaged in producing footage and video material through their own mysterious media company, the al-Sahab Foundation.

What has the proliferation of channels meant to the role of Islam on TV? The answer to this 'a great deal'. As the media in the Western world will also testify, Islam is a most welcome source of subject matter: it involves the individual, the family, gender and other social issues and norms, but also politics and conflict. The whole issue of globalisation is today unthinkable without the Islamic dimension – which often epitomises people's fear of a globalised future. News and debates regularly focus on Islamic issues, and this has now been so for decades.

This also holds true for Arab media, with the added dimension that the religious identity of the vast majority of their viewers is Muslim. And that is significant, not least in a situation where national identity and culture may vary a great deal over the Arab region and beyond. Programmes about for instance Islam and finance, or Islam and child-rearing, are interesting to significant groups among the viewers in all the Arab countries, and beyond. Islam is simply one of a few common denominators amongst the great majority of viewers, so competition between the channels is not least competition over how to present Islamic material. That may not be specifically Islamist, but it will tend to affirm the Islamist outlook that there must be an 'Islamic point of view' on all issues, or an 'Islamic solution' to them.

## The establishment of Islamic channels

As mentioned, in the 1970s and 80s state channels cautiously began to respond to the religious awakening in Arab societies. To take Egypt as an example, the early coverage of specific calendar rituals such as the Ramadan *iftar* (breaking the fast), or the sermon at Arafat during the *hajj*, was gradually expanded, and in the late 1980s, the notification of the call to prayer (the *adhan*) was introduced, inter-rupting the programmes. Moreover, new religious programming was successful: most important was the long-lasting *Nur 'ala nur* ('light upon light') programme, generally hosted by Ahmad Farrag (but introducing many of the television *sheikhs* for the first time) that ran from 1960 to 2005. But mention must also be made of the 400 episodes of *Al-'ilm wa 'l-iman* ('science and faith'), with the medical doctor and Islamic activist Mustafa Mahmud, who among his other objectives strove to demonstrate the scientific sophistication of the Quran. Most Arab countries followed the same path, in cautiously adopting Islamic programmes in order to demonstrate that Islam was an integrated and valued part of the official national culture, while avoiding significant investment of time and money in Islamic programming.

This timidity has been challenged with the arrival of satellite programmes, and even more with the establishment of Islamic channels.
When al-Jazeera launched its 'Sharia and Life' programme in 1996,
it advertised it in pan-Arab newspapers as a complete break with traditional Islamic programming, in that it would tackle controversial
contemporary issues from the point of view of Islamic law (Skovgaard-
Petersen 2004: 153). This type of programme has been copied by several other satellite channels.

In 1998 *Iqra'* ('read!'), the first fully Islamic channel, was launched
as part of the Arab Radio and Television (ART) subscription pack-
age. After a couple of years it was followed by other channels with
Islamic names and programming. There are currently around 50
such channels, and according to the Egyptian representative of one
of the most successful of these, *al-Resalah* ('the message', 2006), they
compete over some 10–15 per cent of the television market. *Iqra'*
and *al-Resalah* are Islamic channels comprised in larger portfolios
of channels, some of which broadcast very different content, such as
video-clips with female singers, or American films. The two channels
are owned by Saudi media moguls – Saleh Kamel and Prince Walid
ibn Talal respectively. A third channel, *al-Majd* ('the glory', 2003), is
owned by a Saudi investment company, and a fourth, *al-Nas* ('people',
2007) by another Saudi businessman, Mansur ibn Kidsa. These four
channels are considered the most watched Islamic channels (Galal
2009: 75).

But there are also a few channels set up by Islamist organisations,
or clearly representing their interests. Hezbollah's *al-Manar* ('the bea-
con') satellite channel, set up in 2000 (a terrestrial channel has existed
since 1991) is an example of this kind: with an Islamic name, and
Islamic preaching, but also with ordinary entertainment, news and in
this case military coverage of the resistance against the Israeli occupa-
tion of South Lebanon (and, since Israel's withdrawal in 2000, occasional coverage of attacks against Israel); it also covers a Hezbollah
view of Lebanese politics. Similarly, in 2006, Hamas in the Gaza strip
launched the *al-Aqsa* channel with a similar mix of politics, resistance
and religion. Finally, in 2006 the Islamic Republic of Iran opened
the religious *al-Kawthar* channel, sometimes but not always with a

specifically Shiite content. A few other channels (*Ahl al-bait*, *al-Anwar*) provide Shiite content.

## The spectrum of Islamic channels

The Islamic channels can be divided into groups of different ideological orientation, or perhaps organised along a spectrum from liberal Islamism to stern Salafism. In the liberal end would be the new channel of the Islam Online website which has some connections to the Muslim Brotherhood, but in Egypt (where it is based) also to the Wasat Party, a quite liberal group who in 1995 broke away from the Brotherhood in frustration with its gerontocratic and authoritarian leadership. *Ana* TV is clearly the channel that has moved furthest in the direction of serving the personal needs of the individual viewer. *Ana* TV has a *fatwa* programme, and it hosts some well-known *sheikhs*, such as Yusuf al-Qaradawi and Ali Jumaa, Mufti of Egypt. But it has an equal number of female and male hosts, and there are as many psychologists among them as there are Islamic scholars. *Ana* means "I" in Arabic, and there are critics who point out that this is an excessively egocentric and individualist name for an Islamic channel, which ought to stress the insignificance and even danger of the self (*al-nafs*) intruding on man's fulfilment of his duties towards God. The producer would maintain that self-improvement within the framework of Islamic ethics, and with a sense of devotion to the local community, is essential to an Arab Muslim audience living in authoritarian and fragmented societies.

Next on the spectrum would be the *Resalah* channel, the most lavish and entertaining offer to viewers of Arab Islamic TV. Established in 2006 in the Rotana family of the Saudi billionaire prince Walid ibn Talal, *Resalah* poached a number of well-known hosts and personalities, particularly from *Iqra'*. With headquarters in Kuwait, and headed by the charismatic *da'i* ('preacher') Tareq al-Suweidan, this channel also has Brotherhood connections. The fare is more specifically Islamic than in *Ana* TV, and the name, ('the message') is a classic term for an Islamic medium. It has, however, also featured non- and even anti-Islamist debaters in its discussion programmes, at least in its early days. The channel educates its audience in Islamic knowledge and promotes the outlook of an Islamic solution in everyday life, for instance in finance and family relations. Much of the same may be said about *Iqra*, the first and most established channel. Based in Saudi Arabia, and more Saudi in outlook, it still caters to Muslims all over the Arab world with a variety of programmes, some of them with female hosts. The last of the middle-of-the-road Islamic channels to be mentioned is *al-Majd*, like *Resalah* and *Iqra'* an all-round religious channel, aiming at being the 'safe' channels for families fearful of the corrupting content that TV might bring into their homes. Those homes, when depicted in the programmes, are Saudi homes: spacious, wealthy, modern and peopled with men in Gulf attire with American-dressed children, living in an apparently all-Muslim society. Much watched in its homeland, *al-Majd* does little to transcend the Saudi setting, and its *fatwa* programmes and general preaching take a conservative Saudi view on social and religious issues (Galal 2009a: 222). *Al-Majd* has expanded, with several channels devoted to special themes such as the Quran, or with targeted audiences such as children.

Finally, at the other end of the spectrum we find the Salafi channels, the most prominent of which are *al-Nas* and *al-Rahma* ('mercy'). These second-generation channels have responded to their mainstream Islamic rivals with a distinct and different formula. Like so many others at the time, the first of these, *al-Nas*, was set up in Cairo in January 2006 as a music and entertainment channel. Failing to attract an audience, it changed track, altering its slogan from '*al-Nas* – the channel for everyone' to '*al-Nas* – the channel that will lead you to Paradise' (Abd al-'Aal 2008). Employing conservative Salafi preachers well known from the cheap cassette sermons sold in the streets all over Egypt, the channel transformed itself into a preaching channel focusing on the salvation of the individual believer, the torments and rewards of the afterlife, and the precise definition of dogma and law, interspersed with blocks of commercials. By the end of 2006, this formula had already ensured it a massive success in Egypt, especially among the lower classes, and it could move into expensive premises in the 'media city' and open subsidiary Salafi channels, *al-Baraka* ('blessing'), *al-Khalijiyya* ('the Gulf') and *al-Hafez* ('the guardian'). In 2007, some of the channel's most famous preachers, led by Muhammad Hassan, broke away and founded their own channel, *al-Rahma* ('mercy'), which features only Salafi *sheikhs* and often employs programme titles close to classical genres of Islamic learning, such as recitation, exegesis, ethics and legal rulings. *Al-Rahma* stresses that it provides a full 'programme of life' for the conscientious Muslim striving to reach the blessings of the 'other reality' (al-Rahma 2009).

The Salafi channels project a different image from the major Arab religious satellite channels. While they do display fancy graphics, for instance with the letters of the Arab alphabet, they tend to avoid the 'feel-good' atmosphere of the other channels. The mood is more sombre, and the typical programme simply features a bearded man who speaks directly to the audience. Opinions other than Salafist are generally rarely voiced, and Islam is projected as a clear and unmistakable doctrine (Field and Hamam 2009: 5). A major difference from the other channels is that female hosts are banned, except in *al-Hafez*, where they sometimes appear, fully veiled (Zaid 2009).

Another point of difference is politics, which the Islamic channels generally do not discuss. The exception here is the group of channels set up by Islamist political organisations (Hezbollah's *al-Manar* and Hama's *al-Aqsa*), or by the state itself (Iran's *al-'Alami*). Islamist actors in talk-shows and other programmes also like to comment on politics, and al-Qaradawi regularly takes up political events in his 'Sharia and Life' on al-Jazeera. Salafi channels, by contrast, display a marked disdain for political subjects. Their interest is primarily individual piety. This has no doubt protected the Egyptian Salafi channels from state interference, but it is also in line with Salafi criticism of Brotherhood Islamism as being over-concerned with politics, and too little with salvation. This rule is broken, though, in the case of very violent events pitting Muslims against non-Muslims, as in the case of the Israeli attack on Gaza in January 2009.

## Programming

Most of the Islamic channels deliver more than religious programmes; many have news and sport, some have documentaries about animal life and the like, and a few have films with family-friendly content but no specific Islamic reference. But many of them are making great efforts to 'Islamise' their menus. This means that tried and tested non-religious programme formats are adopted and given an Islamic tinge, e.g. in 'your money' programmes where Islamic financial instruments are promoted, or in health programmes centred around the 'Prophet's medicine' (quoting *hadith*s on the body and its treatment). Similarly, in cookery programmes Islamic views of specific types of food may be discussed, and meals for Ramadan prepared. Sometimes established formats are directly contested, as when in 2007 the channel *Iqra'* provided an alternative to the popular beauty-contest shows by launching its own 'Iqraa Ms. Ideal Daughter Competition' where headscarf-wearing young girls competed with stories of self-sacrifice for parents and others; some 8,000 girls applied for the competition (Galal 2009a: 176–93). Similarly, the channels have been forced to come up with Islamic versions of childrens' programmes – not all of them successfully, as they tend to become moralistic. The children are assumed to live in a world of good Muslim believers, often with the lifestyle and wealth of the Arab Gulf, far from the realities of most Arab children (Galal 2009a: 226).

The childrens' programmes illustrate a specific problem for the Islamic channels: how to project Islam as relevant, but also as harmonious and individually gratifying, while at the same time making engaging and entertaining television. A look at the fate of some traditional genres of Islamic propagation may illustrate how the logic of the medium is gradually influencing the delivery of the message.

## Preaching and *dawa*

The classic genre of communicating the Islamic message to a great audience is the *khutba*, the Friday sermon. Compared to the Christian experience, the *khutba* as a genre was often formal, consisting of set formulae and Quran quotations. Presumably for this reason, *khutba* collections in manuscript, or later in print, were always relatively rare. In the 20th century, however, a *khutba* from a central mosque became a staple feature of national broadcasting, serving the purpose of presenting religion as part of national culture, and the state broad-caster as a patron of religion. The *minbar* (pulpit) came to symbol-ise official religion: hierarchical, authoritarian and dignified, it was the seat of the religious scholar, *al-'alim*, as the one who knew about religion and passed that knowledge on to believers. For this reason, both the Muslim modernists and the Islamists have generally pre-ferred another word, *dawa*, 'calling to Islam', and selected many other rostrums than the pulpit: Islam was to be lived and applied by all Muslims, not just the scholars, and it could be propagated not just in the mosque, but anywhere. The practice of *dawa* put special empha-sis on reaching people in their workplace and public venues, and the early Muslim Brothers spoke proudly of 'coffee-shop preaching' (Lia 1998: 33). This type of preaching, often much longer, more emotional and more political, has found its way into the media primarily through the cassette recorder and the distribution of cassette tapes, which, as 'small media', are inexpensively produced and distributed and thus more difficult for the state to control. As in Iran during the 1970s, Egypt also witnessed the power of the cassette-tape to relay power-ful emotional Islamic sermons from major oppositional *sheikhs*. The propagation of *dawa* is considered a vocation, and thus carries with it the prestige of the devotee who admonishes his fellow believers, some-times at personal risk.

Although they broadcast Islamic programmes every day of the week, the new Islamic satellite channels generally do not transmit a Friday sermon. Instead, they have adopted the more egalitarian and less formal *dawa*, and developed *dawa* programmes in many differ-ent formats. To this end, they have employed a new type of preacher, selected not for their scholarly credentials but for their telegenic attrac-tion. These preachers call themselves *du'a* ('preachers'), and come in a great variety. On the more conservative channels, such as *al-Nas*, they are predominantly, but not exclusively, dressed as scholars and entitled *sheikh* or 'doctor'. On most other channels, they are often people from other walks of life. Some of them are female, but the most successful are men; some have gained a massive audience, including young peo-ple. The programmes are often organised as a series of presentations and discussions around a theme, which tends to be both general and close to everyday life, e.g. issues of dating and engagement, or parental advice. But there are many other formats, and not all produced in the studio; in 2008, the *Iqra'* channel screened a documentary serial, 'Land of the Prophets' with the Saudi preacher Hassan Shahin, shown visiting the tombs and sites of the Quranic prophets, whose stories he told, together with those of the sites and related pilgrimages. Similarly, the season of the *hajj* (pilgrimage) to Mecca is often marked by documentaries on the history of the *hajj*, its precise rituals and the like.

Many of these preachers run personal websites where they sell their TV material, books and other relevant material and services. The best-known of the new preachers, Amr Khaled, who appears on *Iqra'* and *al-Resalah*, has run traditional serials on the individual prophets, or on the founders of the schools of law. However, he has also combined his appearances with social campaigns, for instance for literacy (from 2007), or his major programme 'Life Makers' (from 2004), which seeks to engage the young in voluntary work for business development, the environment and other causes (Amr Khaled 2009).

## *Fatwas* and counselling

Another classical genre of communication by religious specialists to ordinary people is the *fatwa*. A *fatwa* is the response by a Muslim scholar to a question posed to him about the position of the faith in a legal or theological matter. With the introduction of printing in the Arab world, and the introduction of *fatwa* columns in newspapers and magazines, the scope and character of the *fatwa* genre changed. From being responses to individual believers (who could use a *fatwa* in a court case), the published and public *fatwa*s developed into statements about a point of law or doctrine to the general public (Skovgaard-Petersen, 1993).

The new Arab religious TV channels have all taken to *fatwa*s. All of them have *fatwa* programmes, and their websites also carry a *fatwa* section. In the typical programme, a question from a viewer is quoted, or the viewer presents it over the telephone, and a *sheikh* provides an answer with quotes from the literature of Islamic jurisprudence, or from the Quran or *hadith*s. Whereas a state Mufti must pay attention to the law of the land, *fatwa* programmes on satellite TV are reaching viewers in many different Arab states, and will ignore the relation of the *fatwa* statement to the positive state law, or the specific circumstances, of the *mustafti* (the person asking for the *fatwa*). The sheer number of *fatwa* programmes means that some questions are posed many times. Invariably, the responses will differ, that is, *fatwa*s differing in content will be recorded in response to the same question (and *mustaftis* may, accordingly, 'shop around' for the *fatwa* that suits them best). This '*fatwa* chaos' is itself the subject of discussions and deliberations on Islamic programmes, as it is considered a serious problem that undermines the authority of Islamic jurisprudence and the status of Muslim scholars, the *ulama*.

As in the case of the classical *khutba* (Friday sermon), *fatwa* programmes come across as somewhat formal and top-down. Their authoritative tone is liked by some viewers, however, who want definite answers, but others seem to want something more, or something else. Despite their popularity and number, *fatwa* programmes have been challenged by the rise of a 'sister' genre, the counselling programme (*barnamij al-istisharat*). Here the host may not be an Islamic scholar, but may be a *da'i* (preacher) who will listen to the issue, be interested in the personal details, and show empathy. The camera will often focus on the face of the *da'i*, who will express concern and sympathy. The person with the question or story is present in the programme, sometimes speaking behind a screen to hide his or her identity, e.g. from a violent husband or prying neighbours. The answer may refer to the Quran, but it will be given by a concerned fellow believer who has experienced similar situations, rather than by a scholar who simply states the legal position on the case in hand. Once again, television adds spectacle and a display of emotions to a classic genre, thereby enhancing its appeal and reach, but also altering its content.

## Fiction

Finally, Islamic programming also includes works of TV fiction. In the Arab world, Egypt has been completely dominant in the production of films. Of the more than 3,000 movies produced in Egypt, however, only a few dozens could be labelled Islamic films with a specifically religious content aimed at religious education or promotion (Shafik 1998: 170–4). A few of these films, which were produced from the 1950s to the 1970s, still regularly appear on the Arab TV channels.

Arab TV fiction itself is dominated by the format of the serial, most commonly the so-called *musalsalat ramadaniyya* (Ramadan serials) of 30 episodes, broadcast throughout the month of the Ramadan fast. Again, for several decades Egypt was almost the sole producer, and exporter, of this genre, but in the mid-1990s Syria entered the fray, and after 2000 a TV industry has also emerged in the Emirates. Until the late 1990s the Egyptian serials tended to ignore Islamic subjects, and this is generally the case also with the Syrian and Gulf serials (Abu-Lughod 1993). However, a few serials have been produced about major historical figures of Islamic thought, such as al-Afghani, Ibn Taymiyya or al-Shafi'i.

The Syrians, in particular, have excelled in historical serials, often extolling the virtues of earlier Arab-Islamic civilisation, such as the tolerance, wisdom and quest for knowledge of Muslim Spain or Abbasid Baghdad. But the protracted character of the serials, and the need for dramatic action, almost inevitably ensure that threats to them are not only coming from Muslims' enemies, but also from internal dissent and infighting (Dick 2005). While this may sometimes carry subtle messages about contemporary authoritarianism, or the sorry state of affairs in the Arab world today, it is not an embrace of contemporary Islamist solutions. Even serials on the crusades – such as Muhammad Aziza's *al-Zahir Baybars* (2005), or Najdat Anzur's *The Search for Saladin* (2000) – do not simply buy into the Islamist interpretation of the Crusaders as an early expression of an eternal Christian imperialist drive, but try instead to point to alliances between Crusaders and Muslims and the impact of Islamic civilisation on medieval Christianity. Similar messages can be found in a couple of *musalsalat* about Islamist terrorism – a genre that has appeared since 2001 – where the human costs of terrorism, including Arab sufferings, are graphically depicted, clearly in an attempt to dissuade young Muslim believers from falling prey to militant-Islamist recruitment.

But there are also serials that could be labelled Islamist. Iran has produced a number of high-quality religious serials for the Arab market, recounting the story of the prophets and religious figures from the Quran. The most ambitious of these serials is *Yusuf al-siddiq* ('Joseph the believer in God'), in 45 episodes and in production for four years, broadcast by Iran's state cultural channel in Arabic language, *al-Kawthar*, in 2009. The first was *Maryam al-Muqaddisa* ('the holy Mary'), in 12 episodes, broadcast by Hezbollah's *al-Manar* channel in 2002. In this serial, the virgin Mary is depicted as a devout young Muslim girl with a white and blue headscarf (as known in Christian iconography) and deeply concerned with leading a chaste and God-fearing life in the Temple, some of whose priests are extorting money from the poor of Jerusalem through usurious interest, and conspiring to make the Jewish people rulers of the whole world; here is 'proof', however anachronistic, to confirm contemporary Iranian and Arab conspiracy theories about Jewish and Zionist policies of world domination.

Recent developments in Egypt indicate that the presence of Islam in Egyptian state TV has grown stronger, and drawn closer to Islamist positions. While *musalsal* production is still dominated by the secularist left, Islam is no longer ignored, and some productions even have 'soft' Islamist content. A few production houses have sprung up specialising in religious content, some of them owned by former actors who have 'repented' of their previous lifestyle and now work to promote what is called 'clean cinema', avoiding kissing, unveiling and other scenes deemed reprehensible from a religious point of view. In 2006 the serial 'Heart of the Beloved' (*qalb al-habiba*), starring a handful of such 'penitents', was aired during Ramadan, though with little success – critics pointed to the unreality of scenes where a mother cannot kiss her homecoming son, or a woman remains veiled in her own bedroom.

More convincing have been the serials on Islamic scholars (*ulama*). The Islamist-leaning actor Hassan Yusuf has directed three Egyptian serials on 20th-century Islamic scholars – a novelty in Arab TV drama. One of them (on the TV preacher Muhammad Mitwalli al-Shaarawi) was one of the greatest Ramadan successes of that year (2005). Entitled 'The Foremost of Preachers' (*Imam al-du'a*), it charted the history of

modern Egypt through the eyes of this brilliant preacher and minister of religious affairs, inscribing the late monarchy and the Nasser
and Sadat eras into a new historical framework, that of the struggle
to preserve the Islamic identity and culture of the country under the
onslaught of foreign-inspired ideologies. Egypt's defeat in the Six-Day
War of 1967 is thus interpreted as caused by the lack of Islamic preaching, and consequently combat zeal, in the army. The Islamic awakening, and the new veiling, of the 1970s is depicted as a popular response
to the calls made by Sheikh Shaarawi and his associates, who were
well-known promoters of the headscarf (Van Nieuwkerk 2007). At the
same time, the rise of Islamist militancy is seen as a consequence of
state policy, but also as deviating from the true compassionate Islam
as espoused by Shaarawi. This latter theme, and the absence of criticism of President Mubarak, presumably made the serial acceptable to
the state censors.

The issue of the repentant actors, and their reappearance on screen,
demonstrates yet again the significant differences within Islamic fundamentalism. Many of the actors who decided to withdraw were under
the influence of Sheikh Shaarawi who, although a media preacher himself, was a conservative when it came to the sphere of the arts. This has
also been the position of the Salafis, then and now. At the same time,
the classical Islamism of the Muslim Brothers and the Young Men's
Muslim Association was favourably disposed towards the performing
arts, and had their own troupes performing pious plays (Tamimi 2008).
This line was reinforced with Yusuf al-Qaradawi's book on Islam and
the arts, which stressed that the Muslim should admire beauty, and
that acting, performance, song and music, and even comedy, could be a
force for good (just as they could be a force for evil) (Qaradawi 1998).

## The lure and pitfalls of stardom

Most of the programme formats are centred round hosts, and the stations generally advertise themselves and their programmes by promoting these hosts. They come in a variety of guises, with classical
scholars of Islamic jurisprudence and theology, *ulama*, are still much
in demand, especially on the Salafi channels; on its website *al-Hafez*

provides a list of the *ulama* who appear on its talk shows. Some are entitled *sheikh*, others 'doctor' or 'professor', and (particularly on the Salafi channels) tend to be dressed in turban and gown. As a general rule, the *ulama* are not discussing issues, but explaining and teaching them. They are expected to know the answers, not to strive to reach them.

This is less the case with the other main group, the new preachers (*da'iya*). They typically also have some religious education, but that does not seem to be the point. Such preachers are admired (and marketed) less for their scholarly knowledge, and more for their piety, personality and approach to life. They can therefore often have a more probing attitude to the issue at hand, thus demonstrating how a devout Muslim should approach a subject, rather than simply providing the answer (although they also do this). The new preachers may be men or women, they may be dressed in traditional or Western clothing, and may be oriented towards specific Islamic traditions (such as Sufism) or fields of expertise (such as economics). The important point is that their audiences will feel inspired, and become attached to them. Some of these preachers were discovered while addressing private social groups, and it is precisely this capacity to relate to the audience that ultimately ensures their success. There is a certain animosity between the classically-trained *ulama* and the *da'iya* – the former tend to dismiss the phenomenon of the new preachers as a kind of 'Islam-lite'. Still, the *dawa* tradition makes it difficult for the *ulama* to dismiss the vocation of the lay preacher; besides, so many of the *ulama* appear on TV themselves.

Given the sudden rise of so many Islamic media personalities, it is hardly surprising that there is strong rivalry, and very little common understanding, let alone mutual respect, between them. Their understanding of Islamic law and dogma also varies a great deal. It is, for instance, quite possible to watch one *sheikh* giving a *fatwa* on an issue, and then find another on another channel pronouncing a contradictory *fatwa* on the same issue. While many new preachers state that they are not qualified to give *fatwa*s and do not host *fatwa* programmes, they may still give advice or comments which indicate what they believe to be the position of religion on a specific issue. This 'chaos of *fatwas*',

mentioned earlier, is a much-discussed phenomenon, both in the programmes themselves and on blogs or websites related to them.

In academic writing the 'chaos of *fatwas*' is quoted as an illustration of the 'fragmentation of authority' caused by the new media. But
religious authority has always been fragmented, and all sorts of *fatwas* with very different content have long been circulating in printed
magazines and elsewhere. The new media do not only undermine
authority, they also build it up. As happened with the introduction
of print, the name recognition and audience of the most successful
of the media *sheikh*s has given them an authority unparalleled in
earlier times. Individual television *sheikh*s and preachers are therefore
attractive as members on the boards of charitable societies, public
campaigns, and even pious enterprises or Islamic banks. The name
Yusuf al-Qaradawi in particular is much sought after as an endorsement of any pious Sunni enterprise, and al-Qaradawi is lending his
name to many worthy projects (Tammam 2009: 67). For an Islamist
such as him, the possibility of using the pan-Arab TV channel al-
Jazeera to cement his religious authority has been an invaluable tool
in forming a new Islamic internationalism, unfettered by the interests and control of any one state. Islamic internationalism has for
decades been administered by organisations set up by countries such
as Egypt and Saudi Arabia, and has thus been subject to their for-
eign-policy interests. This is why in 2004 al-Qaradawi used the far-
away and non-Muslim city of Dublin to launch his most ambitious
internationalist project, the International Union of Muslim Scholars
(IUMS) – in this way demonstrating not only his own independence and authority, but also the power and feasibility of the 'Islamic
alternative'.

The extent to which pan-Arab television has become the arbiter
of Sunni religious authority could be seen when the crisis over the
Danish cartoons erupted in early 2006, and when a group of 43 prominent Muslim preachers (*da'iya*) in February the same year launched
a project to end the crisis. The group was seen to represent Muslim
scholarly opinion; it was composed of state muftis, eminent scholar
*sheikh*s, and, for the first time, the new preachers. The project was,
however, contested by Yusuf al-Qaradawi and some other well-known

Islamist figures of the IUMS who wanted the boycott of Danish goods to continue (Skovgaard-Petersen 2009: 297).

Promoted on billboards, in TV commercials and in newspapers advertisements, the names and appearances of new preachers have become famous, even with the many Arabs who do not watch the religious channels; during Ramadan they may even eclipse pop-stars. In addition to their TV appearances, they appear at public and private gatherings, and most of them have websites and run online sales of religious books, DVDs and various religious services. The exposure also makes them newsworthy; they are often quoted, and sometimes attacked, in the other media. Like other celebrities, their private life may be of interest to audiences, including those who dislike their messages; in the autumn of 2008, the anti-Islamist media gleefully reported on Yusuf al-Qaradawi's marital problems with his much younger second wife.

There is, however, a deeper problem about fame. Success itself tends to undermine religious authority. In classical and modern Islamic thought and mores, fame and personal success are looked upon with suspicion – these are the trappings of the worldly life (*dunya*) that believers should avoid because they will corrupt the soul. There is a certain apprehension in Muslim circles about the way the channels promote the *sheikh*s and preachers. Al-Qaradawi himself is struggling with this: in the preface to his memoirs, for instance, he states that such works are an ambiguous genre – being for this world and the self, not for God. Nevertheless, this is such a strong marketing device that practically all the channels provide a list of their 'stars', as they typically refer to them on their websites.

Related to the issue of the commercialisation of personalities is the consumerism of the commercials, which provide essential income for private channels, and are thus not easily dispensed with. The channels allegedly have panels that ensure that commercials are in line with the programming ethics, but here again believers may not agree with such ethics; and the marketing and consumerism are themselves part of the materialism that preachers often mention as a threat to Islam and its believers. That could also be said for the entertainment, the diversion and the clamour for attention in which the channels

participate. Whether they like it or not, religious channels and personalities have become part of some of the developments they are warning
against.

## Concluding analysis

This volume is partly about how fundamentalist religion is employing media, and is itself also transformed in the process. Islamist and
Salafist programmes on Arab satellite TV may provide an important
and topical example of these dynamics. But this is also an empirical
example which challenges much of what is implied by notions such as
fundamentalism and the public sphere.

It may be that the absolutism and inerrancy of essential texts is a
defining characteristic of Fundamentalism; but this would actually
be a matter of dogma to most Muslims, and not just to Islamists.
Moreover, Islamism in the *Ikhwani* (Muslim Brotherhood) tradition
has not been particularly interested in dogma or strict legalism; rather,
it has been concerned about building a modern social life on the *system*
or *principles* laid out in the the Quran and the *hadith*s. Like its intellectual forerunners – the early 20th-century reformists – the Muslim
Brotherhood was calling for *islah* (reform) of Muslim society and of
Islamic thinking, in order to bring them strong and healthy into the
modern age. While the *Ikhwani* tendency in many ways conforms to
this volume's definition of fundamentalism (authoritarian structure,
strict behavioural requirements, moral dualism), when it comes to
its general attitude to modernity and the media it has always been
quite progressive. It also seems necessary to distinguish between the
*Ikhwani* Islamism and its rival Salafism, which is much more focused
on the eternal and unchanging message of textual authority (the
*hadith*s, in particular), rather than on re-interpreting it to make it relevant today. While 20th- and 21st-century Salafism thus seems to fit
the Fundamentalism Project's understanding of its object very well,
Islamism comes in varieties that are sometimes quite dynamic and
less puritan. We have seen how these two tendencies developed rival
organisations and media, as early as the 1920s, and we have seen how
this rivalry has entered a new phase on satellite television.

As noted in the introduction to this volume, the notion of public sphere has, historically, been closely tied to the territorial state, in that media and public were situated within its legal framework and shared its polity. By the 1960s and 1970s, the Arab world certainly provided a good example of congruence of state territory and public sphere, in that states went to great lengths to control all domestic media and to ban attempts by foreign media to cross its borders. Sadly, the regimes also directed discussion and information in the public sphere, and did not allow their citizens freely to contribute to it. Since the 1990s this is, however, no longer possible for the Arab regimes – a new public sphere has emerged that transcends the borders of the individual territorial state. One of the problems this has now led to is that there is no congruence between the relatively free public debate at this level, and the political and legal institutions of the individual country, which have remained more or less the same. Satellite TV, then, suddenly provides the Arab world with all the forums and rostrums needed for public deliberation, but little in the way of political and social institutions to respond to it. The result is the proliferation of TV channels in a deregulated transnational market, determined by commercial and political investments, and by the Arabic language. In this competition, Islamic channels make up approximately 10 per cent of the 500 channels, but many of the others also have Islamic programming. As a source of both the identity and the interests of viewers, Islam is an important theme of and conditioning factor in programming policies. Hence the new Arab television has a lot to offer to Islamists: formerly banned from addressing national TV audiences, they now have access to an international audience of Arabic-speaking Muslims, thus confirming the Islamist idea of the Muslim *umma* (community) as the true basis of the polity. The new transnational Arab audience may not be congruent with the entire *umma*, but the two do have some borders in common, for instance with Israel and Europe. The costs of setting up a satellite channel are no longer prohibitively expensive for many groups; and as talk shows and preaching are relatively cheap programme formats, commercial broadcasting may end up generating a surplus. *Dawa* and business seem to go well together.

Under these conditions it is no wonder that Islamic channels have multiplied. But can we speak of 'Islamist' channels? And can we speak of 'fundamentalism'? The notion of fundamentalism as defined in this volume may partly miss the point that Arabic social and political language has become Islamised to such a degree that we need to focus on what is being said rather than the Islamic idiom in which it is expressed. François Burgat has called this phenomenon 'Muslim-speak', pointing out that it is an idiom that may be used for varying and contradictory purposes. Within the Islamist current there will be those who state that democracy is the very antithesis of Islam, as it is built on man's rule rather than God's, while others will maintain that democracy was invented by the Prophet when he entered Medina, and that consequently any non-democratic polity will be un-Islamic (Burgat 2007: 21). When it comes to Islam on Arab TV, this observation seems apt: there is a lot of Muslim-speak going on, and all sorts of positions are attributed to Islam. The issue of Arabs in Europe would be a case in point, covered as it quite often is within the framework of a Muslim minority with specific needs in a majority society that has strong anti-Muslim elements. The stress is on victimhood, oppression, and the craving for recognition and (what are seen as) equal rights, rather than on Muslim exclusivity in relation to the majority society.

'Muslim-speak' in this broader sense has a significant presence on most channels, but of course especially in the channels with Islamic names and Islamic visual and programmatic identity. Many of these channels could also be labelled Islamist, if by Islamist we do not mean their classical focus on the creation of an Islamic state, but their (equally classical) focus on Islamisation of society and the individual. This is the stated aim of practically all the major Islamic channels. But as we saw with the rise of Islamist and Salafist organisations in the 1920s, there is a clear division between the first and second generation of channels: the aim of the former was to demonstrate that there are Islamic solutions or alternatives to everything, including programme formats. The concern of the second generation, the Salafist channels, is the spread of sin and unbelief in society and among individuals – but to them this is an eternal struggle. These channels must also be seen as a reaction against the first generation, and the new preachers whose formulations of Islam they consider to be theologically misguided or downright wrong. Muhammad Hassan and his Salafist colleagues broke with *al-Nas* not because it was advertising for viagra and other sinful products (at least it had done so all along), but because it was hosting the popular new preacher Amr Khaled and the Sufi Ahmad Abduh 'Awwad (Abd al-Aal 2008).

Television has provided Islamists and Salafists with a new and powerful platform to relay their message and to recruit new adherents. It is the fiction of the all-Islamic channel with its head-scarf-wearing hostesses and bearded hosts, and its audiences, the all-Islamic society, cleansed of vice and peopled with God-fearing Muslims, which appears before the eyes of the viewer. From talk shows to fiction and preaching, television programmes present an outlook on the world infused with the Islamist or Salafist understandings of ethics, history, politics and social life. This is indeed an Islamic solution.

But what about the other side of the coin – the logic of the media? That logic entails channels and programmers broadcasting television that audiences want to watch, and thus turns their attention to audience tastes, to innovations, and to the adaption of the formats and messages. We have seen how the classical *khutba* is abandoned on Islamic TV, and how counselling programmes and talk shows have a growing appeal, even if they, too, must regularly be improved and overhauled. This logic seems inescapable: even the most Salafist of the channels, *al-Rahma*, asks its visitors to rate its programmes and come up with suggestions for new ones. And *al-Hafez* decided to introduce the female host (albeit fully veiled), clearly to enhance its attraction for a wider range of viewers.

And as we know, the media is not so distinct from the message. In 2005, the young Saudi preacher (*da'i*) Ahmad al-Shuqayri introduced a daily Ramadan show for youth on subjects such as 'the generation of Saladin', 'gender culture of the Prophet' or 'how can my love for the Prophet grow?' After five seasons (in Ramadan 2009) his young crew went to Japan, and each night a new feature showed how the Japanese manage to be ultra-modern while preserving their inherited culture. Good television for youth, but *dawa* only in the most stretched understanding of the term. Few of the Japanese depicted in the programme were, after all, Muslims. What to some is a laudable and innovative

Islamisation of foreign formats may to others be to profane the purity of their religion.

The overall message of the Islamic channels – whether Islamist or Salafist – is the demonstration of an Islamic solution that covers all walks of life, for the individual and society. This is both a stated intention and the implied message of the programme menu as a whole. But this message is contradicted by the space allotted to them on the screen; whatever the Islamic channels come up with, they are just another offer on the long menu of Arabic-language television. On any given day, viewers will zap through Islamic content on one channel, a Western romance on the next, and video-clips on the third. The channels become an Islamic choice among other choices, to be actively selected only by those who have the pious inclination to do so. The programmers sole response to this reality is to try to devise formulas where they cover all the issues and interests of the viewers, thus keeping them tuned in. But this, again, is not intrinsically different from what all the other channels are trying to do. The Islamic channels thus affirm the role of religion as yet another component of a plural modernity, and not its overarching and determining principle.

# Bibliography

'Abd al-'Aal, 'Ali (2008) 'Salafiyun wa qanat an-nas'. *Al-Islamiyoon*, 7 May 2008. At *http://islamyoon.islamonline.net/servlet/Satellite?c=ArticleA_C&cid=1209357 345783&pagename=Islamyoun/IYALayout*, accessed 12 December 2009.

Abu-Lughod, Lila (1993) 'Finding a place for Islam: Egyptian television serials and the national interest'. *Public Culture*, Vol. 5, No. 3, pp. 493–513.

Al-Rahma (2009) At *http://www.alrahma.tv/Pages/Static/?type=RahmaMessage*, accessed 12 December 2009.

Amr Khaled (2009) At *http://amrkhaled.net/index.html*, accessed 3 December 2009.

Brunner, Rainer (2004) *Islamic Ecumenism in the 20th Century*. Leiden: Brill.

Burgat, François (2007) *Islamism in the Shadow of al-Qaeda*. Austin, TX: University of Texas Press.

Dick, Marlin (2005) *The State of the Musalsal: Arab Television Drama and Comedy and the Politics of the Satellite Era*. At *http://www.tbsjournal.com/Archives/Fall05/ Dick.html*, accessed 30 November 2009.

Field, Nathan and Hamam, Ahmed (2009) 'Salafi satellite TV in Egypt'. *Arab Media and Society*, Vol. 9, Spring 2009. At *http://www.arabmediasociety.com/*

articles/downloads/20090506151157_AMS8_Field_and_Hamam.pdf, accessed 12 December 2009.

Galal, Ehab (2009a) *Identiteter og livsstil på islamisk satellit-tv*. Unpublished PhD thesis, University of Copenhagen.

—— (2009b) 'Yusuf al-Qaradawi and the new Islamic TV'. In Gräf, Bettina and Skovgaard-Petersen, Jakob (eds.) *Global Mufti: The Phenomenon of Yusuf al-Qaradawi*. London and New York: Hirst/Columbia University Press, pp. 149–80.

Lia, Brynjar (1998) *The Society of the Muslim Brothers in Egypt*. Reading: Ithaca.

Lynch, Mark (2006) *Voices of the New Arab Public*. New York: Columbia University Press.

Qaradawi, Yusuf (1998) *Al-islam wa 'l-fann*. Beirut: al-Maktab al-Islami.

Roy, Olivier (2004) *Globalized Islam: The Search for a New Ummah*. New York: Columbia University Press.

Sakr, Naomi (2001) *Satellite Realms: Transnational Television, Globalization and the Middle East*. London: I.B.Tauris.

—— (2007) *Arab Television Today*. London: I.B.Tauris.

Schulze, Reinhard (1982) 'Die Politisierung des Islam im 19. Jahrhundert'. *Die Welt des Islams*, Vol. 22, Nos 1–4, pp. 103–16.

—— (1993) 'The birth of tradition and modernity in 18th and 19th century Islamic culture – the case of printing'. *Culture & History*, Vol. 16, pp. 29–72.

Shafik, Viola (1998) *Arab Cinema: History and Cultural Identity*. Cairo: American University in Cairo Press.

Skovgaard-Petersen, Jakob (1993) 'Fatwas in print'. *Culture & History*, Vol. 16, pp. 73–88.

—— (2004) 'The global mufti'. In Schaebler, Birgit and Stenberg, Leif (eds): *Globalization and the Muslim World*. Syracuse, NY: Syracuse University Press, pp. 153–65.

—— (2009) 'In defense of Muhammad: 'ulama, da'iya and the new Islamic internationalism'. In Hatina, Meir (ed.) *Guardians of Faith in Modern Times: 'Ulama' in the Middle East*. Leiden: Brill, pp. 291–309.

Talima, 'Isam (2008) *Hassan al-Banna wa tajribat al-fann*. Cairo: Maktabat Wahba.

Tammam, Husam (2009) 'Yusuf al-Qaradawi and the Muslim Brothers.' In Gräf and Skovgaard-Petersen (eds.) *Global Mufti*, pp. 55–84.

Van Nieuwkerk, Karin (2007) 'From repentance to pious performance'. *Isim Review*, Vol. 20, pp. 54–5.

—— (forthcoming) 'Of morals, missions and the market: new religiosity and "art with a mission" in Egypt.' In van Nieuwkerk, Karin (ed.) *Performing Arts, Islamic Ethics and Aethetics*.

Weismann, Itzchak (2003–04) 'The Naqshbandiyya-Khalidiyya and the Salafi challenge in Iraq'. *Journal of the History of Sufism*, Vol. 4, pp. 229–40.

Zaid, al-Sayyed (2009) 'Al-mudhi'at al-munaqqabat: surat al-mar'a fi 'l-fida'iyyat al-salafiyya'. *Al-Islamiyoon* 2 March 2009. *http://islamyoon.islamonline.net/ servlet/Satellite?c=ArticleA_C&cid=1235628736401&pagename=Islamyoun/ IYALayout.* , accessed 12 December 2009.

# Websites of the Sunni TV-stations
## mentioned in the article

*http://www.alresalah.net/*
*http://www.iqraa-tv.net/*
*http://www.almajdtv.net/site/*
*http://www.alnas.tv/*
*http://www.alrahma.tv/*
*www.ana-live.com*

# CHAPTER 12

# RELIGION, FAMILY AND MODERNITY IN ZADIE SMITH'S *WHITE TEETH*

## Priscilla Ringrose

With wry humour, Zadie Smith's bestselling novel, *White Teeth*, winner of the Commonwealth Writers' First Book Prize (2000) and the Whitbread First Novel Award (2000), tackles the relations between religion and modernity, including the rise and reception of new forms of radical Islam.[1] Smith was born in London in 1975, to a Jamaican mother and an English father. *White Teeth* is a rumbunctious, epic novel which follows the fortunes of three 'immigrant' families over three generations throughout the long 20th century – the British and Jamaican Joneses, the Jewish Catholic Chalfens and the Bangladeshi Iqbals. The passages examined are set in multicultural London, from the mid-1980s to the turn of the century, and relate principally to Smith's portrayal of one of the novel's protagonists, Millat Iqbal, son of Bangladeshi immigrants and a convert to a radical Islamic movement. I argue that this novel brings into play two different scholarly interpretations of the origins of contemporary radical Western Islam. The first is Oliver Roy's sociologically-motivated account of Islamic neo-fundamentalism as a global phenomenon, expounded in his book *Globalized Islam* (2004). The second, elaborated by Gilles Kepel in *The War for Muslim Minds* (2004), is a historically-grounded understanding of contemporary radical Islam, which traces its origins to the inter-weaving of different strands of Islamic thought in Saudi Arabia. Finally, with reference to Raymond Williams' theory of cultural mean-ing (1980), I extend Roy's sociological thesis on neo-fundamentalism and modernity to the wider conflict between religion and secularism in the novel, with reference to other members of the Iqbal and Jones families.

## A novelistic approach

Compared to a scholarly analysis, a novelistic approach, such as Smith's, to the phenomenon of radical Islam has its limits, especially when we are dealing with an idiosyncratic and uproariously funny novel. On the other hand, the novelistic genre has textual capacities which are beyond the bounds of scholarly analysis. In looking at the novel's contribution to the debate on the form and functions of contempo-rary radical Islam, I will examine two of these capacities: first, the novel's ability to manipulate the discourse of its protagonists for its own purposes, and second, its ability to 'enter the consciousness' of the other – in both cases I will refer to Mikhail Bakhtin's elaboration of 'double-voiced discourse' (1984: 199). Smith uses the discourse of fun-damentalism against itself as part of a parodic project, which, I argue, serves to highlight the very ironies of the contemporary reinvention of Islam to which Olivier Roy alludes – namely, its unwitting complicity both with the mechanics of secularism and with the post-modern cult of the self. However, Smith also parodies the cocktail of the esoteric and the radical which we find in Gilles Kepel's Saudi-centred account of fundamentalism. Finally, I argue that by entering the conscious-ness of a fictional neo-fundamentalist, Smith allows us to draw a final dividing line between Roy and Kepel.

For Olivier Roy, neo-fundamentalism is a contemporary form of Islam which is growing amongst second- and third-generation migrants in the West. Roy distinguishes neo-fundamentalism from political Islam in that the former is disconnected from the territo-rially-grounded aims of nationalist politics and from the ties of eth-nic affiliation. For Roy (2005-9-18) Islam is essentially a diasporic phenomenon, and is more a product of contemporary globalisation than of the Islamic past: 'Using two international languages (English and Arabic), travelling easily by air, studying, training and working in many different countries, communicating through the Internet and cellular phones, they think of themselves as "Muslims" and not as citizens of a specific country' (ibid). What Roy's scholarly analysis and Smith's parody of neo-fundamentalism have in common is that they both interpret this new form of global Islam as a reaction to socio-logical transformations rather than as evidence of the permanence of unchanging Islamic values.

## Recruiting to the neo-fundamentalist cause

Smith's fundamentalist, Millat, is an ultra-cool teenager, with to-die-for good looks and 'street cred'. But, as Smith tells us, this has not stopped him been 'fucked up' in the playground despite 'his tight jeans and his white rock' (2000: 232). In Roy's terms, Millat repre-sents a classic potential recruit for neo-fundamentalism – a socially marginalised second-generation migrant looking for a reactive identity 'beyond the lost cultures of their parents and beyond the thwarted expectations of a better life in the West' (Roy 2004: 13). This is how Millat puts it: 'He knew that he, Millat was a Paki no matter where he came from; that he smelt of curry; had no sexual identity; took other people's jobs; or had no job and bummed off the state; or gave all the jobs to his relatives ... that no one who looked like Millat, or spoke like Millat, or felt like Millat was ever on the news unless they had recently been murdered' (Smith 2000: 234).

Millat's experiences of exclusion can be read in the context of race relations in 1980s Britain. Early in that decade, riots flared up in urban centres across England, including Brixton (South London), as young 'blacks' vented their anger at society and, in particular, at their treatment by police. A report commissioned to investigate the causes of the riots pointed to police relations and school exclusions as the two main triggers, and proposed new investment in black communities. The report's author, Lord Scarman, identified both 'racial discrimi-nation' and 'racial disadvantage' in the UK, concluding that urgent action was needed to prevent these issues becoming an 'endemic, ineradicable disease threatening the very survival of our society' (Nielsen et al 1984).

The Scarman Report was one of the catalysts for the 'multiculturalism settlement' which was to dominate UK government strategy for two decades. For some, multiculturalism, by challenging 'the myth of an ethnically pure society', functioned as an effective response to the legacy of anti-immigrant Powellism (Kundnani 2002). Critics of multiculturalist policy, on the other hand, would soon claim that by channelling cultural funds to different ethnic groups (achieved via a new class of ethnic representatives co-opted into local politics), the fight against racism was diverted into a fight for culture, obscuring the real problem – that of race: 'Multiculturalism now meant taking black culture off the streets – where it had been politicised and turned into a rebellion against the state – and putting it in the council chamber, in the classroom and on the television, where it could be institutionalised, managed and reified' (ibid). As the 1980s drew to a close, British Blacks and Asians were back on the streets, as members of Muslim communities reacted, sometimes violently, to the publication of Salman Rushdie's powerful and controversial *Satanic Verses* (1988). In January 1989, a group of Muslims in Bradford, West Yorkshire, burnt copies of the novel at the instigation of the city's senior imam (Vallely: 1999).

Returning to the novel, we find Millat, aged 17 in 1990, exchanging words with an old friend, the newly-converted Hifan. Referring to the above-mentioned incidents in Bradford, Hifan entreats Millat to sign up to the radical Islamic movement he has recently joined. In examining their dialogue, I will look at the functions of 'double-voiced discourse' defined by Bakhtin (1984: 189) as 'discourse with an orientation towards another's discourse', where:

> [T]he author ... make[s] use of someone else's discourse for his own purposes, by inserting a new semantic dimension into a discourse, which already has, and which retains an intention of its own ... In one discourse, two semantic intentions appear, two voices.'[2]

These two voices may, as they do here, work against each other, in which case we have the vari-directional form of double-voiced discourse, where 'the speaking voice occupying another's discourse deliberately misbehaves with the intended semantic direction of that discourse' (Aczel 1991: 7). In other words, Smith 'sabotages' the discourse of her neo-fundamentalist protagonists by the use of irony.

In the passage below, two types of discourse are parodied – both the self-important, piously-posturing discourse of the Islamic neo-fundamentalism and the expletive-ridden, street-cool speak of urban youth culture. Smith uses ironic juxtaposition of these two discourses to comic effect, emptying out any serious value from the 'subject' of the conversation – Hifan's account of his conversion and his proselytising of Millat. Instead, the foibles of fundamentalism are mercilessly exposed – its arrogant posturing, its self-important authoritarianism, its magnetic attraction to conspiracy theories and its inflated anti-Western rhetoric, but also, as I will show, its unwitting complicity with the values it loves to hate.[3]

'Look at the suit ... Gangster stylee!' Millat ran a finger down Hifan's lapel, and Hifan, against his better instinct, beamed with pleasure. 'Seriously, Hifan, man, you look wicked. Crisp.'

'Yeah?'

'Better than that stuff you used to go around in back when we used to hang, eh? Back in them Kilburn days. 'Member when we went to Bradford and – '

Hifan remembered himself. Reassumed his previous face of pious determination. 'I am afraid I don't remember the Kilburn days, brother. I did things in ignorance then. That was a different person.'

'Yeah,' said Millat sheepishly. 'Course.'

Millat gave Hifan a joshing punch on the shoulder, in response to which Hifan stood still as a gate post.

'So: there's a fucking spiritual war going on – that's fucking crazy! About time – we need to make our mark in this bloody country. What was the name again, of your lot?

'I am from the Kilburn branch of the Keepers of the Eternal and Victorious Islamic Nation,' said Hifan proudly.

Irie inhaled.

'Keepers *of the Eternal and Victorious Islamic Nation*,' repeated Millat impressed. 'That's a wicked name. It's got a wicked kung-fu kick-arse sound to it.'

Irie frowned 'KEVIN?'

'We are aware,' said Hifan solemnly ... 'that we have an acronym problem.'

'Just a bit.'

'But the name is Allah's and it cannot be changed – but to continue with what I was saying: Millat my friend, you could be head of the Cricklewood branch –'

'*Mill.*'

'You could have what I have, instead of this terrible confusion you are in, instead of this reliance on a drug specifically imported by governments to *subdue* the black and Asian community, to lessen our powers.' (294–6)

'That was a different person.' Hifan's religion is, in true neo-fundamentalist mode, a 'born-again religion', one divorced from his parents' cultural legacy, a symptom of the growing disassociation of faith and pristine cultures. If this moment represents Millat's seduction by Islam, his invitation to be 'born again', then the attraction of this new Islam is first mediated not by reference to 'Koranic exegesis' but by the signifiers of 'gangster cool' – Millat, we are told, is a die-hard fan of *Goodfellas*, Martin Scorsese's gangster movie, set in the predominantly Italian New York City neighbourhood of Brooklyn, and an icon of American popular culture. Millat's infatuation with Western popular culture is, ironically, the prism through which he interprets both the verbal and non-verbal elements of Hifan's Islamic message. Smith plays on the ambiguities of Hifan's vestimentary code, on the plural connotative meanings of the form (the formal male suit), which here has two different but overlapping signifieds. For Millat the suit evokes the machismo and authority of the Hollywood Mafioso; for Hifan it conjures up the machismo and authority of the religious ascetic. But, as

Anne Hollander's historical account of the genesis of the suit informs us, its origins in fact lie in the European upper classes of the latter part of the 17th century (1994: 63–7).

Smith's associative connection between born-again religion and a particular vestimentary item can be understood in terms of neo-fundamentalism's need to invent itself. Since it is a form of Islam which is not founded on tradition but is being reconstructed in the West, 'it has to borrow the different elements it uses to rebuild the body and the daily life of a true Muslim, either from an imagined tradition (for example, the turban or the Pakistani *salwar* and *kameez*, whose origin had more to do with the Roman *camisa*) or from Western sources (rain-coat and gloves for women)' (Roy 2004: 272) – and here we could add the suit for men. It is in this sense, Roy tells us, 'that neofundamental-ism accords with the modern makeshift cultural patchwork where "the social life of things" depends only on the meaning bestowed on them by consumers/actors' (ibid).

Hifan and the movement he stands for are comically deflated not only by the deliberately ludicrous acronym, Hifan's poker-faced lack of humour and his facile naturalisation of his choice of the name KEVIN by reference to 'Allah', but also by the ironic contrast between the suburban localism of Kilburn and the extensive ambitions of the imagined eternal and victorious *universal* nation to which he belongs. Roy argues that neo-fundamentalism is part of a global trend where 'religiosity (self-formulation and self-expression of a personal faith) is gaining the upper hand over religion (a coherent corpus of beliefs and dogmas collectively managed by a body of legitimate holders of knowledge)' (ibid: 5ff). Consequently, the self and hence the individ-ual, are central to contemporary religiosity (ibid: 28). The collusion between Millat's macho Islam and his *private* fantasy of the posturing Hollywood-movie gangster points to Roy's insight into the way neo-fundamentalism becomes an individualistic project, which recalls the general Western trend of the individualisation of religion, and, as such, colludes with the post-modern cult of the self.

Roy points to a second irony – that fundamentalism is leading to increased secularisation – *not* in the sense that 'it is under the scru-tiny of modern sciences, but to the extent that it is debated outside any specific institutions and corporations' (cited in Mamdani 2005). Religion is no longer meted out through established institutions, but experienced by an inward-looking local community of believers (Roy 2004: 28). Anyone, as Smith implies, even the barely converted Millat, can become an authority – here, he is immediately offered the headship of a laughably-localised community of believers – the sub-suburban Cricklewood branch of KEVIN. Moreover, Hifan's appeal to Millat to join up is based on the duty to oppose the machinations of Western governments, rather than to adhere to any specific creed. For Roy, the anti-Western mantra of neo-fundamentalism, by dint of its dependence on anti-imperialistic rhetoric, reveals neo-fundamentalism's hidden parentage, that is to say its neglected connections to the kind of violence (guerrilla warfare, suicide attacks) perpetrated by leftist and Third Worldist guerrilla movements in the 1960s and 1970s (ibid: 41–55). Roy underlines this point by stressing the fact that the most dramatic target of neo-fundamentalists was a symbol of neo-imperialist rather than religious power (Al-Qaeda attacked the World Trade Center and the Pentagon – not Saint Peter's Basilica). For Roy, jihad is arguably 'closer to Marx than to the Koran' (ibid: 41).

Millat's first encounter with Hifan also points to the continuing tensions inherent in multi-ethnic Britain, which can be understood with reference to the distinction between multiculturalism and 'plural monoculturalism' (Sen 2006: 156):

> Does the existence of a diversity of cultures, which might pass each other like ships in the night, count as a successful case of multiculturalism? Since Britain is currently torn between interaction and isolation, the distinction is centrally important and has a bearing even on terrorism and violence. (ibid: 156–60)

The oscillation in Millat's speech between gangster-speak and fundamentalist cliché, or between the signifiers of Western culture and those of Islamic separatism, not only embodies the tension between interaction and isolation to which Sen refers but already hints at the threat of violence and terrorism which he associates with the latter.

## Historical roots of a modern religion

Smith's portrayal of the founder of KEVIN, Brother Ibrahim ad-Din Shukrallah, appears to depart from Roy's transversal account of neo-fundamentalism originating in the spaces of social exclusion in Europe, and instead points to Gilles Kepel's historically-motivated account of the intellectual roots of radical fundamentalism, as elaborated in *The War for Muslim Minds* (2004). This is because Smith locates Shakrullah's radicalisation in Saudi Arabia, putting this kingdom, as Kepel does, 'in the eye of the storm'. Although Kepel explains radical Islam as the product of a linear historical tradition (2004: 152), rather than viewing contemporary Islamic radicals as either 'the direct descendent[s] of an esoteric Saudi Wahhabism' or as 'pre-moderns with access to contemporary technology', he paints a complex picture of them as 'hybrid products of multiple intellectual traditions' (Mamdani 2005). For Kepel, contemporary Islamic fundamentalism emerges from the shifting and complex triangulated relations between the traditional dogma of the ultra-strict and quietist Salafis of Saudi Arabia, the politicised radical thinking of the Muslim Brotherhood which sought to radicalise the dogma in the 1970s, and finally the political interests of the governing Saudi elite with its US 'protectors'. The trajectory of Smith's protagonist, Shakrullah, engages with all three points in this triangle.

Brother Ibrahim ad-Din Shukrallah is a Caribbean convert – he was born Clyde Benjamin in Barbados in 1960 to 'two poverty-stricken dipsomaniacs', and converts to Islam after a vision at the age of 14 (Smith 2000: 469). Later, Shukrullah spends five years studying Islam in Saudi Arabia where he 'became disillusioned with much of the Islamic clerical establishment, and first expressed his contempt for what he called "religious secularists", those foolish ulama who attempt to separate politics from religion. It was his belief that many radical modern political movements were relevant to Islam' (ibid). Because of his views, Shakrullah becomes *persona non grata* in the kingdom, and, after several death threats, moves to England in 1984.

Shakrullah's trajectory evokes elements of Kepel's account of the birth and destiny of the *sahwa* movement in Saudi Arabia. *Sahwa* or 'the religious awakening' emerged in the mid-1980s, as a result of the influence of the politicised Qutb-inspired thinking of the Muslim Brotherhood on the ultra-strict Saudi form of salafism, traditionally controlled by the Saudi Grand Ulema. The waves of Egyptian and Syrian Muslim Brothers who arrived in Saudi Arabia from the mid-1950's onwards had an increasing impact on Saudi society. Although the ruling Saudi dynasty initially forbade these incomers to prose-lytise, this ruling was reversed in 1979, after extreme neo-salafis *not* aligned with the Muslim Brothers attacked the Grand Mosque. The dynasty, suspicious of the attackers' links to the Grand Ulema, turned to the *sahwa* for political support (Kepel 2004: 179). At this time, the *sahwa* also provided the Saudi royals with a much-needed modern rhetoric with which to counter the revolutionary Islamic discourse of Iran, whose polemic against 'the Saudi lackeys of the USA' was becom-ing increasingly threatening (ibid). The *sahwa*, on the other hand, took Saudi support for the Afghan jihad as grounds enough for legitimacy. This accommodation between the ruling elite and the *sahwa* abruptly came to an end when King Fahd requested the help of a US-led coali-tion after the 1990 Kuwait invasion. The *sahwa* publically dissented, and as a result themselves became the target of repressive measures, while the Grand Ulema were brought back into the fold in return for legitimising Saudi military policies (ibid: 181).

Turning back to Smith's novel, elements of Shakrullah's story converge with Kepel's historical account – namely the salafi-style pedantry of his Islamic scholarship, the radicalisation of his faith in Saudi Arabia, and finally his condemnation of the traditional ulema's compromises with the ruling dynasty.[4] Once in England, Shakrullah camped out in his aunt's Birmingham garage for another full five years, during which time '[h]e took his food in through the cat-flap, deposited his shit and piss in a Coronation biscuit tin and passed it back out the same way, and did a thorough routine of press-ups and sit-ups to prevent muscular atrophy" (Smith 2000: 469). Shakrullah withdraws into a world of pedantic and painstaking legalism, glean-ing '637 separate rules and laws from the Quran, listing them in order of severity and then in subgroups according to their nature, ie *Regarding Cleanliness and Specific Genital and Oral Hygiene*' (ibid: 470). Smith, here in Kepel-mode, figures Shakrullah as a true heir of Abdul

Wahhab, the father of Saudi salafism, who, from his power base in central Arabia in the mid-18th century, 'counselled the strictest possible application of the sharia in the most miniscule aspects of daily life and the use of coercion on subjects who did not conform to dogma' (Kepel 2004: 158).

## The monsters of modernity

However, as Shakrullah emerges from the garage to found KEVIN, he appears to create a hybrid 'monster of modernity' (to borrow Mamdani's phase) closer to Roy's syncretic, transversal, global neo-fundamentalism – 'by definition an Islam oblivious to its own history' – than to Kepel's jihadist salafism: '[KEVIN] was a group that took freely from Garveyism, the American Civil Rights Movement and the thought of Elijah Muhammed, but remained within the letter of the Quran ... KEVIN: an extremist group dedicated to direct, often violent action, a splinter group frowned on by the rest of the Islamic community; popular with the sixteen to twenty-five age group, feared and *ridiculed* in the press" (Smith 2000: 470).[5]

Whatever their target, irony and ridicule both have an aggregative function, that is to say they have the capacity to create 'in-groups'. Erving Goffman describes the phenomenon as 'collusive communication' where there are 'those in on it [who] constitute a collusive net and those whom the net operates against, the excolluded' (quoted in Hutcheon 1994: 55). Irony has been theorised as creating in-groups, but it can also be understood as presuming the pre-existence of a like-minded in-group. From this perspective, the condition for irony to function would be the pre-existence of what Hutcheon dubs a 'discursive community' with 'shared knowledge, beliefs, values and communicative strategies' (ibid: 91). In this novelistic context, the discursive community refers to 'us readers' whose particular shared understanding of Islamic fundamentalism enables us to 'get' Smith's ironic allusions to the 'impurity' of this new 'pure Islam'. The exclusiveness implied by the concept of an in-group may presume a simple power relation or equation, namely one of superiority over the ridiculed object. But some irony theorists, such as Kenneth Burke, believe that an author's relation to the object of irony may not be so simple. Irony, usually associated with a polemic edge may, on the contrary, be 'based upon a sense of fundamental kinship with the enemy, as one *needs* him, is *indebted* to him, is not merely outside him as an observer but contains him *within*, being consubstantial with him' (ibid: 54).[6]

With reference to the next excerpt from the novel (below), where Smith enters into the consciousness of the protagonist, I argue that Smith's detached irony, which enables Millat to be 'excolluded', is mitigated by instances of empathy, distinguished by the use of the unidirectional form of double-voiced discourse which 'an intention on the part of the author to make use of someone else's discourse in the direction of its [that is, that discourse's] own particular aspirations' (Bakhtin 1984: 193).[7] On a thematic level, this happens when Smith *humanises* Millat by ascribing to him the everyday emotions of confusion, self-doubt and anger. On a narrative level, this happens when the speaking voice occupying another's discourse momentarily *stops* misbehaving with that discourse and uses it in the direction of the discourse's own semantic intent (in this case, Millat's discourse's semantic intent). The Millat we see here is confused and angry, but he is also, more significantly, imbued with an awareness of the very contradictions which his new ideology embodies:

> It was his most shameful secret that whenever he opened the door – a car door, a car boot, the door of KEVIN's meeting hall or the door of his own house just now – the opening of *GoodFellas* ran through his head and he found this sentence rolling around in what he presumed was his subconscious:
>
> As far back as I can remember, I always wanted to be a gangster.
>
> He even saw it like that, in that font, like on the movie poster. And when he found himself doing it, he tried desperately not to, he tried to fix it, but Millat's mind was a mess and more often than not he'd end up pushing open the door, head back, shoulders forward, Liotta style, thinking:
>
> As far back as I can remember, I always wanted to be a Muslim.

He knew, in a way, this was *worse* but he just couldn't help it ... It was all haraam he knew that.

Worst of all was the anger inside him. Not the righteous anger of a man of God, but the seething, violent anger of a gangster, a juvenile delinquent, determined to prove himself, determined to beat the rest. And if the game was God, if the game was a fight against the West, against the presumptions of Western science, against his brother or Marcus Chalfen, he was determined to win it ... It pissed him off that these were not pious thoughts. But they were in the right ball park, weren't they? He had the funda-mentals didn't he? Clean living, praying, fasting, working for the cause, spreading the message? (Smith 2000: 446)

The author deliberately 'misbehaves' while effecting the incongru-ous substitution of 'Muslim' for 'gangster'. But when she describes Millat's own thoughts about the situational irony we, as readers, observe the author's voice losing its polemic edge: 'And when he found himself doing it, he tried desperately not to, he tried to fix it, but Millat's mind was a mess ... He knew, in a way, this was *worse* but he just couldn't help it.' Here, I suggest, the author and potentially, the reader are 'co-substantial' with Millat, not only because we can identify with the everyday emotions with which he is now associated, but also because his thought processes are mimicking ours – he, like us, is becoming aware of the paradox of his position, which, in Roy's terms, derives from his (and our) consciousness of the contamination of contemporary Islam by modernity. Millat's thought processes break down the barrier between Islam and modernity, threatening the safe boundaries of the collusive community, blurring the divisions between colluded and excolluded – his experiences transverse ours, just as his Islam transverses our modernity.

## Islam as import

Just as the novel brings to bear two internal voices, it is (as we have seen) also in dialogue with two scholarly voices (Roy's and Kepel's), both competing for the signified of Western Islam. In assessing the relative value of these two approaches, Mahmood Mamdani appears to weigh in on Roy's side, pointing out that Kepel's assessment of the state of Islam in Europe reduces Western Muslims to the status of 'conveyor belts'. Kepel does indeed view Western Muslims either as potential *exporters* of modernity to their lands of origin or as *importers* of religiosity to the West (Kepel 2004: 249–51). On the other hand, what both Roy and Smith succeed in doing is to portray Western Muslims not merely as mediators but as 'active subjects struggling to establish a new citizenship in adverse circumstances' (Mamdani 2005). This is why Kepel's version of a Europe overrun by competing versions of Saudi-imported Islam is not enough to explain Millat. Roy's account, by both acknowledging and transcending the historical roots of contemporary radical Islam, accounts for both the Millats and the Shakrullahas of this world.

## Religion and secularism

In constructing her own 'empire's worth of cultural identity, history, and hope' (Intermix n.d.), Smith's colourful cast of characters covers a wide spectrum of religious and secular belongings, in a novelistic universe where neo-fundamentalist Islamists jostle with traditional Muslims, fanatic and 'recovered' Jehovah's Witnesses, newly-converted humanists and die-hard environmentalists. While Roy's *Global Islam*, as we have seen, sheds light on the intimacy between neo-fundamentalism and modernity in the novel, Williams' *Problems in Materialism and Culture* (1980) illuminates the wider question of religion and secularism within the multiplicity of life-worlds which Smith explores.

According to Williams, the self negotiates between three levels of cultural meaning, defined as dominant, residual and emergent cultures (Schirato and Webb 2003: 150–5). Dominant culture refers to the norm of current practices, that is to say 'contemporary doxa that structure identities and actions' (ibid: 150). Such doxa may be represented by nationalism as it shapes identity or neo-liberalism as it affects social structures and practices. Residual culture, on the other hand, forms the basis of traditional beliefs and practices, including religious ones. These may conflict with the dominant culture or constitute a threat to it. Emergent culture influences both dominant and residual culture: 'It includes those meanings, values, ways of being and ways of under-standing that are in the process of being constructed that have not yet been fully incorporated into the social, or defined as part of effective contemporary practice' (ibid).

For Roy, many young British Muslims are 'beyond the lost cultures of their parents and beyond the thwarted expectations of a better life in the West' (Roy 2004: 13). But how do these parents, such as Millat's father Samad, fare in the novelistic multicultural maze that is Smith's South London? Why does Samad not succumb to the temptations of a neo-fundamentalist counter-culture? Roy's deference to 'lost cul-tures' and 'thwarted expectations' may help explain Samad's as well as Millat's experience in the light of Williams' understanding of culture. Samad's disappointment with the West leads him to re-invest himself in the vestiges of a time and space which he once inhabited – in other words, he is Smith's poster-boy for the enduring thrall of residual cul-ture. The further he finds himself drifting from tradition, and the more insecure he feels in the shifting sands of modernity, the more a return to 'tradition' looms large as the only solution.

Samad's sense of insecurity is compounded when he becomes caught up in an affair with his son's teacher, the tantalisingly available Miss Poppy Burt-Jones. The relationship makes him increasingly conscious that both he and his family are slipping further and further from their roots and so he concocts a hapless plan to recover tradition by proxy. He decides to send his sons (later plumping for only one of them, Majid) back to the homeland, in a last ditch attempt to preserve his family from Western secularism and 'moral degeneration':

> To Samad ... tradition was culture, and culture led to roots, and these were good, these were untainted principles. That didn't mean he could live by them, abide by them or grow in the man-ner that they demanded, but roots were roots and roots were good. You would get nowhere telling him that weeds too have tubers, or that the first sign of loose teeth is something rotten, something degenerate, something deep within the gums. Roots were what saved, the ropes one throws out to rescue drowning

men, to Save their Souls. And the further Samad himself floated out to sea, pulled down to the depths by a siren named Poppy Burt-Jones, the more determined he became to create for his boys roots on shore, deep roots that no storm or gale could displace. (193)

But Samad's plan comically backfires. To his despair, Majid is duly returned home to the ancestral homeland but only to be reinvented by Smith as a card-carrying humanist with an unshakeable faith in the certainties of scientific rationalism and the rewards of the English establishment:

> Allah knows how I pinned all my hopes on Majid. And now he says he is coming back to study the English law ... He wants to enforce the laws of man rather than the laws of God. He has learnt none of the lesson dos Muhammad – peace be upon Him! ... all I wanted was now two good Muslim boys ... You try to plan everything and nothing happens in the way that you expected ... There are no words. The one I send home comes out a pukka Englishman, white suited, silly wig lawyer. The one I keep here is fully paid-up green bow-tie-wearing fundamentalist terrorist. I sometimes wonder why I bother. (406–7)

Whereas some of the novel's protagonists, such as Samad, are in the thrall of residual culture but have difficulty living by its principles, others consciously reject inherited traditions but find themselves still bound by them – despite themselves. This is the case for Clara, a beautiful, toothless Jamaican woman who is married to Samad's best friend Archie. Clara rejects the fundamentalism of her obsessively devout Jehovah's Witness mother, but nevertheless finds herself still unwittingly beholden to its laws:

> By February 1975, Clara had deserted the church and all its biblical literalism for Archibald Jones, but she was not yet the kind of carefree atheist who could laugh near altars or entirely dismiss the teachings of St Paul. The second dictum wasn't a

problem – having no ox she was excluded by proxy. But the first was giving her sleepless nights. Was it better to marry? Even if the man was a heathen? There was no way of knowing: she was living without props now, sans safety net. (46)

Clara's self-questioning, Millat's reactive new identity and Samad's nostalgia for home are all symptomatic of lives lived without a life map in a world where 'the signposts established by tradition now are blank' (Giddens 1991 a: 82):

> What to do? How to act? Who to be? These are focal questions for everyone living in circumstances of late modernity – and ones which, on some level or another, all of us answer, either discursively or through day-to-day social behaviour. (Giddens 1991a: 70)

The protagonists in the novel are coming to terms with 'sans safety net', with the lack of ontological security engendered by the loss of traditional roles and certainties (Giddens 1991. a: 82). But while some, like Samad, are terrified by the blank signposts and cling to the 'illusion of destiny', (Sen 2006), Irie, Clara's daughter, welcomes the possibilities which 'blankness' affords with open arms:

> 'These days, it feels to me like you make a devil's pact when you walk into this country ... you want to make a little money, get yourself started ... but you mean to go back! Who would want to stay? Cold, wet, miserable; terrible food, dreadful newspapers ... In a place where you are never welcomed, only tolerated. Just tolerated. Like you are an animal fully house-trained. But you have made a devil's pact ... it drags you in and suddenly you are unsuitable to return, your children are unrecognizable, you belong nowhere. And then you begin to give up on the very idea of belonging. Suddenly this thing, this belonging, it seems like some long, dirty lie ... and I begin to believe that birthplaces are accidents, that everything is an accident. But if you believe that, where do you go? What does anything matter?'

As Samad described this dystopia with a look of horror, Irie was ashamed to find that the land of accidents sounded like paradise to her. Sounded like freedom. (407–8)

According to Turner, globalisation produces a pluralism of 'life-worlds' which threaten the singular claims of any particular tradition, religion or nation (1994: 187). While Smith's benevolent characterisations of a great many and varied life-worlds underline this claim, some but not all of her characters, as we have seen, take on board their creator's insights. And while they negotiate the challenges of modernity, how does Smith herself envision their and our futures?

As Irie and Millat join the full cast of characters who assemble for the novel's final moments, can we read this curtain call as Smith's take on emergent culture? The final chapters of *White Teeth* stage a scientific convention, at which FutureMouse, a genetically engineered mouse which has been programmed to die in carefully designed stages, is presented to the world. But any apocalyptic visions of a technologically-determined emergent culture are put paid to by the mouse being set free from its scientific jailors. Another symbol of the future, what we could call a FuturePerson, is literally embodied in Irie, since she is pregnant with the child of one of the identical twin brothers, Majid or Millat. (She slept with them both within a short period of time, and the unborn child's paternity is therefore forever uncertain). The indeterminacy of the child's paternity subtends the inconclusiveness of the novel's ending, to which Kathleen O'Grady alludes in an interview with the author:

O'Grady: 'We learn of this coming child – Irie's pregnancy – in semi-prophetic, even messianic tones – though not wholly optimistic ones – at the same time that we learn that the cancer-induced, genetically altered FutureMouse escapes from his glass cage. Is this your pronouncement on the coming (3rd generation) of a polyglot, multi-racial England? Are we the FutureMouse finally escaped from the cage?'

Smith: 'It is not pessimistic, but it is a kind of throwing up of hands and all the difficulties with the end of the book, about the end being too fast, and all of the rest of it, are just me not being able to – not having the kind of hardware in my brain – to deal with the software – I couldn't resolve a lot of the issues that the book brought up. In the end I kind of threw up my hands and so do all of the characters really.' (O'Grady n.d.)

What appears here to be an author's admission of abdication may ironically be an outcome of her success in capturing the complexity of perspectives which, according to Smith herself, is the hallmark of the 'interesting' writer: 'The world is very, very complex and the writers who are going to be interesting and who are going to succeed are writers who have the kind of complexity to match the complexity of the world' (O'Grady n.d.). Turning to Bryan S. Turner, we find complexity being defined as a product of globalisation: 'Globalization brings about increasing diversification and complexity of cultures by interposing a variety of traditions within a given community. Cultural globalization therefore forces amongst modern societies...a new reflexivity about the authority of cultures, their social status and the nature of cultural hierarchy (1994: 184).

Paraphrasing Turner, we can conclude that *White Teeth* has done to Smith's novelistic world what globalisation has done to our lives, staged the diversification and complexity of cultures by interposing a variety of traditions within a given fictional community, materialising the ways in which modernisation is undercutting the lure of grand narratives, whether enacted as cultural hierarchies, nationalist rhetorics, imperial hierarchies or religious hegemonies.

## Notes

1. *White Teeth* also won the Guardian First Book Award, the Betty Trask Award and the James Tait Black Memorial Prize for Fiction. In 2002 the story of *White Teeth* was made into a short TV series (Channel 4).
2. My emphasis.
3. Variation in fonts my emphasis, for thematic differentiation.
4. Although Shakrullah's departure from Saudi Arabia in 1984 coincides with the *sahwa*'s ascendancy, rather than its repression, there are precedents for the expulsions of these radicals, even at this time, if their criticism of the Saudi royals became too explicit; see Kepel (2004: 176–7) on the case of Surur.

5. My emphasis.
6. The classic example cited here is Flaubert's 'relation' with his fictional pro-tagonist *Madame Bovary* (Hutcheon 1994: 55).
7. My emphasis.

## Bibilography

Aczel, Richard (1998) 'Hearing voices in narrative texts'. *New Literary History*, Vol. 29, No. 3, pp. 467–500.

Bakhtin, Mikhail (1984) *Problems with Dostoevsky's Poetics*. Ed. and trans. Caryl Emerson. Minneapolis, MN: University of Minnesota Press.

Giddens, Anthony (1991a) *Modernity and Self-Identity*. Cambridge: Polity.

—— (1991b) *The Consequences of Modernity*. Cambridge: Polity.

Goffman, Erving (1974) *Frame Analysis: An Essay on the Organization of Experience*. Cambridge, MA: Harvard University Press.

Hollander, Anne (1994) *Sex and Suits: The Evolution of Modern Dress*. New York: Kodansha.

Hutcheon, Linda (1994) *Irony's Edge: The Theory and Politics of Irony*. London: Routledge.

Kepel, Gilles (2004) *The War for Muslim Minds*. Cambridge, MA: Harvard University Press.

Roy, Olivier (2004) *Globalized Islam: The Search for a New Ummah*. New York: Columbia University Press.

Schirato, Tony and Jenn Webb (2003) *Understanding Globalization*. London: Sage.

Turner, Bryan S. (1994) *Orientalism, Postmodernism and Globalism*. London and New York: Routledge.

Williams, Raymond (1980) *Problems in Materialism and Culture: Selected Essays*. London: Verso.

## Internet sources

Intermix (n.d.) *White Teeth* – Zadie Smith. At *http://www.intermix.org.uk/Books/Books_13_teeth.asp*, accessed 6 May 2009.

Kundnani, Arun (2002) 'The death of multiculturalism', *Institute of Race Relations*. At *http://www.irr.org.uk/2002/april/ak000001.html*, accessed 12 May 2008.

Mamdani, Mahmood (2005) 'Whither political Islam?' *Foreign Affairs*, Vol. 84, No. 1, at *http://www.foreignaffairs.org/20050101fareviewessay84113b/mahmoodmamdani/whither-political-islam.html*, accessed 24 April 2008.

Nielsen, John, Gary Lee and John Saar (1984) 'Rising racism on the continent'. *Time Magazine*, 6 February 1984, At *http://www.time.com/time/magazine/article/0,9171,954150,00.html?iid=digg_share*, accessed 13 June 2008.

O'Grady, Kathleen (n.d.) 'White Teeth: a conversation with author Zadie Smith.' Originally published *in Atlantis: A Women's Studies Journal.* 27:1. 105–111. In *VG: Voices from the Gaps – Women Artists and Writers of Color: An International Website.* At *http://voices.cla.umn.edu/vg/interviews/vg_interviews/smith_zadie. html,* accessed 21 June 2008.

Roy, Olivier (18 September 2005) 'Neo-fundamentalism'. *Social Science Research Council.* At *http://www.ssrc.org/sept11/essays/roy.htm,* accessed 26 February 2009.

# CHAPTER 13

# THE BALL IS NOT ALWAYS ROUND: DELIBERATIONS OVER GLOBAL FOOTBALL AMONG RADICAL MUSLIM 'FUNDAMENTALISTS'[1]

## Moshe Terdman

### Introduction

Football (soccer) is one of the most popular games in the Arab and Muslim nations, as it is in the rest of the world. As in many societies, Muslim and non-Muslim, it is accompanied by social phenomena, which add to its importance not only as a sport but also as a form of ritualised social event, forming specific loyalties across society through supporters' clubs and the like.

While the vast majority of Muslims thus enjoy football, the emergence of radical Islamic fundamentalism – e.g. Islamism (which accepts the nation-state structure) and *jihadi*-Salafism (which rejects the nation-state in favour of resurrecting the caliphate through jihad) – has entailed a new discussion about whether or not football, as a sport and as entertainment, is 'permissible' for Muslims. Some radical Islamists and *jihadi*-Salafis have rejected it, on the grounds that it is a Western or Jewish-Christian import, or (for the Salafis) an 'innovation' without precedents in the traditions deriving from the Prophet Muhammad and his Companions.

However, because of the immense popularity which football enjoys, a total rejection of the game has proved to be an untenable position. This chapter will describe recent deliberations over the permissibility of football among radical Islamists and Salafis. When members of these groups comment on the global sport and entertainment which football represents, they are drawn into the 'globalised public sphere' of football and into the global debate on various topics concerned with the sport. As we shall see, their discussions on the game constitute a distinct 'local' input to this global debate, giving a voice to the virtues and vices of football in relation to such Muslim fundamentalist concerns as *sharia* regulations regarding the permissible and the forbidden, jihad, Jewish-Christian world domination, and war against Islam and Muslims. However, we will also see that not even the most culturally purist of all Muslim fundamentalists – the radical Salafis – are able to withstand the most popular of all global sports.

## 'Islamic' football?

On 25 August 2005, anonymous radical Salafi clerics published in the Saudi Arabian daily newspaper *al-Watan*, an anti-football *fatwa* (ruling). This *fatwa*, as well as other similar anti-football rulings, caused three Saudi players of the well-known al-Rashid club, in the al-Ta'if region, not only to leave the team but also to adopt the belief that football was forbidden by religious law. (One of the three, Majid al-Sawat, was later arrested while planning to carry out a suicide bombing in Iraq.) The *fatwa* declared that it is permissible to play football only when its rules are different from those internationally accepted; the ruling is based on a *hadith* (Prophetic tradition) which forbids Muslims to imitate Christians and Jews.[2]

Thus, for example, the *fatwa* of August 2005 called on Muslim players not to 'play football with four lines [delimiting the field of play], since this is the way of the non-believers'. It further threatened punishment for those who used 'the terminology established by the non-believers and the polytheists, like: "foul", "penalty", "kick", "corner kick", "goal" and "out"'. Furthermore, one should 'not set the number [of players in each team] according to the number of players used by the non-believers' – thus only a larger or smaller number than 11 players could constitute a team. This *fatwa* included further rules, such as wearing normal clothing on the pitch, rather than colourful shorts and numbered jerseys, not playing for two 45-minute halves but rather for one or three periods, etc. The most important statement in the *fatwa*, however, is that 'once you have fulfilled [these] conditions and rules, you must play the entire game with the intention of improving your physical fitness for the purpose of fighting *jihad* for the sake of Allah and preparing for the time when *jihad* is needed'. Moreover, 'when you finish playing, be careful not to talk about the game, and not to say "we play better than the opponents", or "so-and-so is a good player", etc. Moreover, you should speak about your body, its strength and its muscles, and about the fact that you are playing as [a means of] training to run, attack and retreat in preparation for [waging] jihad, for the sake of Allah.[3]

It should be noted that this August 2005 *fatwa* is similar to another, much more detailed, issued in 2002, by the Saudi radical Islamist scholar 'Abdullah al-Najdi, in which he forbade Muslim youths to play football.[4] The *fatwa* of August 2005 was published in June 2006, during the Saudi national team's preparations for taking part in the football World Cup, held in Germany in June–July 2006. This *fatwa* stimulated widespread criticism and rejection among senior Saudi religious scholars, who claimed that the *sharia* permits playing football according to international rules, and even demanded the prosecution of those who had issued the *fatwa*. Sheikh 'Abd al-'Aziz ibn 'Abdullah al-Shaykh, the Mufti of Saudi Arabia, called on the appropriate authorities to 'prosecute those involved in the publishing of these *fatwa*s in a *sharia* court'. Moreover, he also called on the Saudi religious police – 'the proponents of good and combatants of evil' (*hay'at al-amr bil-ma'ruf wal-nahy 'an al-munkar*) – to 'track down those involved and prosecute them, in view of the dangers and the venom with which they were trying to influence society'. He further warned Muslims around the world 'not to act according to any *fatwa* until they have checked its authenticity and source, and verified that it was being issued by people who were qualified to do so ... so that nobody who is not an expert in these areas will come along and issue a *fatwa* that will lead him and others astray'.[5]

Sheikh 'Abd al-Muhsin al-'Ubaykan, an adviser to the Saudi Minister of Justice, said that football is permitted as long as various *sharia* prohibitions are not violated. Thus, according to him, everything emanating from the West but which is not unique to it, such as the use of the terms 'foul' and 'out', the touch- and goal-lines, the referee, etc, is permitted. He also warned young people not to heed *fatwa*s of this kind, and recommended that they approach senior religious authorities and ask them to issue rulings on important issues like these.[6] The echoes of the controversy crossed the Red Sea and reached Egypt, where football is highly popular and where such *fatwa*s were heavily criticised by Egyptian religious scholars. One of them, 'Abd al-Sabur Marzuq, secretary-general of the Supreme Council for Islamic Affairs, stated that football is an inappropriate topic for a *fatwa*, since it is an athletic activity concerning which no revelation has been given by God, and to which the Quran has not referred. He further attacked the anonymous Saudi religious scholars who had issued the August 2005 *fatwa*, and said that 'only those with sick minds and weak souls focus on the players' legs'.[7]

This was only the prologue for what would become a hot debate among radical Salafi scholars during the World Cup in June 2006, a debate which broke out as a result of football's popularity among Muslims. This time the issue concerned watching the games on television.

### Radical Salafis and the opium of football: the debate over watching the World Cup

The World Cup, for which the national teams of three Muslim nations – Saudi Arabia, Iran and Tunisia – had qualified, started on 9 June 2006 and continued until 9 July 2006. Despite the participation of Muslim teams, the games aroused great controversy among radical Islamists and Salafis, who found themselves, perhaps for the first time, debating questions such as whether it was permissible to watch televised football.

Overall, radical Islamist and Salafi scholars denounced the tournament as a corrupt show of Western influence. Even before the World Cup began, one scholar warned his fellow Muslims against what he called 'this plot aiming to corrupt Muslim youth and distract them from *jihad*'. Another called it 'a cultural invasion worse than military war because it seizes the heart and soul of the Muslim'. A Kuwaiti radical *jihadi*-Salafi sheikh, Hamid al-'Ali — one of the leading younger *jihadi* clerics — wrote in the *fatwa* page of his website that 'it is illicit to watch these matches on corrupt television channels while our nation is decimated night and day by foreign armies'. This ruling was circulated later in most of the *jihadi* forums on the Internet.[8] Some Islamists even called for a boycott of what they called 'the Prostitution Cup', following reports that several thousand prostitutes were arriving in Germany for the event. One Islamist, who signed his name as Abu Haytham, wrote that: 'While our brothers in Iraq, Palestine and Afghanistan are being massacred in cold blood by the Crusaders and the Jews, our young people will have their eyes riveted on depraved television sets which emit the opium of soccer to the extent of overdose.' The same author named '12 vices' linked to the World Cup, particularly 'idolatry of infidel players' and the 'distraction of Muslims from *jihad*'.[9]

On 25 June 2006 Abu Basir al-Tartusi, another leading radical Islamist scholar, issued a *fatwa* in which he stated that there is 'no objection to soccer, playing sports as a means of entertainment'. However it is forbidden, according to him, to watch football matches, since it distracts Muslims from the abuses visited on Arabs in Iraq, the Palestinian territories and other places in the Arab and Muslim world. He gave an example that 'in the day of the opening of "the Cup" in Germany, billions of people came to the small screen ... In this day and time the Zionist Jews bombed civilians ... '[10] Moreover, radical Islamists posted a video of their own 'World Cup' on the Internet. The presentation showed scenes of the 9/11 attacks against the USA, as well as footage of killing and torture in the Palestinian territories, the US detention centre at Guantánamo Bay in Cuba and the notorious Abu Ghraib prison in Iraq. The introduction to the footage read: 'At a time when pro-Zionist Arab media are busy broadcasting the World

Cup to divert Muslims away from their religion and from *jihad*... we offer you the three other cups which those media are trying to hide from our nation'.[11]

This anti-football campaign even reached India, where hard-line Muslims in the south tried to dissuade youths from watching too much World Cup football, saying they had 'gone mad' over football. Sattar Pathallur, secretary of the Sunni Students Federation in the Malappuram district of Kerala state, said that: 'Wherever you go, you see [youths] wearing jerseys of various teams. It is like idol worship, which our religion does not promote in any form.' He further said that he 'firmly believed that there was a conspiracy to divert the attention of Muslim youth to an unproductive exercise'. His organisation has been holding religious lessons, rallies and public meetings to dissuade youths from following the sport too keenly.[12] In Somalia, the Council of Islamic Courts, who at the time controlled Mogadishu and part of southern Somalia, banned people from watching the World Cup games.[13]

All the proscriptions, however, were to no avail. The flood of warnings posted on the Internet and even the enforced bans enforced on watching the games, failed to divert all eyes from the matches, judging by the high volume of comments posted by Islamists in online *jihadi* forums. One man, who signed his name Sa'ad al-Wissi, wrote: 'I am an extremist, but I find no problem in watching the matches. Your calls to boycott the World Cup are doomed to fail.'[14] Thus, even some radical Islamists have been able to find ways to exult in triumph over 'the crusaders', '*al-rafida*' (a Salafi term for Shiites) and 'apostates'. An Islamist signing his name as Abu Hamza, wrote a day after Iran lost to Mexico 1–3: 'Praise God! Umar, the Sunni, has crushed the *rafida*.' He was alluding to the fact that two of Mexico's goals were scored by Umar Bravo who, despite his first name, is not of Arab origin but merely shares a first name with Umar, the caliph and Salafi hero who conquered Iran from the Persians (today Shiites) in 640 AD. And John Pentsil, a defender of Ghanaian origins who played for the Israeli team Hapoel Tel Aviv, was roundly insulted for having waved an Israeli flag as he celebrated his team's 2–0 win over the Czech Republic.[15]

But it was the Saudi-Arabian team which was most harshly criticised, since it is allocated vast sums of money, 'instead of giving the money to those who don't have work and to the needy', following their 0–4 loss to Ukraine. Khaled al-Hani wrote: 'Billions of dollars spent on the "Green Falcons" have amounted to nothing. These colossal sums should have been devoted to the many Saudis who slave away day and night for a few riyals in the world's largest oil-producing country.' An Islamist named Bassel wrote that 'our national team is a public disgrace'. This kind of criticism was also published in the *jihadi* forums.[16]

Meanwhile, there were other more moderate Islamist scholars who allowed Muslims to watch the games. Sheikh Faisal Mawlawi, the Lebanese deputy chairman of the European Council for Fatwa and Research, and a leading scholar of the Muslim Brotherhood, stated in his answer to a question on watching football games:

> According to the agreed-upon legal rule, there is nothing unlawful except what God has declared unlawful in the Quran or by His Prophet. Other similar cases can be judged according to these texts. Thus, there is no text that prohibits watching sport matches, and we find no aspect to compare it to the matters that the Almighty prohibited. As for those who say that it is considered to be a waste of time, we tell them that the Prophet Muhammad, peace and blessings be upon him, ordered us to entertain ourselves through lawful means. He, peace and blessings be upon him, said "Entertain your hearts, for hearts become blind when they are tired". Watching matches would be unlawful if they include something unlawful such as watching some players wearing immodest clothes. Also watching matches would be unlawful if one spends an inordinate amount of time doing so or neglects an obligatory religious act.[17]

Another scholar, Dr Jamal al-Din 'Atiyyah, a member of the Islamic *Fiqh* Academy affiliated to the Organisation of Islamic Conference (OIC), stated that:

> There is no harm in watching soccer matches or other sporting matches, on condition that we do not waste most of our time.

Watching such matches will not benefit us; the benefit will be for the one who practices sports.[18]

Moreover, some moderate Muslim scholars issued *fatwa*s allowing the imams to delay prayers, even the Friday noon prayers, 'but within the due time specified for the prayer in a way that does not make people perform it after its due time'. Thus Muslims would not miss the football matches if they coincided with prayer hours. Dr 'Abd al-Sattar Fathallah Sa'id, Professor of the Exegesis of the Quran at al-Azhar University in Cairo, stated that:

Basically, it is an obvious sin to delay Friday prayers or congregational prayers from its due time. However, for the sake of making it easy for people and for the sake of preserving unity among Muslims, it is allowed for the *imam* of a mosque to delay performing Friday prayers for about one or two hours in a way that does not imply neglecting the prayer completely or performing it after its due time.[19]

Besides the issue of watching the World Cup games, one should remember that Muslim players led several European teams in the competition in Germany, among them the legendary French play-maker and three-times FIFA World Player of the Year, Zinédine Zidane. His team mate, Franck Ribéry, also made headlines during his country's opener against Switzerland, raising his hands before the kick-off and praying to God in a typically Muslim fashion. There is information also about the conversion to Islam of Arsenal's Senegalese attacker, and another member of France's national team, Thierry Henry. *Jihadi* forums on the Internet report that Henry was seen praying in a mosque in London. Among other prominent Muslim names in World Cup sides were Holland's Boulahrouz Khalid and Robin Van Persie and Sweden's Zlatan Ibrahimovic.[20]

Zidane and Ribéry played a key role in France's matches in the 2006 World Cup. Lhaj Thami Brèze, chairman of the Union of French Islamic Organisations (UOIF) said: 'We are proud of our French football team and of playmaker Zinédine Zidane.'[21]

## The Islamic religious dimension of football in Africa

Another current issue is the Islamic religious dimension of football in Africa, and its important role in the conflict between Muslim women who wish to improve their status in society and radical Muslim scholars (along with traditional society). This conflict has been taking place against the background of efforts made by contemporary Muslim social, religious and political movements in Africa to develop new forms of social organisations, in particular with respect to seemingly banal features of everyday life such as sport. Thus, every major *madrasa* (traditional Quran school) in Zanzibar is today home to a football team of its own, and the team of Zanzibar's biggest reformist *madrasa*, *Madrasat al-Nur* ('school of the light'), had already won Zanzibar's top-league national championship by the 1990s. Football is also a major feature of the social organisation of the Sufi reformist movement on the Kenyan coast, in particular at Lamu, where the local Sufi brotherhoods have set up teams of their own. The same is true for Northern Nigeria, where the Yan Izala have encouraged the formation of football teams and managed to gain a foothold in Kano, which until recently was controlled by the scholars of the *Qadiriyyah* and the *Tijaniyyah* Sufi brotherhoods, to the extent that many young people tend to take part in the activities of football clubs rather than attending the *dhikr*-groups of the Sufi *sheikhs*.[22]

The popularity of sport in general among Africans, and of football in particular, goes back to the colonial period, when it was a major way of organising activities in the colonial public sphere. In Zanzibar, for instance, both the local elite and British colonial administrators were enthusiastic about a number of outdoor activities, such as football, cricket and scouting. Football was from the outset considered an appropriate sport for the African population, and it became so popular that it was proclaimed Zanzibar's national sport. Moreover, football had rapidly become a favourite sport of the 'Arab' population, and thus all the prominent families were represented in the diverse football clubs.[23]

Football was never regarded in Zanzibar as a feature of 'bad' popular culture by Muslim religious scholars. However, it has recently come to acquire a religious dimension when in 1997 Zanzibari women started to play football, in trousers and *hijab*, in 1997.[24] The female team is called the 'Women Fighters', its name alone hinting that the side is not merely a football team, but is composed of women determined to challenge convention and religion. In a society where the traditional Muslim *hijab* covers women from head to foot, their football outfits have provoked outrage. Ansar al-Sunna, one of the radical Islamic groups in Zanzibar, started to exploit the game for religious and political purposes, attacking women's football as a reprehensible 'innovation'.[25] In addition, some women players have been rebuked by their families and suffered violence. They report their brothers beating them in front of their team-mates. The authorities have also been less than helpful, and the women are forced to practise in makeshift conditions – forced to train on a patch of waste ground, because the men who control the practice pitches exclude them, saying they are always booked.[26] Despite all the challenges, the Women Fighters have about 16 players, ranging in age from 17 to 35. The team has even won games against male teams, and now the team has the backing of the Zanzibar Football Association and Zanzibar's Ministry of Sport.[27]

This women's football team is unusual in the Muslim world; the only other Muslim women's football teams are to be found in Sudan. The foremost Sudanese women's team is called 'The Challenge', one of six teams made up of young women who have battled to break with traditional values in Sudan and who hope to form a competitive national team.[28] The Sudanese women's teams owe much of their existence to the religious freedom which was a key issue in the long years of north-south civil war in their country. Since the peace agreement signed between the two sides in 2005, *sharia* has been more loosely applied in the north. Thus women in Khartoum have been forced in the past to cover their heads and wear long skirts, but the women playing for The Challenge refuse to wear such clothes, since it is difficult for them to play with their heads covered.[29] After years of conflict with the authorities, who blocked their efforts to form a competitive women's league in Sudan, the six female teams eventually played in the first public women's league, which began on 17 February 2006 with a friendly match at Sports City, Sudan University's Department of Sport and Science, between teams from Tahadi and the University. It should be mentioned that the women fund their own activities, without any support from the Sudanese Football Association.[30]

The situation of women's football is quite different in Nigeria. In the Muslim state of Zamfara, in the north of the country, women's football was been banned in January 2000, following the implementation of *sharia* law there. The state director of sport, Shehu Gusau, was quoted as saying that women playing football was 'un-Islamic', and added that 'the sport is against the teachings of Islam'.[31]

At the end of the day, however, Muslim women seem to be breaking loose from their chains, by which they were handcuffed to traditional Muslim society. Football gives them hopes of a better life and future, and serves them as a tool with which to challenge radical Islamists as well as traditional society. The fact that the Zanzibari women succeeded in beating male teams contributes, without doubt, to their self-respect and their determination to improve their status.

## Conclusion

Football is a very popular sport and entertainment in the Arab and Muslim world, as in the rest of the world; people turn to it to keep their minds off the difficulties of day-to-day life, and as an outlet for many emotions. Thus on many occasions and for many people a victory on the football pitch is a means of restoring the 'lost honour' of a country, its people, a tribe or any other kind of grouping.

Radical Islamist scholars do their best, however, to dissuade young people, or people at large, from playing or even watching football. They see it as part of the Western invasion of the Arab and Muslim worlds. Some view the environment of the 'football industry' as a revival of *jahiliyya* – the pre-Islamic period of 'ignorance'. The industry's aim, they claim, is to distract Muslims from their religious duties, such as to pray, or from the politics of the Islamic world and the abuses of the Israelis and the West in the Palestinian territories, in Iraq or elsewhere. Some *jihadi* scholars view the 'local patriotism' of Muslims towards their football team, together with their symbols – flags, colours, vulgar songs, admiration directed towards individual players, in many cases corruption, gambling, etc – as apostasy. Football is also a serious cause of violence all over the world (in 1970 there was even a war between Honduras and El-Salvador following a match between the two national teams), and creates in the Muslim world a kind of *fitnah* – 'inter-communal conflict'.

However, it seems that so far the *jihadi*-Salafi clerics have succeeded in winning only a few people round to supporting their cause. Overall, the campaigns of these radical scholars have failed to convince, especially since more moderate Muslim scholars, even among the Islamists and Salafis, have issued *fatwa*s allowing Muslims to watch football matches. Moreover, Islamic fundamentalist countries and governments, such as those of Iran and Saudi Arabia, invest fortunes in promoting their national teams, and manage to recruit their loyal Islamic institutions to support it. The *jihadi*-Salafis' failure can be felt even among their own radical adherents – they themselves seem to have followed the course of the World Cup, particularly when Iran and Saudi Arabia were playing. It was also a good opportunity for them to attack those countries which they hate most, thrashing their achievements on the football pitch.

Moreover, there are some Muslims, like Zinédine Zidane, who play in European teams, and who seem to become identified with the country in which they play and a source of pride for the Muslim immigrants who reside there. This is the case in France, where Zidane seems to create in the French Muslim population strong feelings of French identity and of integration in France, in addition to their Muslim identity. This potential of Muslim European players to help such integration in new national identities also enrages the most radical Islamists and Salafis, for whom a Muslim belongs exclusively to the Islamic faith community. From their viewpoint, football – being intrinsically bound up for example with national and club loyalties – can only serve to split the faith community into rival factions, and divert attention from the pure faith.

Football is not just a sport but a social and sociological phenomenon too, which is currently gaining in status even in countries with other popular sports, such as the USA, where it is growing in importance among women as well as men. Thus it is only logical for football also to become a tool in the struggle of Muslim women, especially in Africa, to change the social norms surrounding a woman's life and to improve her status. It may seem a paradox that the only Muslim women's football teams can be found in Sudan and Zanzibar, where Islamism rules, but if we consider that women are actively struggling for change in these countries, the rise of female football teams in these countries above others makes perfect sense. This is because Islamist doctrines, whatever their restrictive practices, claim that women's traditional roles in society must change in a 'truly Islamic' society. While conservatives may define such change in ways which are in fact very traditional, progressive women are able to challenge them on the grounds of the 'change for women' doctrine. There is, however, a very important difference between the women's teams in Sudan and those in Zanzibar. In the former country, women play without a *hijab*, while in Zanzibar they must continue to wear it. This difference shows that Islamism has been weakened in Sudan, while in Zanzibar it has succeeded in retaining its force – though not to the extent of managing to ban women from playing football. Thus, the female dimension of the game is becoming a pure social issue, as part of women's struggle for equality in these societies.

Considering these aspects of football, it should not surprise us that radical Islamists and Salafis tend to use football as another tool to mobilise support for their struggle against Western culture, as well as against more moderate Muslims. However, the popularity of the football game among the Arab and Muslim peoples, as well as among the radical Muslims themselves, keeps it alive and survives all the attempts by Islamic fundamentalists to dissuade Muslims from watching or playing it.

In conclusion, football is just one element which the radical Islamists and *jihadi*-Salafi scholars exploit in their social-cultural-political struggle within the Muslim world. Because of the popularity of football, it poses a challenge which is greater and more interesting than that of many other social and cultural phenomena and practices which the radicals also attack. Football is thus a significant test case for the radical fundamentalists' ambitions, and may well prove to be their cultural nemesis.

## Notes

1. This paper was first published in December 2006 by the Project for the Research of Islamist Movements (PRISM), as Terdman, Moshe (2006) 'The ball is not always round: the attitude to soccer between jihadi-radical and moderate Muslims'. *PRISM Papers on Islamist Social Affairs*, No. 1 (December), pp. 1–11. At *http://www.e-prism.org/images/Radical_Islam_and_soccer_-_social_ affairs_-_no_1_-_Dec06.pdf.*

2. Admon, Y. (2005) 'Anti-soccer fatwas led Saudi soccer players to join the jihad in Iraq'. Memri Inquiry and Analysis Series, No. 245. At *http://memri.org/bin/ articles.cgi?Page=archives&Area=ia&ID=IA24505,* accessed 19 December 2006; see at *http://jihadwatch.org/dhimmiwatch/archive/007887.php* – note: there is currently no access to this link, even through Internet archives.

3. Ibid; *Al-Watan* (2005) 'A strange fatwa: soccer is prohibited unless played in pyjamas'. At *http://www.elaph.com/ElaphWeb/NewsPapers/2005/8/85882. htm,* 25 August, accessed 17 December 2006; Saud, Fahd (2005) 'Fatwa prohibiting soccer arouses Saudi debate'. At *http://www.elaph.com/ElaphWeb/ Sports/2005/8/87047.htm,* 30 August, accessed 17 December 2006.

4. See at *http://64.233.183.104/search?q=cache:RzffjqrpZY4J:umanas.netfirms.com/ Soccer.htm+%22%D9%83%D8%B1%D8%A9+%D8%A7%D9%84%D9%8 2%D8%AF%D9%85%22+%22%D9%81%D8%AA%D9%88%D9%89% 22&hl=iw&ql=il&ct=clnk&cd=9&lr=lang_enllang_iwllang_ar* – note: there is currently no access to this link, even through Internet archives.

5. Admon (2005) 'Anti-soccer fatwas'; Al-Basam, Majed (2005) 'New facts exposed by the fatwa and warnings concerning following its fabrications'. *Al-Watan*, 26 August. At *http://www.alwatan.com.sa/daily/2005–08–26/first_ page/first_page01.htm,* accessed 17 December 2006.

6. Admon (2005) 'Anti-soccer fatwas'; see *http://www.soccereconomy.com/world_ sep_02.htm* – note: there is no access to this link, even through Internet archives; *Donia Alwatan* (2005) 'In reaction to a fatwa demanding the Islamization of the games ... a Saudi Judicial Secretary criticized the prohibition of soccer or the change of its rules'. At *http://www.alwatanvoice. com/arabic/news.php?go=show&id=27225,* 26 August, accessed 18 December 2006.

7. *Voice of America News* (2005) 'Leading Egypt cleric wants fewer frivolous edicts'. At *http://www.voanews.com/english/archive/2005–10/2005–10–17-voa31. cfm?CFID=21479830&CFTOKEN=71169137,* 17 October, 2005, accessed 18 December 2006; 'Miss Mabrouk of Egypt' blog (2005) 'The soccer fatwa'. At *http://missmabrouk.blogspot.com/2005/10/soccer-fatwa.html,* 18 October, accessed 18 December 2006.

8. See *http://www.mg.co.za/articlePage.aspx?articleid=275351&area=/breaking_ news/breaking_news__sport/* – note: there is no access to this link, even through Internet archives; see *http://www.tajdeed.org.uk/forums/showthread.php?s= 28a75f0fc6667bc7962b22201e0cdf7f&threadid=42717* – note: there is currently no access to this link, even through Internet archives.

9. See *http://www.mg.co.za/articlePage.aspx?articleid=275351&area=/breaking_ news/breaking_news__sport/* – note: there is currently no access to this link, even through Internet archives.

10. Halima, Abdul Moneim Mustafa (Abu Baseer) (25 June (2006) 'Football ... the World Cup'. At__*http://wincoast.com/forum/archive/index.php/t-34956.html*, 25 June, accessed 18 December 2006.

11. See *http://www.mg.co.za/articlePage.aspx?articleid=275351&area=/breaking_ news/breaking_news__sport/_*– note: there is no access to this link, even through Internet archives; see *http://www.tajdeed.org.uk/forums/showthread.php ?s=28a75f0fc6667bc7962b22201e0cdf7f&threadid=42893* – note: there is currently no access to this link, even through Internet archives.

12. See *http://www.wwrn.org/article.php?idd=21958&con=18&sec=33* – there is currently no access to this link, even through Internet archives.

13. See *http://www.tajdeed.org.uk/forums/showthread.php?s=28a75f0fc6667bc7962b2 2201e0cdf7f&threadid=42383* –_note: there is currently no access to this link, even through Internet archives.

14. See *http://www.mg.co.za/articlePage.aspx?articleid=275351&area=/breaking_ news/breaking_news__sport/* – note: there is currently no access to this link, even through Internet archives.

15. See *http://www.mg.co.za/articlePage.aspx?articleid=275351&area=/breaking_ news/breaking_news__sport/*–there is currently no access to this link, even through Internet archives; see *http://www.tajdeed.org.uk/forums/showthread.php?s= 28a75f0fc6667bc7962b22201e0cdf7f&threadid=42730* – note: there is currently no access to this link, even through Internet archives.

16. See *http://www.mg.co.za/articlePage.aspx?articleid=275351&area=/breaking_news/ breaking_news__sport/* – note: there is currently no access to this link, not even through Internet archives; see *http://www.tajdeed.org.uk/forums/showthread.php?s=2 8a75f0fc6667bc7962b22201e0cdf7f&threadid=42684* – note: there is currently no access to this link, even through Internet archives; see *http://www.tajdeed.org.uk/ forums/showthread.php?s=28a75f0fc6667bc7962b22201e0cdf7f&threadid=42677* – note: there is currently no access to this link, even through Internet archives.

17. *Islam On Line* website (2006) 'Watching football and playing profession- ally'. At__*http://www.islamonline.net/servlet/Satellite?pagename=IslamOnline- English-Ask_Scholar/FatwaE/FatwaE&cid=1148980352168*, 1 June, accessed 18 December 2006.

18. Ibid.

19. *Islam On Line* website (2002) 'Can imam delay a prayer for watching a soccer match?' At_*http://www.islamonline.net/servlet/Satellite?pagename=IslamOnline-English-Ask_Scholar/FatwaE/FatwaE&cid=1119503545316*, 2 June, accessed 18 December 2006.

20. Atta, Ahmad (2006) 'Muslim World Cup players promote image'. At_*http://www.islamonline.net/English/News/2006–06/24/04.shtml*, 24 June, accessed 18 December 2006; see *http://www.tajdeed.org.uk/forums/showthread.php?s=28a75f0fc6667bc7962b22201e0cdf7f&threadid=42685* – note: there is currently no access to this link, even through Internet archives.

21. Abu Abdilla, 'Turn to Islam' blog (2006) 'Muslims in World Cup'. At *http://www.turntoislam.com/forum/showthread.php?t=220*, 7 August, accessed 17 December 2006.

22. Loimeier, Roman, 'Remixes and cross-overs: new concepts of politics and culture in Muslim contexts'. At *http://www.unibas-ethno.ch/veranstaltungen/dokumente/Papers/Loimeier.pdf#search=%22%22Cheikh%20Tour%C3%A9%22%20%22islamic%20reform%22%20%22*, accessed 18 December 2006.

23. Ibid.

24. Ibid.

25. Ibid.

26. Ibid; Giulianotti, Richard (1999) 'Sport and social development in Africa: some major human rights issues'. At *http://www.ausport.gov.au/fulltext/1999/nsw/p18–25.pdf*, 30 July 1999, accessed 17 December 2006; *Global Express* (2002) 'Edition 9: football – a game for change'._*http://www.dep.org.uk/globalexpress/9/page2.htm*, 11 November, accessed 18 December 2006.

27. See White, David and Kamina Holmes (2002) 'Football fever: women kick off debate in Zanzibar'. *New Internationalist*, No. 297. At *http://www.newint.org/issue297/update.htm*, 28 August 2002, accessed 17 December 2006.

28. *Sudan Tribune* (2006a) 'Sudanese women play first competitive soccer'. At *http://www.sudantribune.com/spip.php?article14234*, 24 February, accessed 19 December 2006.

29. Ibid.

30. *Sudan Tribune* (2006b) 'Girls' football kicks off in Sudan'. At *http://www.sudantribune.com/spip.php?article14142*, 18 February, accessed 19 December 2006.

31. See *http://www.dinocrat.com/archives/2005/08/29/islam-and-soccer* – note: there is currently no access to this link, even through Internet archives); *BBC News* (7 January (2000) 'Nigerian state "bans" women's football'. At *http://news.bbc.co.uk/1/hi/world/africa/594912.stm*, 7 January, accessed 19 December 2006.

# INDEX